Holistic Innovation Policy

Holistic Innovation Policy

Theoretical Foundations, Policy Problems, and Instrument Choices

Susana Borrás and Charles Edquist

OXFORD

UNIVERSITY PRESS

Great Clarendon Street, Oxford, OX2 6DP,
United Kingdom

Oxford University Press is a department of the University of Oxford.
It furthers the University's objective of excellence in research, scholarship,
and education by publishing worldwide. Oxford is a registered trade mark of
Oxford University Press in the UK and in certain other countries

Published in the United States of America by Oxford University Press
198 Madison Avenue, New York, NY 10016, United States of America

British Library Cataloguing in Publication Data
Data available

Library of Congress Control Number: 2019930204

ISBN 978–0–19–880980–7

Printed and bound in Great Britain by
Clays Ltd, Elcograf S.p.A.

Preface

What are the theoretical foundations for innovation policy? How do governments identify problems when they design innovation policies? And what is the background for the choice of innovation policy instruments? These are the leading questions that this book aims to address. In so doing, it proposes a problem-oriented approach, building the theoretical foundations for an holistic innovation policy.

We hope that this book will be useful for academics and scholars interested in theoretical and conceptual issues of innovation policy rationales, as well as for practitioners, policy-makers, and politicians who seek an overview of innovation policy instruments, and who also seek insights in specific areas of innovation policy.

In a sense, this monograph is the fruit of what we could coin 'slow academia', a movement that challenges the culture of speed in academia. This is so because each of the ideas contained in the twelve chapters of the book have been discussed innumerable times, either in closed meetings between the two authors, or in specialized seminars and workshops with scholars and policy-makers around the world. Our ideas have been proposed, discussed, refined, reconsidered, elaborated, and finally written in real co-authorship between the two authors, and with the inspiration of generous colleagues who have given us useful (and, at times, hard) feedback on our ideas.

On the occasions when the two authors did not initially agree on some issues and notions, we engaged in a thorough process of discussion, which would usually entail going back to the core axioms of our theoretical foundations, and from there back into further discussions until we reached an agreement. This way of proceeding was not the quickest or easiest, but has resulted in an elaborate and carefully considered framework that we now present in this book. We have taken the time that was necessary in order to come to the core of each of the arguments and ideas, expressing concisely our theoretical foundations. Naturally, this way of working runs counter to quick fixes or fashionable approaches. Our ambition is to contribute to building the theoretical foundations for innovation policy that will pass the test of time.

This book is structured in twelve chapters. Some of them have been previously published in different outlets but have been substantially revised according to the overall aim of this book, providing an encompassing and problem-oriented approach to innovation policy rationales and instrument choice. More concretely, some parts of Chapters 2 and 3 rely partly on the following publications: Edquist, 2005, 2011, 2014d, and 2018b, chapter 4, on Research and Development, was previously published as Borrás and Edquist, 2015b. Chapter 5 on education, training, and skills development is largely based on Borrás and Edquist, 2013c and then later on as a journal article (Borrás and Edquist, 2015a); Chapter 6 on functional procurement is largely based on Edquist, 2014c, 2015, 2016a, 2018a, and 2018b. Chapters 7, 8, and 9 (Borrás, 2016; Borrás and Edquist, 2014) were presented and discussed as draft papers at several international conferences. Chapter 10 is based on Edquist, 2018a and 2018b). Chapter 11 on the choice of innovation policy instruments is largely based on the working paper Borrás and Edquist, 2013a, which was subsequently revised and published as Borrás and Edquist, 2013b. Last but not least, earlier versions of Chapter 12 were presented at international conferences.

Admittedly, writing this book has been a long journey. We have encountered many good colleagues, who have shared with us their views and opinions, giving us advice and good feedback about how to improve our ideas. We are highly indebted to them. First of all, we would like to express our deep gratitude to Cristina Chaminade, who travelled with us until 2009 and helped us during the early phases of this long-term project. Likewise, we are very thankful to Jon Mikel Zabala-Iturriagagoitia who co-authored with Charles articles about innovation-oriented public procurement policy, which has served as the background for further developing the ideas in Chapter 6 of this book.

We are also grateful for the valuable comments from participants at the workshop organized at the Centre for Innovation, Research and Competence in the Learning Economy, Lund University, Sweden, 23–24 May 2017, and the feedback they gave us on the first full draft of this manuscript. In particular, we are thankful for the insightful comments from our good colleagues in the following chapters: Ed Steinmueller and Manuel Godinho on Chapter 2; Elvira Uyarra and Stan Metcalfe on Chapter 3; Diana Hicks and Maureen McKelvey on Chapter 4; Barbara Jones and Ludger Deitmer on Chapter 5; Lena Tsipouri and Jon-Mikel Zabala-Iturriagagoitia on Chapter 6; Åsa Lindholm Dahlstrand and Jonas Gabrielsson on Chapter 7; Nicholas Vonortas and Gabriela Dutrénit on Chapter 8; Matthias K. Weber and Slavo Radosevic on Chapter 9; Massimo Colombo and Rajneesh Narula on Chapter 10; and Jan Fagerberg and Stefan Kuhlman on Chapter 12.

Other people have also been crucial in different ways. First of all, our editor Adam Swallow has encouraged us and shown lots of patience with our slow pace. Before him, David Musson supported and encouraged the overall idea of this book when we first approached him. We are also grateful to three anonymous reviewers for their insightful comments and feedback, which served to improve and make this book clearer and more relevant. Two very diligent student assistants, Eduardo Villacis and Lena Steffen, helped us in gathering data and preparing the figures and tables in the book. And Monica Allen has played a vital role in correcting the language (we are not native English speakers).

Last, and most importantly, we would like to express our greatest gratitude to our respective spouses, Finn and Kirsten, who have been constant sources of inspiration and encouragement during this long journey, and who remind us about the most important things in life: family and friends.

Susana Borrás and Charles Edquist
June 2018

Contents

Contents

List of Figures

List of Tables

List of Boxes

List of Abbreviations

AME	advanced manufacturing and engineering
BAN	business angel network
ERAC	European Research and Innovation Area Committee
EU	European Union
ICT	information and communication technologies
IEP	innovation-enhancing procurement
IPR	intellectual property rights
NIC	National Innovation Council
NSI	national system of innovation
OECD	Organisation for Economic Co-operation and Development
PCP	pre-commercial procurement
R&D	research and development
SI	system of innovation
SME	small and medium-sized enterprises
STEM	science, technology, engineering, and mathematics
TRL	technology-readiness level
UHM	Swedish Procurement Agency
UK	United kingdom
USA	United States of America
VC	venture capital

List of Abbreviations

1

Why We Need an Holistic Innovation Policy

Goals, Problems, and Instruments

1.1 Introduction

This book is about holistic innovation policy: its theoretical foundations, its problem-oriented approach, and its instrument choices. We argue that most innovation policies today are partial rather than holistic. They are partial because they focus only on a few dimensions in the innovation system, rather than having an encompassing view on it. Hence, partial innovation policies leave aside and undervalue crucial problems that deserve policy attention. Developing an holistic innovation policy requires an understanding of the nature and dynamics of innovation processes in the socio-economic context of innovation systems. Equally important, holistic innovation policy also requires an understanding of the nature of the problems in the systems, including the unintended consequences of policy itself.

Over the past decades it has become popular among many governments in the developed and developing world to adopt a series of initiatives influencing the direction and speed of innovation in different ways. National, regional, and local governments seek to provide conditions that foster innovation in their societies and economies. These governmental initiatives are very diverse in nature and aim at different goals, like economic growth and socio-economic development, the improvement of public health, better energy and transport systems in growing cities, or more effective environmental protection. Hence, there is today a bewildering number of cases with very different degrees of success. The situations that these policy interventions address, the resources deployed (monetary, organizational, authority, analytical resources, or otherwise), and the clarity of political goals behind those interventions are not the same. Neither are the outcomes of these policies.

The notion of 'innovation' is hype among political circles. This thrust originates from the widespread view that innovation is a positive source of transformation of the economy and society, and for social progress in general—albeit with some possible negative effects too (Schot and O'Donovan, 2016). This transformative view of innovation has been stimulated by international organizations' analysis and comparative assessments across countries and regions.

However, even if the notion of innovation has permeated much of the political discourse, innovation policies remain skewed, unfocused, and limited. They are partial, not holistic. This is clear when we look at the different areas that most governments focus on when defining their innovation policies. Whereas some areas like scientific production and basic research activities tend to receive a lot of attention from policy-makers, other issues that are absolutely key for fostering innovation in the economy and society have paradoxically received far less attention—for example, the link between skills formation and innovation performance, or the role of prototyping and demonstration: the 'D' in the 'R&D' (research and development) notion. As we will see in Chapters 4 and 5, education, skills formation, and training, as well as prototyping and demonstration activities continue to be undervalued in the design of innovation policies.

Another example of skewed and partial policies is the balance between a supply-side and a demand-side focus in the design of innovation policies. Most government initiatives and areas of attention have to do with the supply side, looking at the provision of specific technological capacities in the economy. It is only very recently that the demand side has received increasing attention (Mazzucato, 2016), focusing on private and public consumption patterns and demand (Edler and Georghiou, 2007; Edler, 2009; Edquist and Zabala-Iturriagagoitia, 2012). This again shows the unbalanced nature of most current innovation policies.

All of the above shows that innovation policies today remain largely skewed and partial. For that reason, they need balance in terms of taking into account all the different activities of the innovation system (not only a few), the different aspects most relevant for the particular country or region, and the actual problems that hinder innovation processes from unleashing their transformative effects in that particular economy and society. In order to achieve these it is necessary to consider developing holistic innovation policies.

Almost three decades of the development and use of the innovation systems approach have put forward valuable insights on the context within which innovation processes take place (Steinmueller, 2006). By understanding that innovation is anchored in a complex context, the systems approach has provided a broad analytical framework to examine how the comparative innovative performance of national or regional economies are related to the performance of socio-economically and politically defined frameworks. This approach has been particularly suitable to see the role of policy fostering innovation as an important dimension within the system.

This extensive literature on innovation has insisted on the need for policy to build effective innovation systems (Mytelka and Smith, 2002), in the sense that they become true selection environments for the evolutionary processes of innovation (Metcalfe, 1995), and effective also in terms of building frameworks fostering the co-evolution of innovations, the economy, and society (Nelson, 2009; Dutrénit et al., 2011).

However, when dealing with innovation policy from a systems of innovation perspective, the literature has continuously suffered from two important gaps.

The first gap is what we might call the 'unfinished business' of the innovation systems literature, when it comes to providing specific and detailed theoretical foundations (including policy rationales) for innovation policy. This unfinished business refers to the large distance that exists today between the very abstract theoretical considerations about the nature of knowledge and the generic precondition of public intervention on the one hand, and the concrete problems that require policy intervention on the other. Because they are so abstract, those general considerations seem poorly equipped to provide a clear theoretical anchorage to the real complex world of policy-making in specific and concrete areas. The system of innovation approach was a great leap forward in innovation studies when it was defined in the late 1980s and early 1990s, but it has so far not been able to provide a specific theoretical background for policy-making.

The second gap has to do with the widespread tendency in the literature to separate the analysis of innovation processes from the analysis of the existing policies. In other words, many studies do not include innovation policy as part of the object of study, as part of the analysis. Instead, in those studies, policy typically comes into the picture in an *ex-post* manner when discussing the 'policy implications' of the findings. This 'policy implications syndrome', as we may call it, means that policy recommendations are being formulated normatively and in a generic manner, rather than concretely and upon the examination of the policy actions and initiatives already in course. For this reason, these policy implications run the risk of being redundant (because the public actions already exist—in which case it is a question of why the existing policies are ineffective). Or they run the risk of being unnecessary (suggesting public action for problems that are not relevant or suitable for public intervention). Even worse, they might suggest some policy interventions in a direction that ignore other more acute problems in the innovation system (turning a blind eye to the 'elephants in the room', particularly when existing policies and public structures are part of the problem). Sometimes this is related to the needs of some specific countries in emerging economies

(Kuhlmann and Ordoñez-Matamoros, 2016). Other times it is related to some generic areas that have been somehow underexplored, as explained above.

This book is about the theoretical foundations of innovation policy. It follows the tradition of addressing innovation policy from the angle of an innovation systems approach (Kuhlmann et al., 2010). In that sense, the book takes the point of departure from the above mentioned gaps in the current literature, and aims at making a contribution to the field with at least two novelties.

The first novelty of this book is to provide a theoretically anchored foundation for innovation policy-making that avoids the traps of too abstract theoretical considerations, or too metaphorical treatments. Therefore, this book provides a mechanism to identify and explain concrete policy problems that tend to afflict innovation processes. Innovation systems are characterized by ten (or more) essential determinants of innovation processes. Explaining the nature and features of concrete policy problems that afflict each of these ten determinants (or activities) is a necessary stepping stone for the identification of viable, relevant, and down-to-earth policy problems and their solutions.

The second novelty of this book is to provide a problem-based approach to innovation policy rationales and instruments, as being part and parcel of the innovation system, and not something that comes afterwards in the analysis. The book offers a critical analysis on policy, its instruments, and its way of pursuing public action in the complex area of innovation. It is not a 'recipe' nor an uncritical 'how-to' guide, ready-made, 'one-size-fits-all' book for policy-makers. Instead, this book aims at providing analytical depth and substantial critical considerations about the ways in which policy might be providing solutions to convoluted policy problems, as well as the negative, unintended consequences that policy itself might pose.

1.2 The Unfinished Theoretical Foundations of Innovation Policy

The question of the theoretical foundations for public action in the field of innovation has been discussed in the innovation literature since the seminal work of Arrow (Arrow, 1962; Nelson, 1959). Following those initial steps, the literature has traditionally pointed at three forms of market failure associated with science and technology inputs in the innovation process. These are the limits of the appropriability of new knowledge (due to its non-rival and non-excluding nature); the uncertainty about the industrial applicability of basic research (or its serendipity) and its ultimately possible industrial utilization; and the information asymmetry in capital markets, between the scientist and the investor (Aghion et al., 2009b).

The rise of the neo-Schumpeterian tradition (Schumpeter, 1942/2005), particularly the institutional and evolutionary economic theories since the early 1990s, has challenged some of the views on the role of technical change in the economy (Nelson and Winter, 1982), with relevant theoretical connotations for the design of innovation policy. The evolutionary and institutional approach sees innovation as a socially embedded process in a complex system where many elements (other than R&D) intervene, and where institutional frameworks play a major role. From this systems perspective, where context matters a lot for innovation, scholars have questioned assumptions of linearity of the innovation process (Kline, 1985; Godin, 2006).

Such considerations are the backbone of evolutionary and institutional economists' recommendation to focus on a wider perspective, one that takes market failure as one among other possible failures (or policy problems), and looks at a wider array of possible failures (Kline and Rosenberg, 1986; Carlsson, 1995; Carlsson and Jacobsson, 1997; Smith, 2000; Klein Woolthuis et al., 2005; Chaminade and Edquist, 2010). Some of the barriers and obstacles mentioned in the literature include infrastructure provision and investments, barriers associated with the transition towards sustainability, innovation lock-in, network barriers, capability and learning issues, or lack of institutional complementarity. It is worth noting that these obstacles and barriers go beyond the traditional concerns of the three market failure rationales mentioned above. Taken together, this approach represents a novel effort to bring forward the importance of the contextual issues, and how these dysfunctionalities might negatively affect patterns and outcomes of innovation activity in its many different dimensions.

However relevant those obstacles and barriers, the theoretical foundations for innovation policy design from the innovation systems approach remain underdeveloped today. Despite the growing amount of literature devoted to these matters, the question of when and how public intervention in the innovation system is motivated or required remains rather open-ended. To be sure, the innovation systems literature provides some relevant blueprints for public intervention. However, oftentimes the theoretical foundations are formulated very abstractly and generically, without a clear description of which problems might afflict the innovation system. Moreover, they tend to disregard the potential problems generated by policy itself.

For that reason, clearly identifying the obstacles and barriers in the innovation system is a necessary first step for defining the scope and the nature of policy-making. We need a process in which a series of observations from theory, from innovation processes, and from the real world of policy-making are used to develop specific views about the obstacles and barriers that often afflict innovation systems. This will not only bring policy practice closer to the scholarly work, but it will also provide critical clues for further theoretical development. The latter refers to the process of theorizing, which entails a certain degree of real-life observations in the context of discovery, as well as considerations from previous findings (Swedberg, 2012). To be sure, theorizing is a process by which abstractions are developed in this context of discovery and into a gradual approximation towards the final development of a theory (the product of theorizing) (Sutton and Staw, 1995). 'Perhaps the ultimate trade-off is the one between process and product, between theorizing and theory, between doing it and freezing it' (Weick, 1995, p. 390).

Hence, the ambition of this book is to provide a solid theorizing process that will ultimately, in the future, bring forward a fully fleshed theory about the design of holistic innovation policy. In other words, this book constitutes an early step into the theorizing process that consists of building some stepping stones that bridge the gap between the observations of the real world of innovation policy-making, with the stringency and strengths of analytical scholarship. In order to do so, this book puts a particular emphasis on observing in detail the obstacles and barriers that are most often afflicting innovation systems. Thus, this book is a theorizing endeavour observing and identifying specific obstacles and barriers in the real world of innovation processes and the systems in which they are contextualized.

With this purpose in mind, the leading questions of this book are related to identifying and developing the theoretical foundations of innovation policy: towards what specific dimensions and problems in the innovation system should governments direct their attention? Can policy solve all types of problems in the innovation system—and if not, which ones? What should public policy try to do and what should it not? What are the unintended negative consequences of innovation policy? What specific policy instruments and combinations thereof are most suitable for solving different problems in different innovation systems?

1.3 What Goals? What Problems?

Policy rationales are the set of underlying reasons—the logical basis—for the course of a public action; in this case, for policy intervention. Therefore, a rationale can be seen as a consistent and well-defined argumentation that is used to justify (*ex-ante* or *ex-post*) the decision and shape of a policy intervention. They can be *ex-ante* in the contexts of political discussions and negotiations. They can also be *ex-post* in situations where policy-makers are arguing about decisions that were made previously, in the absence of explicit formulations. This argumentation, logical basis, and reason can be very differently formulated, but in the context of our current endeavour policy rationales are essentially the result from the process of theorizing. By collecting and putting experiences and observations from the real world into the context of discovery, the process of theorizing brings concrete phenomena into broader scholarly discussions. This is to say that, necessarily, these scholarly discussions will be related to a certain level of concreteness and move into a more general level of discussion.

A good starting point for such an endeavour is to ask questions about the specific goals of innovation policy, e.g. public health, economic growth, and environmental protection. What are the ultimate goals of innovation policy? The identification of clear goals gives an important sense of directionality and an ultimate purpose of policy intervention. This might sound trivial, but real-life goals are not always explicitly formulated or obvious.

Thereafter, at a more concrete level, the question that emerges is, what specific problems are innovation policy aiming to address? As we will discuss later, not all problems associated with innovation are amenable to being addressed by public interventions. For that reason, it is paramount to identify those problems in a clear way. Describing the specific nature of the innovation system suggests observations about the unwanted or harmful situations that need to be overcome and that are amenable to policy intervention. It is a matter of identifying the obstacles and barriers which typically and most often tend to afflict the good functioning of the innovation system, when aiming to achieve the ultimate goals suggested above.

The issue that arises at this point is how to identify the problems and how to formulate them. Here we need to revert to the characteristics and nature of the innovation system. This book focuses on ten crucial activities that define an innovation system, and looks into them one by one in order to identify the problems. Hence, based on our previous discussions above, this book will undertake the process of theorizing in three interrelated steps.

Firstly, it describes the features that characterize the specific activities and dimensions in the innovation system. This serves as guidance to proposing a mechanism or method for identifying policy problems in the system. Such policy problems may be mitigated by means of innovation policy instruments that are related to the activities.

Secondly, this book looks into the problems generated by policy intervention itself. This is an important matter, as governmental failure might be an important source of problems in the innovation system. Policies may be designed in a way that generate unexpected negative effects (for example, by distorting incentives).

Thirdly, this book identifies a series of more specific obstacles and barriers that might plague each of the different ten activities and dimensions in the innovation system, and which might be addressed by public policy (see Section 12.4). This is done taking into account the available policy instruments, the choices between them, and their implementation.

1.4 Instrument Choice and the Learning Policy-Maker

The choice of policy instruments is a crucial matter in the process of designing or, more correctly said, of constant redesigning of innovation policy. Yet, the availability of instruments and the logic behind their choice is always constrained by budgetary as well as politico-administrative matters and other circumstances. Yet, the specific forms of instrument mixes that governments develop through time, in new combinations, have to be based on a systematic review and appraisal of the obstacles and barriers that innovation encounters in a given country, region, or municipality. To do otherwise might run the risk that innovation policy becomes too conservative (without any significant or relevant changes in the instrument mix), and hence an oxymoron. Yet, policy-makers are always bounded one way or another (by limited resources, information, etc.); and, even if their choices might not be entirely free, their decisions have to be adaptive and based on continuous learning from experience.

Policy-making is certainly not always a rational and mechanistic process. On the contrary, it has been famously described as a process of 'muddling through' (Lindblom, 1959). This is so because the problems that policy-makers are dealing with are complex, interrelated, and ever changing. Moreover, policy-makers have limited resources, limited information, and operate within values-based political systems that determine political priorities (Forester, 1984). Furthermore, policy operates in a context of uncertainty, which means that there are no 'ready-made' or 'one-size-fits-all' policy solutions. For all those reasons the real life of policy-making tends to be incremental and based on gradual adjustments of existing instruments, rather than on great leaps or sudden deep changes. Hence, it is more accurate to talk about the constant redesign of innovation policy-making, transforming, and changing it in a gradual manner, according to what is needed but also to what is feasible.

Policy-making is about choice, implicit or explicit, by action or inaction. There are also some elements of serendipity in policy-making, as sometimes charismatic individuals are able to take the initiative and act as policy entrepreneurs (Breznitz, 2007) in specific circumstances and windows of opportunity (Citi, 2014). At other times, loosely defined ideas become fashionable, promoting some specific solutions in the absence of identified problems or clearly defined goals. And at other times, societies might have anti-government and anti-policy discourses overemphasizing the role of the free market, while their governments are simultaneously developing highly sophisticated and encompassing forms of public intervention. All of this shows how complicated innovation policy-making can become.

Policy-makers operate in a context where their policy initiatives need to be relevant and realistic. This requires not only high-level political will in the country, region, or municipality, but also, very importantly, the acceptance and adaptation of the relevant stakeholder groups in the economy and society while implementing the policy instruments.

This latter remark brings us to a key dimension in policy-making, namely, the participation of stakeholders in policy-making. The participatory nature of policy-making has been advanced in the new forms of governance, where public and private actors co-create and collaborate intensively in the definition and solution of complex collective problems (Pierre and Peters, 2005). Governance refers here to these forms of interaction where the state or public actors are one among other actors engaged in these collective processes, yet, an actor that (in most cases, not all) has particularly strong resources (authority, budget, etc.) and hence is not simply 'an additional' actor.

In the field of innovation policy, participation has been mainly addressed at regional and municipal levels, sometimes in the form of conditionality from external funding (donors or international organizations) (Diez, 2001). But it has also been extended to non-parliamentary forms of public participation at the national level (Joss, 1999), typically in the form of broad societal consultations and discussions, as well as participatory forms of technology assessment and forecasting (Weber et al., 2012; Schot, 2001). This is mostly associated with the need of broad societal debates about the consequences of specific innovations, as much as about the general societal priorities for the direction of socio-technical progress and innovation in the society, and its self-defined limits (Schot and O'Donovan, 2016).

Our book follows this participatory tradition, acknowledging that these broad and open debates are the way forward to democratizing important decisions about the collective future of a society. But also, they are the way to limit the harmful effects of sectoral interests capturing policy decisions. This latter point is not trivial in innovation policy. The large budgetary allocations of national and regional R&D public expenditure, and the regulatory frameworks authorizing (or not) new products, are two areas that typically attract a substantial number of private vested interests. Striking a balance between those in ways that the collective will is ultimately respected is not easy at times.

This book takes these issues into consideration when examining one by one the different areas of innovation policy-making, as the dynamics might differ according to these areas. Enhancing the absorptive capacity of governments, reinforcing their internal knowledge capabilities, and intensifying their intelligence sources about the problems of its innovation system is a useful way to immunize policy-makers to the arguments of vested interests, while letting them keep a solid overview of other interrelated issues in innovation. This has to do with policy-learning (Borrás, 2011).

The literature on organizational learning, and particularly the seminal work of James March, shows that past experience is ambiguous and therefore learning (as a process of sense-making of that experience) can take several forms. It can be a process of trial and error and/or a process that links past experience with abstract analytical frameworks (March, 2010). Our book follows that second type of learning process. It aims at developing a solid theoretical and conceptual framework that will serve the double purpose of guiding policy-makers in their co-evolving and participatory learning processes, and of advancing the social sciences' theoretical foundations of innovation systems and innovation policy.

Stan Metcalfe's view that 'the evolutionary policy-maker adapts rather than optimizes' (1995, p. 418) is particularly salient here. Adaptive (learning) policy-makers muddle through, inducing gradual (yet substantive) change, participating with a wide array of stakeholders in open discussions and co-creation of solutions, while keeping a solid and independent overview. Acknowledging the multiple and highly diversified state of traditions and politico-administrative systems, this book recognizes that there are no silver bullets or ready-made solutions. Instead, it aims at stimulating theoretically solid critical thinking among policy-makers and researchers. On that basis we propose a mechanism of identifying policy problems and mitigating them by proposing relevant policy instruments.

1.5 The Contents of This Book

The next two chapters constitute the conceptual backbone of the book. Chapter 2 comes to grips with the nature of innovation and of the innovation system, and in so doing it identifies ten specific activities that define an innovation system. The ten activities are specific elements directly related to the performance of innovation, which collectively shape the way in which innovation takes place in a specific economy. It develops and presents the theoretical basis, i.e. the specific assumptions and conceptual underpinnings, for the development and presentation of the holistic innovation policy approach.

Chapter 3 develops the core of the argument regarding the specific assumptions and theoretical propositions about the role and limits of innovation policy. The theoretical basis for the holistic approach to innovation policy proposed in this book includes the identification of the concrete policy problems that afflict the innovation system, including the unintended consequences when implementing policy. Following from that, the chapter argues that most innovation policies across countries are still partial, not holistic; that innovation policy must be separated from research policy; and that innovation policy-learning can only take place using an analytical model that helps understanding what worked, how, and why.

Chapter 4 focuses on knowledge production as one of the ten activities in innovation systems. It addresses questions like: Who produces scientific and technical knowledge these days? What type of knowledge is being produced, and for what purpose? Why are firms and governments funding R&D? It studies the role of public policy in knowledge production (especially R&D activities) relevant for the innovation process from a perspective of innovation systems. It examines how public actors have traditionally approached the issue of building, maintaining, and using knowledge in their innovation systems. It also identifies four typical policy-related obstacles and barriers associated with knowledge production in an innovation system. Next, it elaborates a set of overall criteria for the selection and design of relevant policy instruments addressing those barriers. Most importantly, the chapter argues that in most countries, innovation policy continues to be subsumed under research policy. An holistic and problem-oriented innovation policy requires that innovation policy and research policy are separated from each other in the design phase—but they must support each other when implemented (in the same way as many other policy areas have to be coordinated with each other).

The main question that guides Chapter 5 is how governments are focusing (and must focus) on competence-building (education, training, and skills formation) when designing and implementing innovation policies. After a brief literature review, this chapter suggests a typology of internal/external and individual/organizational sources of competences that are related to innovation activities. This serves to examine briefly the most common initiatives that governments are taking in this regard. The chapter identifies three overall obstacles and barriers in innovation systems in terms of education, training, and skills: the insufficient levels of competences in a system, the time lag between firms' short-term needs for specific competences and the long time required to develop them, and the imbalances between internal and external sources of competences in firms. On this basis, the chapter elaborates a set of overall criteria for the (re)design of policy instruments addressing those obstacles and barriers.

Chapter 6 looks at innovation-related public procurement as a specific form of innovation policy instrument operating from the demand side, as opposed to R&D that operates from the supply side, and has dominated—and is still dominating—innovation policy. The demand side of innovation policy may affect both the rate and direction of innovation processes. This could particularly be realized if an increasing part of the products (goods, services, and systems) are procured on the basis of descriptions of problems (societal, environmental) and functions, rather than on the basis of descriptions of products. Public procurement amounts to about 15 per cent of GDP in the whole of the European Union (EU), i.e. €2.0 trillion. Part of this enormous sum is already being used for supporting innovation by means of functional procurement and there is potential for much more of it to be used in that way. In this way, functional public procurement can become the most important instrument among all innovation policy instruments. It would then also be an important element in the transformation of innovation policy from being partial and linear to becoming increasingly holistic.

Chapter 7 addresses organizations and organizational change, which are crucial elements in innovation systems. Yet, their role is so ubiquitous that it is difficult to grasp and examine from the perspective of public policy. Besides, links between the literature at firm and systems levels on the one hand, and public policy studies on the other, are still scarce in this field. The purpose of this chapter is to define the conceptual background of innovation policy in relation to the role of organizations, looking in particular at the role of entrepreneurship and intrapreneurship as examples of organizational change. In so doing, this chapter aims at making three contributions. Firstly, it defines the role of entrepreneurship and intrapreneurship in the innovation system, a crucial topic in understanding innovation dynamics and its blurring borders. Secondly, it identifies the obstacles and barriers related to entrepreneurship and intrapreneurship in innovation systems and examines the choice of policy instruments to solve them. Thirdly, it discusses the limits of public policy and suggests key issues in the design of innovation policy.

Chapter 8 focuses on networks and complex forms of interaction in the innovation system. The logic behind this is that innovation systems cannot be conceptualized without understanding the networks that are formed by different actors in the system. These interactions take many different forms and dynamics, some of which have received specific attention in the literature, ranging from broad notions like social innovation and open innovation, to more specific forms of business-related and business-driven innovation interactions like firms' strategic R&D alliances, global and/or localized innovation networks, and user-driven innovation. This chapter aims at providing an encompassing view of these different notions, putting them directly into the theoretical context of the innovation systems approach. This is done not only for the sake of conceptual clarification, but above all for identifying the concrete obstacles and barriers associated with these interactions that might plague the innovation system. This serves as the basis for distinguishing and classifying the wide diversity of network-oriented innovation policy instruments that governments have deployed through time. Just as in other chapters of this book, the unexpected negative consequences of these instruments are also examined as part and parcel of possible obstacles and barriers in the innovation system. Last, the chapter puts forward a set of criteria for the design and redesign of these instruments according to the specific features that define the obstacles and barriers in the system (and of policy itself).

Institutions (understood as 'rules of the game') are constitutive elements of innovation systems, and therefore cornerstones of innovation policy. Focusing on soft and hard regulation, Chapter 9 identifies salient regulatory areas from the perspective of the innovation system. When addressing the effects of regulation on innovation, the chapter argues that there are three key issues that need careful empirical analysis. One is whether regulation is effective and efficient in terms of reducing uncertainty and generating incentives. Another is whether it is able to generate wider social benefits for the innovativeness of the economy at large. A third issue is the extent to which regulation is adapting to new (social, economic, and technological) contexts and is socially legitimate and accepted.

Chapter 10 examines small firms' access to venture capital for financing innovation processes. We go to great lengths to discuss where, i.e. in which situations, private funding is not available and why this is so. We address the rationales for public intervention, i.e. in which situations policy should be pursued. We also address the policy instruments for financing innovations that the state has available. We present a description and analysis of the provision of risk capital by the Swedish state. We describe a situation where unintended consequences of the policy pursued led to the non-fulfilment of the additionality condition. We also describe how this mistake has begun to be attempted to be resolved after discussions in the Swedish National Innovation Council, a government investigation, a bill from the government to the parliament, a decision there and the subsequent creation of a new public risk capital company, wholly owned by the Swedish state with a capital of 5 billion Swedish crowns (€0.55 billion). This means that we address innovation policy (re)design in action.

Chapters 4 to 10 examine different crucial areas or activities in innovation policy, the obstacles and barriers that emerge around them, the innovation policy instruments different governments have used, and the typical unintended negative consequences of policy. These three dimensions have been examined in order to identify some crucial aspects when designing or redesigning innovation policy instruments.

Chapter 11 focuses more concretely on the different innovation policy instruments as a whole. The purpose of this chapter is to discuss the different forms of intervention by governments, to explore the political nature of instrument choice and design (and associated issues), and to elaborate a set of criteria for the selection and design of the instruments in relation to the formulation of an holistic innovation policy. The chapter argues that innovation policy instruments must be designed and combined in ways that address the problems identified in the innovation system. These mixes are often called 'policy mixes', although we prefer the expression 'instrument mixes'. The problem-oriented nature of the design of instrument mixes is what makes innovation policy instruments 'holistic'.

The concluding Chapter 12 takes stock of the detailed considerations in its different sections, looking into a series of fundamental issues related to holistic innovation policy design. Most of all, this chapter summarizes previous chapters' identification of the problems, obstacles, or barriers that can afflict innovation systems. Together, the previous chapters provide an encompassing set of theoretical foundations behind the design of holistic innovation policy, which includes not only framing the problems in the innovation system, but also considerations about the most suitable policy instruments for the tasks at hand, including the unintended consequences that might be posed by policy instruments themselves. Readers who prefer to cut to the main arguments of the book may read Chapter 12 independently.

2

Innovations

A Systems Activities Approach

2.1 Introduction

'Innovation' and 'system of innovation' (SI) are notions that have gained substantial currency over the past few decades. Seen as a crucial dimension of economic growth and prosperity, as a source for improving social development, public health, environmental protection, etc., social scientists and policy-makers have tried to understand and decipher in which way and how to foster innovation. This includes influencing the rate (speed) and direction of innovation processes.

Analysts, policy-makers, and politicians have also tried to reflect critically about the boundaries of innovation, its trade-offs, and possible ethical dilemmas. However, no matter how fascinating these endeavours are, there continues to be a lack of conceptual clarity regarding what exactly innovation is, what exactly SIs are about, and what governments can do about problems afflicting them. Much of the lack of clarity these days has to do with the rapid blurring of the meaning of 'innovation'. This is due to a certain 'inflation' in its academic and conventional use, as well as within the rapidly changing context of innovation processes.

This chapter looks into these key conceptual and contextual matters as a way of setting up the foundations of the rest of the book. In particular, it focuses on two interrelated items. Firstly, the issue of 'what innovation and innovation systems are', which is not a trivial matter. The widespread use of the concept of 'innovation', in many different areas with many different meanings, requires clarification. We will delve into considerations about concept-stretching. Thereafter, we will formulate explicitly our own definitions of 'innovation', 'system of innovation', and other key concepts that will be used in this book. We clarify terms and notions, making clear what we include in these concepts and what we do not include, i.e. where the boundaries are. The presentation and discussion of these definitions will be embedded in theory, i.e. the relations between some of the concepts are also addressed.

Secondly, this chapter focuses on what 'happens' in SIs, which means that we address the 'activities' in SIs. This is our way of explaining what we mean by *the systems activities approach*. In so doing, we address the 'activities' in SIs by identifying ten activities that influence innovation processes. This chapter is devoted to unfolding, one by one, each of these ten activities, specifying the key activities in a dynamic perspective. The identification and definition of these ten activities is an essential stepping stone for Chapter 3.

It is important to note that our conceptual specifications do not exclude the possibility of alternative definitions of these concepts. Stipulative definitions are not right or wrong; they are good or bad for certain purposes. We choose the definitions and conceptual specifications below simply because they serve our purposes and we consider them to be reasonably clear. There are myriad other possible ones and it is futile to argue about them. Hence, we present our concepts briefly, without arguing in detail for our choices or explicitly comparing with the choices of others. We hope that our specification of the basic concepts provides a clear and solid basis for the analysis in the rest of this book. Hence, we present definitions that suit the purposes of our analysis, briefly and sharply. The concepts we chose, of course, stem from the history of the analyses of innovation processes, innovation systems, and the analysis and design of innovation policy.

2.2 What Is an Innovation?

Innovations are defined here as new creations of economic or societal importance, usually performed by firms. However, firms do not normally innovate in isolation, but in collaboration and interdependence with other organizations (actors or players), which are parts of SIs. These organizations may be other firms (suppliers, customers, even competitors) or non-firm entities such as universities and financing organizations. Innovations may be brand new, but are more often new combinations of existing elements, i.e. existing knowledge elements can be integrated into an innovation. Hence, innovations certainly do not need to be based on new scientific breakthroughs.

Innovations can be new or improved products or processes. New—or better—products (product innovations) may be material goods or intangible services; it is a question of what is produced. New—or better—processes (process innovations) may be technological or organizational;[1] here, it is a question of how the products are produced. Innovations are certainly not only technological and material.

Process innovations have been product innovations in earlier incarnations. This means that product innovations play a more dynamic role in the renewal of an innovation system and an economy than process innovations (Edquist et al., 2001a).[2] In this taxonomy, only goods and technological process innovations are material; the other categories are non-material and intangible. Thus, for example, innovations in service products are considered to be non-material or intangible innovations. So too are organizational process innovations.

Of great importance, however, is that the new creations do not become innovations until they are actually commercialized or diffused (i.e. spread) to a considerable degree. The development of a prototype or a test series are not enough for research results to qualify as innovations. New creations that are not commercialized or diffused in other ways are not innovations at all (OECD, 2005).[3]

The innovation concept used in this book is wide and includes product innovations as well as process innovations. It also includes the creation as well as the diffusion of new products and new processes to additional firms (possibly in other countries).[4] And it includes innovations in all sectors of society, the public as well as the private sector.

---

[1] Organizational innovations here capture forms within the production process, as they correspond to technological innovations—it is not meant to capture new organizations, such as firms or public agencies.

[2] Note that 'process innovations' are not the same as innovation processes', used later.

[3] This definition is based on the 2005 edition of the OECD Oslo Manual, which is the standard basis for work on innovation within the OECD and the EU—and elsewhere. During the phase of the work with this book when we checked the copy editing (late October 2018), the *Oslo Manual 2018* was published. The following is a quote from the OECD trailer: 'The *Oslo Manual* distinguishes between innovation as an outcome (an innovation) and the activities by which innovations come about (innovation activities). This edition defines an innovation as "a new or improved product or process (or combination thereof) that differs significantly from the unit's previous product or processes that has been made available to potential users (product) or brought into use by the unit (process)"'; http://www.oecd.org/sti/inno/oslo-manual-2018-info.pdf. We decided to make no changes in the text of this book caused by the new edition. However, we want to point out the following:

- The *Oslo Manual 2018* definition of innovation is more similar to the definition in this book than to definitions in previous editions of the Oslo Manual.
- It is interesting that the new Oslo Manual talks about innovation 'activities'.
- To qualify as an innovation the new product or process must have been made available to users.

[4] It might also be useful to distinguish between incremental and radical innovations and between science-based and experience-based innovations. A general remark is that the notion of innovation in a general sense is so comprehensive and heterogeneous, that it is useful to create various taxonomies of innovation and deal with the different categories of innovation separately, when describing and explaining innovation processes. However, different taxonomies will not be discussed in any detail here.

However, in recent years, there has been an 'inflation' in the use of the innovation concept. Innovation has become a buzz word on the lips of scholars from various disciplines, policy-makers, consultants, etc. This tremendous attention has produced a large variation of understandings and meanings of innovation. There is currently a great number of notions like 'open innovation' (Chesbrough, 2003; OECD, 2008), 'service-sector innovation' (Miles, 2005; Rubalcaba, 2006), 'innovation in the public sector' (Bartlett and Dibben, 2002; Hartley, 2005), 'frugal innovation' (Zeschky et al., 2011; Prahalad, 2012), 'employee-driven innovation' (Høyrup, 2010), etc.

We do not undertake a literature review of the many recently proposed widenings of what innovation can be because it is beyond the scope of this book. As an example, we will just mention 'social innovation', a concept that has become increasingly popular (Domanski et al., 2014; Nicholls et al., 2015; Maclean et al., 2013). When used, the concept of 'social innovation' often means making innovations with the objective of solving social problems or meeting social challenges. 'Social innovation' refers to highly respectable and very important issues. However, we believe that it is not useful to regard them as a certain class of innovation, just as we do not want to consider scientific progress (like Albert Einstein's general theory of relativity), institutional change (like changes in constitutional law), or new cultural achievements (a new film) to be innovations. We prefer to see some of these 'open innovations', 'social innovations', employee-driven innovations, etc. as ordinary product and process innovations (see definition above) that have consequences for solving social problems and for mitigating social challenges. Hence, social innovations are a matter of objectives and directionality (and consequences) of pursuing innovation processes and innovation policies.

In this book, only product and process innovations as specified above are therefore considered to be innovations. This means that new markets, new research results, new patents, new organizations, new institutions, etc. are not called 'innovations' here. We prefer to defend some limits to what is included in the category of innovation, and be clear about the boundaries of the concept. We strongly stress the crucial role of new markets, new research results, new institutions, new organizations, and new institutions in innovation systems—but we do not call them 'innovations'. These phenomena are instead determinants of innovations and are here dealt with in terms of 'activities' in innovation systems that influence the development of (product and process) innovations. The main part of this chapter is devoted to an identification and discussion of these key activities.

The development of innovations can be regarded as investments that are subject to risk and uncertainty. Some people might believe that 'more innovation is always better'. However, this is not the case. We cannot take for granted that more innovation is better. At the same time we cannot determine how much innovation is 'optimal'. This is certainly a dilemma that is not solvable and we have to live with it and deal with it. Neither can we argue that innovations are always good nor bad. They are not value neutral. There are, for example, innovations that destroy the environment and there are others that improve environmental conditions. It is in such contexts that innovation policy tries to influence the direction of innovation processes by pursuing certain objectives (Edquist, 2011; Section 3.6. of this book).

The definitions of the key terms introduced in this chapter and in Chapter 3 are summarized in Box 2.1. Some of them will be discussed in more detail in later sections of this chapter and in Chapter 3. This is particularly true for

---

Box 2.1 DEFINITIONS OF KEY TERMS

Innovations	New creations of economic significance, primarily carried out by firms (but not in isolation). They include product innovations as well as process innovations.
Product innovations	New—or improved—material goods as well as new intangible services; a matter of *what* is produced.
Process innovations	New ways of producing goods and services. They may be technological or organizational; a matter of *how* things are produced.
Creation versus diffusion of innovations	This dichotomy is partly based on a distinction between innovations that are 'new to the market' (brand new, or globally new) and innovations that are 'new to the firm' (being adopted by or diffused to additional firms, countries, or regions). In other words, 'new to the firm' innovations are actually (mainly) a measure of the diffusion of innovations. For many small countries, diffusion (absorption from abroad) is, relatively speaking, more important than the creation of new innovations.
Systems of innovation	Include innovations as such as well as determinants of innovation processes—i.e. all important economic, social, political, organizational, institutional, and other factors that influence the development and diffusion of innovations. SIs are also called innovation systems.
Main role of SIs	To pursue innovation processes—i.e. to develop and diffuse innovations.
Activities in SIs	Those factors and actions that influence the development and diffusion of innovations. The activities in SIs are the same as the determinants of the main role of innovation systems, i.e. to drive or enhance innovation processes. (A list of activities is presented in Box 2.2.) The same activity (e.g. R&D) can be performed by several categories of organizations (universities, public research organizations, firms). And the same kind of organization (e.g. universities) can perform more than one kind of activity (e.g. research and teaching).
Components of SIs	Include both organizations and institutions.

(continued)

Box 2.1 CONTINUED	
Constituents of SIs	Include both components of SIs and relations among these components.
Organizations	Formal structures that are consciously created and have an explicit purpose. They are players or actors.
Institutions	Sets of common habits, norms, routines, established practices, rules, or laws that regulate the relations and interactions between individuals, groups, and organizations. They are the rules of the game.

Source: Edquist 2011

activities in innovation systems, and concepts related to innovation policy in Chapter 3 of this book.

2.3 What Is an Innovation System?

The processes through which innovations emerge are complex; they (often, but not always) have to do with the emergence and diffusion of new knowledge elements, as well as the 'transformation' of these into new products and new production processes. The behaviour of organizations (such as firms[5]) is also shaped by institutions—or rules of the game—that constitute incentives and obstacles for innovation. These organizations and institutions are components of systems for the creation and commercialization of innovations. Innovations emerge in such SIs. The constituents of SIs include the components (organizations and institutions) of the systems as well as the relations among those. The main role of SIs is to pursue innovation processes.

The so-called linear model dominated innovation studies and innovation policy in the early days (Bush, 1945). This linear model was based on the assumption that innovations are applied scientific knowledge. The model was called 'linear' because innovations were assumed to be generated by a process consisting of well-defined, consecutive stages, e.g. basic research, applied research, and development work, resulting in new products and processes that ultimately influence growth and employment as well as societal and environmental problems. It was a supply and technology-push view.

However, research does not automatically lead to innovations, and innovations need not be preceded by research. Scientific knowledge that may lead to

[5] Innovation systems cannot be internal to (large) firms, but firms are the most important organizations in innovation systems.

inventions is not sufficient; it has to be transformed into commercialized innovations in order to mitigate societal and environmental problems and create growth and employment. The goal should never be to enhance innovation as such or in the abstract. Innovations should always have a purpose. Innovations themselves, as such, are not interesting, but their consequences are.

Some research results are never transformed into innovations, and research is only one of the many determinants of the development and diffusion of innovations. Above all, research is never sufficient to achieve innovations, and it is certainly not always necessary. Most innovations are developed without a direct basis in new research.

The SI approach, which has diffused rapidly during the latest decades, has completely replaced the linear view in the field of innovation research. This approach is very different from the linear approach. It is usually, in its different versions, defined in terms of determinants of innovation processes, although different determinants are emphasized in different versions (Freeman, 1987; Lundvall, 1992; Nelson, 1993; Braczyk et al., 1998; Carlsson, 1997; Cooke, 2001a; Bergek et al., 2008). The SI approach is also used in policy contexts by regional organizations (Cooke et al., 1997), national governments, public agencies, and international organizations such as the Organisation for Economic Co-operation and Development (OECD), EU, the United Nations Conferences on Trade and Development, United Nations Industrial Development Organization, etc. We will address innovation policy and the SI approach in more detail in Chapter 3.

The pioneers in the development of the SI approach were the books of Lundvall, and of Nelson and Rosenberg.[6] Both define national SIs (NSIs) in terms of determinants, or factors, affecting innovation processes, although they point out different determinants as important in their definitions (Chaminade and Edquist, 2006; Edquist, 2014d). Lundvall writes that the 'structure of production' and 'the set of institutions' together define an SI (Lundvall, 1992, p. 10). Nelson and Rosenberg emphasize the organizations that support R&D—that is, the organizations that support the creation and dissemination of knowledge—as the main source of innovation (Nelson and Rosenberg, 1993).

If all the factors that influence innovation processes cannot be included in the definition, we have to choose the potential factors that should be excluded, and motivate why. This is difficult, because at any given moment we do not know, systematically and in detail, what all of these determinants are. It seems risky to exclude certain potential determinants, as these may prove to be important when our knowledge has increased. Thirty-five years

---

[6] What follows in the rest of this section is based on Edquist 2014b.

ago, for example, it was natural to exclude interaction between organizations as a determinant of innovation processes. Today, we know that these are very important (Camagni, 1991; Edquist and Johnson, 1997; Edquist, 2005; Cunningham and Ramlogan, 2016; Haakonsson and Slepniov, 2018). Therefore, a broad definition, including all possible determinants, is highly preferable.

Interactive learning has been central to the concept of NSIs from the beginning (Lundvall, 1992). The main components of an innovation system are often said to be organizations and institutions. In our view these two categories should be clearly distinguished from each other, but they are often not. For us more useful stipulative definitions follow.

Organizations are formal structures (e.g. hierarchies) that are consciously created and have an explicit purpose. They are actors or 'players'. Examples include companies, universities, and policy organizations.

For their part, institutions are laws, rules, regulations, routines, and habits. They are the 'rules of the game'. Institutions may be external to organizations, or located inside them. Organizations may influence institutions and they may be influenced by them. Key institutions in innovation systems are patent laws, national laws, and rules that govern the relations between companies and universities, rules governing the approval of drugs, rules and laws governing public procurement, etc. (Edquist and Johnson, 1997).[7]

Most of the attention in innovation research has long been paid to the components (organizations and institutions) of SIs in a static way, e.g. by Lundvall, and Nelson and Rosenberg. Less has been said about the processes that occurs within the systems and how they change. We choose such a dynamic approach and we label it a 'systems activities approach'.

As we have seen, traditional SI approaches, such as Lundvall (1992) and Nelson and Rosenberg (1993), focused strongly upon the components within the systems, i.e. organizations and institutions. Since the late 1990s, some authors have addressed issues related to the specification of activities influencing the main role of SIs (Galli and Teubal, 1997; Liu and White, 2001; Johnson et al., 2002). Such a focus on 'activities' (also sometimes called functions) within SIs emphasizes strongly what 'happens' in the systems—rather than their components. In this sense the systems activities approach pursued here provides a more dynamic perspective—an issue to which we will return in Section 2.4.[8]

---

[7] To study the relations between them, they must be conceptually distinguished from each other. For Nelson and Rosenberg (1993), 'institutions' are the same as different kinds of 'organizations' ('players'), while the term 'institution' primarily means 'the rules of the game' for Lundvall (1992). Hence, the term 'institution' is used in different senses in the literature, and institutions and organizations are often not clearly distinguished from each other.

[8] The focus on activities here does not mean that we disregard or neglect the organizations and institutions that constitute the components of SIs. When addressing activities it is also necessary to address the organizations (or organizational actors) that carry out these activities and the

We chose the term 'activities' to denote the determinants that influence the development, and diffusion and use of, innovations. Examples are R&D (as a means for the development of economically relevant knowledge that can sometimes provide a basis for innovations—Chapter 4 of this book), or the financing of the commercialization of such knowledge, i.e. transformation into innovations (Chapter 10 of this book). An alternative term to 'activities' is 'functions' (Hekkert et al., 2007; Bergek et al., 2010). We chose the term 'activities' in order to avoid the connotation with 'functionalism', the traditional approach in classic sociology. Classical functionalist sociologists tended to focus on the consequences of a phenomenon rather than on the causes (determinants). Our focus is on the causes (determinants) of innovation (Edquist 2005: footnote 16), rather than its consequences. As mentioned above and below, other colleagues prefer the term 'function' to denote almost the same thing.

One way to address what occurs within SIs is as follows. On a general level, the main dynamics of the innovation system is to drive or enhance innovation processes, i.e. to develop and disseminate innovations. What we call the activities in innovation systems are those that affect the development and diffusion of innovations. Examples of such activities are R&D and financing, as mentioned above. As we will see in Section 2.5, there are many other activities.

There are many specifications and definitions of the SI approach. For us, innovation systems should be defined as ones that include 'all important economic, social, political, organizational, institutional and other factors that influence the development, diffusion and use of innovations', as well as the innovations themselves (Edquist, 1997, pp. 3, 11–12; 2005, pp. 184 and 190–1, 2011; Borrás and Edquist 2013a and 2013b).

Hence, innovations can be seen as the output, whereas the innovation system is also constituted by a set of activities or determinants that influence such output. This is a wide definition; much more comprehensive than earlier ones. At the same time, the innovation system should not be considered as being the same as the whole economy or the whole society. It is much more sensible to limit the notion of innovation system to be constituted by innovations of various kinds and all the activities or determinants that influence their development and diffusion. The activities that are performed in innovation systems will be detailed later in Section 2.4.

Innovation systems may be national, regional, or sectoral. These three perspectives may be clustered as variants of a single generic SI approach (Edquist and Johnson, 1997). Much of the discussion here is based on the premise that the different variants of SI coexist and complement each other

institutions (institutional rules) that constitute incentives and obstacles affecting the innovation efforts of these organizations.

(Tödtling and Trippl, 2005) (Amable et al., 1997). Whether the most appropriate conception of the SI, in a certain context, should be national, sectoral, or regional depends, to a large extent, on the questions one wants to ask.

We believe that a systematic emphasis on activities or determinants within SIs will become crucial for the development of both innovation theory and innovation policies in the future. It is also by influencing the determinants of innovation that enterprises and public agencies can influence the innovation processes through their strategies and policies.

SIs are not 'machines' that produce innovations in a mechanical or automatic way. They are systems in which the different activities are partly self-organized. Part of this coordination is performed by the self-organization of markets. And another part of the necessary coordination of the activities is achieved by means of policy and politics—as we will discuss in Chapter 3, and in much of the rest of this book.

2.4 Key Activities in Innovation Systems

No consensus has yet emerged among innovation researchers as to which specific activities (functions, determinants) should be included. This is because innovation research has not yet been able to identify in a specific enough manner the determinants of the development and the diffusion of different kinds of innovation. The state of the art is simply not advanced enough—and this provides abundant opportunities for further research. In Box 2.2 we present a hypothetical list of ten activities. This list of activities is based on the literature and on our own knowledge about innovation processes and their determinants, as discussed earlier (Edquist, 2005; Edquist and Chaminade, 2006; Chaminade and Edquist, 2010 and Edquist 2011). The activities are not ranked in order of importance, but the list is structured into four thematic categories:

I. Provision of knowledge inputs into the innovation process (e.g. research, education, training, and competence development).

II. Demand-side activities (e.g. public procurement for innovation, or articulation of new product quality, or safety requirements).

III. Provision of constituents of SIs, for example creating and changing organizations (e.g. entrepreneurship), creating and changing institutions, networking, and interactions.

IV. Support services for innovating firms (e.g. financing innovation processes or incubation of innovative firms).

The different activities can each be considered to be determinants of the development and diffusion of innovations. The list is certainly preliminary.

Box 2.2 KEY ACTIVITIES IN SYSTEMS OF INNOVATION

I. **Provision of knowledge inputs into the innovation process**

　　1. *Provision of R&D results* and, thus, creation of new knowledge, primarily in engineering, medicine, and natural sciences.
　　2. *Competence-building*, e.g. through individual learning (educating and training for the labour force for innovation and R&D activities) and organizational learning. This includes both formal and informal learning.

II. **Demand-side activities**

　　3. *Formation of new product markets*, for example through public procurement of innovation.
　　4. *Articulation of new product quality requirements* emanating from the demand side.

III. **Provision of constituents for SIs**

　　5. *Creation and change of organizations* needed for developing new fields of innovation. Examples include enhancing entrepreneurship to create new firms and intrapreneurship to diversify existing firms, and creating new research organizations, policy agencies, etc.
　　6. *Interactive learning, networking and knowledge integration* among different organizations involved in the innovation processes. This implies integrating new knowledge elements developed in different spheres of the SI and coming from the outside with elements already available in the innovating firms.
　　7. *Creation and change of institutions*—e.g. patent laws, tax laws, environment and safety regulations, R&D investment routines, cultural norms, etc.—that influence innovating organizations and innovation processes by providing incentives for and removing obstacles to innovation.

IV. **Support services for innovating firms**

　　8. *Financing of innovation processes* and other activities that may facilitate commercialization of knowledge and its adoption.
　　9. *Incubation activities* such as providing access to facilities and administrative support for innovating efforts.
　　10. *Provision of consultancy services* relevant for innovation processes, e.g. technology transfer, commercial information, and legal advice.

Source: adapted from Edquist, 2005 and 2011.

Extra activities may be added as our knowledge about determinants of (different kinds of) innovation processes increases.

Our specific definition of innovation systems (presented in general terms in Section 2.3) is based on a particular specification of the SI approach where the ten activities (or determinants of innovation processes) define an innovation system. This definition of an SI is much broader and more general than other variants (e.g. Lundvall's and, especially, Nelson and Rosenberg's).[9]

---

[9] Nelson and Rosenberg's definition, organizations that support R&D, is actually very close to being linear.

It includes all determinants of innovation processes (as well as the innovations themselves).

The concept of 'innovation ecosystem' is increasingly used. As we see it, the biological analogy 'eco' adds nothing of substance at all. This is pointed out by other authors, who also claim, 'Innovation ecosystems is not yet a clearly defined concept, much less a theory. Moreover, the idea carries pitfalls, notably its over-emphasis on market forces, and its flawed analogy to natural ecosystems' (Oh et al. 2016, p. 1). Our activities approach to SIs is a more clearly defined notion, and much more useful as a basis for pursuing innovation policy (as we will see in Chapter 3).

It is important to keep in mind that the activities are not ranked according to importance. Together, they all refer to different dimensions of determinants of innovation processes, which complement each other in different ways—sometimes potentially overlapping and reinforcing each other, sometimes pulling in different directions.

The list of activities (sometimes called functions in other lists) in Box 2.2 is preliminary, and one among several possible lists of activities. It will certainly be revised when our knowledge of the determinants of innovation processes has improved. Nonetheless, this list can still be used as a checklist or signpost to discuss the factors that—probably—affect innovation processes. This is important, as innovation processes are very complex and influenced by a variety of factors. Among other things, the list can serve as a tool to avoid simplistic mono-causality, i.e. an overly strong emphasis on one single activity (be it research or seed funding) and a neglect of others (be it innovation-enhancing public procurement or entrepreneurship). Innovation processes are certainly multicausally determined, i.e. partially influenced by several or many activities or determinants. This is important when we causally try to explain innovation processes and when we want to select innovation policy instruments to mitigate policy problems (see Chapter 3).

The list in Box 2.2 may thus be useful in assigning causes to policy problems and to identify possible policy instruments to solve the policy problems. If the main cause of a policy problem is a lack of research, then R&D should be in focus. If the cause is a lack of demand for certain kinds of product innovation, then a demand-side instrument such as innovation-enhancing public procurement can be used. At least the most important causes of the development and diffusion of innovations need to be identified, in order for policy-makers and politicians to be able to identify innovation policy instruments that can solve or mitigate the policy problems. All ten activities in Box 2.2 can be related to several innovation policy instruments. In fact, several instruments might have to be considered for each of the ten activities in the innovation system, i.e. it can even be a matter of choosing from among scores of instruments (Borrás and Edquist, 2013b, and Chapter 11 in this book).

Therefore, our approach is *broader* than corresponding approaches because we focus on all the activities in SIs (rather than on the components in the systems). Furthermore, it is *dynamic* because we focus on the changes associated with determinants. For example, we address 'creating and changing organizations' and 'creating and changing institutions', rather than organizations and institutions as such in the list of activities (see Box 2.2). Our focus on 'activities' emphasizes strongly what happens in the systems—rather than their components. In this sense the activities approach provides a more dynamic perspective than other perspectives, such as Lundvall's and Nelson and Rosenberg's.

We believe that understanding the dynamics of each of the activities and the division of labour between private and public organizations in performing them is important to describe, explain, and influence innovation processes. It is a useful departure point for discussing the role of the state (public organizations) in influencing the direction and speed of innovation processes by means of innovation policies.

The list of ten activities is an effort to organize the determinants of innovation processes in SIs. The list should be seen as an effort to theorize about determinants of innovations in innovation systems. In other words, the list is a theoretical effort to create some order in a number of determinants of innovations previously identified by the rich literature of evolutionary and institutional economics of innovation.

2.5 Specification of the Activities in Systems of Innovation

In this section we will describe in more detail some of the activities listed in Box 2.2.

2.5.1 *Provision of Knowledge Inputs to the Innovation Process*

2.5.1.1 PROVISION OF RESEARCH AND DEVELOPMENT RESULTS
'Research and experimental development (R&D) comprise creative work undertaken on a systematic basis in order to increase the stock of knowledge, including knowledge of man, culture, and society, and the use of this stock of knowledge to devise new applications' (OECD, 2002, p. 30). According to the Frascati Manual, the term R&D covers three activities: basic research, applied research, and experimental development. Basic research is experimental or theoretical work undertaken primarily to acquire new knowledge without any particular application or use in view. Applied research is also original investigation in order to acquire new knowledge, but is directed

mainly toward a specific practical aim or objective. Experimental development is systematic work, drawing on existing knowledge gained from research and/or practical experience, which is directed to producing new materials, products, or devices, to installing new processes, systems, and services, or to improving substantially those already produced and installed (OECD, 2002, p. 30).

Here, we want to distinguish, to the largest possible extent, between determinants of innovation processes and innovation processes as such. Obviously, 'Experimental development', according to the Frascati definition, highly overlaps with innovation activities.

R&D results are an important basis for some innovations, particularly radical ones in engineering, medicine, and the natural sciences. R&D resulting in radical innovations has traditionally been an activity partly financed and carried out by public organizations. This applies to basic research, as well as to applied research in some countries, conducted in public universities and public research organizations. NSIs can differ significantly with regard to the balance between these two kinds of organization in the provision of R&D. In Sweden, less than 5 per cent of all R&D is carried out in public research organizations. In Norway, this figure is more than 20 per cent.

Such data may be a way of distinguishing between different types of NSIs. In most low- and medium-income NSIs in the world today, little R&D is carried out and the bulk of this is performed in public organizations. Some high-income countries spend considerable amounts of their GDP on R&D, and much of that is carried out by private organizations. This includes not only some large countries such as the USA and Japan, but also some small- and medium-sized countries such as Sweden, Denmark, Switzerland, and South Korea.

Because innovation processes are evolutionary and path dependent, there is a danger of negative lock-ins, that is, trajectories of innovation that lead to low growth and decreasing employment. Potentially, superior innovation trajectories may not materialize and the generation of diversity may be reduced or blocked. In such situations, the state should favour experimentation and use R&D subsidies and public procurement for innovation, for instance, to support possible alternatives (Edquist et al., 2004).

In sum, public organizations may influence the R&D activity in different ways ranging from allocating funds for specific research activities in public universities and research centres to stimulating alternatives via R&D subsidies. However, more analysis is needed in order to understand the interrelationships of R&D, innovation, productivity growth, the role of R&D in innovation in different sectors, and the impact of different instruments on the propensity of firms to invest in R&D.

2.5.1.2 COMPETENCE-BUILDING

Here we use the definition of (Johnson et al., 2002) of *competence-building* that includes formal education and training, the labour market dynamics, and the organization of knowledge creation and learning within firms and in networks. Knowledge is a 'stock' category and learning is a 'flow' category adding more knowledge to the existing 'stock'. Competence-building includes processes and activities related to the capacity to create, absorb, and exploit knowledge for individuals and organizations. Obviously, this includes formal learning as well as informal learning.[10] In addition, informal learning is vital for innovation processes and, therefore, an important part of (the activity of competence-building in) SIs.

n most countries, much of the education and training that are important for innovation processes (and R&D) are primarily provided by public organizations—schools, universities, training institutes, and so on. However, some competence-building is done in firms through learning-by-doing, learning-by-using, and learning-by-interacting—which are informal activities. Competence-building may increase the human capital of individuals: that is, it is a matter of individual learning, the result of which is controlled by individuals.[11]

The organizational and institutional contexts of competence-building vary considerably among NSIs. There are, for example, significant differences between the systems in the English-speaking countries and continental Europe. However, scholars and policy-makers lack good comparative measures on the scope and structure of such differences. There is little detailed knowledge about the ways in which the organization of education and training influences the development and diffusion of innovations (Toner and Woolley, 2016; Lorenz et al., 2016; Lorenz, 2011). As labour, including skilled labour, is—still—the least mobile production factor, domestic systems

---

[10] Formal learning is planned learning resulting from activities within a structured learning setting; it often takes place within a teacher–student relationship, such as in a school system. Informal learning occurs outside formal learning and teaching settings, often through the experience of day-to-day situations. It is a part of 'lifelong learning', extending for decades after formal schooling. Formal learning is often a foundation for informal or ongoing learning.

[11] There is also organizational learning, the result of which is controlled or owned by firms and other organizations. Organizational learning leads to the accumulation of 'structural capital', a knowledge-related asset controlled by firms (as distinguished from 'human capital'). An example of such an asset may be a patent, based on learning pursued by individuals but often owned by firms. Organizations have an interest in transforming individual knowledge into organizational knowledge, e.g. through codification of individual knowledge into operation manuals (Edquist et al., 2001b).

for competence-building remain among the most enduringly national of elements of NSIs. However, international mobility of labour is in the process of increasing.

Competence-building should not, however, be limited to human capital. Organizations may have competences that exceed those of the employees.[12] Human capital is hired by the company but is always owned by individuals. There are ways in which the firm can capture individual knowledge and transform it into organizational knowledge. There is also learning at the social level, i.e. neither individual nor organizational learning, but involving society outside these spheres. Organizing the processes of learning within the firm and in networks is part of the competence-building activity (Lundvall et al., 2002). Many individuals belong to many networks, both formal and informal, where learning takes place. Individuals may have attachments other than employment organizations, such as labour unions, technical societies, and Rotary Clubs. Scholars started to analyse such processes in the late 1990s, but many questions remain unanswered (Edvinsson and Malone, 1997; Lorenz and Lundvall, 2011).

2.5.2 Demand-Side Activities

2.5.2.1 FORMATION OF NEW PRODUCT MARKETS

In the very early stages of the development of new fields of innovation, there is uncertainty about whether market demand exists.[13] The state might need to intervene in the market from the demand side for market creation (Mazzucato, 2016). There are two main reasons for this: a market for certain goods and services might not exist, or the users of goods and services might not be sophisticated enough to provide the required feedback to the producers with regard to new needs.

One example of market creation is in the area of inventions. The creation of intellectual property rights (IPR) through patents gives a temporary monopoly to the patent owner, which is intended to enhance commercialization by making the selling and buying of technical knowledge easier.[14] Policy-makers may also enhance the creation of markets by supporting legal security or the formation of trust.

---

[12] Of course, the competence of an organization may also amount to less than the sum of the individual competencies, the organization thereby being dysfunctional.

[13] In this sub-section we will address 'Formation of new product markets' as well as 'Articulation of product quality requirements' (see Box 2.2).

[14] Paradoxically, then, a monopoly is created by law in order to create a market for knowledge: that is, to make it possible to trade in knowledge.

Another example of public support to market creation is the creation of standards. For example, the NMT 450 mobile telecom standard created by the Nordic telecommunication companies in the 1970s and 1980s—when they were state-owned monopolies—was crucial for the development of mobile telephony in the Nordic countries. This made it possible for private firms to develop mobile systems (Edquist, 2003).

In some cases, the instrument of public procurement for innovation has been important for market formation (Edquist et al., 2000b, 2014; Edquist and Zabala-Iturriagagoitia, 2012, 2015; Edquist, 2014c, 2015). In other words, a market emerged because the public sector demanded products and systems that did not exist before the public procurement for innovation. This has been—and still is—an important instrument in the defence sector in all countries. It has also been important in infrastructure development (telecoms, trains, etc.) in many countries. Moreover, public policy may influence demand—and thereby diffusion of innovations—when public agencies require a certain product mix, such as a minimum share of electricity based on renewable resources or cars powered by electricity or fuel cells.

The provision of new markets is often linked to the articulation of product quality requirements. Articulation of quality requirements emanating from the demand side with regard to the characteristics of the new products is important for product development in most SIs, enhancing innovation and steering processes of innovation in certain directions (see Sections 3.5 and 3.6 for a discussion of the meaning of the term 'direction'). Most of this activity is performed spontaneously by demanding customers in SIs, as a result of interactive learning between innovating firms and their customers. However, product quality requirements may also be a consequence of public action, for example, regulation in the fields of health, safety, and the environment, or the development of technical standards. Public procurement for innovation normally includes a functional specification of the product or system wanted, and this certainly means demand articulation that influences product development significantly.

Functional procurement can be defined as the procurement of products by a public authority/unit that describes a function to be performed (or a problem to be solved) instead of describing *the product that is to perform the function*. In functional procurement, a public agency specifies *what* is to be achieved rather than *how* it is to be achieved. Functional regular procurement is pursued by means of functional specifications instead of product specifications. Hence, it is a matter of the *manner* in which a procurement call is set up and the tender documentation is formulated. Needs are translated into functions to which potential suppliers can respond. Needs are accurately identified and presented as requirements in terms that suppliers can respond to. It *opens up* for innovation but does not *require* it. Innovations are not excluded or disadvantaged, as they are in product procurement.

31

2.5.3 *Provision of Constituents for Systems of Innovation*

2.5.3.1 CREATION AND CHANGE OF ORGANIZATIONS

As pointed out, organizations are considered key components in SIs. Entry and exit of organizations, as well as change of incumbent organizations, are therefore important activities contributing to the change of SIs as such. Organizations include not only firms, but also universities, research institutes, financing bodies, and so on. But since firms are ultimately responsible for commercializing new products, we will focus mainly on the creation and change of firms.

The creation and change of organizations for the development and diffusion of innovations is partly a matter of spontaneous firm-creation (through entrepreneurship) and diversification of existing firms (through intrapreneurship). However, public action can also facilitate such private activities by institutional change, for example, by changing tax laws. Mergers between firms are also organizational changes. New R&D organizations (public research organizations and universities) as well as innovation policy agencies are also created through political decisions.

One important role of policy is to enhance the entry and survival of new firms by facilitating and supporting entrepreneurship. Compared to incumbents, new entrants are characterized by different capabilities, and they may be the socio-economic carriers of innovations. They bring new ideas, products, and processes. Hence, public agencies should create an environment favourable to the entry of new firms and the growth of successful small and medium-sized firms. Survival and growth of firms often require continuous (or at least multiple) innovations, particularly in high-tech sectors of production.

Enhancing entrepreneurship and intrapreneurship may be a way of supporting changes in the production structure in the direction of producing new products to a larger extent. There are three mechanisms by which the production structure may change through the addition of new products: existing firms might diversify into new products (as has happened often in Japan and South Korea, for example); new firms in innovative product areas might grow rapidly (as many have in the USA, for example); foreign firms might invest in new product areas in a country (Ireland, for example).

Adding new products to an existing bundle of products is important, since the demand for new products might grow more rapidly than for old ones—with accompanying job creation and economic growth. New products might also be characterized by high productivity growth. Public agencies could therefore create opportunities and incentives for changes in the production structure.

In any SI it is important to study whether the existing organizations are appropriate for promoting innovation. How should organizations be changed or engineered to induce innovation? This dynamic perspective on organizations is crucial in our version of the SI approach (the systems activities approach). Creation, destruction, and change of organizations were very important in the development of strategies in the successful Asian economies and they are crucial in the ongoing transformation of Central and Eastern Europe and Latin America. Hence, organizational changes seem to be particularly important in situations of rapid structural change which, in turn, is linked to building the capacity to deal with such changes. Policy issues in this context concern how policy-makers may help develop alternative patterns of learning and innovation, and nurture emerging sectoral SIs (Edquist et al., 2004).

2.5.3.2 INTERACTIVE LEARNING, NETWORKING, AND KNOWLEDGE INTEGRATION

As we have pointed out, relations among SI components (i.e. organizations such as firms, universities, public agencies, and institutions such as established practices, rules, and laws) are a basic constituent of SIs. Relations facilitate interactive learning which, in turn, is a basis for innovation. The SI approach, emphasizing interdependence and non-linearity, is based on the understanding that firms normally do not innovate in isolation, but interact with other organizations through complex relations that are often characterized by reciprocity and feedback mechanisms in several loops. Innovation processes are not only influenced by the components of the systems, but also by the relations among them. This captures the non-linear features of innovation processes and is one of the most important characteristics of the SI approach.

The interactive nature of much learning and innovation implies that this interaction could be targeted much more directly than is normally the case in innovation policy today (Oerlemans and Meeus, 2005; Lundvall and Johnson, 1994). The SI approach should not only focus on the organizations of the systems, but also—and perhaps primarily—on the relations among them. Relations between organizations might occur through markets and other mechanisms. This implies integrating new knowledge developed in different spheres of SIs and coming from outside with knowledge already available in the innovating firms. It is a matter of 'learning linkages' across the boundaries of organizations.

Most of the interaction between organizations involved in innovation processes occurs spontaneously when there is a need. The activity of (re)combining knowledge—from any source—into product and process innovations is largely carried out by private firms by means of self-organization. They often collaborate with other firms, but sometimes universities and public research organizations are also involved. The long-term innovative performance of firms in science-based industries strongly depends on the interaction of firms, universities, and research facilities. If they are not spontaneously operating smoothly enough, these interactions should be facilitated by means of policy. Here, institutions are important, as we will see in Section 2.5.3.3.

Relations between universities and public research institutes, on the one hand, and firms on the other are coordinated only to a limited degree by markets. Policies help coordinate relations in different ways and to different degrees, reflecting differences across NSIs—but sometimes they are not coordinated at all. Incubators, technology parks, and public venture capital funds might also help in a similar way. This means that the public sector might create organizations to facilitate innovation. At the same time, however, it might create the rules and laws that govern these organizations and their relations to private ones—that is, create and change institutions (Edquist et al., 2004).

2.5.3.3 CREATION AND CHANGE OF INSTITUTIONS

Institutions are normally considered the second main component in SIs, in addition to organizations. Creating, demolishing, and changing institutions are crucial to the maintenance of SIs' dynamism. Important institutions in SIs are IPR laws, procurement regulations, technical standards, tax laws, environment and safety regulations, R&D investment routines, procurement rules, firm-specific rules and norms, and many more. They influence innovating organizations and innovation processes by providing incentives (or obstacles) to organizations and individuals to innovate.

IPR laws are considered important as a means of creating incentives to invest in knowledge creation and innovation (and, as argued earlier, they create markets). We have already mentioned the important role of institutions in facilitating the interaction of organizations in Section 2.5.3.2. Public agencies may, for example, support collaborative centres and programmes, remove barriers to cooperation, and facilitate the mobility of skilled personnel among different organizations and regions (Edler et al., 2011). This might include the creation or change of institutional rules that govern the relations between universities and firms, such as the one in Sweden stating that university professors shall perform a 'third task' in addition to teaching and doing research: that is, interact with the society surrounding the university, including firms (Edquist et al., 2004) and wider society as well (Tsipouri, 2012). There are institutions that influence firms and there are institutions that operate inside firms (for taxonomies of institutions see Edquist and Johnson, 1997).

Some institutions are created by public agencies. They are often codified and constitute policy instruments (such as the aforementioned IPR laws). Public innovation policy is partly a matter of formulating the rules of the game that will facilitate innovation processes. These rules might have nothing to do with markets, or they might be intended to create markets or make the operation of markets more efficient. Many institutions (such as laws and regulations) are publicly created and therefore easy to modify by governments. However, others are created by private organizations, such as through firms' routines, norms, and culture. They develop spontaneously over time and are much more difficult to influence by public agencies.

As in the case of organizations, it is important to study whether the existing institutions are appropriate for promoting innovation and to ask the same question of how institutions should be changed or engineered to induce innovations of certain kinds. Here, too, the evolution and design of new institutions were very important in the development strategies of the successful Asian economies and in the ongoing transformation of Central and Eastern Europe and Latin America. Hence, again, institutional (as well as organizational) changes are particularly important in situations of rapid structural change.

2.5.4 Support Services for Innovating Firms

2.5.4.1 FINANCING OF INNOVATION

Financing of innovation processes is absolutely crucial for turning knowledge into commercially successful innovations and to facilitate their diffusion. The significance of the financing of innovation processes is certainly not reflected in the space it receives here—and the heading 'support services' is not intended to downgrade its importance. Financing comes primarily from private actors within innovating firms (internal capital markets), stock exchanges, venture capital funds, equity firms, banks, or individuals ('business angels'). However, in many countries—including the USA—public agencies provide financing in the form of seed capital, for instance, in support of innovation activities.

As with public intervention in general, public funds (financial subsidies) should only come forward when firms and markets do not spontaneously perform this activity well enough (for example, when there is uncertainty or when risk is too great). But the question is not just when the public sector should finance innovation activities but also how: that is, what should be the instruments and what should be the appropriate balance between public and private funding in a particular SI.

2.5.4.2 INCUBATING ACTIVITIES

Incubating activities include the provision of access to facilities and administrative support for new innovating efforts. In recent decades, incubating activities have been carried out in science parks to facilitate the commercialization of knowledge. That this activity has become partly public has to do with the uncertainty characterizing early stages of product development, which means that markets do not operate well in this respect. In addition, universities have started their own incubating activities to commercialize the results of their research activities.

However, innovations are also emerging in existing firms through incremental innovation and when they diversify into new product areas. In those cases, the innovating firms normally provide incubation themselves. There is a need to better understand the conditions under which incubation needs to be a public activity and when it should be left to the private initiative.[15]

[15] In this book we include the discussion of incubation activities when addressing Financing of innovation. In addition, we choose not to discuss Provision of consultancy services at all in this book (see Box 2.2).

3

Innovation Policy

An Holistic and Problem-Based Approach

3.1 Introduction

This chapter presents a conceptual basis for what innovation policy is and how it is, and should be, pursued. Policy-making (the design of policy and its implementation) is done in the specific context of the SI. Naturally there is large diversity between innovation systems. This means that there are many different situations and specific policy problems according to the idiosyncrasies of each economic and social system in which innovation processes take place. Innovation policy aims at influencing the speed and direction of innovation processes. For that reason, policy is inextricably linked to the dynamics of the SI, which it aims at redressing, shaping, and transforming. This large diversity of innovation systems means that there are no ready-made solutions that policy can provide: there is no one-size-fits-all innovation policy. Policy must be designed and implemented according to the concrete policy problems that afflict the SI.

This chapter develops the core of this approach. It does so by stating a series of assumptions and propositions about the role and limits of policy, and by presenting a method to identify the policy problems that afflict the SI (see Section 3.5). The holistic approach to innovation policy is an analytical model based on the innovation system's ten activities and on a problem-based approach to policy-making. That approach also includes the unintended consequences that often emerge when implementing policy. All this is important in light of policy-learning because learning can only take place when evidence is confronted with a specific analytical model that is able to explain why things work or why not.

It is important to point out that innovation policy is not included as one of the ten activities (see Box 2.2). The simple reason is that public innovation policy is part and parcel of all ten activities. That is, all the activities are carried out by organizations in SIs and these organizations normally include both private and public organizations for most activities. As an example, in all SIs, R&D is funded and performed by public organizations (public universities, public research institutes) as well as by private organizations (enterprises, private universities, private non-profit research organizations). This also applies to education (although the balance between private and public here varies greatly between different national innovation systems). This is the way public actors can influence the context in which innovators operate, i.e. the activities that influence innovation processes. What is important is the division of labour between private and public organizations with regard to the implementation of each of the ten activities.

The chapter proceeds as follows. Section 3.2 defines what an holistic innovation policy is, and is not. A fully holistic innovation policy is currently not practised anywhere, as most countries in fact are conducting partial innovation policy for different reasons. Section 3.3 addresses this, and argues that most innovation policies today are still following a linear model, although there are some attempts trying to gradually introduce a more holistic approach.

Section 3.4 argues that research policy is still hegemonic, and that innovation policy continues to be subsumed under research policy. For that reason we claim that innovation policy needs to be pursued separately and independently from research policy. That would contribute to ending the dominance of the linear view that still directs much of innovation policy-making. Section 3.5 develops the notions of policy problems and additionality and how they can be identified and secured. Building on the existing literature, the section looks into what policy problems are, and how they relate to issues of policy intervention and additionality. Section 3.6 addresses the objectives of innovation policy.

Section 3.7 discusses the limits of innovation policy. Here the focus is on the policy problems that are generated by the deficient previous design and implementation of policy, including the selection of policy instruments. This is so because policy is part and parcel of the SI. Many different types of unintended negative consequences might be related to policy implementation. Therefore, it is equally important to consider those in order to understand what went wrong. This is what will ultimately allow true policy-learning. That remark brings forward the last important argument of this chapter, that innovation policy-learning is only possible when evidence is confronted with a set of specific assumptions and expectations. That is ultimately one of the goals of this book. Section 3.8 discusses the next steps, while Section 3.9 summarizes the arguments in this chapter.

3.2 Partial and Holistic Innovation Policies

In recent years, innovation policy has increasingly been discussed using terms such as 'broad-based innovation policies', 'systemic innovation policies', 'a demand-pull view', and 'demand-oriented policy instruments' (van den Ende and Dolfsma, 2002; Edquist et al., 2009; Godin and Lane, 2013). These terms refer to a wide or comprehensive view of innovation policy. We prefer to call this view *the holistic approach to innovation policy* (see below for explicit definition).[1] We have previously dealt with holistic innovation policy in, for example, (Borrás and Edquist, 2013b; Edquist 2014a, 2014b, 2014c, 2014d). Holistic innovation policies are also, in different senses, addressed by Boekholt (2010), Weber and Truffer (2017), and Fagerberg (2017).

An holistic innovation policy requires a very broad definition of innovation system and a broad view of the determinants of innovation processes, which we also call activities in innovation systems.[2] It should indeed take into account all the determinants of innovation processes in the whole innovation system. Our list of ten activities as part of an innovation systems definition is an attempt to provide such an holistic approach. As a matter of fact, pursuing an holistic approach to innovation policy is very closely related to the choice of a broad definition of the concept of SI (Borrás, 2009), which was presented in Chapter 2. They presuppose each other. Having chosen a broad version of the SI approach, this leads to an holistic policy; it is 'in the cards'. And an holistic innovation policy requires a comprehensive version of the SI approach.

Innovation policies are actions by public organizations that influence the development and diffusion of innovations. A crucial question is then what these 'actions' are. We make a distinction between partial and holistic innovation policy. These two kinds of policies are here used as 'opposites' to each other. They can also be seen as variations between the extreme points on a scale, and hence we can talk about the degree to which an innovation policy is partial or holistic. Hence, there is a continuum from directly partial to fully holistic innovation policies.

An holistic innovation policy is, in this book, *defined as a policy that integrates all public actions that influence or may influence innovation processes.* It takes all activities in innovation systems into account (e.g. the ten activities). As mentioned, an holistic policy requires a broad version of the SI approach as its basis, including all the activities influencing innovation processes. Our list of ten activities (Box 2.2) as part of an innovation system definition is an attempt to provide such an holistic approach in a preliminary and instrumental way.

---

[1] The term holistic innovation policy in our sense of the word was first codified and specified in Edquist (2014d) and then used in Edquist (2018a, 2018b).

[2] Determinants of innovation processes, activities in innovation systems, and factors influencing innovation processes are here treated as synonyms.

Demand-oriented innovation policy instruments must certainly be a part of an holistic innovation policy, although their inclusion alone is not sufficient for innovation policy to warrant the name 'holistic'. Examples of demand-side innovation policy instruments are innovation-enhancing public procurement of various kinds (Edquist and Zabala-Iturriagagoitia, 2012, 2015), standard-setting, subsidies or tax incentives to support demand, and enhancing articulation of user needs (Edler, 2006). The use of these instruments is being encouraged by the European Commission but is still not widely used in the Member States. However, their use has enormous potential as innovation policy instruments (Edquist, 2014a, 2014d, and Chapter 6 in this book).

In partial innovation policies, only instruments from one or a few activities are included in the policy. One example, or a specific and common case of partial innovation policy, is based on the so-called linear view, which is very much focused on the activity of R&D (see Section 2.3). This is a supply-and-push view based on scientific knowledge, which is not sufficient to produce innovations. Some research results are never transformed into innovations, and research is only one of the many activities influencing the development and diffusion of innovations (see Section 2.3). A fully holistic innovation policy explicitly integrates all public actions that influence or may influence innovation processes—for example, by addressing all the activities influencing innovation processes in a coordinated manner.

3.3 All Innovation Policies Pursued Are Partial—Most of Them Are Linear

As mentioned in Chapter 2, during the latest decades the linear model has been completely rejected in innovation research and has been replaced by the SI approach (Lundvall, 1992; Nelson and Rosenberg, 1993; Edquist, 1997, 2005). Innovation policies are, however, normally practised in a partial way, focusing on only a few of the ten activities in Box 2.2. There can be many different partial innovation policies, as it depends on what specific activities the policy focuses on. However, partial innovation policies are most often based on the linear view of innovation because they typically focus strongly on research. Hence, a linear innovation policy is a special case of partial innovation policies, and the most common one. Currently, innovation policies in all countries are partial and, within this category, most of them are linear. This means that innovation policy as currently practised is lagging behind the research undertaken by innovation scholars.

We have argued that there is a trend for innovation policies to become less partial and more holistic, through some gradual policy reforms (Biegelbauer and Borrás, 2003; Borrás, 2003, 2015). However, the development of fully holistic innovation policies requires that all the ten activities of innovation processes are taken into account when selecting policy instruments. We have proposed that this is done by means of a wide version of the SI approach. However, the use of the innovation systems approach for actual policy purposes is still often a matter of lip service. That is, the content of innovation policies is still dominated by the linear model. Let us give an example by summarizing some empirical results from a recent study.

The European Research and Innovation Area Committee (ERAC) of the European Commission ran a mutual learning seminar in the spring of 2014. The topic was 'Efficiency of Research and Innovation Systems for Economic Growth and Employment'.[3] As part of that project, a questionnaire was designed and sent out to the twenty-three EU Member States that had indicated an interest in participating in the project.[4] The process, the seminars, and the results are published in detail in Edquist (2014a, 2014d). Only the conclusions from that study are presented here.

The responses to the questionnaire indicate that 'provision of R&D results' (see Box 2.2) was regarded by participants as the most important activity in terms of resources spent for innovation policy purposes and that little innovation policy was considered to be demand-side oriented. This also applies to the responses to the question of whether public procurement for innovation was used as an innovation policy instrument. In other words, the innovation policies practised were all partial and most of them linear. Clearly, those countries that are striving in the direction of pursuing an holistic innovation policy have a long way to go.

Innovation policy design is, accordingly, certainly lagging behind innovation studies when it comes to being broad-based, demand-oriented, or holistic. This is clearly an example of a disturbing failure when it comes to communication between innovation scholars and politicians in the field of innovation.[5] This may be a strong reason to directly involve innovation scholars to a much higher degree in the design and implementation of innovation policy. There is a great deal that policy-makers and, in particular, politicians can learn from innovation studies, not only in principle or analytically, but also regarding policy design and policy practice.

Why then is innovation policy still mainly linear and not holistic, even if the linear view has been completely abandoned in innovation studies? Why is innovation policy behind?

---

[3] ERAC is a strategic policy advisory committee (DG RTD) whose principal mission is to provide strategic advice to the European Council, the European Commission, and EU Member States on research and innovation issues that are relevant for the development of the European Research Area. ERAC asked Charles Edquist to design and organize the initiative on research and innovation systems.

[4] Nineteen countries responded.

[5] Such communication seems to work much better in the field of the environment and climate.

Policy-makers in the field of innovation who attend scholarly conferences on innovation are more often than not in favour of holistic (broad-based, comprehensive, demand-oriented, etc.) innovation policies. They too have abandoned the linear view, having learned from innovation research. As a result, the division between 'linear' and 'holistic' is located within the community where innovation policies are designed and implemented. This community is composed of policy-makers (administrators/civil servants) and elected politicians. Perhaps the dividing line lies between these two groups mainly because politicians, who actually make the decisions, may be believers in the linear view in an unreflected way. There may also be disagreements between (the leadership of) different ministries, e.g. between the ministry of finance and other ministries or between the ministry of research and the ministry of industries.

It is also a fact that policy-makers in areas other than innovation policy are influencing innovation policies to remain linear, especially policy-makers and politicians in the field of research policy. A partial explanation that innovation policy is still predominantly based on the linear model is that the research policy community is much better organized than the innovation policy community. The 'research policy people' want to keep innovation policy as an area that is dominated by research policy—as an appendix to research policy.

The fact that innovation policy is very often treated as a sub-category of research policy is a significant obstacle in the process of establishing innovation policy as an independent policy area. This continued integration of design of research policy and innovation policy tends to cement the linear character of innovation policy, and to cement partial innovation policy—rather than developing an holistic innovation policy. In Section 3.4, we will discuss the reasons and mechanisms for avoiding this situation.

3.4 The Relations between Innovation Policy and Research Policy

Developing an holistic innovation policy would mean to establish it as an independent policy area. This would, in this respect, make it similar to research policy—which has been an independent policy area in many countries for decades. But it would also make innovation policy partly independent and separate from research policy. This would be a major change, as innovation policy has been treated as an 'appendix' to research policy for a long time. We argue that such a separation between innovation policy and research policy is a very important improvement for developing a truly holistic approach. It is also an important precondition to make the linear view lose its hegemonic dominance over innovation policy.

Of course, if we use broad definitions of innovation policy and research policy (as we propose), there must be overlaps between the two policy areas with them 'intruding' into each other's 'territories'. This can be generalized: they also intrude into the territories of other policy areas, such as labour market policies, education policies, public procurement policies, defence equipment policies, energy policies, transport policies, health-care policies, environmental policies, and regional policies. The effect of the resulting 'intrusion' or 'trespassing' makes it clear to everyone that policy areas do overlap and that they therefore have to be coordinated. It must also be mentioned that most parts of the 'territories' of the two policy areas discussed here do not overlap with each other.

Innovations emerge in complex systems where many partial determinants have an influence on innovation processes (see Box 2.2). Research is certainly not always a basis for innovations, and much research funding is intended for basic research and research in areas with little relation to innovation. Since research and innovation are different, we must distinguish between innovation systems and research systems. We should therefore not talk about 'research and innovation systems', which is actually a very common expression. Research policy and innovation policy are self-evidently also different. They have different objectives, influence different things, and use different policy instruments. A separation between the two is an obvious way of facilitating the transformation of innovation policy from linear to holistic. It may lead to better policies in both cases.

In the discussion above about the relation between policy areas, it was noted that it is natural that policy areas are partly overlapping. Research-related innovation issues should be addressed within research policy and innovation-related research issues within innovation policy. Innovation policy and research policy should be separate from each other in the design phase—but it must be ensured that they support each other when implemented (in the same way as many other policy areas have to be coordinated with each other).

In Sweden, innovation policy is gradually being established as an independent policy area. At the same time there are strong tendencies transforming this policy area into an increasingly holistic one (Edquist, 2018a, 2018b). Indications in this direction are that:

- A National Innovation Council (NIC), chaired by the Swedish prime minister, was created in February 2015. The discussions in the NIC address all the potential determinants of innovation processes, not only research. (There is another council for research that has existed for decades.[6])

---

[6] The existence of two councils creates space for a separation of the two policy areas. For the benefit of developing an innovation policy independent of (but coordinated with) research policy, it is a great advantage that there are two different councils.

The NIC describes its purpose on its website as such: 'The Innovation Council is needed to develop a coordinated and integrated innovation policy'. That the NIC has been created and is chaired by the prime minister has certainly increased the status and importance of innovation policy in relation to other policy areas in Sweden. In other countries, such councils focus predominantly on science and/or research and treat innovation, if at all, as an 'appendix' to research (Schwaag-Serger et al., 2015).

- Sweden has a minister of enterprise *'and innovation'* for the first time, a role established in September 2014. This is also an upgrading of the importance of innovation policy, and in Sweden this ministry is one of the largest.

Sweden also has, for the first time, a minister for whom public procurement is a main responsibility. He has developed a National Public Procurement Strategy in which functional procurement that enhances innovation is a very important element. Functional procurement is potentially a very powerful innovation policy instrument, and it operates from the demand side. Therefore, the policy emphasis on functional procurement can serve to balance the dominance of research, i.e. the supply side, in Swedish innovation policy. If the strategy is successfully implemented, functional procurement will develop into a major contribution for developing an holistic innovation policy in Sweden. Functional procurement is further addressed in Chapter 6.

In the *Research Europe* issue of March 2015, the following was reported: 'The establishment of the innovation council means that research policy and innovation policy will be separated, with research issues dealt with by a separate group. According to Stefan Löfven (the Swedish Prime Minister), the council is intended to take a holistic and realistic approach to innovation' (Maukola, 2015, p. 17).

To sum up, Swedish politics over the last three to four years has certainly changed in the direction of developing an holistic innovation policy. This means that Sweden has the potential of becoming the first country that breaks with the linear model in its innovation policy and continues to develop innovation policy in an holistic direction. This is very much thanks to the creation and operation of the Swedish NIC, the fact that the prime minister is its chairman, and the emphasis on functional procurement that can serve to enhance innovations when pursuing public procurement in NIC and by the minister in charge. In other words, although holism may develop without the existence of a NIC, the Swedish NIC has been very important as a governance tool to develop along this trajectory. These developments are discussed in much more detail in Edquist (2018a, 2018b).

3.5 Policy Problems and Additionality: Reasons for Policy Intervention

The design and implementation of public innovation policy should focus on addressing and solving what we call 'policy problems' in the SI—see Box 3.1.[7] These problems must, of course, be identified in the process of *ex ante* policy

---

Box 3.1 POLICY PROBLEMS

What is a policy problem? A policy problem is always related to low innovation performance of the innovation system. The performance of an innovation system is the relationship between what goes into (a certain part of) the system and what comes out; it is a relation between innovation inputs and innovation output. The output is—simply—innovations. There is a policy problem when there is low innovation performance (output as compared to input) of the SI.

How can we identify 'policy problems'? The existence of a policy problem in a concrete context (region, country, sector, etc.) has to be identified through empirical analysis. This book provides the theoretical and conceptual foundations upon which that analysis can be based.[8] This means that empirical analysis of policy problems needs to measure the innovation output in the specific countries, regions, or sectors under review. Policy problems cannot be identified through comparisons between an empirically existing system and an optimal one, as we are unable to specify an optimal SI. In other words, a 'policy problem' exists if the objectives in terms of innovation intensities are not achieved by private organizations (see Section 3.6 about objectives of innovation policy). If there are no policy problems, there is no need for an innovation policy. If the innovation system performs badly due to low innovation performance, it must have to do with some obstacles and barriers in the determinants of innovation processes, for example some of the ten activities listed in Box 2.2.

What obstacles and barriers are there in innovation systems? Obstacles and barriers are the deficiencies, imbalances, etc. in the activities of the innovation system that might be the causes behind low innovation performance in that system. There are a number of possible obstacles and barriers for each of these activities, which might lead to low innovation performance in a system, or in a part of a system. The existence of these obstacles and barriers in a specific innovation system of a country or region needs to be analysed empirically.

---

[7] We use the term 'policy problem' instead of 'market failure' in order to avoid the connotations associated with the traditional economics notion of 'market failure'. This is a conscious and intentional choice. A 'market failure' implies a comparison between an existing SI and an ideal or optimal system. Since it is not possible to specify an optimal innovation system, the notion of 'market failure' loses its meaning and applicability. Not to lead thoughts in wrong directions, we therefore prefer to talk about 'policy problems' instead of 'market failures' (Edquist, 1993, 2011). Our notion of 'policy problem' is wider than 'market failure'. For example, it includes policy problems generated by policy itself.

[8] This is one reason why the measurement of innovation output as well as of the determinants of such output is of utmost importance in innovation studies as a basis for the design of innovation policy. We have gone into these issues in quite some detail recently in Edquist

design. No policy at all is better than a policy that does not target identified specific policy problems (Edquist, 2011). The question is, then, how this policy problem identification can be undertaken.

There are three sub-questions here:

- What is a 'policy problem'?
- How can we identify 'policy problems'?
- What obstacles and barriers are there in innovation systems?

Policy-makers need to know what to do in order to mitigate innovation performance problems. Policy-makers and politicians must choose the adequate policy instruments. The choice of instrument has to be based on the causes or explanations of low innovation performance. If private organizations perform the necessary activities well, there will be no innovation policy problems in the sense above. If the private actors perform them badly, or if they cannot or will not perform the activities that are necessary or important for the innovation system, there is a need for public intervention. An example is the early stages of the development of innovations where there is uncertainty or too high risk for private actors to supply risk capital.

Innovation policy is the set of public interventions that are directed towards influencing the context in which firms and other innovators operate (and through this, influencing innovations). In other words, innovation policy is about influencing the determinants of the SI, e.g. the ten activities that influence innovation processes.

A quick glance at the ten activities specified in Box 2.2 reveals that each of them is normally performed partly by private organizations and partly by public organizations.[9] As innovation policy is comprised of actions by public organizations that influence innovation processes, policy is a part of the ten activities. This is the reason why innovation policy is not included as a separate activity in Box 2.1. Naturally, the division of labour between the public and private realms varies between countries/regions and changes over time. Likewise, the division of labour between different levels of government might vary greatly (particularly in federal states like Canada, the USA, and Germany, or supra-national political systems like the EU).

This brings us to another crucial issue: why and in which situations should innovation policy be pursued and when should it not, i.e. what is the rationale

et al. (2018). In that article we show that the European Innovation Scoreboard claims to measure innovation performance, but that it fails to do so in a meaningful way. The reason is a flawed methodology. Performance and productivity of innovation systems are also emphasized in (Edquist 2011).

[9] It is infrequent that an activity is performed by private or by public organizations exclusively. Both private and public organizations are normally involved in the performance of each activity.

for innovation policy? Two conditions must be fulfilled for there to be reasons for public innovation policy intervention in a market economy:

- private organizations must prove to be unwilling or unsuccessful in achieving the objectives[10] formulated; i.e. a policy problem must exist; and
- the state (national, regional, local) and its public organizations must also have the ability to solve or mitigate the policy problem.

This means that only tasks that are important for the SI, but are not carried out by private organizations, should be stimulated or performed by public organizations—and, of course, only if they have the ability to do so. Hence, it is important to find out (a) what is important for the SI, and concurrently (b) what private actors are not doing. If private actors can perform the important activities in principle but do not do so spontaneously, innovation policy should give them incentives to do it. If they still cannot or will not, then public organizations must do it themselves as a part of innovation policy. Policy problems, in our sense, have a dual character, where the two parts are linked to each other (Edquist 2011, section 3).

The concept of 'additionality' is important in this context and is closely related to the identification of policy problems (Bergman et al., 2010; Georghiou, 2002). It is sometimes called 'market supplementation', meaning supplementing what market actors (can) do. Additionality is a matter of the division of labour between what private organizations are carrying out in innovation systems and what is carried out by means of policy intervention.

Innovation policy pursued by public organizations is sometimes needed, but must not replace, duplicate, or crowd out what private actors (can) accomplish. Public action should supplement private action. Central here is that activities that are important for the system should be performed by public organizations only if they are not (or cannot be) carried out by private organizations. If public-sector organizations try to pursue everything that private actors do, there is no limit to public intervention, and a planned economy is waiting around the corner. There would be duplication, crowding out, and competition between private and public actors, and therefore very large public resources would be unnecessarily used.[11]

When we know the policy problems in an SI, we want to use policy instruments to do something about them. We also have to know the (main) causes of the policy problems beforehand in order to be able to select policy

---

[10] 'Private organizations' refers to firms, but also to other types of privately owned organizations, including non-profit, hybrid organizations, and/or civil society organizations undertaking innovations. We will address objectives of innovation policy in Section 3.6.

[11] However, there may be cases where the public sector can do things better than the private sector, or one may not want the private sector to have control over a certain area of technology. In such cases, limited exceptions from the principles proposed here may be motivated.

instruments intended to mitigate or solve the problems. This means that we have to grapple with the fact that dealing with causal explanations in the social sciences is a very demanding task—an issue to which we will return in Section 12.5.

Related to this issue is the question of how innovation systems change. They are not automatic and rigid machines. Rather, they are systems in which the different activities are partly self-organized. Part of the coordination of the systems is performed by self-organizing through markets. Another part of the coordination is achieved by policy and politics. The systems may be partly self-transforming. Self-organized systems can change because of crises or other shocks. Changes in the objectives of innovation policy can also change the operation of the systems. We have also stressed (in Chapter 2) that we focus more on changes of institutions and organizations than on the institutions and organizations as such.

As mentioned earlier, our focus on 'activities' within SIs emphasizes strongly what happens in the systems. We focus more on issues of dynamics and change than on individual determinants in a static way. In this sense, the activities approach provides a more dynamic perspective than other perspectives. Our approach can therefore capture how various activities that influence specific innovation processes may change the performance with regard to these innovations—and thereby how the whole system changes. We study how the activities change and provide a dynamic basis for innovations which, as such, are novelties introduced into the innovation system and the society.

Policy plays a crucial role in the change of innovation systems. Policies are designed because of problems in the systems. The design and implementation of policies are conscious efforts to actually change the systems. Additionality and market supplementation means that policy operates in a different way than markets and can therefore be an important mechanism of system change.

3.6 Objectives of Innovation Policy

The design of an innovation policy includes analysing innovation intensities, determinants (activities) of innovation processes, and innovation policy instruments. The latter two are closely related, i.e. the instruments are actually (partial) determinants of innovation processes. However, as such, the above says nothing about the objectives of innovation policy. They have to be specified separately. Once we have specified the objectives of innovation policy and have a general picture of the policy problems, including their main causes, it is possible to design policies to attempt to solve or mitigate the policy problems.

Here, we make a distinction between ultimate and direct innovation policy objectives. Ultimate innovation policy objectives may be economic (growth, employment, competitiveness, etc.), environmental, social, or they may be related to health, security, etc. The ultimate objectives overlap strongly with what is often called (global) challenges (Kuhlmann and Rip, 2014; Foray et al., 2012; Weber and Rohracher, 2012). Direct innovation policy objectives must be identified and specified in innovation terms, i.e. in terms of problems associated with low innovation performance that can be solved or mitigated by means of innovation policy instruments.

Innovation policy instruments cannot influence the ultimate objectives (e.g. growth, the environment, or the health system) in a direct and immediate sense, but only indirectly. These instruments can only influence innovation processes. Policy problems to be solved by innovation policy must be identified and specified in innovation terms. That is, the ultimate socio-political objectives must be 'translated' into concrete policy problems directly related to innovations. For example, we need to know how the ultimate objectives of economic growth and environmental protection are related to (certain kinds of) innovations, and how these innovations can be enhanced.

Fulfilling direct objectives is a means of (indirectly) achieving ultimate objectives, i.e. in a mediated way. Hence, innovation policy instruments are selected to achieve direct objectives, and thereby indirectly to achieve the ultimate objectives (Borrás and Edquist, 2013b). To solve or mitigate a policy problem of low innovation performance by means of innovation policy we need, of course, to know (be able to measure) the innovation intensities. Ideally, we also need to know which determinants/activities influence innovation intensities and how (Edquist, 2011; Borrás and Edquist, 2013b).

Of course, the ultimate objectives of innovation policy and the balance between them are, and should be, determined in a political process. The specification of innovation policy objectives is accomplished in a complex process, which, in democratic societies, involves executive government initiatives, parliamentary discussions, and civil society and media involvement. This includes the formal political process, such as elections, parliaments, and governments, but also political activities across this formal process, such as public debates, contestation and demonstrations, as well as lobbyism.

Naturally, politicians are not interested in innovations per se, but in their consequences for social and economic development, such as economic growth, job creation, protection of the environment, and other ultimate objectives mentioned above (Borrás and Edquist, 2013b).

49

Once we have specified the (ultimate and direct) objectives of innovation policy and have a general picture of the policy problems and their causes, it is possible to design policies to attempt to solve or mitigate those policy problems. Policy objectives are essential in order to give a sense of direction to innovation policy. They are implemented through the use of specific policy instruments.

A useful way of analysing the role of policy instruments in the innovation system is to relate different possible instruments to each of the ten activities. In the real world, however, the instruments of innovation policy are rarely used alone. Normally, they are combined in specific mixes of different instruments and used in a complementary manner. Instrument mixes are created because the solution of specific policy problems requires complementary approaches to the multidimensional aspects of innovation-related policy problems (Borrás and Edquist, 2013b, chapter 11).

3.7 The Limits of Innovation Policy: Implementation and Policy-Created Problems

Innovation cannot solve all problems, and innovation policy cannot solve all problems either. Some social problems are complex and cannot be solved by means of innovation at all. Examples of this are social problems (like social exclusion or mobbing in schools) that have to be addressed by political and legal processes and policies.

Likewise, not all the problems that have to do with the innovation system performance can be solved by innovation policy. This is because there are certain limits to what innovation policy can do. There are cases where identified policy problems can, in principle, be solved by innovations and innovation policy—but public organizations do not have the ability to solve them either. In other words, they are not solvable in that particular country or region due to the limitations of those particular public organizations (see Section 3.5). In addition, problems can be created by innovation policy itself.

In the previous sections we have argued that the identification of specific policy problems afflicting the innovation system is necessary for the design of innovation policy. Naturally, this includes those policy problems that might be generated by policy itself ('policy-created problems'). This refers to the unintended consequences of policy interventions when implementing policy instruments. In other words, one important argument of this book is that we should not disregard the problems that are generated by the negative effects (or lack of effect) of innovation policy initiatives themselves. Policy-generated problems, including lack of additionality, may have its roots in a lack of analysis of the reasons for and suitability of public intervention, in lobbyism, or in using the wrong policy instruments.

One such source of policy-created problems is cases where the additionality condition was not fulfilled when the policy was initiated. We could give many examples here. One is that practically all state risk-captial funding in Sweden was allocated to late stages in the innovation and firm-building process—where plenty of private capital was available. This problem is addressed in Chapters 10 and 12 in this book.

Lack of additionality has potentially several roots, most likely related to the lack of previous analysis and careful discussion of reasons for public intervention. This calls for more effort into identifying and analysing the policy problems in the SI and the potential solutions that might come from public action, securing the effectiveness of innovation policy, and in particular its additionality. We believe that it should always be established that the additionality condition is fulfilled before policy action is taken. This requires a solid conceptual and theoretical framework to provide underpinnings of such analysis, ultimately guiding policy decisions when devising and reshaping relevant policy instruments. It also requires an ability to empirically measure performance and productivity of innovation systems, i.e. innovation outputs and inputs, as we have strongly argued (Edquist et al., 2018b).

Our impression from interacting with politicians and policy-makers in the field of innovation policy is that some politicians are not particularly used to thinking in additionality terms. At the same time it is important that the state and its organizations are doing only things that private organizations cannot or are not doing, i.e. that public organizations, through policy intervention, are acting in a way supplementing what market actors do and/or stimulating private actors.

To find out whether or not policy is generating problems itself, and in particular if the additionality condition is being fulfilled, detailed analyses are required. Admittedly, this is not that easy to establish in an exact manner due to the methodological issues related to causality in the social sciences, including statistical analyses and evaluation studies. Having said that, however, it is possible to gather evidence about policy-generated problems.[12] This provides a very important guidance for policy-makers, meaning that the decision to pursue innovation policy intervention (or not) needs not (only) to be a matter of political ideology. It can be discussed and debated on the basis of ultimate and direct goals, identification of specific policy problems, and the suitability of instrument selection.

---

[12] The example of the supply of risk capital in Sweden is addressed in Chapter 10.

3.8 Next Steps

We have described seven activities listed in Box 2.2 in some detail.[13] As indicated earlier, the following chapters will focus on these seven activities. The difference in the number of activities is not an issue, as we have stressed that the list of activities is preliminary and will be subject to change in the future when our knowledge on determinants of innovation processes has improved. In addition, it is a matter of choice to divide activities in more or less specific categories. The important thing, in our approach, is that we, in principle, want to capture all determinants of innovation processes, no matter how they are sub-divided.

The seven activities addressed are determinants of innovation processes, and they constitute the basis for selecting policy instruments when pursuing innovation policy. The next steps of this book will be to devote one chapter to each of these seven activities (Chapters 4 to 10). On this basis, in Chapter 11, we will discuss the selection of innovation policy instruments. Finally, in Chapter 12, we will present the conclusions and implications of the approach in this book.

3.9 Concluding Remarks: The Holistic Innovation Policy Approach as an Analytical Framework

This book attempts to develop the theoretical foundations of the holistic innovation policy approach. In so doing it provides a conceptual and analytical framework for gathering evidence and making sense of it. Holistic innovation policy is a policy that takes into consideration the whole innovation system, meaning a policy that is designed to look into all determinants of innovation processes, for example the ten different activities that characterize the innovation system.

Unfortunately, most innovation policies designed today are far from that, because they are still only partial. Partial innovation policies are those which take into consideration only a few of the many different determinants of innovation processes and activities in the innovation system. Those partial policies that focus mainly on R&D as policy instruments are the most common partial policies. For that reason we suggest in this chapter that research and innovation policies must be separated in order to avoid the hegemony that research policy still exercises over innovation policy today.

---

[13] We dealt with the two demand-side activities in Box 2.2 as one activity in Section 2.5.2; we included incubation in the financing activity, and we did not address the provision of consultancy services at all in this book. The activities excluded here are described in Edquist (2011).

The holistic innovation policy approach can be used as well as an analytical framework to gather evidence and make sense of it. Here, it is important to distinguish between three different items.

Firstly, it is important to understand what the policy problems that afflict the innovation system are. Those problems might, however, most relevantly be addressed and solved by policy intervention only under specific circumstances. For example, any policy intervention must be additional to private action. Moreover, public organizations must have the ability to solve or mitigate the policy problem. This means that much more effort and evidence-based analysis should be invested in securing that the additionality condition is fulfilled when innovation policies are designed and redesigned.

Secondly, it is important to understand which the most commonly used policy instruments currently used are. Innovation policy is not a *tabula rasa*, meaning it is not something to be created *ex-novo*, because many instruments are already there. That means that a host of valuable evidence is already available to be gathered and analysed. Understanding and analysing the most commonly used policy instruments will give a critical and attentive view into how innovation policies are actually being framed. This is important given that policy instruments are one of the core elements that form innovation policy.

Thirdly, there are a number of possible unintended consequences generated by policy itself. This is an important consideration, as the reality of policy implementation brings forward new situations to the performance of the innovation system. Without analysing that reality of policy implementation, and without considering the problems that are generated by policy itself, the analytical framework will remain too abstract and disengaged with real-life innovation policy-making. Unintended consequences are typically the lack of additionality, but also a long list of possible problems like lack of flexibility, focus on quantity not quality, and balanced support to some areas while disregarding other important areas, etc. A profound analysis of an holistic innovation policy approach requires having an integral view on the implementation side. It is typically here that some issues like undefined goals or ill-designed instruments come forward and hit the reality of partial innovation policies.

The following chapters (4–10) of this book will focus on different activities in SIs. In particular, they will look at some crucial activities like education and training, R&D, entrepreneurship, and venture capital. Each of these chapters will carefully consider what and why that activity is crucial for the innovation process and innovation system. This will serve to engage in a detailed discussion about the deficiencies and/or policy problems that might afflict the innovation system in that particular activity. These chapters will also look into the deficiencies and policy problems that are generated by policy itself.

Here, the issues of lack of additionality, unbalanced approaches, or badly implemented instruments will emerge. Governments and states must be aware of these when redesigning and considering policy changes.

An overview of the most typically used innovation policy instruments will be presented in Chapter 11. This will explain the way in which the state is addressing some of the policy problems identified. That will be done with a critical eye, because sometimes certain policy instruments are more fashionable than others, and they may be designed in ways that might not always be clearly addressing identified policy problems or fulfil the additionality condition. Finally, Chapter 12 will return to some of the topics that we have addressed in Chapters 2 and 3.

4

Knowledge Production and R&D

4.1 Introduction

What type of knowledge is being produced, and for what purposes? Why are firms and governments funding R&D? What problems are they addressing? What problems might this funding generate? How is public R&D funding distributed and allocated? This chapter aims at providing a consistent conceptual and theoretical framework for innovation policy rationales based on the innovation systems approach. This will serve to capture and analyse critically the role of research policy in relation to an holistic innovation policy. As we saw in Chapter 2 of this book, innovations can be defined as new creations of economic significance. Following most of the literature in these matters, innovation is related to the emergence, combination, and diffusion of knowledge, and its transformation into new products and new processes. Seen from this perspective, innovation is intrinsically related to knowledge, which can be either entirely new knowledge, or it can be old/existing knowledge that is being combined and used in new ways. For this reason, the production of knowledge and its development is a fundamental activity of any innovation system, albeit certainly not the only one or the most important one.

This chapter proceeds as follows. Section 4.2 discusses the role of knowledge production in the innovation process from a perspective of innovation systems. It pays special attention to R&D as a specific and crucial activity related to knowledge production. In so doing this section examines who produces R&D, and what type of R&D. After that, the chapter examines, in Section 4.3, the R&D-related problems that innovation policy aims at addressing. This is crucial because decisions to allocate public funding have traditionally been justified on very different grounds, and are in fact addressing different types of problems. The production of knowledge is an extensive topic. Therefore, the remainder of the chapter focuses on four key topics related to public R&D funding in innovation policies, which have been experiencing important transformations over the past two decades. These are the transformations in direct and indirect public funding of knowledge production (Section 4.4); the increasing attention given to the 'development' side of R&D (Section 4.5); the rapid transformations in the governance of research universities (here mainly the autonomy of universities—or lack thereof—and the measurement of research universities outputs) (Section 4.6); and the problems that are generated by policy itself (Section 4.7).

Finally, the concluding section (4.8) argues critically that in most countries innovation policy continues to be subsumed under research policy, and that an holistic, problem-oriented innovation policy requires that innovation policy and research policy are separated from each other in the design phase—but it must be ensured that they support each other when implemented (in the same way as many other policy areas have to be coordinated with each other). In order to do so, the section elaborates on a set of overall criteria for the design of holistic innovation policy instruments addressing the problems identified in the chapter.

4.2 Conceptual Underpinnings: Knowledge and R&D in the Innovation System

The innovation systems approach sees the production of knowledge (and R&D in particular) as a crucial element in any economy and society. It is crucial, but not as the 'linear view' suggests. In contrast to the automatic, direct, mono-causal link between the 'amount' of knowledge and R&D activities and the innovativeness of that economy suggested by the linear model, the innovation system perspective sees this relationship as much more complex.

From the current perspective of innovation systems, we might distinguish the broad definition of knowledge with the more specific definition of R&D. Box 4.1 clarifies conceptually 'knowledge production', 'research', and 'development'.

Box 4.1 KNOWLEDGE PRODUCTION, RESEARCH, AND DEVELOPMENT: CONCEPTS

Knowledge production refers to the creation of new knowledge. This is the widest concept and does not necessarily refer to scientific and technical knowledge, but to all manner of new knowledge.

Research refers to the production of new knowledge using scientific and technical methods.

Development refers to the production and the adaptation of new knowledge in its use context, typically related to processes of prototyping, demonstration, testing, certification, modelling, scale modelling, proof of concept, and clinical trials.

As Box 4.1 indicates, 'knowledge' is the broadest notion. Hence, knowledge is not the same as R&D, which refers to the type of new knowledge produced using scientific and technical methods. An example of this is a patient organization which produces relevant knowledge by collecting information about some observed secondary effects of a specific drug. This knowledge is relevant for the patients themselves, as well as for authorities and the producing firm. The knowledge of the patient organization might not necessarily be the direct result of R&D activities, just the collection and desktop interpretation of specific observations.

What is knowledge, and what type of knowledge exists? This a very relevant question, because there are a multitude of different views on knowledge types (Steinmueller, 2006). One of the most influential understandings of knowledge and knowledge types was done by ancient Greek philosophers. The Greeks distinguished between 'episteme', a form of knowledge that is based on disinterested understanding and contemplation (not involving the act of doing manual work), and 'techné', which is the context-based, applied knowledge that derives from manual work and craftsmanship. This is behind the conventional division between basic science and applied science (Stokes, 1997).

Another widely used distinction examines the ultimate purpose and drive of knowledge production. Here, the distinction is between curiosity-driven and utility-driven knowledge (Strandburg, 2005; van den Hove, 2007). Partly overlapping, there is also a distinction between knowledge that is a fundamental discovery and knowledge that is a technical invention. The latter has been quite relevant in political and legal discussions of patent law, when trying to determine the limits of what type of knowledge can be patented.

This latter remark brings forward another distinction, namely the one between tacit and codified knowledge. The debates around their respective nature, and their relative importance in the knowledge-based economy, have been heated (Cowan and Foray, 2000) (Johnson et al., 2002; Nightingale, 2003). The backdrop of these discussions has been the so-called 'patent era', or the increasing trend in knowledge appropriation and commercialization through the issuing of patenting rights (a form of codified owned knowledge) (Gabrielsson et al., 2012, 2013; Foray, 2001).

These discussions evolved towards a somehow similar approach, namely the different types of 'knowledge bases' in innovation systems. Here the distinction has been made between STI (Science, Technology, Invention) and DUI (Doing, Using, Interacting) types of knowledge (Jensen et al., 2007). Or in another version, analytical knowledge base and synthetic knowledge base in local or regional economies (Asheim and Coenen, 2006; Chaminade, 2011). All innovation systems have both types of knowledge bases, but it might be that in some systems one of the knowledge bases dominates the other. The relative presence of these knowledge bases shapes the particular dynamics of innovation in a system.

Naturally, the borderline between basic and applied science; between *techné* and *episteme*; between curiosity-driven and utility-driven knowledge; between fundamental discovery and technical invention; between tacit and codified knowledge; between synthetic and analytical knowledge bases, are very fluid and can always be challenged. However, they are still valid for analytical reasons: they can help in grasping the complex dynamics, processes, and purposes of knowledge production and its uses; and most importantly, they can help in understanding on what grounds policy-makers have made decisions. This is to say, we are not interested in an ontological discussion about the nature and types of knowledge per se, nor on what types of knowledge are more important in the innovation system and for innovation policy. Rather, we are interested in understanding the way in which these distinctions have been influential in innovation policy-making, and in crucial decisions regarding the allocation of private and public investment.

This chapter focuses on a specific sub-set of knowledge production, namely the knowledge that is produced through 'research' and 'development' activities. As seen in the definitions of both terms in Box 4.1, R&D is an heterogeneous activity. A useful way of studying R&D in an innovation system is to consider the actors that are producing it. This can provide a snapshot into the 'who' and 'what' of R&D activities at a specific point in time, and its changes through time. Naturally, these are schematic and representative tools that could be combined with indicators and other analytical instruments.

Following from the discussions above on the nature of knowledge and the context in which it is produced, and being particularly inspired by the Pasteur's Quadrant (Stokes, 1997) and its subsequent elaborations (Guinet, 2009), we might consider two crucial dimensions for the study of R&D and knowledge production in an innovation system (see Figure 4.1).

The first dimension follows from the discussions above, in particular about fundamental discovery and technical invention, which serves as an heuristic to grasp the different logics behind R&D.

The second dimension looks at the exploration or exploitation of knowledge (March, 1991). This is the distinction between R&D that is directed more towards the exploration of new frontiers of knowledge, and the R&D activities that are geared towards the exploitation of that knowledge with a specific purpose (profit or non-profit). In most Southeast Asian countries, emphasis on the exploitation and development side of R&D activities was a strategy for the rapid catch-up process in the 1970s and 1980s, combining the imitation and

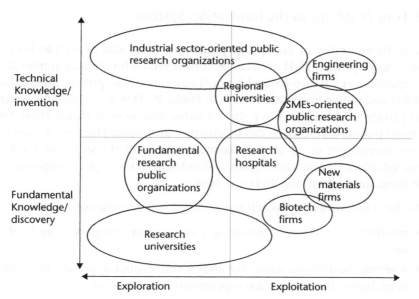

Figure 4.1. Mapping R&D organizations in innovation systems: a generic illustration

Source: own elaboration

exploitation of existing knowledge with its further development at the product level (Kim, 1997).

The mapping of Figure 4.1 visualizes the spaces the R&D producers occupy along these two dimensions. The specific types of organizations located in these two dimensions illustrate a generic example. In analytical terms, mapping the different R&D organizations of an innovation system along these two dimensions allows the identification of strengths and weaknesses in terms of possible duplications, as well as empty spaces of R&D activities in a system. These R&D-performing organizations can be very diverse, like research universities, public research laboratories (Crow and Bozeman, 1998), and research hospitals. Figure 4.1 can also help in comparing R&D strengths and weaknesses across countries or regions, which might be useful for the design of innovation policy.

R&D investments are funded and performed very differently across countries. This has to do with historical as well as socio-economic structures. In the figures below it is worth noting the large differences in terms of the funding sources of R&D, as well as the performing organizations (the organizations actually conducting R&D activities). When discussing the problems in innovation systems, these funding and performing differences must be taken into account.

4.3 Four Problems in the Innovation System

Given the centrality of knowledge production for social as well as for economic development, R&D needs to be considered an investment (rather than an expenditure).[1] Hence we make a distinction between private investments in R&D and public investment in R&D. Public R&D policies have no control over private investments. They should rather supplement them. These (private and public) investments can be different in terms of the time perspective of the investment (long or short term), in terms of the different levels of expected risks and potential results, and in terms of the types of organization that fund and perform the R&D activities.

An R&D investment approach has to do with the following questions:

- whether the innovation system as a whole is investing adequate levels in R&D;
- whether the different sources of R&D investments, e.g. private and public, in an innovation system are supplementing each other;
- whether the innovation system is able to deal with the high uncertainty and large time lags between investment and its different types of returns; and
- whether R&D investments in the innovation system are generating adequate social rates of return and social benefits.

These four questions are directly related to four possible main imbalances and deficiencies of R&D investments in the innovation system. It is important to note that together they are also related to another typical issue in innovation policy: the overemphasis of R&D activity over the other nine activities in the innovation system (see Box 2.2). These problems are important because public budgets are limited, and public funding of R&D competes with other important policy areas (like health, environment, defence, education, etc.). Therefore, it is important to understand the crucial role that public R&D funding plays, as well as the main problems it faces. Box 4.2 summarizes these main problems, and the following sub-sections examine each carefully one by one.

4.3.1 Inadequate Levels of R&D Investment

Evolutionary and institutional economic theory has largely challenged the notion of equilibrium and optimality (Metcalfe, 1995, 2007; Freeman and Soete, 1997). Innovation systems are very different from each other and are

---

[1] R&D has traditionally been accounted for as 'expenditure' rather than 'investment' in public budgets. Yet, this is currently changing. In the spring of 2013, the USA began considering R&D within its public budget, formally recognizing R&D as an investment.

Box 4.2 KNOWLEDGE PRODUCTION, RESEARCH, AND DEVELOPMENT: MAIN IMBALANCES AND DEFICIENCIES

Inadequate levels of R&D investments
Poor complementarity of R&D investments
High levels of uncertainty and large time lag between investment and private returns
The 'research paradox' and low levels of social rate of return of research

constantly changing. Therefore, policy is about making decisions based on adapting and learning, rather than decisions that are following a single one-size-fits-all optimal model for all systems. In other words, as we say in this book, innovation policy is about making decisions on the basis of a diagnosis of the problems that are specific and individual to each innovation system.

When talking about the possible obstacles and barriers in an innovation system, there might be inadequate levels of R&D investment. Determining the levels of R&D is essentially a political process. Societies must define explicitly their own aspirations for economic growth and for other ultimate socio-political goals. From that point of departure, it can be useful to analyse the extent to which the levels of R&D investment in an innovation system are adequate to fulfil those self-defined goals. Adequate means here that there is no underinvestment or overinvestment. Identifying whether the levels of R&D investments are adequate requires a careful analysis of the socio-political goals and the idiosyncrasies of each innovation system. It is not an analysis that proposes a single pre-defined optimal level of R&D investment that is the same for all innovation systems. The EU 3 per cent of R&D expenditure target, as an example of a one-size-fits-all level of R&D investment, is inadequate for most EU economies. Innovation systems are highly diverse, and therefore it is impossible to determine one single level for all systems. Levels of investment are different, because socio-political goals are different and because innovation systems are different.

Therefore, a problem-oriented approach to innovation policy has to undertake such a careful analysis. This analysis might find that there are inadequate levels of R&D investment, either because there is an overinvestment in R&D (typically in some high-income countries) (Aghion et al., 2009a) or because there is an underinvestment in R&D (typically in low- and middle-income countries) (Romero-Jordán et al., 2014).

4.3.2 Poor Complementarity of R&D Investment

Poor, or a lack of, complementarity of R&D investments may be a second imbalance of some innovation systems. There are roughly four funding sources of

R&D investment. These are private for-profit R&D investment (typically by firms), private non-for-profit R&D investment conducted/funded by philanthropic or charitable organizations, public R&D investment conducted/funded by national public authorities, and international (private, philanthropic, or public) funding sources. Thus, one place to start when examining levels of R&D investment in an innovation system is to look at the relative shares of these four funding sources and to look at what exactly they are funding. These shares vary considerably across countries.

A general tendency is that in those countries with higher levels of innovativeness in their economies, the share of private for-profit R&D investment tends to be proportionally higher than the share of public and philanthropic sources (philanthropic sources are 'private non-profit' sources). In some countries, the level of international inward R&D investment is also extremely high. These are countries either with some specific cultural and historical ties to other large R&D investing countries, or with extremely low levels of domestic R&D investment for which the little external investment in absolute terms is proportionally high. Figures 4.2 and 4.3 show some key items in the distribution of R&D funding and performing across countries.

Figure 4.2 shows the funding sources of R&D expenditure per GDP in a selected number of countries. That is, the origin of the money spent on R&D. It is worth noting that Israel has by far the largest share of funds from abroad (2 per cent of GDP) compared to the rest of the countries. This indicates the ability of this country to attract foreign R&D funds (most likely from its traditional relation to the USA and its participation in EU framework programmes). Likewise, it is worth noting that the share of funds coming from

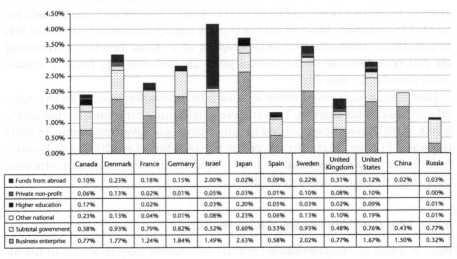

	Canada	Denmark	France	Germany	Israel	Japan	Spain	Sweden	United Kingdom	United States	China	Russia
■ Funds from abroad	0.10%	0.23%	0.18%	0.15%	2.00%	0.02%	0.09%	0.22%	0.31%	0.12%	0.02%	0.03%
▦ Private non-profit	0.06%	0.13%	0.02%	0.01%	0.05%	0.03%	0.01%	0.10%	0.08%	0.10%		0.00%
■ Higher education	0.17%		0.02%		0.03%	0.20%	0.05%	0.03%	0.02%	0.09%		0.01%
☐ Other national	0.23%	0.13%	0.04%	0.01%	0.08%	0.23%	0.06%	0.13%	0.10%	0.19%		0.01%
☐ Subtotal government	0.58%	0.93%	0.79%	0.82%	0.52%	0.60%	0.53%	0.93%	0.48%	0.76%	0.43%	0.77%
▨ Business enterprise	0.77%	1.77%	1.24%	1.84%	1.49%	2.63%	0.58%	2.02%	0.77%	1.67%	1.50%	0.32%

Figure 4.2. R&D expenditure as percentage of GDP by funding source, 2013

private non-profit sources are large in countries such as Denmark, Sweden, and the USA (with more than 0.10 per cent of GDP), whereas they are very small in the other countries. Regarding business enterprise R&D funding, Japan, Sweden, Germany, China, and Denmark seem to have the largest shares (above 1.5 per cent of GDP), proportionally larger than in other countries in Figure 4.2. Finally, regarding higher education, all countries show very little funding originating from this source. The figure shows the wide diversity across countries when it comes to sources of funding R&D activities in NSIs.

Figure 4.3 provides data for the same countries on the levels of R&D expenditure by performing sector. That is, the sector that actually receives the funding and carries out the R&D activities. This figure shows the relative position of R&D organizations and sectors within the NSI. In Denmark and Sweden, the higher education sector performs a very large share of R&D activities (1.02 per cent and 0.9 per cent of GDP, respectively), which corresponds to the traditionally very strong position of universities in the Danish and Swedish NSIs, relative to other countries. By the same token, countries such as Russia, China, the USA, Japan, Germany, and France show very high levels of R&D performed by government organizations (typically public research organizations), with around or above 0.30 per cent of GDP.

There is a relevant observation when comparing business enterprise engagement across both figures. Looking at Figure 4.2, Denmark, Germany, Israel, Japan, Sweden, and the USA are the countries with the highest level of business enterprise-performed R&D activities (with around 2 per cent or above). These are, at the same time, the countries that have more than 2.5 per cent overall GDP

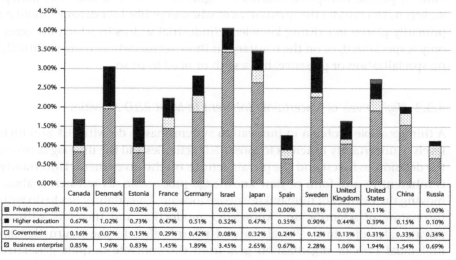

	Canada	Denmark	Estonia	France	Germany	Israel	Japan	Spain	Sweden	United Kingdom	United States	China	Russia
Private non-profit	0.01%	0.01%	0.02%	0.03%		0.05%	0.04%	0.00%	0.01%	0.03%	0.11%		0.00%
Higher education	0.67%	1.02%	0.73%	0.47%	0.51%	0.52%	0.47%	0.35%	0.90%	0.44%	0.39%	0.15%	0.10%
Government	0.16%	0.07%	0.15%	0.29%	0.42%	0.08%	0.32%	0.24%	0.12%	0.13%	0.31%	0.33%	0.34%
Business enterprise	0.85%	1.96%	0.83%	1.45%	1.89%	3.45%	2.65%	0.67%	2.28%	1.06%	1.94%	1.54%	0.69%

Figure 4.3. R&D expenditure as percentage of GDP by performing sector, 2013

expenditure in R&D. It is worth noting that a similar picture emerges in Figure 4.3, but with some remarkable variation. In Germany, Japan, and Sweden, business enterprises fund around 1.9–2.0 per cent of that expenditure itself; whereas in Denmark, Israel, and the USA, business enterprises perform more R&D activities than those they themselves fund, implying an important transfer of funds from other funding sources like foreign, public, or private non-profit.

Having seen the relative proportion of R&D investment funding sources and performing sectors, one might need to have a closer look at how the overall investment is distributed across different knowledge areas in the innovation system. In other words, in what type of R&D does a particular innovation system tend to specialize, and in what areas are the different funding sources invested. From the point of view of innovation, policy-makers should examine and determine whether or not the different sources of R&D investments (public, private, philanthropic, or international) are complementary.

Complementarity is important because one crucial issue that public R&D investment would like to avoid is a displacement effect on private sources of investment, which economists have defined as the 'crowding-out effect' of public R&D funding, substituting private investment (Jaffe, 1998). In the terms of Chapter 3, we want additionality rather than crowding out. As seen in Figure 4.2, in countries such as the United Kingdom (UK), Sweden, and Denmark, where large philanthropic foundations devote considerable amounts of resources to R&D funding (particularly in the biomedical and life sciences fields), the national government must also examine the extent to which there is an overlap or lack of complementarity between its own public R&D investments and those of the philanthropies (which are the same as private non-profit sources in Figures 4.2 and 4.3). Likewise, policy-makers must consider the question as to whether public investment should be primarily placed in existing knowledge/industrial sectors in which the economy is specialized, or on the contrary, in those sectors where there is virtually no specialization or presence, but a wish or need to be so.

4.3.3 *High Levels of Uncertainty Inherent to Most R&D Activities*

A third possible problem in innovation systems has to do with risk and high levels of uncertainty inherent to most R&D activities and the time lag between the decision to invest and the private returns on the investment. Uncertainty is inherent to any form of new knowledge production, as research is about moving the frontier of human knowledge forward. Uncertainty has to do with the nature of scientific and knowledge production and therefore with its private rates of return. 'Private rate of return' refers to the return that an individual firm or organization gets from the concrete outputs generated from the R&D investments.

Several studies indicate that there are very different rates of private return across firm cases and across technologies (see (Hall et al., 2010) for a literature review), and that these have a skewed distribution (Scherer and Harhoff, 2000). Besides, in addition to being extremely uncertain, the time lag between the investment in research activities and their outcomes in terms of innovative impact may be very long. It may take approximately fifteen to twenty years to build up a research environment, and it often takes even longer to get relevant research results. This important time lag is a problem for private firms—and for public research investment—to find suitable funding sources in order to position themselves in new research areas, or to redirect or reorient existing R&D activities.

The time lag can be particularly problematic in times of financial constraint. As the financial and economic crisis of 2007 clearly demonstrated, some Southern European countries have disregarded the long-term effects of public R&D investment against the short-term needs of cutting public expenditure. This (at times, massive) discontinuation in public R&D investment may become very problematic for the future competitiveness of those economies. Furthermore, this will be aggravated by the brain drain of young researchers, which will together represent a net loss of competences (skills and expertise) as well as R&D outputs. Other than public budget retrenchments, the time lag can be particularly problematic in areas that require high levels of R&D investment (large and expensive laboratories and equipment, such as nuclear research or space research) and where their outcomes take a long time to materialize.

4.3.4 *The Research Paradox and Low Levels of Social Rate of Return on Research*

The fourth main type of R&D-related problem in innovation systems has to do with *the research paradox, and low levels of social rate of return*. The 'research paradox' refers to the paradox of high levels of investment in research activities in a country, vis-à-vis the poor results of that investment, when it comes to the aggregated level of innovation performance in the economy and of innovative social solutions. This refers to the social rate of return on research. The social rate of return is a notion that includes the private rate of return (the concrete outputs from the investment) plus other broader outcomes[2] from that investment in the form of knowledge and market spill-overs. Hence, the

---

[2] The literature on impact assessment distinguishes between output, outcome, and impact. Output refers to the concrete results from the R&D activities; outcome refers to the wider set of effects associated with these outputs; and impact has to do with the broader social dimension of the results of the R&D activities. These three notions are directly associated respectively to this book's definition of 'private rate of return', 'social rate of return', and 'societal benefit'.

Box 4.3 BASIC CONCEPTS ASSOCIATED WITH RATES OF RETURN ON R&D INVESTMENT

Private rate of return on R&D: The firms' rate of return on their own R&D investment.

Social rate of return: The rate of return which includes not only the private rate of return, but also the knowledge and market spill-overs of R&D activities (see below).

Spill-over (general): An unintended transfer of market benefits to other market agents without any payment involved.

Knowledge spill-over: Knowledge created by one agent which is used by another agent without compensation, or with compensation less than the value of the knowledge.

Market spill-over: When the market for a new product or process creates benefits to the consumers and to other producers through better products and lower costs.

Technology transfer: 'Trade in technology which occurs when an agent sells a piece of technology with a price attached to the transaction.' Hall et al., 2010, p. 25.

Source: own elaboration

---

social returns on R&D are larger than those of private returns, and are closely intertwined with spill-overs (Audretsch and Feldmann, 2004) (Feldman, 2000). Box 4.3 distinguishes between these concepts.

As we saw above, policy-makers must place R&D investment in ways that do not displace private R&D investment, and achieve additionality. In order to do so, the rule of thumb says that public policy should fund those projects which yield high social rates of return, but which have low commercial prospects in the short run (Jaffe, 1998). Determining *ex-ante* which project will have these two features is, however, a very difficult task, given the unpredictability of the R&D investment's results.[3] One way of doing that would be to put the private returns of R&D investment into a broad context (Teece, 1986).

Teece suggests that there are three factors that determine an individual firm's ability to obtain profits from its own innovation. According to him these are: the appropriability regime (the way in which the patent system works for product innovations, and the relative irrelevance of patenting process innovations), the complementary assets of the firm (marketing, post-sale services, etc. are crucial for an innovation to be successful), and the dominant design paradigm (the competition the new product faces in the market).

---

[3] A parallel policy-design problem is in the area of public risk capital funding for early-stage innovation processes. If private capital is available, there is, of course, no need for public funding. This means that *a public funding agency shall not compete with private organizations in an 'unfair' manner on the basis of public taxpayers' money*. On the contrary, the public agency shall add something to the innovation system that no other actor is able to contribute, i.e. 'additionality' shall be at hand. This means that *private initiatives shall not be duplicated or crowded out by public actors*. This issue is analysed in detail in Chapter 10.

A similar contextual approach has recently emerged in examining the rates of social returns. This is the case of research evaluation studies, which is currently moving away from the traditional focus on aggregated social returns of R&D investment, in terms of knowledge or market spill-overs. Instead, they are looking at the social benefits of research and science policy programmes from the perspective of grand social challenges, beyond considerations related to economic benefits (Kuhlmann, 2003; Rotolo et al., 2013; Wallace and Rafols, 2015). This is an important issue, far more so when the goals of public R&D programmes are not just advancing economic goals, but also other broader social goals like improved public health services, carbon-free and renewable energy sources, or consumer protection. This is related to what Bozeman and Sarewitz term the 'public value' of R&D, the overall impact of R&D activities on the public goals stated in their related policy documents, which are broader than just the scientific or economic goals (Bozeman and Sarewitz, 2011). This approach is a promising new venture in the study of the impacts of public R&D policies on the basis of self-defined 'grand social challenges' (Kuhlmann and Rip, 2018).

Above we examined the four main barriers and deficiencies in innovation systems when it comes to R&D investment (insufficient levels of R&D investment, lack of complementarity between the different investment sources, high uncertainty and time lag, and the 'research paradox' and poor social rates of return). Through time and space, different policy-makers have dealt with these problems in different ways, and using a wide variety of policy instruments. Seeking to foster the levels of private investment in R&D, to secure private rate of return, and to find solutions to complex social challenges, policy-makers have devised and deployed different tools, and have historically 'experimented' with different policy instrument mixes.

Among the most widely used instruments are:

- Direct public funding of research-performing organizations (like public laboratories, large public research organizations, or public research universities).
- Competition-based public funding to R&D conducted by a consortia of firms and research organizations.
- Specific forms of taxation to give incentives to R&D expenditure by private firms.
- Regulation of intellectual property rights (patents, copyrights, etc.).
- Specific forms of public-private partnerships (typically in the funding and exploitation of large research infrastructures).

These are just a few types of policy instruments devoted partly or entirely to stimulate indirectly or directly the undertaking of R&D. Some of these instruments are examined in detail in other parts of this book (see Chapter 11).

The next three sections of this chapter focus on three specific forms of innovation policy intervention, discussing and introducing some of the most salient transformations and aspects associated with R&D in the innovation system. They are by no means the only relevant areas. Yet, they are three areas that represent large public budgetary allocations on R&D, and areas that have witnessed profound transformations in the choice of policy instruments over the past few decades. These are the changing policy instruments in public research funding, the growing relevance of 'development'-focused instruments, and the deep ongoing transformations in research universities.

4.4 Recent Trends in Research Public Funding and Its Changing Policy Instruments

Public funding of research activities has been changing in most countries over the past few decades, in ways that we examine below. First, however, we need to distinguish between direct and indirect public funding of research activities. Direct public funding refers to government budgetary allocations for research activities. At first glance, these are relatively easy to identify. However, public research funding is sometimes so widely distributed across different levels of government (national, sub-national, local) and across different types of public agencies, that it might not be so simple to uncover the exact total figure of public funding.

Indirect public support, for its part, refers to the tax incentives (or other types of monetary) incentives in the form of depreciations and exemptions to firms (and other taxable organizations) for the research activities they have conducted (Köhler et al., 2012). This is an indirect support in the sense that it exempts research activities from some specific taxation obligations, with clear monetary effect for the firms in question. Direct and indirect public funding of research is a vast topic, and there is abundant empirical literature. For this reason, this section focuses on the first type of incentive because it is arguably an area that has seen major reforms and changes over the past few decades.

When examining direct public funding of research, two broad trends are worth considering. The first has to do with the increase of competitive public funds for research vis-à-vis traditionally non-competitive public funding. The second trend has to do with fundamental changes in mission-oriented and diffusion-oriented public funding of research. We examine these two trends below.

Governments have supported research activities since the inception of the modern state. Traditionally, this support has taken the form of direct public endowments to public (or private) universities, as well as the creation and financial support to different types of public research organizations. Studies show important differences across countries in terms of the size of project-based funding (vis-à-vis other types of funding) and in terms of the distribution among different types of beneficiaries (firms, universities, or public research organizations) (Lepori et al., 2007, 2009).

The time-limited and performance-related allocation of public research funding has had a particularly important impact for universities (Hicks, 2012). If performance measurement of research organizations is conducted only on the basis of scientific rather than socio-economic contribution, these allocation mechanisms might run counter to most governments' intentions to enhance the diffusion and technology transfer of publicly funded research.

The second dominant trend over the past decades has been some changes in the orientation of the public funding. In his seminal work, Henry Ergas distinguished between two types of public research and technology policy styles (Ergas, 1987). Mission-oriented research policies are those where big science is deployed to meet big problems. This is when public funding of research is dominated by programmes serving specific government missions and targeted research in some areas (defence, agriculture, health, energy, etc.). By contrast, countries with a diffusion-oriented policy 'seek to provide a broad capacity for adjusting to technological change throughout the industrial structure' (Ergas, 1987, p. 196).

As indicated above, many countries have engaged in significant reforms of their public support policies towards research. A quick look at cases such as France, Germany, or Denmark tend to indicate that there might be a process where these diffusion-oriented countries have introduced important elements of mission-oriented policy (Borrás, 2011). For example, the creation since 2001 of three different strategic research councils (and their merger into one in 2015) indicates Danish willingness to address more targeted public funding of applied research. To be sure, Denmark remains a country with a mainly diffusion-oriented approach, but the introduction of these important instruments has kicked off a relative mission-oriented focus in Danish public funding compared to earlier.

Something similar has happened in Germany, which proposed its first high-tech strategy in 2006. By contrast, France has introduced a significant number of instruments and organizational restructuring towards more diffusion-oriented policy, like the creation of the National Research Council, which funds research projects on a competitive basis, and the creation of the Poles de Competitivité and Carnot Institutes, which focus on industrial innovation and competitiveness. This is quite remarkable for a country that tended to be one of the clearest examples of mission-oriented policies in Europe. The extent to which these changes are expressions of convergence across some countries (or not) is still a question that remains empirically unanswered. One might expect that the extensive exchange of ideas and cross-country comparative analyses at international level, like the EU, the OECD, or the World Bank, might have generated some learning among policy-makers (Borrás, 2015).

4.5 Development: the Crucial Little Brother

Development is the 'D' of the R&D acronym. It encompasses various crucial and interlinked activities in the innovation process, like prototyping, demonstration, testing, certification, modelling, scale modelling, proof of concept, and clinical trials. Broadly speaking, 'development' or 'product development' refers to the formulation of an entirely new product or process that addresses specific needs, or the modification of an existing product or the process of adapting it to a new need.

By definition, 'development' is application-related, meaning that it encompasses a set of activities whose direct purpose is to design a suitable product or process (suitable in terms of complying with user needs; and, depending on the sector, complying with the legal requirements of safety, too). Development is also highly specific to its sector context, meaning that the precise steps and activities of the development depend to a large extent on the specific features of the industrial/knowledge sector in question (Zabala-Iturriagagoitia, 2012). For example, the development of products in the aeronautic sector typically involves different forms of prototyping and scale modelling, whereas the development of products in the pharmaceutical sector involves several steps in clinical trials.

In contrast to the 'R' of R&D, the different set of activities defined here as 'development' has received surprisingly little attention from scholars of innovation processes. Admittedly, the debate on different types of knowledge (see sections above) has involved issues related to 'development', but typically in an indirect way and without taking into consideration the differences among these (i.e. clinical trials are quite different to prototyping). There are, though, some relevant studies that analyse the social organization of development activities and their respective design-related challenges (Carlsen et al., 2014; Hsu and Fang, 2009). However, these studies rarely include generalizable findings that can be used in broader analyses of innovation processes in an innovation system. Box 4.4 provides our definitions of some of the most important generic types of development activities.

Multiple types of development activity are performed by very diverse organizations. Sometimes these activities are conducted inside firms' own R&D labs, other times they are outsourced to specialized external organizations/firms or testbeds (contexts where prototypes are tested), of typically private or semi-public nature. These organizations normally sell their services to companies or

---

Box 4.4 GENERIC TYPES OF DEVELOPMENT ACTIVITY

Prototyping: An early sample of a product in order to test its design, its functionality, and/or its material components. There are different types/processes of prototyping in various industrial sectors. Prototyping usually involves sequential tests of the design of relatively generic features of the final product.

Computer modelling: A prototype designed and tested by computer software, not involving a physical artefact, but simulating digitally the expected features of the product. It is currently a common development activity in several engineering sectors.

Clinical trials: Sets of tests in medical research and drug development that prospectively assign human participants to health-related interventions in order to evaluate their health outcomes (typically the drug effects and their safety).

Product certification: The documentation that a certain product has undertaken and successfully passed a series of performance tests indicating that the product in question complies with pre-determined criteria typically defined by regulations and/or (semi-) mandatory technical specifications set up by governments and/or standardizing bodies. Certification is conducted by certifying laboratories/organizations or testbeds, typically of a semi-public nature.

Source: own elaboration

---

to governmental agencies and might sometimes enjoy (generous) state support for some basic costs. Traditionally, these organizations have operated in their national/sub-national contexts. However, their activities have become more internationalized over the past decades, probably due to an accelerated internationalization of certification and standardization of processes, as well as cross-border regulations and trade agreements.

Seen from the perspective of innovation policy, these activities are crucial for issues of scaling up. Scaling up refers to the process from the laboratory/ finding/research to the pilot phase, and thereafter into full-scale development. Processes of scaling up refer to developing innovations in their socio-economic context (e.g. the development of smart city sensors and innovative solutions for traffic congestion; or the full-scale industrial production of a new product, like a new type of 3D printer). But it also refers to high-growth firms, the so-called 'gazelles'—young firms (up to five years old) with extraordinary rapid growth (greater than 20 per cent annually) (OECD, 2007).

The 'development' activities mentioned earlier might be very important aspects of these different (but at times intertwined) processes of scaling up. Policy-makers are naturally aiming to foster scaling-up processes through different mechanisms. One of those is the organizations mentioned earlier, which are crucial in terms of bridging the world of research and new knowledge production with the world of industrial application, commercial use, and regulatory compliance.

Another important policy activity towards 'development' is the assessment of technology-readiness levels (TRL). This is a set of guidelines put forward by policy-makers in order to assess the technological maturity of specific items, in order to be used in decisions about the incorporation of specific technologies and related solutions to public policy purchases or specific public programmes (like in the defence or aerospace sectors, with heavy public involvement). Initially developed in the USA, the TRL scale has been expanding to other areas and is currently used not only for public-sector innovation and public acquisitions, but also in R&D competitive funding decisions.

Unfortunately, most of these 'D' activities have tended to sail under the radar of policy debates. The dominance of 'R' in most discussions related to the funding and organization of R&D activities has tended to advance at the detriment of 'development'. The result of this is that this little brother has tended to remain underexamined and underconsidered among policy makers. This is a major issue because it reinforces the 'research paradox' and underestimates the importance of the social rate of return on research investments, as mentioned in Section 4.3.

4.6 Research Universities: A Top-Down Revolution

Universities are absolutely central organizations in any innovation system. There are, however, many different types of universities and many different ways in which national and regional governments interact with, regulate, and fund their universities. In this section we focus on universities that undertake considerable research activities and examine three key issues which are having a profound effect on universities, namely, the deep transformation of university roles and organization in some countries; the move towards detailed measurement of the quantity and quality of universities' research outputs; and the recent emergence of global university rankings.

The relative presence and weight of universities in innovation systems varies considerably from country to country. As shown in Figure 4.2, in Sweden and Denmark, universities tend to conduct around 1 per cent of the country's overall GDP expenditure on R&D; while this is much lower in other countries such as China and Russia with around 0.10 per cent; or the USA, UK, and France with around 0.5 per cent. This depends on the features of the innovation system, and on the relative tradition of research universities (Mowery and Sampat, 2005). Since the turn of the twentieth century, strong research-based universities in the USA grew (Geiger, 2004) and have recently become an example for developments in this direction in Asia, Latin America (Altbach and Balán, 2007), and not least in Europe (McKelvey and Holmén, 2009).

Over the last two decades, research universities have moved from a relatively unnoticed life outside public scrutiny towards being seen as core elements for the innovation performance of a national economy. During this period, universities have been seen as performing a series of different tasks (Uyarra, 2010): the production of scientific knowledge (university as a 'knowledge factory'), the sharing of knowledge with firms ('a relational university'), the commercialization of their research output ('an entrepreneurial university'), activities related to boundary spanning in the innovation system ('a systemic university'), and their active contribution to economic development in their local area ('engaged university'). These tasks and roles overlap to a degree, and most universities have introduced significant organizational changes responding to these external demands and political expectations. These organizational changes are closely linked to the introduction of top-down reforms of university governance and by the introduction of more competition-based R&D funding allocations to universities.

First and foremost, the reforms of university governance in Europe, Asia, and elsewhere have been guided by national governments' wish to make universities strategic actors in the innovation system. However, the ultimate ability of universities to become strategic actors and develop their organizational role as such depends largely on the overall framework of university governance in that country (Whitley, 2008). More concretely, this refers to the extent to which universities exercise authority over their input and output, and over their internal processes. Regarding inputs and outputs, this has to do with the universities' dependence on state funding, on their ability to employ directly their scientific staff, and on their ability to select students, whereas their authority over internal processes relates to their discretion for establishing and closing departments, for promoting scientific groups, and for defining their own performance goals. In other words, their ability to become a strategic actor in the innovation system depends on their degree of organizational, regulatory, and financial framework.

The second key feature of the recent and profound transformation in higher education is the remarkable thrust towards the detailed measurement of the quantity and quality of universities' research output. This measurement includes databases on university international publications, the widespread use of citation analyses of university professors, the introduction of university and scientific discipline levels of peer-review exercises, and perhaps the most politically visible of them all, the introduction of a large number of university rankings. Different countries have taken very different approaches towards this matter. In any case, the growing attention towards measuring university R&D output has been equally prominent in developed and developing countries.

Figure 4.4 provides a look at the relation between levels of scientific and technical publications in international journals per capita, by the level of R&D expenditure on higher education in the country. This figure does

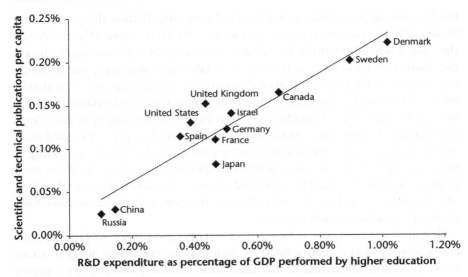

Figure 4.4. Scientific publications and R&D expenditure on higher education

not represent any inference analysis of the relation between both (as further analysis would be needed). It just plots a line in the figure with the indicators on both axes, offering a first look at how both indicators might relate to each other.

The initiatives taken by governments can be seen as an attempt to measure (and reward) universities' performance. This is the case, for example, of public initiatives that aim at measuring cross-university performance. Perhaps one of the most far-reaching (and controversial) initiatives in this regard has been the Research Assessment Exercises by the UK government (Hicks, 2012), which has recently introduced measurements of societal effects. Other initiatives, however, have come from private (or non-governmental) organizations. This is the case, for example, of databases and software tools measuring and ana-lysing scientific citations, like *Google Scholar* or Hartzing's *Publish and Perish* software tools. These new entrants in the market of publishing and citation indexes have been game changers in the field, providing free and easily accessible information to users and challenging incumbents.

A third important transformation of universities has to do with the advent of international university rankings. These rankings are mainly private initia-tives, which had a profound impact on universities' political and self-perception during the 2000s. The publication in 2003 for the first time of the 'Academic Ranking of World Universities' by Shanghai Jiao Tong Univer-sity created a wave of discussions about the quality of higher education worldwide. Since then, the number of university rankings has grown rapidly. Today, the most well-known rankings are produced by a series of private or semi-public organizations including the Shanghai Ranking Consultancy, Times Higher Education-Thomson Reuters, Quacqarelli-Symmonds, CWTS Leiden, Taiwan Higher Education Accreditation and Evaluation Council, the Centre for Higher Education Development/*die Zeit*, and Reitor.

The European Commission and the OECD, too, have launched their own ranking projects, namely, the European Multidimensional University Ranking System (U-Multirank) and the Assessment of Higher Education Learning Outcomes Project (AHELO), respectively. Almost since the creation of all these rankings, there has been growing criticism regarding several important aspects. The European University Association pointed to the fact that the rankings tend to be elitist, focusing only on the research-heavy, oldest, and largest universities worldwide (European University Association, 2011).

More problematic perhaps is the growing view that the methodologies of these rankings are not transparent (methodologies and data not—sufficiently—available), use disputable data (most of them are self-reported data, or subjective reputation survey data), or provide problematic measuring (lack of normalization of the data). Sometimes the methodologies and composite indexes have changed rapidly, rendering virtually incomparable results of the same ranking through time (Hazelkorn, 2013). Yet, regardless of these issues, it is obvious that the rankings have had a tremendous impact in real life. They have exposed higher education to international comparison, and governments and university leaders alike have had to deal with them. It has been virtually impossible to ignore them, most probably because their comparative effects have caught the eye of the media and prompted public debates. These problems, along with similar issues in other areas of research evaluation, have led to a heightened concern among experts. Experts are concerned that these procedures are not done properly and hence might damage the research and scientific systems. Their concerns are behind initiatives such as the 'Leiden Manifesto', which aims at providing a set of principles to guide research and university evaluation activities.[4]

4.7 Problems Generated by Policy Itself

The previous sections brought to the fore a series of issues directly related to policy-making. As mentioned at the outset of this book, in industrialized societies (developed or developing), public policy action is intrinsically embedded in the innovation system. This means that public action is today a reality, and part and parcel of the innovation system as such. Therefore,

---

[4] http://www.leidenmanifesto.org/.

Box 4.5 SUMMARY OF THE FIVE UNINTENDED NEGATIVE CONSEQUENCES
OF POLICY

- Lack of additionality and crowding out.

- Public R&D support does not promote disruptive knowledge.

- Unbalanced public support between curiosity-driven R&D and strategic R&D; and/or between 'research' and 'development', and between other types of knowledge.

- Focus on the quantity not on the quality of R&D.

- Undefined goals of public R&D investment.

---

when examining obstacles and barriers in innovation systems, we must also refer to the unintended negative consequences which are related to the role of public action itself. Five unintended negative consequences generated by ill-designed innovation policy are identifiable, as summarized in Box 4.5.

4.7.1 *Lack of Additionality and Crowding Out*

The first negative consequence is *the lack of additionality and/or the crowding-out effect of public R&D funding* on private R&D investment. Traditionally, it is expected that public investment in R&D will generate an additional effect on private R&D investments. This is typically the logic behind the requirements of industry involvement in some publicly funded R&D projects, or the requirements of co-funding from private actors as an indication of their commitment and real interest in the research activities funded by public sources. However, some situations might emerge when such additionality is not being achieved (public R&D funding is not able to generate or stimulate similar or relevant levels of private R&D investments), and even when there is a direct negative effect of public R&D investments substituting or crowding out private R&D investments. Economists have been largely interested in these types of policy-generated problems, showing cases where such problems are visible.

> Additionality is a key concept of innovation policy evaluation and refers to the question what difference a policy makes. The concepts of input additionality (i.e. additional inputs that would not have been created without a government intervention) and output additionality (i.e. outputs exclusively attributable to government intervention) are widely considered as the hallmark of the neo-classical policy rationale, which ultimately seeks to remedy market failures.
>
> (Gök and Edler, 2012, p. 307)

More recently, the literature has begun to offer different understandings of the notion 'additionality'. Following Autio et al., 'first-order additionality' relates to this 'market failure' approach of economics in terms of the private rates of return as defined above in this chapter; and 'second-order additionality' with the notion of social rates of return (Autio et al. 2008). More recently, the notion of 'behavioural additionality' has gained increasing attention, referring to the need that policy focuses on generating and increasing cognitive, knowledge, and networking capacities in the different types of agent in the innovation system (Lipsey et al., 2005; Georghiou and Clarysse, 2006). This literature stems mainly from evaluation and impact assessment studies, and has used this notion of 'behavioural additionality' in different manners. Economic studies analysing the 'crowding-out' effect of R&D public investments have also been rather extensive. These are more focused on the negative effects of public R&D investment on private levels of R&D investment. We look carefully into this in Chapter 10 when dealing with public funding of venture capital activities (Leleux and Surlemont, 2003). Although extensively discussed in the theoretical economic literature, it is worth noting that crowding-out effects are very difficult to determine empirically (Lach, 2002; Wallsten, 2000).

4.7.2 Public R&D Support Does Not Promote Disruptive Knowledge

The second unintended consequence of policy is *when public R&D support does not promote disruptive knowledge*. This has to do with a certain tendency towards risk aversion and traditionalism in public R&D funding. In spite of political rhetoric, sometimes public R&D support programmes are not designed in a way that promotes the most cutting-edge or novel type of knowledge production. Strong continuation of research funding lines, logics, and targets might secure stability in the funding of R&D environments (universities, public research organizations, or firms). The extent to which that continuation is positive for the overall innovation system depends very much on the ability of these environments to generate R&D outputs that are significant and valuable assets for the innovativeness of the economy. This is what economists have referred to as 'technological or innovation lock-in' in innovation systems, which is not only a matter of firms' own investment decisions, but of the inability of public R&D investment to break such negative lock-in dynamics and to generate true new disruptive knowledge.

4.7.3 Unbalanced Public Support between Different Types of R&D

Unbalanced public support between different types of R&D is a third type of unintended consequence generated by policy itself. For example, too much emphasis on 'R' (research activities) in relation to 'D' (development activities) might not have a positive effect on overall innovation performance. Specific overfunding of research (most typically public investment) might be observable in some prestige projects, where governments have funded research facilities, infrastructures, and equipment without considering the context (geographical, socio-technical, and the like) in which that investment is done, and without considering how this knowledge will be exploited in relation to 'development' activities.

The notion that the more quantitative investment in research, the more innovation will automatically come out of this is popular today. Sometimes there is an overwhelming focus on increasing the level of public and private funding on research activities without much consideration on the less attractive but no less crucial 'development' activities. Recent studies suggest that large publicly funded projects are sometimes proportionally less productive than small publicly funded projects (Fortin and Currie, 2013). A similar issue might emerge between small and large firms' investment in R&D and their respective yields in innovation performance. Knowledge-intensive small and medium-sized enterprises have traditionally been seen as relatively weaker compared to large knowledge-intensive firms. This particular concern is behind the creation of the Small Business Research Initiative programme in the USA in the 1980s, supporting small business research (Black, 2006).

4.7.4 *Focus on Quantity—Not Quality—of R&D*

The fourth type of unintended consequence associated with public R&D investment in the innovation system has to do with *the unsophisticated use of indicators and performance measures of R&D activities* and their outputs and outcomes. The ability to quantitatively measure R&D and innovation activities (and their outputs) has improved dramatically over the past few years (Moed et al., 2010). The creation of new databases and of new measurement methodologies have revolutionized the fields of research evaluation and the comparative studies of national innovation systems (Schmoch et al., 2006; Molas-Gallart, 2012). In spite of this, policy-making tends sometimes to be based on rather simple measurement techniques that do not reflect sufficiently well the complexity of factors that interplay in the performance of R&D activities and their associated impacts and effects. Somehow, too much emphasis has been put into the measurement of quantitative effects, whereas the more subtle qualitative effects are left aside.

Worse, quantitative measurements are used by policy-makers uncritically without considering what is being measured or how. Take, for example, the recent case of university rankings. Some of these rankings use inconsistent methodologies across time (making them unsuitable for comparison over time), use only self-reported data by universities (with all the reliability problems that this represents), and lack any theoretical reasoning behind the specific ponderation of variables in their aggregate indexes. In spite of these severe problems, university rankings are today extensively used in the public domain as comparative indicators of quality. However, their methodological inconsistency, data unreliability, and poor theoretical basis render them problematic as a form of measurement. If taken too seriously, these rankings might induce poorly considered policy action and decisions on public R&D investment.

4.7.5 Undefined Goals of Public R&D Investment

A fifth set of policy-generated unintended consequences on R&D activities relates to *the undefined goals of public R&D investment*. For many decades, the development of public R&D investment has been conducted within the parameters of very broadly defined political goals. Naturally, this is not a problem on its own. The deficiency has to do with the lack of a broad view of the overall expected outcomes of such an investment and their alignment to well-defined goals. Typically, policy-makers put too much emphasis on improving the private rates of return of firms' receiving public funds, rather than other issues.

We know from the discussions in this chapter that the social rates of return of R&D investment are extremely important and can at times exceed those of private returns due to spill-overs (including not only market benefits but also knowledge spill-overs) (Álvarez and Molero, 2005). Likewise, the social benefits of public R&D investment are much broader than just issues of economic growth, such as improved public health, improved living conditions for ageing societies, energy efficiency, etc.

However, public investment has not always focused on those broad social rates of return or on societal benefits. Sometimes it has just focused on increasing the aggregated levels of private return, which is a narrow focus, undermining the possibility of other societal effects. An example of the latter is the motto 'from research to bill' (*fra forskning til faktura*), that dominated Danish research policy in the early 2000s. Under this motto the aggregate level of private rates of return was perceived as the ultimate goal of public R&D investment. This is a deficiency insofar as it ignores the wider effects of knowledge production, for example, in the form of social rates of return. Some governments are increasingly turning their interest in the role of R&D investment to address grand social challenges, yet the exact formulation of policy instruments that convey that goal into specific decisions of public R&D investment are still scarce.

4.8 Conclusions

When examining advanced market-based countries, most of them show that innovation policy is subsumed under research policy. That means that research is considered to be the first priority, and innovation is a secondary type of area, somehow subsidiary to research activities. This approach is problematic insofar as it disregards other fundamental activities in the innovation system (covered in the chapters of this book). Subsuming innovation policy to research policy is the same as developing a partial innovation policy, as described in detail in Chapter 3. In this book we argue instead that innovation policy and research policy should be separated from each other in the design phase—but they must also support each other when implemented (in the same way as many other policy areas have to be coordinated with each other—see Chapter 3). In other words, an holistic innovation policy should encompass the different activities of the innovation system, among them, the production of knowledge and research.

Yet, this is not enough. As stated in Chapters 2 and 3 of this book, an holistic innovation policy is problem-oriented. That means that it focuses on the problems in the innovation system that are solvable by public initiatives, and on the problems that policy itself has generated. Based on this problem approach, the lessons from the issues discussed in this chapter allow identifying and developing a series of criteria for such a design.

As examined above, economic approaches from the 1950s and later have tended to focus on two rationales for public R&D expenditure, namely, the *additionality* of public R&D expenditure vis-à-vis private expenditure (in a way that does not 'crowd out' or substitute private expenditure); and the need to introduce public regulation to secure the *appropriability* of knowledge production by firms conducting R&D activities, as a way to overcome the lack of incentives in the market due to the public nature of knowledge. This chapter has examined the set of possible problems related to R&D in the innovation system in relation to a much wider set of possible bottlenecks and negative issues. For that reason additionality and appropriability are two issues among other equally relevant issues that innovation policy must consider when designing its specific instruments for intervention.

In this chapter we brought forward a set of criteria for the design of innovation policy that is based on empirical observations and on the analysis of the deficiencies and imbalances in R&D activities. Hence, our perspective is not so much based on theoretical considerations about the nature of knowledge, but about the real context in which knowledge and R&D are being produced and used. In so doing, we aim at bringing forward a much more realistic picture of the actual and direct obstacles and barriers associated with R&D activities, and of the dilemmas and challenges that policy-makers are currently facing when making decisions about the allocation of public budgets and the organization of R&D activities in the system.

As expressed earlier, our point of departure is the understanding that R&D is not an expenditure but an investment. Therefore, policy-makers must consider the distribution of this investment according to the different types of investment (long–short term, high–low risk, and results), and across the different overall goals it aims at achieving (economic growth, improved public health, energy efficiency to combat climate change, better solutions to traffic and mobility in metropolitan areas, etc.). This also means that governments must examine the private and social rates of return, as well as the overall social benefits of this public investment.

All in all, the investment approach means a perspective where policy-makers must look carefully at the three large sets of issues, namely, the inadequate levels and unbalanced investment of R&D activities in an economy and society, the undefined goals of public R&D investment, and the problems directly related to policy-making.

The following criteria for the design of innovation policy emerge from the discussions above. Firstly, *innovation policy must secure minimum levels of private and public investment* (according to politically defined goals that are not only economic growth, productivity, and job creation, but also goals that address grand societal challenges like climate change, ageing societies, public health, etc.). Secondly, *innovation policy must secure the diversity of knowledge production and R&D activities*, and a certain balance between different types of R&D activities, namely 'research' and 'development', between knowledge-intensive large and small firms, large and small collaborative R&D projects, as well as in the different forms of knowledge appropriability.

Thirdly, *public R&D investment must focus primarily on enhancing the social rates of return in an innovation system*. This is because policy-makers must be aware and encourage processes of knowledge spill-overs, while securing certain levels of appropriability. Because appropriability will invariably be imperfect, policy-makers must be attentive to the positive spill-over effects of knowledge production in a system to a point where private incentives to invest in R&D are not undermined.

Fourthly, *public investment in R&D must be risk-taking*. We know that the return on investment in R&D is skewed, which is due to the high levels of unpredictability of R&D investment. This gives policy-makers leeway to think strategically, designing policy in a way that takes into account the unavoidable skews of any such investment's return. The risk of public R&D investments, however, must never become so high that it jeopardizes the entire innovation system and its future dynamism.

Fifthly, *public investment in R&D must be patient*. We know that there is a long time lag between the public (and private) decision to invest until investment yields returns. This is actually part of the risk that public action might be willing to take. But such patience must not be blind. Policy-makers might define some guideposts and milestones regarding the performance of that investment along the way.

Sixthly, *R&D public funding must be adaptable* and able to fund totally new knowledge that is able to introduce disruptive innovation. This is to say that policy-makers must avoid problems of lock-in in the investment of some specific scientific and industrial areas. Yet, public funding must also avoid inconsistent or arbitrary policy targets, as it takes at least fifteen to twenty years to build strong research groups. Hence, it is necessary to strike a balance between problems of institutional inertia and interest capture in R&D areas of investment, on the one hand; and volatile and arbitrary funding that might result in inconsistency, on the other hand.

Last but not least, R&D investments and organizational public decisions must be based on intelligent and reliable data-based performance measurements of the innovation system, not least for universities (avoiding the misuse of unreliable university rankings and other simplistic benchmarking exercises).

5

Education, Training, and Skills Formation

5.1 Introduction

In the rich literature on innovation, studies have pointed to the crucial role of knowledge production in innovation systems, in particular the role of R&D (Jasanoff, 1995; Salomon, 1977; Guston, 2000). However, in the same literature, there is widespread recognition that the mere existence of advanced scientific and technical knowledge (and its production and transformation into prototypes) does not automatically generate innovation (which includes commercialization of products and processes; see Chapters 1 and 2 of this book). Some of the crucial elements that 'translate' knowledge into innovation are the ways in which skills and expertise are developed and used by individuals and organizations. The combination of knowledge, skills, and expertise is generally referred to as 'competences'.

The role of competences in innovation systems is complex. This complexity has resulted in the fact that different strands of the literature have addressed these issues from various angles, using concepts that are sometimes partly overlapping. For that reason, conceptual clarity when dealing with these matters is crucial. Some of the most used notions refer to 'competence', 'resource', 'capacity', 'capability', and 'skills'. Whereas some authors in the literature use these words interchangeably, basically referring to the same thing, other authors have distinguished among them in their conceptual frameworks (Smith, 2008; Vincent, 2008; Dietmer, 2011).

There is extensive literature about competences and innovation at the firm level as well as at the system level, as this chapter will briefly review. One aspect, however, that tends to be understudied in that literature is the role of innovation policy-making. Even if part of the literature deduces some broad 'policy implications' from the findings, the research rarely takes into account the public action that innovation policies have already put into place.

This chapter focuses on competences and competence-building from the perspective of innovation systems, and in particular from the perspective of public policy-making. Hence, the main question it addresses is how governments are focusing, and can focus, on competence-building through education, training, and skills formation when designing and implementing innovation policies. With this approach, the chapter aims to contribute to putting aspects of innovation policy at the forefront of studies about how education, training, and skills formation affect innovation performance in a system.

This chapter examines how governments in different countries and at different times have actually approached the issue of building, maintaining, and using competences in their innovation systems. On this basis the chapter identifies and turns a critical eye on some important unresolved obstacles and barriers related to competences in the system. Last but not least, this chapter elaborates a set of overall criteria for the selection and design of relevant policy instruments addressing those obstacles and barriers.

5.2 Conceptual Clarification and Definitions

The most widespread concepts in innovation and economics literature addressed here are essentially three: 'core competencies', 'dynamic capabilities', and 'absorptive capacity'. 'Core competencies' is a concept that has been developed in the literature of strategic management (Prahalad and Hamel, 1990). In their highly influential chapter, Prahalad and Hamel define the firm's core competencies '[as] the company's collective knowledge about how to coordinate diverse production skills and technologies' (p. 1). Firms must focus on these core competencies in order to exploit emerging markets and create new markets. Hence, strategic managers must identify the core competencies in their firm in order to organize a new 'strategic architecture'. The chapter inspired a new Schumpeterian focus in the literature on the interplay between tacit knowledge and codified knowledge dynamics in managing innovation through these core competencies (Nonaka, 1994).[1]

The notion of 'dynamic capabilities', defined a few years later, took a similar point of departure (Teece et al., 1997; Teece, 2010). The definition is quite similar to the one above, as these authors see dynamic capabilities as 'the firm's ability to integrate, build, and reconfigure internal and external competences to address rapidly changing environments' (Teece et al., 1997, p. 516). But they position this notion in a wider analytical framework where they see the competitive advantage of firms being defined by their distinctive

---

[1] Tacit knowledge (as opposed to codified knowledge) is knowledge that is difficult to transfer to another person or organization by means of writing it down.

processes and asset positions, as well as the evolutionary paths firms adopt and the technological dimension of the particular market in which firms operate.

From the point of view of innovation systems, these two notions of 'core competencies' and 'dynamic capabilities' have interesting analytical strengths. Firstly, they emphasize the interaction between the firm and its external context when developing competences (Dutrénit, 2004). They also position the development of the competences of the firm in relation to different types of knowledge. And last but not least, they see the development and use of competences in relation to possible issues of path dependency (or current options being dependent on past decisions), a central feature of evolutionary economics (Garrouste and Ioannides, 2001).

The notion of 'absorptive capacity' is slightly different from the two above. The definition of 'absorptive capacity' is: 'the ability of a firm to recognise the value of new, external information, assimilate it, and apply it to commercial ends' (Cohen and Levinthal, 1990, p. 128). This notion is anchored in the knowledge and learning approach to the firm, and in the view that firms interact with their environment in the process of acquiring/developing their own innovativeness. The analytical advantage of 'absorptive capacity' is its strong, intuitive message that absorptiveness varies across firms depending on the level and type of their own internal knowledge, and that this affects innovation performance (Murovec and Prodan, 2009). More recent studies have discovered, however, that the effect of absorptive capacity on the innovativeness of the firm is positive only up to a certain level. When firms become too dependent on external sources of knowledge, they tend to be less innovative (Flatten et al., 2011; Laursen and Salter, 2006). In order to be adaptable, and tap into external sources of knowledge, small and medium-sized firms tend to use technology watch on a regular basis (Zabala-Iturriagagoitia, 2014).

Taken together, these concepts of 'core competencies', 'dynamic capabilities', and 'absorptive capacity' have inspired studies in their respective areas for several decades and continue to be very valuable conceptual tools, particularly in the fields of innovation management, international business, and strategic management, where they were originally created.

However, as mentioned in the introduction to this chapter, they suffer from an important limitation. They tend to disregard the role that education, training, and skills formation frameworks generally play in the development of these competences, such as primary education systems, vocational training arrangements, etc. In other words, they tend to underestimate the social and formal embeddedness of these competences. Firms are highly dependent on the ability of the innovation system to provide them with some fundamental assets that they can develop as their internal competences (Porto Gómez et al., 2018).

The remarks above underline the need to move from an individual-firm perspective of these previous notions, towards a view where the innovation system is seen as having a series of formal educational, training, and skills formation frameworks that generate and develop competences that are vital for the innovativeness of firms. It is worth noting that policy might be crucial in the definition of these institutional frameworks. This shows that there is a limitation in the three concepts. In order to redress this, this chapter refers to 'competences' in a slightly broader manner than the three approaches mentioned above, and in so doing it includes these frameworks (and innovation policies in particular) as essential for the formation and development of competences.

In this chapter, we define competences as the set of knowledge, skills, and expertise that individuals and organizations have (Box 5.1). They can be seen as a set of acquired abilities and aptitudes to carry out specific activities, often including a given set of (analytical, physical, etc.) techniques and methods, and/or they are based on certain levels of past experience. Hence, competences are an outcome or a result of a process to which individuals or organizations are exposed (a training scheme or a series of new tasks). The literature has generally identified different types of competences (management competences or skills), STEM competences (science, technology, engineering, and mathematics), or more general social and communication competences (Curtin et al., 2011; Smith et al., 2012; see Chapter 3).

Competence-building, for its part (see Box 5.1), is the actual process of formal or informal development or acquisition of specific competences by individuals and organizations. It should be noted that we take our point of departure from the perspective of the learning economy put forward by Lundvall and others, as a suitable first step into this theme of competence-building (Andersen et al., 2002). This view is that innovative performance within an economy is largely dependent on the learning of organizations and individuals, understood as their constant ability to adapt to the rapidly changing external context, based on their competences and their ability to build those competences constantly.

Box 5.1 CONCEPTUAL CLARIFICATION ON COMPETENCE AND COMPETENCE-BUILDING

Competences refer to the set of knowledge, skills, and expertise that individuals and organizations have.

Competence-building is the process of formal or informal development and acquisition of specific competences by individuals and organizations.

The motivation behind this focus on competences and competence-building is the acknowledgement that the pace of innovation and change in other dimensions of the economy and society has a direct impact on the way in which (innovative) firms operate (OECD, 2011). In a rapidly changing (and globalizing) context, firms and other innovating organizations must be able to adapt to these changing conditions. Therefore, in order to stay competitive and produce new products and processes, these organizations constantly need to keep upgrading their competences. They need to adapt and change by combining these competences differently and organizing production and innovation processes inside and outside the firm in different ways. As Lundvall and Borrás put it: 'In a context of increased market competition and rapid innovation, firms are faced with non-price competition factors . . . A firm's capacity to learn and transform in this new context is a crucial competitiveness factor. There is a definite need to rebuild the skills of the individual and the technological and organisational competencies of the firm' (Lundvall and Borrás, 1998, pp. 34–5).

This chapter focuses on competences (and competence-building), rather than on 'learning' as such. The organizational and institutional contexts for competence-building vary considerably among national systems of innovation. There are, for example, significant differences across educational and vocational training systems (Brockmann et al., 2011; see Sections 5.3 and 5.4 below), as well as ways of organizing training and labour market regulations, with significant differences in terms of innovation performance (Lorenz, 2011). The matter of competence and competence-building is particularly relevant for developing countries and their processes of catch-up (Fagerberg and Srholec, 2009).

5.3 Internal and External Sources of Competence

From an innovation system perspective, one of the most important aspects is the process by which competences are created, maintained, and developed.[2] There are, in principle, an 'unlimited' number and type of competence that firms and innovation-supporting organizations have and need in order to keep pace with rapidly changing market and societal contexts, such as globalization. As firms operate in a wide variety of markets and try to develop competitive advantages in special segments of local or global markets, it is virtually impossible to provide an exhaustive list of competences that firms need, as it will always vary according to different markets and contexts. This

---

[2] As implied above, these competences are not the same as the creation of R&D results.

variety of competences becomes even more apparent when we keep in mind that innovation is not solely an issue of commercialization of products per se, but also an issue of providing specific novel solutions to complex grand social challenges (like poverty, security, or ecological sustainability) in a mediated way. Hence, firms and other innovating organizations have a wide diversity of needs in terms of the competences required to keep them at the frontier of market competition, or at the frontier of problem solving.

Having said that, we would like to make a general distinction among the different competences that a firm or innovative organization might need at its disposal, as well as the traditional mechanisms and processes of competence-building associated with them. First, we want to mention that competence is a 'stock' concept and competence-building is a 'flow' concept. Further, we make a distinction between *individual* competences and *organizational* competences. And last but not least, we distinguish between *internal* and *external* competence. Table 5.1 summarizes these distinctions.

Individual competence-building refers to the acquisition of information, knowledge, understanding, and skills by individual people, through participation in some form of education and training, whether formal (for example in educational institutes) or informal (for example 'learning-by-doing' in the workplace). Individual competence-building largely consists, unlike R&D, of the dissemination of existing competencies, even if they are new to the individual concerned (Jones and Miller, 2007). The result of individual competence-building is an increased stock of *human capital*.

Table 5.1. Internal and external sources of competence for a firm

	Definition	Content
Internal competences	A. Organizational competences developed by a firm or acquired from outside. They are an integral part of a firm, and often called 'structural capital'.	Information and knowledge competences in the organization that are embodied in databases, customer directories, organizational routines and procedures, as well as in trademarks, patents, copyrights, trade secrets, etc.
	B. Individual competences (human capital) acquired through employment. They are less firmly integrated within a firm.	Human capital: formal primary, secondary, and tertiary education of the employees. Vocational training and continuous skills development at the workplace. Reverse brain drain and immigration of high-skilled workers (see below).
External competences	Competences that remain outside the firm, but can be acquired through exchange/collaboration.	University–industry interactions for human resources development. Lead-user interactions. Crowdsourcing.

Source: based upon Borrás and Edquist, 2015a

Individuals exert substantial control over firms' human capital. A firm where an individual is employed can profit from the latter's human capital only as long as the employee continues in the firm's employment. All firms exist under the threat that the most skilled of their employees may leave for a competitor or create a competing firm, once they have accumulated experience and built up a contact network. Employee ownership programmes and stock option programmes to tie key employees to a firm are therefore becoming more common. The power balance between some employees, defined in terms of their significant human capital, and the owners and managers of firms has changed because of the increased importance of human capital.

There are some other forms of competences, however, which are not directly related to individuals and therefore cannot easily leave a firm. These may be termed *organizational competences*. Generally speaking, these are embedded in the working processes of a firm or organization as such. These can also be termed 'structural capital' (OECD, 2001). Such capital is retained by a firm independently of the presence of particular employees. Structural capital includes the information and knowledge in the organization that is embodied in, for example, databases, customer directories, organizational routines and procedures, and technical manuals. It also encompasses assets such as patents, copyrights, trade secrets, and other kinds of intellectual property rights. These are controlled by a firm; they belong to a firm independently of the individuals who are employed at any one time. Similarly, the knowledge and skills encapsulated in firms' routines and work processes may, in certain circumstances, be retained and transmitted to new employees when they join. They have also been included within much broader concepts related to firms' investments, such as 'intangibles', 'intellectual capital' (Sanchez et al., 2000; Guthrie and Petty, 2000), or more recently 'knowledge-based capital' (OECD, 2012a).

Competences might be internal or external to a firm or organization. *Internal* competences can be of an organizational kind as specified above (structural capital). They are often developed by a firm, but they may also be acquired by a firm from outside. Regardless of their origin, they might become an integral part of a firm.

Internal competences can also be of an individual or human capital kind (see above). They are acquired by the firm through employing people. But as these employees may leave a firm at any time, this kind of internal competence is not as securely integrated in a firm as internal organizational competences.

External competences, which refer to those assets, resources/skills, and abilities that remain outside a firm, are also very important for a firm's innovation process. These are not an integral part of a firm, as they continue to be owned by external actors and partners. Yet the firm or organization in question might need to tap into them in order to be able to reach its own innovation targets.

This type of external source of competence is particularly relevant from the perspective of the innovation system, as it is related to the firm's collaborative patterns.

5.3.1 Internal Competences

Turning now to internal competences and competence-building, it is important to understand that, even if these competences are an integral part of a firm, the firm does not acquire, maintain, and develop them in isolation from its context. On the contrary, these internal sources of competences typically originate and are developed inside as much as outside the firm. The internal competences of a firm in the form of 'structural capital' are ultimately owned by the firm. Likewise, 'human capital' is only accessible to the firm as long as the employees remain employed at the firm. For example, when a company employs an engineer and puts her to work on specific projects, the quality and innovativeness of her work would depend very much on the tertiary education she received in the formal education system, but also on the specific training, skills, and competence she has developed within that company. These refer to human capital (or individual-level competences), but her contribution to the innovativeness of the firm will also depend on the particular way of organizing the use of her specific competences inside the firm (organizational routines and processes), as well as her access to relevant data-sets, software, patents, etc. Hence, structural capital and human capital in the firm complement each other.

We have previously discussed internal organizational competence, which is an integral part of a firm. The example of our female engineer, however, emphasizes two specific areas of competence-building that we would like to focus on from an innovation system perspective, namely, formalized education (primary, secondary, and tertiary education levels), and vocational training and continuous skills development at the workplace (Carneiro, 2003), including technical vocational training and apprenticeship (Ludger et al., 2013).

Looking at the internal sources of a firm's competences, perhaps one of the most crucial areas in an innovation system is the quality and organization of primary, secondary, and tertiary education. It occurs externally, but the result of it can be acquired by firms. The exact way in which levels and types of formal education affect innovation performance in an innovation system is still partly an open research question. Many studies have focused on the link between educational levels and quality of education on the one hand, and economic growth on the other, but few have related these to innovative performance. One of the latter studies shows that countries investing in the quality of mathematics and science education at all levels (primary, secondary, and tertiary) are more likely to perform better in innovation terms

(Varsakelis, 2006). Other studies show the cumulative interaction between the development of new products and the levels of skill in the workforce (Toner et al., 2004). Figure 5.1 shows the possible relation between the number of graduates in STEM, and government expenditure on education.

Levels of educational attainment have been increasing over the past decades; around one third of 25–34 year olds in OECD countries have tertiary educational levels (OECD, 2011). There has also been substantial growth in the proportion of the population with a doctoral degree compared to recent decades. However, some OECD countries have suffered a relative decline in the percentage of graduates within science and engineering education, and some countries have faced problems of skills shortage (OECD, 2011). Education is, of course, also crucial for developing countries: newly industrializing countries have put considerable effort into boosting levels of education as the means for economic growth and innovation. Whereas this is the case for Asian countries such as South Korea and Taiwan, it has been less so for Latin America and the Caribbean (De Ferranti et al., 2003). Figure 5.2 shows data for twenty economies with mid-range innovation output scores, according to Global Innovation Index 2015 data. It is worth noting in the figure the wide spread of the levels of government expenditure on education, which ranges between approximately 4 per cent and 9 per cent of GDP. Likewise, it is worth noting a similarly wide spread in terms of STEM graduates per thousand inhabitants. Furthermore, and perhaps most importantly, looking at the

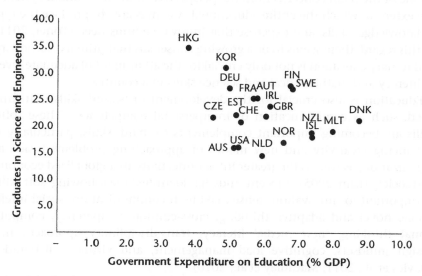

Figure 5.1. Graduates in STEM per thousand inhabitants and government expenditure on education, top 20 economies

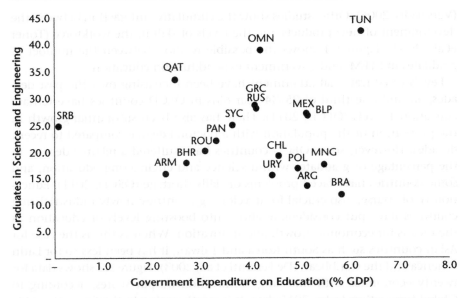

Figure 5.2. Graduates in STEM per thousand inhabitants and government expenditure on education, mid-range innovation economies
Source: Global Innovation Index 2015

shape of the observations in Figure 5.2 there is no obvious relationship between both indicators.

One of the main concerns from the perspective of the innovation system is the extent to which the entire educational system is able to produce the type of knowledge, skills, and expertise that innovative firms need (Toner, 2011). In this regard, there seems to be a growing consensus that primary, secondary, and tertiary education is not only crucial for the attainment of adequate levels of literacy and mathematical and science skills in a country.

Education is also crucial for the development of 'softer' skills that firms need, such as communication or interpersonal competences. These softer skills are becoming important complements to 'hard' skills, particularly in enhancing creativity and new modes of approaching problems inside an organization, as well as for greater interconnectivity in a globalized economy and society (Lam, 2005). A recent study has identified the following 'soft skills' as important for innovation: sense-making in communication, social intelligence, novel and adaptive thinking, cross-cultural competency, computational thinking, 'new media' literacy, trans-disciplinary approach, new design mindsets, cognitive load management, and virtual collaboration (Davies et al., 2011; Macaulay et al., 2010).

The quality and organization of vocational training and continuous skills development at the workplace is an important element when considering the internal sources of innovative firms' knowledge competences and processes of competence-building. There are naturally many different ways of organizing vocational training and skills development, as this is typically a topic where national and regional institutional frameworks play a fundamental role (Brockmann et al., 2011). These authors have shown the large differences in the understanding of core ideas about education, training, and skills formation; and how those core ideas have affected the system and the practices at the national level. For its part, the more recent literature on 'varieties of capitalism' has been interested in how vocational training is organized differently across countries. Their findings show that vocational training arrangements have been evolving differently across countries according to employee and employer relations, as well as business and politics relations (Harhoff and Kane, 1997) (Culpepper and Thelen, 2008), and that they have had different results in terms of innovation performance (Bosch and Charest, 2008).

Figure 5.3 shows the percentage of firms offering formal training in upper-middle-income economies, according to data from the Global Innovation Index 2015. It is worth noting the relatively high number of firms in those countries offering training, spanning from the highest with around 80 per cent of firms (China) and the lowest with around 50 per cent of firms (Malaysia). Whereas the definition of what constitutes formal training might vary across countries, these data are positively surprising, showing

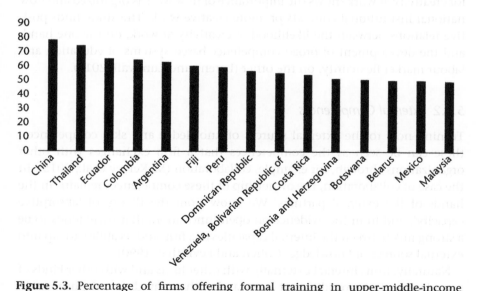

Figure 5.3. Percentage of firms offering formal training in upper-middle-income economies, 2015

Source: Global Innovation Index 2015

the engagement of firms in formal training and their need to provide workers with more specific skills.

The traditional way of looking at skills and training is to observe that labour markets are imperfect, and therefore there are different expectations regarding investment in vocational training at the firm level (Acemoglu, 1997). However, this has long been surpassed by the view that vocational training and continuous skills development at the workplace are related to the creation of quasi-public goods in the economy. This is so because the 'stickiness' of knowledge in a given territory means that the overall outcome of skills development tends to revert to the entire local economy via localized knowledge spill-overs. It is worth noting here that the notion of a link between continuous vocational training and innovation performance is widely accepted (Makkonen and Lin, 2012; OECD, 2011).

Admittedly, the relationship between levels of vocational training at the workplace and innovation performance in an economy is mediated by many complex dimensions, not least the organizational dimension at the firm level. Naturally, vocational training and continuous skills development has to do with building knowledge competence in the human resources at the firm level (Smith et al., 2012). But it has also to do with the way in which work is organized and, in particular, whether these skills development and organizational forms do in fact allow for creativity and employee-driven innovation patterns within the firm (Høyrup, 2010). A recent study on the preconditions for creativity at work shows the importance of how work is organized and how national institutional contexts promote creative work. The study finds positive relations between the likelihood of creativity at work, on the one hand, and the development of broad competence-based systems of education and labour market flexicurity, on the other (Lorenz and Lundvall, 2011).

5.3.2 External Competences

Turning now to the external sources of knowledge and skill competences, these can be seen as the competences that a firm exchanges with other organizations through, for example, collaboration (McKelvey et al., 2015). In the case of collaboration, the ownership of these competences remains in the hands of the external partners. We know from the theory of 'absorptive capacity', and from the evidence on open innovation, that there tends to be a strong link between the internal capacities of a firm and its ability to tap into external sources of knowledge (Cohen and Levinthal, 1990).

Naturally, firms interact externally with other firms and with other kinds of organization in many different ways and with many different purposes in relation to knowledge and skills. We would like to briefly mention three, which we believe are crucial from the perspective of innovation systems:

1 university–industry relations that aim at developing human resources;
2 relations to lead users as key external sources of knowledge for innovation processes; and
3 crowdsourcing as a new form of collective pooling of knowledge resources in an innovation system.

There are many other forms of external interactions. We argue, however, that these three are crucial for two reasons; firstly, because they are among the most common forms for firms' external interaction in innovation systems; and secondly, because they show high components of training, experience, and/or skills development in a way that a firm can potentially benefit from external sources of knowledge.

Looking at the first, there are many different forms of university–industry linkages. From the current perspective, several countries use university–industry relations in order to encourage university researchers to obtain firm-level expertise, skills, and competences. This can be achieved, for example, by co-funding industrial PhDs who are co-located in the firm and the university, by supporting university researchers' internships in firms, and by other types of liaison programmes. The overall goal of these programmes is to develop 'firm-oriented' and other types of 'soft skill' competences.

The second area that is worth looking at when examining the most important external sources of knowledge for innovative firms are lead users. 'Lead users' are highly competent and knowledge-producing consumers and users of specific products who get involved in a tight collaboration with the producing firm, giving the firm valuable information and feedback about the further development of the innovative product. Lead users are more generally associated with user–producer relations (Lundvall, 1988), and to notions of user-driven innovation (von Hippel, 2005), both forming the backbone of the innovation systems approach.[3]

Last but not least, a third crucial external source of knowledge and skills that has emerged relatively recently is crowdsourcing. There are many interpretations of crowdsourcing (Estellés-Arolas and González-Ladrón-de-Guevara, 2012), but a review of the literature defines crowdsourcing as participatory online activities in which individuals or organizations propose the voluntary undertaking of a task which typically involves the pooling of knowledge resources, and is therefore associated with innovative activities. From an innovation system point of view, crowdsourcing can be seen as competence-building by the mobilization and combination of knowledge resources in the wider society. Crowdsourcing creates online-based communities of

---

[3] In Chapter 6 we address another kind of user–producer relation that can enhance innovations, i.e. functional public procurement.

individuals and organizations with different competences and problem-oriented approaches. It is typically based on social media (Schenk and Guittard, 2011).

5.4 Policy Initiatives

Having addressed internal as well as external sources of competence in firms and organizations, the question that arises is: what are governments doing about this? How are governments securing the creation, maintenance, and development of competences in the innovation system? What are the current or typical policy initiatives undertaken by governments in terms of this particular activity? And what are the main focuses of these policy initiatives? These are crucial questions to ask, as many countries are engaged in different types of public action that relate to issues of competence creation, maintenance, and development, with direct and indirect effects on the innovative performance of firms and other organizations in the system.

The three traditional cornerstones of public action for competences and competence-building in an innovation system are:

(1) the regulation, organization, and funding of education systems (primary, secondary, and tertiary—both public and private);

(2) the support and incentive schemes for vocational training systems; and

(3) migration policies (including both immigration and reverse brain drain).

5.4.1 *Education Policy*

Regarding educational and vocational training policy initiatives, we note that public action to a large extent regulates, organizes, and (partly) finances formal education and vocational training. At the core of policy intervention is the collective understanding that there is a need for public action, either by public means alone or in collaboration with private for-profit and non-profit actors, when the levels and types of competences in the system are perceived to be insufficient. This may mean that the division of labour between public and private action in the field of education may need to change, or that the character of already existing public action should be modified. As Section 5.3 showed quite clearly, competence-building in an innovation system is a complex matter. This is because the issue of 'competences' is very broad, spanning from the individual (person-focused) to organizational competences (firm level). But it is also because 'competences' are difficult to identify concretely, and because their actual use in the economy strongly depends on organizational and cultural dimensions.

One example of recent education policy schemes that relate to innovation is the USA's focus on STEM education. In the USA, as in many other advanced economies, there has been a lively debate over the past couple of decades on the adequate levels and quality of STEM education and the fact that students' enrolment in STEM education has not grown as much as in other areas. This has motivated a wave of public and private initiatives in the USA focusing on STEM education, ranging from the creation of non-profit associations promoting and lobbying for STEM education[4] to a series of governmental initiatives at the federal and state levels. A report by the US Government Accountability Office in 2005 identified 207 education programmes, which were specifically established and run by thirteen federal agencies, to increase the number of STEM students in the country (US Government Accountability Office, 2005). The total expenditure on these programmes in 2004 was about 2.8 billion USD, of which more than 70 per cent was provided by the National Institutes of Health and the National Science Foundation. However, some of these programmes were very small.

This topic appeared in the political spotlight again when the 2006 PISA survey (Program for International Student Assessment) showed that USA students ranked 21st out of 30 in science literacy, and 25th out of 30 in mathematics. The President Obama administration launched the 'Educate to Innovate' campaign to raise awareness of the importance of STEM. This initiative was intended to supplement the existing federal agencies' programmes in the field. The initiative followed from the focus of the Obama presidency on advanced manufacturing industries, particularly the Advanced Manufacturing Partnership launched in 2011, and the creation of the federal-level National Network for Manufacturing Innovation in 2012.

5.4.2 *Vocational Training Policy*

Policy initiatives in the area of competence-building consist as well of vocational training and continuous skills development. These are crucial policies for innovation, and considerable focus has been put on competence-building in the workplace. 'Policies to promote the learning necessary for skill and competence upgrading at the firm level cannot ignore the potential of the workplace and the strong incentives for upgrading what employers can provide' (Steedman, 2003, p. 210).

---

[4] Examples of these non-profit organizations in the USA are FIRST, a civil society association created in 1989 to conduct activities that motivate young people to pursue STEM education and careers; STEM-coalition, a sector organization advocating policy-makers for STEM education in US policy-making institutions; and Innovate+Educate, an industry-based organization formed in 2009, which involves industry in STEM education and the innovation-based workforce in the USA.

There are, of course, many different vocational training systems and programmes. One interesting example is the 'Apprentice service' of Semta, at the UK Sector Skills Council for Science, Engineering, and Manufacturing Technologies. This organization runs a programme for apprentices in the UK advanced manufacturing and engineering (AME) sector, and pays specific attention to the needs of small and medium-sized enterprises (SMEs). Semta creates individualized programmes for firms in the AME sector to develop, train, and fund apprenticeship schemes. The AME sector is highly dependent on getting access to the right (high) level of skilled workers, and one way is through apprenticeships. The problem many SMEs face is their lack of capacity to organize and finance encompassing programmes that provide the skills their apprentices need, and that secure quality training and certification. The organization of these individualized programmes requires the pulling of resources from different sources according to funding possibilities (age of the apprentice, region where the firm is based, etc.). It also requires specific knowledge competences, e.g. finding suitable trainers and designing the adequate educational framework.

Having addressed some examples of policy initiatives in education and vocational training, it is also important to determine their effects. However, the existing evidence in the literature is rather scarce. Starting with primary, secondary, and tertiary education policy initiatives and structures, there is very little focus on education schemes and innovation system dynamics in research. Some of this literature has focused on regional/local patterns (OECD, 2001; Kitagawa, 2004). A similar situation emerges from the literature on vocational training. See Jones and Grimshaw (2012) for a recent review of the literature on evidence on which policy schemes for vocational training are reflected in firms' innovative performance, and a description of some public schemes for vocational training in different countries. Following these authors, some of the findings in the literature indicate that the more flexibility there is between educational organizations and workplace training programmes, the more positive the outcomes in terms of firms' adaptability. In addition, long-term financial schemes and principles of skills formation schemes seem to give the certainty and stability needed for securing the participation of relevant stakeholders (Jones and Grimshaw, 2012).

5.4.3 *Migration Policy*

As mentioned above, the third traditional policy area related to competence and competence-building is migration policy, in which countries determine the levels of access of foreign labour to the domestic labour market. Following Jones, there are basically three types of migration policy regarding highly skilled workers: 'point-based' policies (assigning points to applicants regarding their education level and other factors), employer-based policies (employers' job offers), and hybrid policies combining both. It is unclear which of these different types, and different policies, achieve their goals of covering deficiencies of competences in the innovation system (Jones, 2012).

Another important aspect regarding migration policy schemes has to do with reversing 'brain drain'. For many low- and middle-income economies, the problem of 'brain drain' has been a source of major concern. Countries make substantial efforts to create a highly educated workforce, but this investment does not revert to their economy if those highly skilled workers move to another country, which is highly relevant given current patterns of globalization (Borrás et al., 2009). Reversing flows of highly skilled workers is a very difficult matter for policy-makers because many different factors are at play, from good job opportunities and employment conditions to personal reasons or contextual/scientific motivations.

Several countries have addressed this issue by various combinations of activities. One such approach has been to target individuals directly, offering very rewarding job conditions. A case in point is the ICREA programme of the regional government of Catalonia in Spain, which attracts top scientists worldwide and offers them excellent working conditions. Although the programme does not target nationals only, more than 50 per cent of their excellence-based grantees were of Catalan origin during the period 2001–11 (Technopolis Group, 2011). On this evidence, it may be argued that the programme indirectly served as a platform for reintegrating Catalan scientists from abroad.

Another, yet quite different, approach is the Chinese government's public action in relation to 'brain circulation'. After many years of concern over the loss of talent, particularly the so-called 'new Argonauts' to the Silicon Valley (Saxenian, 2006), the Chinese government set up a programme in 2001 to encourage Chinese students who had settled abroad to return for short visits and relate to ongoing research activities in China, even if they intended to continue living abroad. This 'diaspora option' (Kutnetsor, 2006), recognizing the difficulties of reversing brain drain as such, used the strong ties of the Chinese scientific diaspora to develop innovativeness in China (Zweig et al., 2008). This also indicates that there are social and cultural differences in the ways in which societies deal with the contributions of migrants and with the returnees of expatriates working abroad.

5.5 Obstacles and Barriers in the System and in Policy-Making

Following the previous identification of policy initiatives for competence-building and competence maintenance, it is worth examining now some of the possible obstacles and barriers in the innovation system. The innovation systems approach emphasizes that innovation is always performed in specific contexts. Hence, our starting point is to consider innovation policy as part and

---

Box 5.2 GENERAL DEFICIENCIES AND IMBALANCES

- Insufficient levels of competence in an economy, and/or net losses of competences.
- The time lag between firms' short-term needs and the long time required to develop competences.
- Imbalance between internal and external competences, which generate excessive insulation against or dependence on external sources.

---

parcel of the innovation system. This is so because innovation policy's overall intention is to shape the context in which innovation activities take place. Accordingly, when examining obstacles and barriers in the innovation system, we include the effects (or lack) of public policy initiatives.

In our complex societies, whether in advanced market economies or in emerging market economies, the role of public action is 'everywhere'. Consequently, it is sometimes difficult to distinguish between when deficiencies and imbalances in an innovation system are the direct outcome of some socio-economic or technical features as such, or when they are related to the dynamics induced by public policy. Because both are intertwined, we need to examine them together. This is particularly relevant for our current focus on competences and competence-building in innovation systems. In many countries the educational and vocational training frameworks rely strongly on public policies. Thus, when asking, for example, about the extent to which the vocational training framework in a specific country stimulates innovation, it is virtually impossible to ignore the central role that policy-makers have in shaping that framework.

From the previous sections of this chapter, three general types of deficiencies and imbalances in the innovation system seem to come to the fore—summarized in the Box 5.2.

5.5.1 *Insufficient Competence Levels*

The first has to do with *insufficient levels of competences in an economy*. This might be because the economy is not able to create the competences that its firms need for a sustained level of innovation performance, or because there is a net loss of competences due to negative migration flows into the country or region. Developing competences in an economy is not just related to the levels of educational attainment or vocational training. The competences of an economy are also highly dependent on the continuous development of skills and expertise in the organization of work. There is widespread recognition today that this type of 'know-how', based on skills and expertise, is important for the levels of competences in an economy.

As a consequence, there has been a political debate over the past few years, particularly in Europe and the USA, about the effects of offshoring manufacturing activities on the levels of competences in the economy. The concern is that the past decades' offshoring of firms' manufacturing activities to countries with lower wages represents a loss of jobs and of competence development in the home country. Skills and expertise are based on workers and middle-level managers having hands-on experience in the organization of production. Workers engaged in product and process innovation require a deep knowledge of the product and its production process, which cannot be attained in research laboratories alone. Besides, advanced forms of manufacturing depend not only on substantial levels of scientific-technical knowledge, but also on skilled and experienced workers (Bessen, 2015).

Policy initiatives like the High-Tech Strategy in Germany (in 2006) and the USA's National Network for Manufacturing Innovation scheme (in 2012) focus on advanced manufacturing sectors, and therefore aim indirectly at boosting the development and retention in the country of competences in the form of highly skilled workers and expertise in these cutting-edge industrial areas. Still, it is less clear whether these and similar policy initiatives will eventually counteract firms' continuous offshoring of manufacturing activities.

5.5.2 Time Lags

A second issue has to do with *the time lag between firms' needs for specific competences in the short term and the long time needed to develop them.* When discussing the acquisition and development of competences in an innovation system, demand for labour plays a key role. Naturally, this demand must be met by the supply of labour; namely the specific competences of the labour force in the innovation system. Imbalances in the innovation system come when the provision of such skills and competences (the supply) is subject to educational programmes that are—and often have to be—designed on a long-term basis, whereas the demand in the labour market is typically more an issue of covering the short- to medium-term needs of firms. This time lag between the supply and demand sides becomes particularly important with regard to higher education (universities), where there is much specialization.

It takes many years to educate a chemical engineer with a specialization in a certain technical area, but this competence might become obsolete relatively quickly. Several situations might occur here. One is when there has been an 'overproduction' of a specific kind of chemical engineer, which the local economy cannot absorb. This is most acute in situations of rapid industrial restructuring. Another possible situation is when rapid technological development makes the content of educational programmes (partly) obsolete in the short term. For reasons of legal commitments, it might take universities quite a few years to be able to terminate an educational programme.

The above shows that several factors are at play in these time-lag imbalances; these are the dynamics of the labour market itself, the dynamics of technological change, and legal-institutional frameworks. Thus, policymakers are always confronted with the fundamental question of how to best define and determine the types of competences and skills that the economy will need in the future. This is not just the case for the public education sector itself, but for the private education sector as well.

In many countries, private education receives direct or indirect public subsidies, and it is typically subject to some national/regional publicly defined framework (i.e. regulatory frameworks regarding academic titles, accreditation criteria for higher education institutions, quality measurements, etc.). Policymakers are therefore confronted with a great amount of uncertainty when it comes to the future needs of the innovation system. And the problem is that the labour market demand of today does not necessarily predict demand in the future. Whereas current deficiencies might indicate future needs in terms of, for example, the number of medical doctors or engineers, determining what specialization will be most acute in the future is much more difficult.

5.5.3 *Imbalance between Internal and External Competences*

A third set of potentially problematic issues in an innovation system is *the imbalance between internal and external competences*, which may result either in isolation from, or in an excessive dependence on, external competences. This has to do with the notion of absorptive capacity, which refers to firms' capacity to tap into sources of external knowledge, and to combine this knowledge with their own internal knowledge in order to generate innovations. The development of innovation systems is highly related to their absorptive capacity (Castellacci and Natera, 2013). However, securing the right balance between internal and external competences might prove to be difficult in reality.

Firms that rely too much on internal competences might run the risk of isolation and lose the opportunity to acquire new knowledge and skills available elsewhere. On the other hand, firms that rely too much on external competences might become too dependent on externally dominated knowledge resources and might rapidly lose absorptive capacity, thereby their competitive edge. Hence, keeping the balance between internal and external competences is crucial for the development of the innovation system—and for firms.

From the point of view of the policy-maker, this is an important matter, though a difficult one to tackle. When discussing competences in innovation systems, policy-makers might have a natural tendency to think exclusively in terms of competences that are solely internal to firms. The theory of absorptive capacity tells us that external competences are very important too, in the sense of both external to the firm and external to the innovation system as a whole. This latter consideration emphasizes striking a balance between the types of competences to be developed inside an innovation system, country/region, or an economy, and those to be tapped from outside.

5.6 Concluding Remarks: Policy Design for Competence-Building

There is a wide consensus that competences play a central role in innovation systems and in the dynamics of economic growth. For that reason, innovation policy typically has strategic issues to tackle concerning the development and acquisition of competences. Competences have been defined here as the set of knowledge, skills, and expertise that individuals and organizations have. Likewise, competence-building is the process of formal or informal development and acquisition of specific competences by individuals and organizations.

Following the literature on these matters, this chapter has argued that competences can be internal or external sources to firms. 'Internal' refers to competences that are an integral part of the firm at a specific point in time. 'External' refers to the competences that firms exchange with other firms or agents (for example by collaboration) at a particular point in time. As we have indicated, the employment of human capital is less secure internally than other types of capital. Naturally, external competences can become internalized at a certain point if the firm decides to acquire them, or vice versa. The point at stake here is whether to 'own' (internal) or to use without owning (external). This crucial decision is pertinent to any type of organization (public or private) and—by extension—to the innovation system as a whole.

After providing some examples of policy action in this area, this chapter has also identified some deficiencies and imbalances that typically occur in innovation systems. These can be essentially summarized into three categories. The *first* has to do with the insufficient levels of competences in an economy and/or the net loss of competences in that economy. The *second* is the time lag between firms' short-term needs and the long time required to develop future competence (in the national context). The *third* is the possible imbalance between internal and external sources of competences, which might generate either excessive isolation from or excessive dependence on external knowledge.

The general criteria for the design of innovation policy that we suggest in this chapter focus on the imbalances mentioned above. Therefore the first criterion is the *creation, retention, and attraction of competences in a country or region*. There is a widespread understanding that modern economies have a positive bias towards skilled labour (against unskilled labour), and that this is related to technological change. This is what has been termed the 'Skill Biased Technological Change' hypothesis, which has been confirmed empirically in most developed countries—see Piva et al. (2006) for a review. Policy-makers must secure adequate levels of skill in an economy, but this might not happen automatically for several reasons, as we have seen above.

The second criterion is *the identification of the specific types of competences that are needed currently and in the future*. It might be too obvious to say that countries, regions, and cities need to identify their present and future needs of knowledge, skills, and experience for their innovation system and their economy more broadly (Edquist et al., 2001b). However, many countries and regions actually do not have any systematic monitoring mechanisms for this (Jones and Grimshaw, 2012). Yet, determining the types of competence that an innovation system needs is a daunting task for policy-makers given the bewildering complexity and variety of competences that innovative firms and organizations need, now and in the future. Several sets of statistics, survey analyses, and foresight exercises are policy instruments which can be used in this regard (Borrás and Edquist, 2013b).

The third criterion is *keeping a sound balance between internal and external competences in firms*. This is to avoid too much emphasis on internal sources of competences (which would create an isolated situation) and to avoid too much 'invent elsewhere' situations by which firms become too dependent on external sources of knowledge. This requires considering the 'give and take' of firms' interaction with other organizations, as well as the internationalization of competences in an economy.

The three aspects examined here are not only relevant for the design of innovation policy. They are also the foundations of a theoretical and analytical framework for the study of the multiple linkages of competence-building dynamics, the public schemes to develop them, and their final effects on the innovation system. As stated earlier in this chapter, public action is a *sine qua non* element of an innovation system. For this reason, studying competences and competence-building in a system requires taking on board existing public action.

These remarks lead us to pinpoint important gaps in the literature that warrant further research efforts in the near future. One of these gaps is the lack of empirical studies that look at the effects of education and vocational training schemes, as well as migration and brain-circulation policies, on innovation performance in innovation systems. One question that remains unanswered is what specific effects several decades of migration policy schemes for skilled and trained workers have had on different dynamics of the innovation system.

Another highly relevant question is the time-line evolution in the composition of skills and expertise on the one hand, and the innovative performance of a specific economy on the other. Can we see specific patterns in terms of competences and their development that are associated with the particular evolution of the innovation system?

Finally, there is a lack of attention paid to competences and competence-development in the public sector itself. Here the question is how the competences and competence-building in public, semi-public, and non-profit private organizations also affect the level of innovation performance in a system. This article has focused primarily on the competences of firms as a crucial asset for their ability to innovate. However, it is important to keep in mind that competences and competence-building remain central to any kind of public or semi-public organization in an innovation system. This question is particularly relevant when looking at innovation processes in the public sector.

6

Functional Procurement as Demand-Side Innovation Policy

6.1 Introduction

Public procurement occurs when public agencies (national, regional, local) purchase products (goods, services, systems). The rationale, purpose, and starting point of public procurement should always be to solve societal problems, to satisfy human needs, or to meet global challenges, such as environmental or health problems. This chapter is aimed at everyone who is involved or interested in public procurement, and especially how it can influence the direction and speed of innovation processes, as an instrument of innovation policy operating from the demand side.[1] How can we achieve an increase in the use of innovation-enhancing public procurement in policy-making? What types of procurement initiative have the potential to influence innovations most? And how can these be designed and implemented to increase their use?

One purpose of this chapter is to show how public procurement can be a driver of innovation for the purpose of solving societal problems. In Sweden, the policy questions related to public procurement and innovation have partly been handled by the Swedish National Innovation Council (NIC) over the last few years. This chapter illustrates how procurement issues have been addressed by the NIC and discusses the policy-learning that can be derived from such experience. Special emphasis will be given to the development of the actual policy with regard to functional procurement in Sweden. It will also be discussed whether Sweden can serve as a role model for other countries in this respect. The NIC and its operation have been addressed in detail in Edquist (2018a, 2018b).

---

[1] This chapter is partly based on Edquist 2014c, 2015, 2016b, 2017, 2018a, 2018b, Edquist et al. 2018a, and Wesseling and Edquist, 2018, but also on earlier publications on innovation-related public procurement co-authored with Jon Mikel Zabala-Iturriagagoitia: Edquist and Zabala-Iturriagagoitia 2012, 2015.

Innovation policy includes, in principle, all actions by public organizations that influence innovation processes (see Chapter 2). The choice of which innovation policy instruments to consider within the instrument mix when designing a certain policy intervention is a very important part of the formulation and design of an innovation policy (Borrás and Edquist, 2013b). There are many innovation policy instruments to choose from.[2] The choice must naturally depend on the kind of problem that needs to be solved and the (main) causes behind that problem. A combination of two or more instruments is often used to solve specific problems. They are thus combined into an 'instrument mix'.

Historically, innovation policy has been strongly dominated by supply-push oriented instruments (measures), primarily R&D funding. This linear view actually still dominates in practical innovation policy (Edquist 2014d and Chapter 3 in this book), but no longer so much in policy analysis—and certainly not among innovation researchers. The linear view has actually been completely rejected in innovation research, being replaced by the systems of innovation approach, but it still prevails in innovation policy-making. The innovation systems approach dates back to the works by Chris Freeman in the 1980s and it is, in its different versions, normally defined in terms of determinants of innovation processes, although different determinants are emphasized in different versions (Freeman, 1987; Lundvall, 1992; Nelson and Rosenberg, 1993; Breschi and Malerba, 1997; Carlsson, 1997; Cooke, 2001b; Bergek et al., 2008; Cooke et al., 1997; Edquist, 1997, 2005). In Chapters 2 and 3 of this book we identified and described ten such determinants.

There seems to be a considerable time lag between progress with regard to innovation studies and the implementation of its academic findings in the design of innovation policy.[3] The demand-side factors that influence innovation processes are emphasized to a much greater extent in the innovation systems approach than in earlier theoretical approaches (Edquist, 2005, 2011). This points to a failure in using innovation studies' results in the design of innovation policy and the choice of innovation policy instruments (Weber and Truffer, 2017). On the one hand, it points to a failure in the effectiveness of how scholars engage with the innovation policy community to disseminate their findings. On the other, it also shows a clear failure on the demand side, namely, the lack of interest or lack of absorptive capabilities at the political as well as the policy side, to learn from the state of the art in innovation studies.

---

[2] The number depends of course on how 'well' one divides the different main instruments into sub-categories. At times, there is, for example, talk of innovation-enhancing procurement as one general category. Here we divide this category into distinctly different types.

[3] For the empirics on this, see Edquist 2011, 2014a, 2014b, 2014d, and 2016b.

In this chapter we concentrate on one group of demand-side innovation policy instruments: public procurement that can enhance innovation.[4] It may affect both the speed and direction of innovation. The purpose is to show how public procurement can be a driver of innovation (Edquist et al., 2000b). The reason for choosing innovation-related public procurement in particular is that it is potentially by far the most powerful kind of demand-side innovation policy instrument available (Uyarra and Flanagan, 2010). Public procurement amounts to 15–20 per cent of GDP in the whole of the EU, and it may amount to the enormous sum of €2.0 trillion (Kahlenborn et al., 2011).

A small part of this enormous sum is already being used for supporting innovation, and there is potential for much more of it to be used in that way. This could particularly be realized if an increasing part of the products (goods, services, and systems) are procured on the basis of descriptions of problems (societal, environmental) and functions, rather than on the basis of descriptions of products. In this way, innovation-enhancing public procurement can become the most important instrument among all innovation policy instruments, based on the sheer size of public procurement. It would then be an important element in the transformation of innovation policy from linear to holistic.

The remainder of this chapter is structured as follows. Section 6.2 presents a taxonomy of different types of public procurement relevant for innovation, with a strong emphasis on functional public procurement. After discussing the importance of functional procurement for innovation (Section 6.3), we address the obstacles to pursuing it and how to overcome them (Section 6.4). In Sections 6.5 and 6.6, we describe and analyse how functional procurement became government policy in Sweden in 2016 and whether Sweden can be a role model for other countries in this respect. Section 6.7 summarizes the discussion and deals with combinations of different kinds of public procurement.

6.2 Innovations and Procurement: Definitions and Taxonomy

A central question is how innovations can be achieved by means of public procurement. Hence, it must be possible to distinguish between public procurement that leads to innovation and that which does not. Therefore, it is necessary to revert back to Chapter 2 in this book for the definition of innovation. Innovations are new creations of economic or societal importance, usually performed by firms. Innovations can be new or improved products

---

[4] Other demand-side innovation policy instruments are standard-setting, subsidies, or tax incentives to support demand, enhancing articulation of user needs, etc.

or processes. New—or better—products (*product innovations*) may be material goods or intangible services; it is a question of *what* is produced. New processes (*process innovations*) may be technological or organizational; here, it is a question of *how* the products are produced. Of great importance, however, is that the new creations do not become (successful) innovations until they are actually commercialized or diffused (i.e. spread) to a considerable degree; the end products have to be deployed in commercial volumes. The development of a prototype or a test series is not enough for new creations to qualify as innovations. New creations that are not commercialized or diffused in other ways are not innovations (see Chapter 2).

Public procurement is related to demand and occurs when a public agency or unit (national, regional, or local) purchases a product (i.e. a good, a service, or a combination of these as a system). There are different kinds of public procurement. The procurement categories addressed below have different goals and characteristics and are implemented in different ways.

Existing ('off-the-shelf') products are purchased in *public regular procurement*, and the procuring authority or unit does not, in this case, demand any innovations (new products) from the bidders. Regular procurement may, for example, be the purchase of pens, paper, towels, trains, telecommunication services, cars, etc. In regular public procurement the procuring part normally describes the desired product and its characteristics in the tender documentation (i.e. *förfrågningsunderlag* in Swedish). We also call this *product procurement*.

A large number of regular public procurements are perfunctorily conducted, i.e. the procuring agency or unit describes the same product as in previous procurements in a routine manner (Edquist, 2014c), by means of product procurement. These products must obviously be existing ones, since they can be described by the procuring organization. They may even be obsolete. If that is the case, qualitatively superior products (i.e. innovations) will be excluded in the procurement process. A routine of simply describing previously procured products makes it difficult or impossible for new products (innovations) to be accepted. This is a major obstacle to innovation. You get what you ask for—even if it is an obsolete product. Such repetitive product procurement leads to lock-in situations and inertias sooner or later. It would be very important to better understand, and in detail, the underlying reasons for this behaviour. It would, for example, be very important in an attempt to change such behaviour.

6.2.1 *Innovation-Enhancing Procurement*

Public *innovation procurement* takes place when a public agency or unit prepares and places an order to fulfil certain functions within a given time period, where a product to fulfil these functions does not exist at the time of the order.

The purpose is to satisfy unmet socio-economic or environmental needs or to mitigate global challenges—which are often national and regional at the same time. This type of procurement *must* result in some form of product innovation before delivery can occur (although the new product can be used as a process). Product development is needed, but not necessarily R&D. It must result in innovation and delivery of a more advanced product. In other words, public innovation procurement is always innovation-enhancing (if not failing altogether).[5]

We will now specify three existing kinds of public procurement that we call 'innovation-enhancing procurement' (IEP), as they may directly influence innovation:

1 direct innovation procurement;
2 catalytic innovation procurement; and
3 functional regular procurement.

The sub-category *direct innovation procurement* occurs when the procuring authority or unit is also the (end) user of the product that results from the procurement (if successful). The procuring agency uses its own demand or need to promote an innovation. This is the 'classical' case. Direct innovation procurement has long been practised in Sweden and other countries. Several examples are described and analysed (Edquist et al., 2000b; Edquist and Zabala-Iturriagagoitia, 2012; Edquist, 2015), e.g. the transmission of electricity at 400,000 volts and the first electronic telecom switch. In Sweden, such procurement has led to tens of thousands of jobs and billions of euros in export incomes.

The sub-category *catalytic innovation procurement* occurs when the procuring public agency operates as a catalyst, part-financier, and/or knowledge resource for the (end) users, which are represented by a 'purchase group'. In this kind of procurement, the need lies 'outside' the public procuring organization, which acts as a coordinator. The procuring agency, although not being the end user of the resulting product, has the task of 'purchasing' the new product 'on behalf of' other actors, both private and public. The agency thus acts as a 'catalyst' for the development of innovations for wider use, and not for the direct satisfaction of needs of the procuring organization. The purpose of conducting innovation procurement may, for example, be to mitigate global challenges.

This concept as specified here was first formulated in Edquist and Hommen (1999) and further developed in Edquist et al. (2000b). There are different

---

[5] The notion of 'innovation-friendly procurement' is also around. It is, however, a rather vague term and is therefore not used here.

definitions of catalytic public innovation procurement (e.g. in the Dutch SBIR program) which are not considered here. Sweden has had a long and successful experience of catalytic innovation procurement by carrying out sixty catalytic procurements around the turn of the century; for example, the procurement of a Freon-free refrigerator that uses only half the amount of electricity compared to existing ones at the time.

Functional regular procurement can be defined as the procurement of products by a public authority or unit that describes a function to be performed or a problem to be solved (functional specification) instead of describing the product that is to perform the function. In functional procurement, a public agency specifies what is to be achieved rather than how it is to be achieved. Hence, it is a matter of the manner in which a procurement call is set up and the tender documentation is formulated. It might lead to innovations or it might not.[6]

Functional regular public procurement is a special kind of public regular procurement. It is innovation-enhancing in the sense that it opens up for innovations, but it does not require innovations. The old product can still be procured (if it fulfils the—functional—specifications) and functional procurement is therefore not innovation procurement. If an innovation is not required in functional procurement, the risk of failure is smaller with functional procurement than with innovation procurement (which also, by the way, requires functional procurement)—see also below. In short, functional procurement is regular procurement (since it may result in the procurement of existing products), but it also allows for the procurement of new products (innovations), without requiring them.[7]

An example of functional procurement might be a public transportation agency, or a local government offering to buy a specified maximum decibel level in apartment buildings close to a road or railway—instead of describing a noise barrier (e.g. a fence) in the tender documentation. The targeted decibel level can be achieved by suppliers/innovators in many ways (an earth wall, trees and plants, 'quiet' asphalt, lower speed, a device that 'bends' sound upwards, something not yet imagined by anyone, etc.)—and which particular method or device does and should not matter.

Another example can be procuring ambulance services. The call for tenders should not specify where the ambulances are to be placed, but how quickly

---

[6] The perspective on functional procurement has been developed in Edquist 2014c, 2015, 2016a, 2016b, and 2017. Note that EU procurement directives also stress the importance of functional procurement for innovation—see Section 6.3.

[7] According to EU directives on public procurement, there are different 'procurement procedures' through which public procurement initiatives can be undertaken and which allow for dialogues to be pursued in early stages. Examples are open, restricted, and negotiated procedures, competitive dialogues, and design contests. 'Functional procurement' is not such a formal procurement procedure.

they can reach the people who need them. The supplier is the one who should make the decision on where they are to be placed to minimize their time to reach the patients and, hence, maximize their effectiveness. Thus, one should not specify technical solutions or describe products (including services) in procurement—or even be too precise in the description of functions to be performed or problems to be solved.

In the autumn of 2016, the Swedish Procurement Agency (UHM) published on its homepage detailed descriptions of seven cases of functional procurement to serve as role models. There are many additional cases of functional regular procurement in Sweden. Two examples are the procurements of 'wound care' (instead of bandages) and plastic aprons for surgery, pursued by the health-care part of the Skåne region. Many previously unrecorded cases have also 'emerged' when the issue has been publicly discussed in Sweden. It is likely that cases also exist in other countries.

When considered together, we call the three categories specified above 'innovation-enhancing procurement' IEP). Given that IEP is very much an evolving field, a need might emerge to include other kinds of procurement, or to divide the previous types into different sub-categories if they have a bearing on innovation and can be separated from each other.

This typology and the categories included are by no means a list of 'procurement procedures' in the legal (EU directive) sense of the word. As a matter of fact, this chapter is not a systematic discussion of such procedures at all; they are mentioned only in passing in a few places. Instead, this chapter deals with matters of substance with regard to innovation-enhancing public procurement.

A new procurement procedure of relevance, however, is included in the 2014 EU Procurement Directives. It is called 'innovation partnerships'. This procedure is applicable when there is a need for a new innovative product that cannot be met by suppliers at the time. This procedure may include R&D as well as manufacturing of the products.[8]

Hence R&D as well as innovation and manufacturing are stressed to a larger extent than before, and partly in a combined way, in this procurement procedure. In the context of innovation partnerships, there is, however, no mention of functional specifications, although such specifications seem to be necessary when the characteristics of the product are not known, judging from the arguments presented above. The general resistance by many procurement administrators to use functional specifications might make them abstain here, too. It would have therefore been pedagogical to mention that functional specifications can be advantageous in this context as well.

---

[8] At the time of writing (May 2018), this procedure has not been used to any substantial extent.

Innovations may, of course, sometimes occur 'spontaneously' in regular procurement, if the product description is generic enough to include innovations (better products) that emerge anyway. One of the roles of innovation policy is, however, to create the conditions for the systematic emergence and development of innovations that help address and respond to socio-economic and environmental needs, both in the present time and in the future. Therefore, innovations may be highly stimulated by functional procurement.[9]

6.2.2 Pre-Commercial Procurement

We did not include Pre-Commercial Procurement (PCP) in the taxonomy of IEP above. The reason is that it cannot be accurately labelled product procurement or innovation procurement. The following comments on PCP are included only because the phenomenon has often—mistakenly—been considered to be innovation procurement. See Edquist and Zabala-Iturriagagoitia (2015) for a comprehensive discussion on why PCP cannot be regarded as innovation procurement.

PCP takes place when an expected R&D result or solution is procured by a public agency, i.e. it implies direct public R&D investments (or R&D subsidies). PCP is an approach to procuring R&D services, which involves risk-benefit sharing and does not constitute state aid. As indicated above, a product must be commercialized or spread in the economy or society to be considered an innovation. Commercialization is not allowed to be part of the PCP process, according to World Trade Organization, Agreement on Government Procurement, and EU regulations.

PCP is exempted from a large part of EU procurement rules. 'Pre-Commercial Procurement (PCP) means the procurement of research and development services...where there is a clear separation of the research and development services procured from the deployment of commercial volumes of end products' (Regulation (EU) 2013; also quoted in Note to ERAC 2016: footnote 2). PCP is not intended to lead to the procurement of a certain number of (non-existing) products. A buyer of such products is not at all involved in the public procurement (unlike the cases of regular procurement and innovation procurement). An innovation is not the result of the PCP process as such. PCP precludes innovation as a part of the procurement.[10]

---

[9] Over the last three years or so, we have gradually developed the perspective on functional procurement in Edquist 2014c, 2015, 2016a, and 2017. This has occurred in interaction with the colleagues in the Swedish NIC where Charles Edquist has been a member since February 2015—see Section 6.5.

[10] That this is so has been shown in detail (Edquist and Zabala-Iturriagagoitia 2015, 2012; Edquist 2015). The concept of IEP is a much wider term than the old concept of 'public procurement of innovation—PPI', as it includes 'functional regular procurement'. However, it excludes PCP for obvious reasons. We have previously discussed taxonomies of various categories

In other words, the buying of end products in commercial volumes is not included in PCP. In this sense, PCP is not innovation procurement (but procurement of R&D), although it can precede innovation—and thereby influence innovation processes from the supply side, but not from the demand side. So do many other determinants of innovation that we do not call IEP.

Hence, PCP is a supply-side policy instrument in relation to innovation—not a demand-side policy instrument. However, PCP is a demand-side policy instrument in relation to research, and it is even functional procurement of research results (Edquist and Zabala-Iturriagagoitia 2015). The PCP type of public procurement may also be called 'contract research', which is public R&D financing that is highly problem-oriented and targeted. It thus differs considerably from general public R&D financing, or tax deduction that companies in many countries can use for R&D expenditure.

In PCP, the financing organizations are often research-funding organizations (such as Swedish VINNOVA), which are normally not the end users of the R&D services procured. The end users are those organizations that have applied for funding from, for example, VINNOVA and pursue PCP projects.

The four kinds of IEP discussed here should not be confused. They are different; they have different goals and are implemented in different ways. The four kinds of procurement addressed here need different organizational set-ups. In direct innovation procurement and functional regular procurement, the organization that will use the product is also pursuing the process of procuring the innovations. In catalytic innovation procurement, several other kinds of organization are also involved—as catalysts, part-financiers, or knowledge resources for the (end) users. Functional regular procurement may lead to innovations or not. PCP means procurement of research results, not innovations.

This means that the four categories should be dealt with in partly different ways. It is therefore necessary that we have terms and concepts for the different specific kinds of procurement to understand the differences and commonalities between them.

Naturally, the four categories of procurement can be used and combined with each other (and with other innovation policy instruments) in a complementary manner within an instrument mix. However, it is important to define the concepts precisely and separate them, instead of lumping them together. For analysts, it is important for concepts to be defined precisely so that the phenomena they denote can be clearly understood. For policy-makers, clear concepts are important for deciding what they should do, e.g. which goals to set for a certain type of procurement, what is to be procured, and how the procurement is to be conducted.

---

of public procurement at great length. See Edquist 2014c, 2015, 2017; Edquist and Zabala-Iturriagagoitia 2012, 2015. These taxonomies cannot be repeated in a systematic way here.

6.3 The Importance of Functional Specification for Innovation

In this section it will be argued that explaining and defining functional specifications rather than traditional descriptions of product/process characteristics is the key to all three categories of IEP and also to PCP. Hence, 'functional specifications' and 'functional procurement' will be focused on here.

The category 'functional regular procurement' is, of course, regular procurement (as it may result in the continued procurement of existing products, if no better products come forward). But it also allows for the procurement of new products (innovations), thanks to the functional specification.[11] Functional regular procurement can be considered to have the largest potential for innovation of the four categories of innovation-related procurement addressed here.

However, functional procurement is much more important for innovation than that. In passing, we have also mentioned that *public innovation procurement* (direct as well as catalytic) must also be pursued by means of functional specifications. Product procurement is not possible in this case since an innovation (commonly a new product) is required and it is not possible to describe a non-existing product. Functional public procurement opens up for innovations in *all* public procurements—not only those requiring innovations (i.e. innovation procurement).

The same is actually true for PCP. PCP is a matter of buying research results that solve certain problems. These research results are not known and cannot be described *ex ante*—which implies that PCP is normally a matter of functional procurement (of research results).

The general conclusion is that functional procurement is needed for all four different kinds of procurement addressed here.

A common belief is that private firms are often open to innovation when they buy from each other—and they often require improved products, i.e. product innovations, or they use functional specifications. Public procurers do so more rarely (Edquist 2014c). This means that both they and their suppliers are left behind. To achieve innovation through public procurement it is, somewhat paradoxically, more important to emphasize functional procurement than to pursue innovation procurement. From the point of view of enhancing innovation, the main dividing line is between product

---

[11] Obviously, functional public procurement can take the form of regular procurement or lead to innovations. (Direct or catalytic) innovation procurement is, however, always functional procurement. Product procurement can only be regular procurement.

procurement and functional procurement, i.e. between two different ways or modes of pursuing public procurement.

The European Commission provides procurement rules in the form of directives, which are translated into national laws by Member States. The process is not ratification, but Member States are mandated to adopt the rules described in the directives in their national legislation (not necessarily word for word, but national changes can be made as long as they are not in conflict with the directive). The directives are applicable for all kinds of public procurement, including the three kinds of IEP discussed here. However, they are not valid for PCP, which is governed by other EU rules.[12] These procurement rules are very complicated and it is often said that they should be simplified (Edquist and Zabala-Iturriagagoitia, 2012).

'Functional (regular) procurement' is not one of the so-called 'procurement procedures' in the EU regulatory framework for public procurement specified in the legislation, which has to be followed by all EU Member States. This is a legal fact and cannot be changed in the short term. Functional procurement/ specification is not a procurement procedure. Despite this, functional procurement is necessary in all innovation procurement, direct as well as catalytic. It can simply apply functional (or performance) specifications in the tender documentation for the procurement. Several of the existing 'procurement procedures' can be used for this purpose.

However, the concept of 'functional demand' is—and was—found in EU and national legislations, such as in Sweden. Swedish law states, for example, 'A procuring agency may set the technical specifications as performance or functional demands' (SFS 2007: 1092, LUF chapter 6 paragraph 3; SFS 2007: 1091, LOU 2007: 1092). The procurer may thus choose to describe a function or a product in the tender specifications. There are actually no legal limits to this and 'functional demands' can always be used in tender specifications without changing any laws or rules. The procurer may thus choose to describe a function or a product in the tender specifications. Or he can use a combination of both.[13] It is highly relevant to point this out, as it was strongly argued that functional demands could not be used in public procurement at the time of the publication of Edquist (2014c). It was even argued that it was not legally allowed by EU directives to pursue functional procurement, on the basis of functional specifications.

---

[12] Making use of the exemption of the Article 16(f) old Directive 2004/18/EC and recital (47) the new Directive 2014/24/EU. The latter EU directive refers to PCP 'which deals with the procurement of those R&D services not falling within the scope of this Directive'.

[13] We consider performance and functional demands as synonymous in the text quoted, which means that functional procurement is possible also with 'performance requirements'—e.g. the tender can specify a certain amount of energy reduction relative to the best available technology without specifying how this energy reduction is to be achieved. In other words, a performance requirement as the one here is the same as a functional requirement.

EU procurement directives on public procurement are very important for all procurement in the EU. In the new Directive 2014/24/EU of 26 February 2014 it is written:

> The technical specifications drawn up by public purchasers need to allow public procurement to be open to competition as well as to achieve objectives of sustainability. To that end, it should be possible to submit tenders that reflect the diversity of technical solutions standards and technical specifications in the market place, including those drawn up on the basis of performance criteria linked to the life cycle and the sustainability of the production process of the works, supplies and services.
>
> Consequently, technical specifications should be drafted in such a way as to avoid artificially narrowing down competition through requirements that favour a specific economic operator by mirroring key characteristics of the supplies, services, or works habitually offered by the economic operator. *Drawing up the technical specifications in terms of functional and performance requirements generally allows that objective to be achieved in the best way possible. Functional and performance-related requirements are also appropriate means to favour innovation in public procurement and should be used as widely as possible.* (EU 2014: Recital 74, emphasis the authors)

It is remarkable that the EU directive so strongly stresses functional requirements and emphasizes that they 'should be used as widely as possible' to favour innovation (and competition) in public procurement. The rationale is to avoid favouring specific companies by defining the requirements too narrowly. Luckily, this emphasis also favours innovation, although it may only be the secondary reason for emphasizing this approach. In other words, the use of functional requirements in public procurement not only supports innovation, but also serves as a powerful instrument of competition policy. The mechanism is that opening up for competition between different products to satisfy the same need or solve the same problem is an important means of increasing competition.

6.4 Obstacles to Functional Procurement and Ways of Overcoming Them

There are several important obstacles to the increased use of functional procurement. We have dealt with obstacles to innovation procurement and ways of overcoming them (Edquist, 2014c, 2015). These are the weaknesses of public organizations, the identification of needs and problems, the specifications of functions, the competence-building in procurers and procurement support, risk aversion, the lack of interactive learning, and restrictive procurement regulation.

6.4.1 *Weakness of Public Organizations*

At a time when there were large direct public innovation procurements in Sweden, the procuring public organizations were strong and not governed by short-term considerations (e.g. quarterly reports). Organizations such as Vattenfall (electric power), Televerket (telecommunications), and SJ (railways) were able to have a long-term strategic vision. This has since changed. Televerket is now listed on the stock market and has a large proportion of private shareholders; in addition, it has been merged with the previously Finnish state-owned monopoly to form TeliaSonera. Vattenfall and SJ function pretty much as private enterprises.

This leaves only limited room for manoeuvre for public organizations in their use of resources to create incentives to develop new products of increased quality and/or lower costs in the long term. Hence, the capacity of these public organizations to be strong procurement actors has been considerably weakened. As a consequence, they tend to restrict themselves to regular procurement of existing 'off-the-shelf' products (Skogli and Nellemann, 2016).

6.4.2 *Identification of Needs or Problems*

We have emphasized that the goal of public functional (and innovation) procurement is not primarily to support or stimulate the development of new products, but to focus on solving problems. Needs or problems must be the point of departure for every functional procurement. One should never start with the product or specify what it should look like.

The most important task in preparing functional procurements is to identify the problems to be solved and the needs to be satisfied by means of the procurement. It is a question of specifying the goals (problems and needs). Developing an ability to identify needs and problems and evaluate the feasibility of proposed solutions is important. This might sometimes be quite difficult.

6.4.3 *Specification of Functions*

Identified societal needs and problems must be translated and transformed into functional requirements. This specification of functions is an early stage of the procurement process, and comes directly after identification of needs and problems. This applies to direct and catalytic innovation procurement as well as to functional procurement. Function-specification may be a very simple task, as in the decibel case (see Section 6.2.1). In other cases it may be a complicated and at times demanding task.

Neither the detailed design nor the basic design of any product should be specified by the procuring authority or unit. It is important that the procuring authority or unit should limit itself to specifying the functional requirements. If not, the creativity and innovativeness of the potential suppliers will be hampered. It may also lead to development being locked into wasteful and ineffective paths. By the same token, overly detailed function specifications may also be an encumbrance for innovation. It may be an obstacle to the simultaneous procurement of more than one attempt to meet the same functional demands, but in different ways. The products must be designed by the potential innovators/suppliers.

Let us present an example that will illustrate why the procuring authority or unit should not specify the technical requirements. When SJ procured a fast train called X2000 in the 1980s, it insisted on a locomotive-drawn train. X2000's competitor, the Italian model Pendolino, had a motor in each carriage. This made Pendolino much more flexible, giving it an advantage in all export markets. The end result is that Pendolino is used in a host of countries, while X2000 is only used in Sweden. The Swedish solution was falling behind in terms of international technological competition. This illustrates the effect of a lack of competence in a procuring agency. It is also an example of the devastating effect that overly specific technological requirements may have on the outcome. SJ should have specified only functional requirements such as speed, safety, comfort, and so on, rather than making the specific requirement that the train should be locomotive-drawn (Edquist et al., 2000a).

6.4.4 Competence-Building in Procurers and Procurement Support

Functional specification can be demanding in terms of competence and ability, and the lack of such competence can be an obstacle to functional procurement. Hence, the procuring authority or unit must see to it that it develops the competence to make functional specifications directly related to the needs and problems that it wishes a product (good, service, or system) to deal with. Accordingly, the competence will have to be problem-specific, sector-specific, and even product-specific. Needless to say, this cannot be provided by an organization that offers procurement support to all the procuring authorities and units.

However, generic procurement support is also necessary.[14] General support may comprise legal advice, support in the procurement process, preparation, implementation of the bidding procedures, and so on.

As we have seen, however, there is a fundamental difference between regular product procurement and functional procurement. The latter may

---

[14] In Sweden, such generic support has, over time, been provided by several public organizations. This support was in September 2015 moved into a separate public agency that has procurement support as its main responsibility.

require more competence since it is a matter of innovative new thinking and perhaps buying products that do not already exist.

Therefore, a considerable part of procurement support ought to be directed towards functional procurement. The most important contribution that can be made through procurement support is to provide support for the implementation of functional procurement. People with specific competence in functional procurement must be employed by the procurement-supporting organization. This organization should also collect and describe cases of successful functional procurement and produce a manual for pursuing functional innovation procurement. Another important task for such organizations is to create and collect statistics about innovation procurement of various kinds.

6.4.5 Risk and Risk Aversion

Conducting regular procurement is often easier and incurs less risk than carrying out functional procurement. The larger risk associated with functional public procurement affects procuring organizations as well as employees, and it reduces their propensity to carry out functional procurement. Administrators often prefer to cut and paste from the previous call for tenders and describe the product. They often believe that it is much more complicated to describe functions. This may be true in some cases, but certainly not in the decibel example referred to in Section 6.2.1. This risk aversion has its basis in the procuring authority's or unit's competence and the complicated and at times ambiguous legislation with which they must deal. As a procurer or administrator, one does not want to break the law or risk legal proceedings.

If functional procurement is to be carried out on a large scale, one may have to accept risks that are larger than in regular product procurement, where buying existing products 'off the shelf' is the norm. However, the risks associated with regular functional procurement are smaller than risks associated with innovation procurement, as the latter requires new products. The development of these innovations might fail—possibly because of tender specifications that are too demanding.

If the management and staff of a procuring authority or unit are to be induced to take larger risks, they should be 'protected' by politicians. The enormous volume of public procurement supports this argument. A certain number of risky projects may be taken on by an organization as part of a larger 'portfolio' in order to spread the risk. On the other hand, the media often criticize failures and tend to single out individual politicians, rather than accept isolated instances of failure as natural in relation to the large volumes of procurement. This may be reflected in opinion polls. Thus, considerable political skill is required to direct attention to procurement portfolios as a whole (Edquist et al., 2014).

This certainly looks like a catch-22. Regardless, it is necessary for politicians to encourage absorption of these risks so that risk-taking in the procuring authority or unit does not become too much of a disincentive for increased functional and innovation-enhancing procurement.

6.4.6 Lack of Interactive Learning and Procurement Regulation

Public procurement (including innovation and functional procurement) is governed by European procurement legislation. The directives are quite complicated. The concept of 'innovation procurement' cannot be found in European procurement legislation. However, as we have seen, 'functional demands' are a part of the legislation (Section 6.3) and can always be used in tender specifications.

EU procurement regulations have functioned as a significant obstacle to public procurement intended to lead to innovations. The EU regulations on state support constitute a part of the regulations intended to ensure that competition in the common (EU) market is not distorted. The regulatory framework for procurement has therefore, to a large extent, been dictated by the wish to promote 'perfect competition' which, in reality, is not perfect at all. There are also obstacles resulting from inadequate knowledge of the regulations and a 'fear' of them (see Section 6.4.5).

These regulations have been discussed and criticized in political and academic debates (e.g. Martin, 1996; Edquist et al., 2000b; Edler and Georghiou, 2007; Rolfstam, 2009). Such discussions, in fact, led to changes in the regulations in the 2000s. For instance, EU procurement directives were changed to enable certain possibilities of dialogue (or interactive learning) between the procuring authority or unit and suppliers (Edler and Georghiou 2007, p. 960). Such dialogue is a necessity if the parties to a functional or innovation procurement process are to understand each other and be able to practise 'interactive learning', which is an important source of innovation. In 2014 new directives were also added (EU 2014).

There are reasons to continue these discussions and introduce more changes in the regulations, in particular changes that enhance innovations in procurement processes. There is also room for considerable simplification of the directives.

6.5 The Pursuit of Functional Procurement as Innovation Policy in Sweden

The systematic use of functional procurement as an innovation policy instrument may be under way in Sweden. After the September 2014 election, new prime minister Stefan Löfven appointed a minister for public administration for whom the responsibility for public procurement is a very important duty. From September 2015, this minister (Ardalan Shekarabi) created a new separate public agency, *Upphandlingsmyndigheten*, or UHM, with support to innovation-related procurement as an important task.

In February 2015, Prime Minister Löfven created the NIC (*Nationella Innovationsrådet*).[15] He personally chairs the five–eight hour meetings that occur four times per year—something that is extremely uncommon for corresponding (science and technology/innovation) councils in other countries. This is evidence of his dedication to dealing with innovation policy. Our impression is that this dedication is not only a political priority of his, but also a personal interest. With his background as a trade union negotiator and leader, he understands the importance of innovation for the economy and for society—e.g. for productivity, wages, profits, and taxes.[16]

The NIC consists of ten external advisors from industry, unions, and academia, including three university professors, one union representative, and representatives of large and small firms. In addition to Prime Minister Löfven, the four ministers of finance, enterprise/innovation, higher education and research, international development cooperation, and climate participate in the meetings. The small secretariat of the Swedish NIC is placed under the auspices of the Office of the Prime Minister, i.e. above all ministries.

The NIC is thus not a science/research and technology/innovation policy council. It deals with all the determinants of innovation in an holistic manner. Hence, it is dedicated to dealing with innovation policy in a much broader sense than most of the science, technology, and innovation policy councils in other countries, which are strongly dominated by a focus on issues of research (Edquist, 2018a and 2018b).

The Swedish NIC also partly deals with research policy issues, but in the broader context of innovation. This approach is similar to the way the Swedish Research Policy Council (which is a separate council that has existed for decades) is dealing with innovation policy. This means that the areas of responsibility of these two councils partly overlap.[17]

For the benefit of developing an innovation policy independent of (but coordinated with) research policy, it is a great advantage that in Sweden two separate councils exist: one for research policy and one for innovation policy. The establishment of this organizational structure means that Sweden has the potential to become the first country to break with the linear model in its

---

[15] When forming his government after the election in September 2014, Prime Minister Löfven also changed the name and responsibility area of the minster of enterprise (Mikael Damberg) into 'Minister of Enterprise *and Innovation*' (emphasis ours).

[16] The description of NIC here is based upon detailed accounts in Edquist, 2018a, 2018b.

[17] It is actually common that some policy areas partly overlap, leading to possible coordination problems (Edurne et al., 2014).

innovation policy and to develop an holistic innovation policy. It is, potentially, a basis that will allow Swedish innovation policy to escape the linear model.

The importance of innovation-related public procurement was a topic that I addressed in a presentation on innovation policy at the first meeting of the NIC in February 2015. In November 2015, a meeting to discuss public procurement was organized by the main secretary of the NIC (Wille Birksten) between Annelie Roswall-Ljunggren, the state secretary to Ardalan Shekarabi, and Charles Edquist, member of NIC. At that meeting, functional public procurement was emphasized. In December 2015, functional procurement as a very important innovation policy instrument operating from the demand side (and therefore potentially balancing the linear view) was discussed with the prime minister. Throughout 2015, we also gradually developed the analysis of innovation-related procurement in the direction of increasingly stressing the importance of functional procurement. The result was published in an op-ed article in the daily economic newspaper *Dagens Industri* in February 2016 (Edquist, 2016a).

A National Public Procurement Strategy was simultaneously being formulated by Ardalan Shekarabi during the first half of 2016. How enhancement of innovation can become a part of this strategy was discussed in some detail at two NIC meetings (in February and June) during the spring of 2016, after presentations by Ardalan Shekarabi. As regards the relations between innovation and public procurement, the discussions in NIC led to a gradual reorientation. An initial focus in the presentation on 'innovation-friendly public procurement' was changed to a focus on functional innovation procurement as an innovation policy instrument. In May 2016, Charles Edquist was called in for discussions of a draft of the national public procurement strategy with Ardalan Shekarabi. The discussion at that time focused only on how functional procurement can be used to enhance innovation. This influenced the procurement strategy, as can be seen in the excerpts from the strategy in the list of bullet points below.

The Swedish government collectively took a decision to adopt the National Procurement Strategy on 30 June 2016. Functional procurement is an important element in that strategy (Regeringskansliet Finansdepartementet 2017).[18] One of the seven parts of that strategy has the title 'Public procurement that enhances innovations and alternative solutions'. The following are quotes from this section:

- 'There is a large potential in using procurement as an instrument to enhance development and innovation.'

---

[18] In the sections enhancing innovation in the Swedish National Procurement Strategy, the strongest emphasis is on functional procurement. PCP plays no role in the strategy.

- 'The public sector can also enhance innovation in suppliers by, in procurement, demand functions rather than ready solutions.'
- 'By requiring functions instead of having specific requirements with regard to goods and services, the creativity and ability to innovate of the potential suppliers are enhanced.'
- 'To demand functions can increase competition in the procurement, since a larger number of firms and organizations can respond to the tenders, which is beneficial particularly for small and medium-sized firms.'
- '[Y]our agency formulates functional requirements and emphasizes the result that shall be achieved instead of specific requirements with regard to the goods and services.'
- '[Y]our agency uses assistance from the initiatives and means of support that The National Agency for Public Procurement has developed to formulate functional requirements in procurement.' (Regeringskansliet Finansdepartementet, 2017, pp. 18–19)

The fact that functional public procurement is an important part of the National Public Procurement Strategy will not mean any substantial new costs (except for education and training) in the budget.[19] It will be an alternative way of using the funds that are already allocated to public procurement of goods, services, and systems to solve problems and mitigate challenges. The size of the funds allocated to public procurement in Sweden is, as mentioned, 700 billion Swedish crowns (about 20 per cent of GDP).[20] The additional costs for education and training and other 'transaction costs' related to changes in organizational routines within affected public agencies can be estimated to be a small fraction of 1 per cent of this (Edquist 2014b).[21]

Product procurement can be transformed into functional procurement. A considerable proportion of all regular procurement should be described in terms of functions to be fulfilled or problems to be solved. In the Swedish context, our proposal has been that the proportion of the regular procurement volume (state, county, and municipality) to be described in functional terms should increase by five percentage points every year over the next five years. When 25 per cent has been achieved after five years, the programme should be re-evaluated and new decisions should be made (Edquist 2014b).

---

[19] However, as we will see, the socio-economic benefits may be enormous.

[20] As mentioned, €2.0 trillion is used for public procurement in the EU.

[21] This means that the finance minister has not, in the NIC, expressed any objections to functional procurement. Instead, she may see a possibility of using existing resources in a way leading to more creativity, more innovation, and more competition—and to productivity growth in the end.

For Sweden, our proposal means that functional public procurement would amount to 175 billion crowns after five years. This is actually 5 per cent of Swedish GDP. The total Swedish public research budget is about 35 million crowns per year, i.e. a fifth of the above. Measured in economic terms, a transformation such as the one proposed here is an extremely powerful innovation policy instrument. How much innovation this would lead to is, however, impossible to say in detail *ex-ante*.

If 10 per cent of the 700 billion crowns used for public procurement would stimulate innovation in the future, this corresponds to 70 billion crowns (€8 billion). Given that the publicly funded annual research budget in Sweden is 35 billion crowns (€4 billion), the application of this new strategy has great potential to increase the resources that will be used to obtain products of a higher quality (innovations). This, in turn, could lead to better needs satisfaction and/or problem-solving and lower costs in the long run.

The main reason for this proposal is that its implementation would release enormous creativity and innovativeness among suppliers—and for the public sector—within a very large proportion of the economy as a whole. The proposed approach would also lead to increased competition, not only among different potential suppliers of similar products, but also among radically different products that solve the same problem. All this leads to a higher quality of public services (i.e. to innovations in the public sector). Functional public procurement has thus the largest potential to enhance innovations of all kinds of public procurement. This potential has, so far, been harvested to a very limited degree (Edquist et al., 2018a). Estimates of the (small) quantity of functional procurement in Sweden are presented in Edquist (2014c). The small quantity indicates that there is a huge unleashed potential.

6.6 The Implementation of Functional Procurement to Influence Innovation

The implementation of the Swedish National Procurement Strategy started after summer 2016. The UHM has been given the task of providing special support by taking initiatives and providing support to formulate functional specifications in public procurement. When an existing organization with existing personnel and given competencies is given new tasks, there is always a danger that the new tasks are less focused, due to a lack of knowledge, organizational inertia, and resistance to change. It then becomes an issue for the leadership of the agency—and learning may be necessary also for the supporting organization.

In December 2016, the Swedish government also gave an assignment to UHM to enhance innovation procurement by giving support to 'procurement groups' (*beställargrupper*) to be formed by procuring agencies at a national, regional, and local level that have similar needs for innovative solutions (i.e. bundling of demand). The general director of UHM (Inger Ek) said in a conference organized by UHM on 21 November 2016 that they are pushing functional procurement. At the same conference, the minister in charge (Ardalan Shekarabi) said that all public state agencies have been given instructions to pursue IEP.

In Sweden, all the public central state agencies are controlled by the government. The ministries under which they operate can instruct them to pursue functional procurement through their annual 'letters of regulation' (*regleringsbrev*). However, the regional and local governments have a large degree of independence from the national state. Hence, they cannot be directly instructed by the central state to pursue functional procurement. However, regional and local governments are also governed by democratically elected bodies. They may take similar decisions with regard to functional procurement as the central government has done. Two things facilitate this. The recent national government strategy is certainly serving as an example for regions and local communities. In addition, there are cases of functional procurement that have already been pursued at the regional/local level. Hence, there is a spontaneous interest in pursuing functional procurement among some regional and local bodies, which will most certainly be strengthened by the existence of the national strategy.

The support from the procurement agency to the functional procurement part of the Swedish National Public Procurement Strategy seems to have been rather vague and slow over the first nine months. This might change, however, judging from an interview with Inger Ek in May 2017. In a supplement to the biggest Swedish economics newspaper, she is quoted on the front page as saying, 'We want to open up for innovation and new ideas by means of buying function instead of product' (Inger Ek, interview, 2017). This is very promising, if enough competence and resources are recruited, mobilized and allocated for this purpose.[22]

The minister in charge (Ardalan Shekarabi) and the director-general of the Innovation Procurement Agency (Inger Ek) were invited to a meeting with the NIC on 19 March 2018 to report on implementation. The minister stressed at that meeting that the legal rules are not the main problem, but the application of those rules. The director-general emphasized strongly innovative solutions

---

[22] It may be noted that the statement by Inger Ek is quite similar to a sentence in Section 6.3: *To achieve innovation through public procurement it is, somewhat paradoxically, more important to emphasize functional procurement than to pursue innovation procurement if the objective is to achieve innovation by means of public procurement.*

in public procurement and that such solutions can best be enhanced by means of functional procurement.

Charles Edquist stressed that a concrete plan of action for implementation of functional procurement is badly needed, but not in existence. The unanimous view among the members of the NIC was that it is very important that the issue has been advanced and that developing competence and educational programmes with regard to functional procurement is very important. One member of NIC (Ola Asplund) said, 'We are on our way to get this big stone moved'.

To achieve innovations in public procurement, it is important that the functional specifications are not accompanied by other requirements that may restrict access to the process for small and innovative firms. It is crucial that other restrictive conditions like product descriptions are not included in calls for tender. At Region Skåne, which is a very advanced procuring organization in the Skåne region in Sweden, Louise Strand (Director of Procurement) calls this an 'innovation-friendly washing machine'. Restrictive clauses might concern requirements of reference deals, size of the company, size of the tender, restrictive intellectual property rights conditions, disproportionate financial and technical guarantees from tenderers, etc.

It is important to provide support for the implementation of functional procurement. Such support should have the development of capability to pursue functional procurement as an important ingredient. On this basis, education and training of procurement administrators is needed. People with specific competence in functional procurement must also be employed by the procurement-supporting organization. This organization should also collect and describe cases of successful functional procurement and produce a manual for pursuing functional innovation procurement. Part of this support should be provided by the procurement agency (UHM), but also other actors (universities, consultancy firms, etc.) may have to be involved.

6.7 Combinations of Different Types of Procurement

We have mentioned the interrelationships between different types of procurement in several sections of this chapter. In order to implement these different types effectively, it is of utmost importance to clearly distinguish them from one another. Unfortunately, this is not always done. In this section we will summarize, in a more systematic way, the interrelationships between different forms of procurement and their significance. A conclusion is that it is important that the right type of procurement should be used to respond to the right type of problem or need. It is also important that they complement each other in an instrument mix that effectively targets and mitigates the problem being addressed.

Furthermore, functional and innovation procurement should be combined with innovation policy instruments other than the different types of procurement. One should consider the whole process of innovation and the determinants of innovation (Dalhammar and Leire, 2012; OECD, 2016). (For a discussion on the relation to non-procurement innovation policy instruments, see Borrás and Edquist, 2013a and Chapter 11 of this book.)

The entire process of functional (and innovation) procurement is inclusive of many stages, from identification of the needs and problems, to functional specification, to R&D, product development, commercialization, delivery, and finally to meeting and solving the original needs and problems. Note that this is not a process that begins with research and ends with products (innovations). In other words, it is not a linear process in the traditional sense. It begins with needs and demand, which must be identified and prioritized by policy decisions. Moreover, there is considerable feedback between the constituent parts of the process. Interactive learning and cooperation between organizations are central mechanisms in most innovation processes, for example those which occur through functional procurement that are enhancing innovations.

The results that are achievable with the help of functional procurement are highly significant in that they may contribute to meeting social needs and solving societal problems, as well as mitigating global challenges. They can, for example, constitute partial solutions to environmental problems. All such problems cannot be solved only by innovations, but many cannot be solved without them. They can also contribute to creating growth, jobs, and profit for those companies that may be encouraged to develop new products before their competitors as a result of functional procurement, as well as by public agencies. The measures suggested in this chapter should be implemented to make this potential become a reality.

Despite the lack of data, we shall, partly on qualitative grounds and very preliminarily, suggest some implications concerning which types of innovation-related procurement that will be important in the relatively near future—if political efforts are made. Currently, the potential for performing direct innovation procurement is limited, partly because of the weakening of public organizations. The possibilities for pursuing catalytic innovation procurement are considerably larger if political initiatives are taken. The greatest potential is in transforming regular public procurement into catalytic innovation procurement and, above all, into functional procurement. However, both require political intervention in the form of demanding procurement to be conducted as functional procurement.

As we have seen, different types of procurement can be combined with one another. Although PCP is not product procurement or innovation procurement, it is relevant to address PCP in relation to such kinds of procurement and in a general innovation policy context. For instance, PCP-funded research on one hand, and functional or innovation procurement on the other, can be combined with each other, as they cover different 'parts' of the innovation process. It may also be useful to let PCP and regular procurement complement each other. For example, a prototype that results from PCP may be taken further by means of regular procurement.

The combination of PCP and regular procurement can also be seen as an alternative to innovation procurement, as the combination covers a large part of the innovation process. If the result of PCP (e.g. a prototype) needs to be further developed before it can become a new, finished product (i.e. an innovation), functional procurement (or even innovation procurement) can also be used as a complement to PCP. PCP can be a part of innovation procurement (the R&D phase), but it is not innovation procurement, as a prototype, and not a commercialized product, is the possible result.

As can be seen, our predictions are highly dependent on whether political initiatives are taken. This is not surprising, as it is state agencies, counties, and municipalities that can create demand by means of public procurement. They constitute the demand and they are the market (except when it comes to catalytic innovation procurement).

Even if the resources presently being devoted to innovation-related procurement in Sweden and in other countries are small in monetary terms, the interest in innovation policy instruments that operate from the demand side is on the increase. Public functional procurement is by far the most important of these instruments. Functional procurement can be developed into the most important innovation policy instruments in Sweden's innovation strategy, if the necessary political initiatives are taken. There are also prospects for diffusion to other countries.

The EU Commission has taken an initiative that may facilitate the diffusion of functional procurement to make public procurement more innovation-enhancing. They organized a mutual learning exercise on 'Innovation-related public procurement', which ran through 2017 and part of 2018. Fifteen EU Member States participated in this exercise, which included six meetings. The topics addressed were developing a strategic framework, capacity-building, financing, and evaluation of IEP and PCP.[23]

As mentioned in Section 6.5, functional public procurement is an important part of the National Public Procurement Strategy that was decided upon by the Swedish government in June 2016. As also mentioned, this will not mean any

---

[23] The reports are available at https://rio.jrc.ec.europa.eu/en/library/mle-innovation-related-public-procurement-final-report. Charles Edquist was the chairman of this project and wrote a summary report, 'Developing a strategic framework for IEP and PCP' (Edquist, 2017); Edquist et al. 2018a is the final report of this project.

substantial new costs, but an alternative method of using the funds that are already allocated to public procurement. The funds will be used to obtain higher-quality products (which will lead to better needs satisfaction and problem-solving) and at lower costs in the long run. At the same time, there will be creation of new jobs, exports, profits, and welfare.

If the implementation process continues well, functional public procurement may develop into the most important instrument in Swedish innovation policy. Sweden could be the first country in the world to systematically use functional public procurement as an innovation policy instrument on a larger scale. Since this instrument operates from the demand side, it constitutes a supplement to research policy and other instruments that drive innovation from the supply side. It could thereby contribute to transforming Swedish innovation policy from a linear one in an holistic direction.

7

Change of Organizations

Entrepreneurship and Intrapreneurship

7.1 Introduction

For more than three decades, evolutionary and innovation system perspectives have emphasized not only the importance of the knowledge base and dynamic competences of firms, but also the role of national institutional configurations in explaining different levels of innovation performance and economic growth across countries. The systemic view brings to the fore the multiple forms of interactions and processes across and within organizations when conducting innovation processes. At the core of all this is the endogenous view that innovation is essentially a socio-economic process embedded in idiosyncratic organizational and institutional contexts (Hage, 1999).

Some of the most valuable literature-review articles have pointed to different perspectives in terms of economic theories of the firm (Pitelis, 2010), different approaches to organizational change (Lam, 2005; Crossan and Apaydin, 2010), and multiple determinants of innovation, inside and outside the firm (Crossan and Apaydin, 2010). These are valuable insights into the vast field of business studies at the organizational and firm level. From the point of view of innovation systems (Teixeira, 2014; Jordan et al., 2008), firms are the core organizations performing innovation activities. The capacity of these organizations to successfully conduct those processes internally, to engage with their external context when 'capturing' new opportunities, and to develop the necessary knowledge that lies behind the new products or processes is an essential feature of the innovation system.

The purpose of this chapter is to develop a conceptual basis for addressing innovation policy in relation to organizations, paying particular attention to entrepreneurship and intrapreneurship, which is a key topic within the broad concept of organizational change. In so doing, the chapter relies on the knowledge-based views of business organization, on recent advances in the field of public policy, and on the innovation system perspective.

The chapter addresses issues of conceptual clarity relating to entrepreneurship and intrapreneurship in the context of innovation systems. The argument is that one of the probable reasons for the gap between the literature of entrepreneurship/intrapreneurship and public policy is the division of labour between the social sciences focusing on the private sphere and on the public sphere, respectively. Business studies focus on firms and the knowledge-based dynamics created and used in entrepreneurship/intrapreneurship, and in innovation processes, whereas public policy studies focus on (the changing role of) public organizations and their interaction with society more generally. Another probable reason for the gap between the literature of entrepreneurship and of public policy might be that the notion of 'entrepreneurship' has had many different meanings.

These remarks suggest that part of the problem with these gaps might reside in conceptual issues, which in turn hinder theoretical and policy-oriented developments (Radosevic and Yoruk, 2013). With this in mind, this chapter tries to provide useful definitions of entrepreneurship and intrapreneurship, and their roles in the innovation system. Thereafter, the chapter draws on the lessons from previous literature on organizational change and innovation, bringing forward previous suggestions on linking entrepreneurship and intrapreneurship studies to innovation systems (Lundvall, 2007; Radosevic, 2007). Hence, this chapter will refer to Schumpeter and recent entrepreneurship and intrapreneurship literature in order to identify the general obstacles and barriers associated with entrepreneurship and intrapreneurship in the innovation system. This will serve to examine the existing sets of policy instruments that policy-makers have in order to address these obstacles and barriers.

7.2 Entrepreneurship and Intrapreneurship as Examples of Organizational Change

In earlier chapters of this book we define innovation as new creations of economic or societal importance, usually conducted by firms. Therefore, the process of innovation often has to do with the knowledge base and capabilities of organizations; more precisely, the way in which organizations use and create those resources internally, and the way in which they act externally in relation to other organizations, to the market, and to the innovation system. Organizations are defined here as: 'formal structures with an explicit purpose and consciously created. They are players or actors' (Edquist and Johnson, 1997, p. 47). Organizations are therefore to be distinguished from institutions in the innovation system. Whereas organizations are the actors and agents who actually carry out innovation activities (or indirectly support these activities), institutions are not at all actors or agents. Institutions are the formal or informal 'rules of the game' that shape the conditions under which organizations (inter)act. This conceptual distinction is paramount to the understanding of the differences between the behaviour of the units of action (the organizations—as the actors conducting or supporting innovation activities), and the overall framework that shapes the conditions for such action (the institutions—as formal/informal rules of the game).

When stating that innovation processes are conducted by organizations, we refer to the fact that innovation is essentially a social process generated within and across organizations as units of action. Innovation within organizations refers to the fact that innovation is a process that is intrinsically related to the way in which organizations structure their processes internally. The social interactions that take place within organizations are crucial to understand the patterns of innovation of a firm. Saying that innovation is a process that takes place across organizations is a reference to the growing evidence that innovation does not only happen inside organizations, but also in different forms of interfirm and interorganizational interactions, usually as strategic alliances or innovation networks (to be addressed in Chapter 8).

There are many different types of organization in an innovation system. Organizations do not only include private firms, but also other innovation-active organizations with different ownership and purposes, like research universities, business consultancy services, venture capital firms, standardization bodies, governmental regulatory agencies, etc. This large number of organizations can be bewildering and difficult to grasp. From an innovation system perspective, it is paramount to understand the diversity and complexity of organizations in the system, as a way to identify positive and negative organizational dynamics in the innovation system that might be addressed by innovation policy. A tentative typology of innovation-related organizations in an innovation system might serve this analytical purpose. This will provide a broader contextualization of innovation activities and the agents of innovation.

We can distinguish between two dimensions. The first dimension refers to the involvement of the organization. Here we might distinguish between organizations that are directly involved, conducting innovation activities, and organizations that are indirectly involved, regulating or supporting the innovation activities of other organizations. This distinction is relevant from the perspective of our definition of innovation as a new creation of economic significance. Hence, those organizations directly involved in these new creations belong to our first type, whereas those organizations that are not directly but only indirectly involved in these new creations (regulating them, approving them, testing them, supporting their development, etc.) belong to our second type.

Table 7.1. Types of organization in the innovation system according to their involvement and purpose

	Direct involvement: conducting innovation activities	Indirect involvement: regulating/supporting innovation activities
Business organizations: private for-profit purpose	Firms in the manufacturing and service sectors directly conducting product and process innovation activities.	Organizations and firms selling services which support innovation activities conducted by other firms, i.e. venture capital firms, consultancy firms, etc.
Public organizations: public purpose	Publicly owned organizations directly conducting innovation-related activities for the public good, i.e. public research universities, public research laboratories, public research hospitals, etc.	Publicly owned organizations regulating or/and supporting innovation activities for the public good carried out by other organizations; i.e. public regulatory agencies in innovation-related areas (medical devices and pharmaceuticals, food and consumer safety, energy sector, ICT sector, etc.), patent offices, competition regulatory authorities, public vocational training schools and organizations, etc.
Hybrid organizations: combined purposes and ownership	Private or semi-public not-for-profit organizations, or semi-public organizations with mixed purposes directly involved in innovation-related activities, i.e. public-private partnerships building and managing research infrastructures.	Private not-for-profit organizations or semi-public organizations with mixed purposes supporting innovation activities carried out by other organizations, i.e. philanthropic organizations supporting innovation-related activities, scientific associations, standardization bodies, etc.

Source: own elaboration

The second crucial dimension in our typology of organizations has to do with the explicit purpose for which they were consciously created. Here we can distinguish between three types.

The first is private organizations with a for-profit purpose. These are typically different forms of private firms, which produce new goods and services in the manufacturing and service sectors. But they can also be private for-profit organizations that indirectly support innovation activities, like business services or other for-profit organizations.

A second, large type, is made up of public organizations, which are defined here as organizations with the ultimate purpose of producing public goods. They are typically owned by the state or some other form of public authority, and they are subject to public regulations and procedures. This is naturally a large group, with organizations like public research universities, public research institutes, and laboratories all directly involved in innovative activities; but also organizations like public regulatory agencies, which indirectly regulate innovation activities, exercise different forms of public entrepreneurship (Klein et al., 2010) and have different strategic capabilities (Klein et al., 2013).

The third large type is composed of hybrid organizations, defined here as organizations which have combined purposes and ownership (for-profit and non-profit purposes—and public-privately owned). Examples of this type of organization are private not-for-profit organizations like scientific associations, or standardization/certification bodies.

These distinctions are summarized in Table 7.1.

This chapter focuses on entrepreneurship and intrapreneurship as examples of organizational change. This is because firms are key organizations in innovation systems, therefore entrepreneurship can be largely seen as enacting innovation in a Schumpeterian way. In other words, entrepreneurship and intrapreneurship are not only about the creation of new firms but essentially about who carries on innovation. Section 7.3 delves deeper into this matter and provides a definition of entrepreneurship and intrapreneurship in line with the literature.

7.3 Definitions

Innovation is purposefully undertaken by firms and other organizations seeking to create novelty in order to gain comparative advantage (Metcalfe 1995). For this reason, variation and the selective environment in which firms operate are two crucial themes in evolutionary economics when discussing technological change and innovation through time. Regarding the first, Metcalfe reminds us that the generation of variation (of knowledge and innovation) is crucial to understanding the dynamics of change. This is strongly based on the process of selection and the environment in which this selection takes place, which is not only an external cross-organizational issue but also internal to the organization.

> The concept of a selective environment requires careful handling. In the simplest cases, it can be equated with a market mechanism within which users and suppliers interact in traditional fashion. However, this represents only one level and mode of selection. Any framework in which agents interact in order to choose between competing patterns of behaviour has selective properties. In particular, organisations create their own internal selection environments to choose between competing alternative futures and their associated patterns of behaviour.
>
> (Metcalfe, 1995, p. 29)

These two items—innovation as the outcome of a cross-organizational selection environment and innovation as the outcome of internal based selection—bring us to the issues of entrepreneurship and intrapreneurship.

Starting with the first, the indisputable landmark in economic theory on entrepreneurship, innovation, and economic growth is Schumpeter's notion of creative destruction (Schumpeter, 1942/2005). This pattern of innovation is characterized by the centrality of individual entrepreneurs and small-firms creation, and was a highly dominating view among pioneers of entrepreneurship and small business research (Landström, 2005). This has been labelled 'Schumpeter Mark I', in contrast with 'Schumpeter Mark II' where patterns of creative accumulation that take place as innovation activities are conducted mainly inside large firms.

> The first [Schumpeter Mark I] represents a widening pattern: concentration of innovative activities is low, innovators are of small economic size, stability in the ranking of innovators is low and entry of new innovators is high. The second represents a deepening pattern: concentration of innovative activities is higher than in the first group, innovators are of larger economic size, stability in the ranking of innovators is greater, and entry is lower.
>
> (Malerba and Orsenigo, 1996, p. 451)

The empirical findings of Malerba and Orsenigo show that these two patterns of innovation are related to different technologies. Their argument is that technologies provide properties of the knowledge base, therefore the opportunity and appropriability of different technologies is key to understanding cross-national differences according to technological specialization. These empirical findings indicate that possible debates about whether large or small firms are the most important for innovation are fruitless, and that it might be worth looking at the synergetic effects of large and small firms (Baumol, 2002). In the same vein, the external and internal dimensions of these processes, entrepreneurship and intrapreneurship, may be seen as two distinct but interrelated socio-economic phenomena.

According to one author, 'entrepreneurship consists of *the competitive behaviors that drive the market process* (Kirzner, 1973)' (cited in Davidsson, 2016, p. 6). This definition is succinct and gives a clear delineation of the role of entrepreneurship in the innovation system. As Davidsson argues, it is a definition that sees entrepreneurship from the perspective of behaviour and its outcomes.

> The behavior part is necessary in order not to lose track of the fact that micro-level decisions and actions are needed for any change to be introduced. As regards the outcome part, I argue that when we think of entrepreneurship as a societal phenomenon, it is a distinctive advantage to include an outcome criterion and make clear, for example, that mere contemplation over radically new ideas or vain introduction of fatally flawed ones do not amount to 'entrepreneurship'. Entrepreneurship makes a difference, or else it isn't entrepreneurship.
>
> (Davidsson, 2016, p. 6)

In a certain sense, this definition manages to somehow incorporate two different approaches to entrepreneurship. The first approach has to do with the focus on entrepreneurship as a process. This follows the work of William

Gartner (1988), who in the 1980s introduced the understanding of entrepreneurship from a process perspective, changing the traditional individual view on the entrepreneur that dominated the field for a long time. Gartner's view is that entrepreneurship is a process related to the creation of new firms, and hence to 'enacting innovation' as an organizational process. The second approach has to do with the view on entrepreneurship from an opportunity perspective. This has to do with Scott Shane and Sankaran Venkataraman's seminal paper on entrepreneurial opportunities, and their outcomes when those opportunities are exploited (Shane and Venkataraman, 2000).

To be sure, the links between entrepreneurship and innovation are varied and complex (Audretsch et al., 2011), and there is a vast body of literature on them. Yet, for the purposes of this chapter, we follow the definition of entrepreneurship proposed by Davidsson above.

Our definition of innovation earlier in this chapter (new creations of economic or social importance, usually performed by firms) refers to the outcomes of entrepreneurial activities understood as processes of innovation. Therefore, not all forms of entrepreneurship or intrapreneurship will be innovative.

Figure 7.1 shows new firm registrations per thousand population, according to data from the Global Innovation Index. It is worth noting the great diversity across a number of different countries. This diversity might be due to different factors, for example, favourable regulations and taxation conditions, as well as levels of entrepreneurship.

Turning back to the goal of this chapter, which is examining the role of organizations and in particular entrepreneurship and intrapreneurship in the

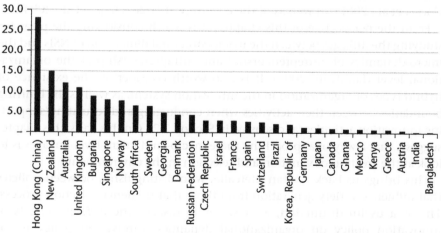

Figure 7.1. New firm registrations per thousand population, 2015
Source: Global Innovation Index 2015

innovation system, there are three recent trends in the literature which are worth highlighting (see the definition of intrapreneurship below).

Firstly, there are very interesting attempts to bridge the gap between the agency-focused entrepreneurship literature and the institution-focused literature on national systems of innovation (NSIs) (Ács et al., 2014). '[The] routine-reinforcing perspective of NSIs has proven difficult to reconcile with the individual-centric, routines-breaking emphasis of the entrepreneurship literature' (p. 478). Hence, the way in which entrepreneurship is linked to social attitudes (van Praag, 2011) and to the individual traits of the entrepreneur/intrapreneur (Shane, 2003) needs to be complemented with an institution-based approach to entrepreneurship.

The second recent trend is the introduction of the concept of 'social entrepreneurship', acknowledging that entrepreneurship and innovation are not only related to private for-profit organizations, but also to public and hybrid types of organization (Steyaert and Hjorth, 2006). This has stimulated efforts to use Schumpeter's theory about entrepreneurship and creative destruction to study social change more broadly (Swedberg, 2006).

Thirdly, there has been an increasing focus on studying organizational change and innovation inside (large) firms (Lazonick, 2005); what we call intrapreneurship. This is reflected in recent analytical efforts behind the notion of 'employee-driven innovation' (Kesting and Ulhøi, 2010), as well as in the rapid growth in books and studies on how to manage innovation processes inside a firm (Tidd and Bessant, 2013). These two broad but different approaches to intrapreneurship are highly related to the importance of organizational forms, learning, and decision-making processes inside the firms for understanding the innovative performance of the individual firm (Aragón-Correa et al., 2007), as well as of the economy at large (Drejer et al., 2004).

From the perspective of this chapter, it is worth considering the pleas for studying the linkages between the macro-structural dimension of NSIs and the micro-dynamics of entrepreneurship and intrapreneurship at the organizational level (Lundvall, 2007). It is also worth considering the existence of hybrid types of organization in the innovation system, as well as the blurring boundaries between their activities when conducting and regulating/supporting innovation activities (as discussed in Section 7.2). On this basis, this chapter suggests that a way of approaching these macro- and micro-level linkages is to look at the creation of variation and selection in the environment.

This brings us back to Stan Metcalfe, who distinguishes between policies that influence variety generation from those that influence selection process. This is a useful distinction, as it serves to discern the different effects of innovation policy on organizational dynamics. Innovation policy is—or should be—a broad policy, encompassing a wide set of public policy areas of action (Borrás, 2009) and largely overlapping with other policies like energy, health, telecommunications, or competition (see Chapter 3). It is worth noting here that Metcalfe's distinction has to do with the role of the state as well, either as supporting some dynamics (creating variation) through the encouragement and enabling of organizations, or as regulating these dynamics (pursuing selection) through the control and constraining of organizations' behaviour. Whereas the first concerns the support of innovation activities by encouraging clusters (Pitelis, 2012), the second refers to the regulation of innovation activities by for example defining the costs and conditions for firms' market entry (Prantl, 2011). Section 7.4 examines both.

7.4 Policy Instruments for Entrepreneurship and Intrapreneurship

Entrepreneurship is typically an issue that attracts considerable attention from governments because it is seen as a source of present and future economic growth and dynamism. For that reason, governments have put forward different policy instruments that are combined in specific mixes (Borrás and Edquist, 2013b). In a seminal chapter, Henrekson and Stenkulas identify generic types of policy instrument that have potentially important effects for entrepreneurship and intrapreneurship (Henrekson and Stenkula, 2010). Thereafter, they classify them according to four tenets (Baumol et al., 2007). These four tenets are ease of starting a business, rewards for productive entrepreneurial activity, disincentives for unproductive activity, and incentives to keep winners on their toes.

Looking carefully at these tenets, we can see that the first two correspond to what Metcalfe sees as creation of variation, whereas the latter two refer to creation of selection environment. Policy instruments that typically and most clearly affect the creation of diversity are regulations of business creation, capital constraints, labour market, and social security; or direct support to entrepreneurial activity like start-up incubators. The reason is that they have most effect on how easy it is to create a new business. They are incentives for productive entrepreneurial activity.

On the other hand, regulations like taxation laws, bankruptcy laws, competition laws (particularly anti-trust and merger control), intellectual property rights, and trade regulations all create a selection environment by means of disincentives for unproductive activity and incentives to keep winners on their toes.

Besides these policy instruments, this chapter argues that there is another broad type of policy instrument, focused on stimulating behavioural change. Entrepreneurialism is not just a matter of market or institutional conditions, but also an issue of cultural and social attitudes. Many national, regional, and local governments have created a series of instruments to motivate, inform, and educate potential entrepreneurs (Audretsch et al., 2006). Examples of these are entrepreneurship schools at technical universities; information and coaching packages; awareness-raising campaigns about entrepreneurship; entrepreneur business angel meetings and events; and entrepreneurship prizes and awards (Hart, 2003). Yet, these schemes might have very different effects (Ramlogan and Rigby, 2012b).

Taken together, policy instruments can be divided into three big groups. The first group consists of policies that aim at creating variation in the environment in order to stimulate the creation of entrepreneurial opportunities and the subsequent processes of exploiting them into innovative outcomes. The second group of policies has to do with policy-makers' intentions to create a selection environment from which the processes of entrepreneurial and intrapreneurial activities are framed, securing a level playing field that stimulates those entrepreneurial innovative processes. The third group of policies towards entrepreneurship are those directed towards promoting the entrepreneurial culture and spirit through indirect actions like information, coaching, campaigns, awards, etc. Table 7.2 summarizes these three sets of policy instrument.

Regarding the intrapreneurship dimension, it is worth noting here that recent decades have seen some OECD countries promoting the distribution of best practices of innovation management activities as a form of promoting organizational change inside firms and other organizations (Freitas, 2007). These public initiatives seek explicitly to enhance the innovation management competences inside firms, helping them with business management tools and approaches that can inspire and stimulate the business community. Some of those are schemes launched at the national level, whereas others are mostly designed and carried out by regional and local governments.

Table 7.2. Policy instruments for entrepreneurship

Policy instruments creating variation	Policy instruments creating a selection environment	Policy instruments promoting entrepreneurial culture
Business creation laws	Taxation laws	Entrepreneurship education
Regulations on capital constraints	Bankruptcy laws	Information and coaching packages
Support to venture and risk capital	Competition laws (particularly anti-trust and merger control)	Awareness-raising campaigns
Labour market and social security regulations		Entrepreneurship awards
Incubators	Intellectual property rights	Meet business angel events
Support packages to start-ups	Trade regulations	

Source: own elaboration

Naturally, some of these governmental initiatives for entrepreneurs and intrapreneurs are not carried out by public organizations in isolation, but in close cooperation with private and hybrid organizations, which have closer ties to the market and society. This is to say that public policy must be seen as supporting organizational capacities as a way of fostering innovation. Whereas the 'arm of the state' is most visible in regulations and binding laws (like competition law, taxation law, or trade law), many other supportive measures aimed at entrepreneurship and intrapreneurship are designed and implemented by interaction between multiple agents. This is particularly the case for the more 'cultural' dimension of entrepreneurship policy (like entrepreneurship awards).

In order to elaborate further on innovation policy design, Section 7.5 examines the bottlenecks and imbalances in an innovation system with regard to entrepreneurship and intrapreneurship.

7.5 Bottlenecks Associated with Entrepreneurship and Intrapreneurship

When the notion of 'innovation system' was put forward and developed in the early 1990s, the main focus was on countries with advanced market economies. Many important cross-country comparative studies at the time focused on Western countries, or on OECD countries. The traditional case studies were Japan and the Scandinavian countries, all with high levels of existing and newly entering innovative firms, and with a number of organizations supporting and regulating innovative activities. In a sense, the literature of that time took for granted that NSIs invariably had strong innovative firms, strong entrepreneurs, strong intrapreneurs, and well-functioning organizational support for these. However, these implicit assumptions came into question with the subsequent expansion of this analytical framework into the fields of regional economics and development economics (Lundvall et al., 2009). Weak regional and national economies do not have strong entrepreneurs and intrapreneurs, let alone a group of organizations supporting and regulating such activities.

The above reminds us of the importance of not taking for granted these conditions for organizational change in general, and for entrepreneurship and intrapreneurship in particular. Taking a step back, we might need to look at this matter from a systems perspective. Looking at the way in which organizations (individually and collectively), suffer from some obstacles and deficiencies in the innovation system is a paramount step to take in relation to the design of innovation policy. From this perspective, this chapter identifies at least four possible bottlenecks in the innovation system (see Box 7.1).

> **Box 7.1** ENTREPRENEURSHIP AND INTRAPRENEURSHIP: POSSIBLE
> OBSTACLES AND DEFICIENCIES
>
> Weak level of entrepreneurship and new entrants in the economy.
> Low quality of entrepreneurship.
> Low organizational capacity and innovation by established firms.
> A poor selection environment that does not reward entrepreneurial activity.

The *first* bottleneck has to do with a weak level of entrepreneurship and low number of new entrants in the economy. The number of new entrants in the economy and their ability to create new business models that challenge established firms are paramount for any economy or innovation system to stay competitive. Levels of entrepreneurship matter for the performance of the innovation system, either with new science-technology-based firms (i.e. spin-offs from universities, or high-tech start-ups; Dahlstrand, 1997; Politis et al., 2012), or new and innovative firms which are not science-based (i.e. new firms entering mature sectors by bringing substantial novelties through process innovation; Audretsch et al., 2011; McKelvey and Ljungberg, 2017).

Some examples of well-functioning local/regional innovation systems show the strong link between entrepreneurship and innovative performance in high-tech sectors (Gabrielsson et al., 2014). Other successful examples of relations between entrepreneurship and innovation include local innovation systems based in low-tech or medium-tech sectors, and with less geographically concentrated dynamics. Naturally, there is no one-size-fits-all, or minimum level of 'critical mass' of entrepreneurship in an innovation system beyond which there is invariably a problem. However, this does not hinder identifying a bottleneck when the levels of entrepreneurship are not sufficiently high to keep up with the 'mortality' of firms and the subsequent effects on economic growth and jobs. This leads to the next issue, namely the origins of bottlenecks, which might be difficult to determine. A bottleneck might be a matter of socio-cultural dynamics (generalized risk-averse social attitudes, or lack of societal reward/recognition of entrepreneurs), or a matter of policy-generated problems, either because important variation-creation policies mentioned in Table 7.2 are ineffective or simply absent.

A *second* possible bottleneck in an innovation system has to do with low-quality entrepreneurship. This is a very important matter because not all entrepreneurship is the same, nor is it automatically linked to innovation. Acknowledging this, some recent studies define the quality of entrepreneurship in terms of its ability to grow rapidly. They measure the quality of entrepreneurship by 'linking the probability of a growth outcome (e.g., achieving an IPO [initial public offering] or a significant acquisition) as a function of start-up characteristics observable at or near the time of initial business registration' (Guzman and Stern, 2017, p. 63). The empirical findings show great geographical variation in the quality of entrepreneurship (Guzman and Stern, 2016). From the perspective of the possible bottlenecks that might afflict innovation systems, entrepreneurship might not have sufficient quality to enhance rapid growth. It can be the case that a region or a country has both high and low quality entrepreneurship, for example, the establishment of many new coffee shops but few IT firms. Even if fast-growing firms or 'gazelles' might not be the solution to all problems (Nightingale and Coad, 2014), it is also true that low levels of entrepreneurial quality do in fact pose an important bottleneck in the innovation system.

The low organizational capacity and innovation by established firms constitute the *third* possible type of bottleneck. It refers to a fundamental issue of the internal managerial processes and intrapreneurship inside firms (Drejer et al., 2004), which might not be sufficiently strong to keep up their competitive advantage vis-à-vis rapidly changing market and innovation contexts. Clearly, weak intrapreneurship is an issue that is as relevant to SMEs as it is to large firms.

As we have seen in this chapter, firms are currently exposed to very rapid changes in terms of increased globalized market competition and rapidly changing technological developments, with consequences such as the shortening of product life cycles, and new entrants and competitors into core business areas. These contextual changes offer new opportunities to any established firm, but they also pose important challenges to them. From an innovation system point of view, the bottleneck might arrive if and when a large number of firms in an economy are weakly or not sufficiently engaged in innovation activities to keep up with the rapid pace of contextual change. Low innovation performance levels of firms in a given economy might rapidly erode the competitive basis of those firms.

A *fourth* type of bottleneck is associated with the selection environment. This is a type of bottleneck that is related to the conditions under which possible entrepreneurs and intrapreneurs operate. It refers to problems when a selection environment is not operating in a way that rewards productive entrepreneurial activity, generates incentives to keep winners on their toes, and provides disincentives for unproductive activity (Henrekson and Stenkula, 2010). Again, the bottlenecks might be generated by the environment itself, or by ineffective or absent policies. This is to acknowledge that policy is not always a solution; it might even be part of the problem. Therefore, any analysis about the conditions under which innovation systems stimulate entrepreneurship must take these policies as part of the equation.

7.6 Concluding Remarks

Having seen that organizations, entrepreneurship, and intrapreneurship are ubiquitous social phenomena, we may now come back to the issue of the role of public policy and its limits. In its previous sections, this chapter has discussed bottlenecks that public policy might need to address, types of initiatives that have been launched in order to address them, and the extent to which policy initiatives themselves might sometimes become part of the problem rather than part of the solution. However, the issue of the limits of public action has remained unaddressed.

This chapter's identification of different organizations based on their public, private, and hybrid purposes (in Section 7.2) serves to recognize that any form of public action is organizationally embedded, and not only in a set of specific political values, collective ethos, or particular history. The nature, dynamics, and composition of these particular ecologies of organizations are crucial aspects when considering the role of public policy and its limits.

This refers to two interlinked issues. Firstly, that public policy must target specific challenges and bottlenecks in a system, and those might differ considerably across regions or countries according to the features of their economy and innovation system. Furthermore, each country or region has a specific composition of organizations, meaning that there is no 'natural' or pre-determined definition of the boundaries between public, private, and hybrid organizations. Variations between innovation systems are significant.

The second issue is concerned with the fact that entrepreneurship and intrapreneurship are socially embedded phenomena, hence subject to territorial dynamics as much as to functional dynamics (Lindholm Dahlstrand and Johannisson, 2013). This view on the double nature (the geographical anchorage as well as technological and sectoral dimension) of entrepreneurship activities has triggered an effort to see entrepreneurship in a contextual manner, beyond the personality of heroic individuals.

For these reasons, this chapter suggests that policy should focus directly and explicitly on improving the context in which entrepreneurial and intrapreneurial activities take place. This is essential in order to address the four bottlenecks identified earlier: weak levels of entrepreneurship/new entrants in the economy, low-quality entrepreneurship, low organizational capacity and innovation by established firms, and poor selection environments that do not reward productive entrepreneurial activity. For that reason policymakers must secure the creation of variety, a well-functioning selection environment, and a positive social attitude towards risk-taking and entrepreneurship/intrapreneurship activities.

8
Interaction and Networking

8.1 Introduction

Innovation systems cannot be understood without conceptualizing the interactions between different actors in the system and the knowledge integration and interactive learning that takes place. It is so that they are called 'systems' because these interactions were found to be very important for innovation processes. For example, the Lundvall version of the system of innovation (SI) SI approach was based on empirical studies of user–producer interactions (Lundvall, 1985). These interactions take many different forms and dynamics (Mowery and Rosenberg, 1998). The literature has approached the study of those interactions with the use of broad notions like open innovation and the network society, as well as with the use of more concrete analysis of specific forms of interactions among different types of actors (firms, universities, and other organizations) like innovation networks, industrial clusters, or firms' user-driven innovation strategies.

This chapter aims at providing an overview of these different concepts, putting them directly into the theoretical context of the innovation systems approach. In particular, Sections 8.2 and 8.3 will start with a broad mapping of concepts on innovation-related interactions, and thereafter will examine in a more focused manner some useful typologies of innovation networks. This is done not only for the sake of conceptual or typology clarification; but as a first step for identifying the concrete bottlenecks and deficiencies associated with these interactions in innovation systems, which in turn should be addressed by innovation policy.

Innovation-related interactions are complex and rapidly changing. Individual inventors and entrepreneurs, small and large firms, research universities, public laboratories, civil society organizations, municipalities, public agencies, and other innovators interact in many different ways, in order to bring specific forms of innovative solutions to the market and to society. These interactions are very different in nature, and in their ultimate purposes and goals. Most of the time, these interactions do not encounter any barriers or pose any obstacles. However, at times these interactions suffer from barriers that become difficult to overcome. Likewise, interactions might themselves constitute obstacles to innovation activities, particularly when there is too much collusion among actors and too little competition (Section 8.4). When such barriers reduce the overall innovativeness of the economy and society it is time for policy-makers to step in.

The identification of the barriers and problems that are amenable for policy action (Section 8.5) serves to approach the diversity of network-oriented innovation policy instruments that governments have been deploying through time (Section 8.6). Reviewing them will allow this chapter to put these instruments more explicitly in relation to the very diverse goals they might eventually fulfil. Indeed, as in the other chapters of this book, this is done critically, assessing not only the features that characterize the instruments but also the possible situations in which policies and policy instruments have become part of the problem (Section 8.7). This means that the failures of these policies and policy instruments are also examined as part and parcel of the possible deficiencies afflicting the innovation system. Section 8.8 puts forward a set of criteria for the design and redesign of these instruments according to the specific features that define the bottlenecks in the system (and of policy itself), which might eventually serve as a guiding post for policy-evaluation exercises.

8.2 Networks and Interactions in Innovation Systems

Innovation is a socially embedded activity. This is the reason why innovations are often pursued by firms through complex interactions with their surrounding environments. Since its formulation in the early 1990s, the SI approach has paid particular attention to the interdependence and non-linearity of the innovation process. Therefore, it has examined in detail the fact that firms and other organizations do not normally innovate in isolation. Instead, they interact with other organizations through complex relations that are often characterized by reciprocity and feedback mechanisms. This focus on inter-organizational relations in innovation processes is inherent to organizational and institutional analyses developed in the 1990s. These analyses tend to contrast with previous ideals of individual (almost heroic) innovators/inventors/entrepreneurs. They were seen as conducting innovative activities mainly inside the organization, in isolation from their surroundings. Whereas these types of inventor/innovator/entrepreneur might still exist, today a growing number of innovators (in developed as well as developing countries) are engaged in one way or another in collaborative relations with other organizations in their local environment or abroad (Bartels et al., 2016).

A long list of surveys and empirical findings tends to underline this overall collaborative trend in innovation activities, particularly among firms (Freeman, 1991; Garcia and Calantone, 2002; Phelps et al., 2012). Particularly relevant, and emerging from this large literature, the notion of 'open innovation' was developed in the mid-2000s, partly on the basis of the SI approach. Essentially, it puts forward the notion that firms are (and should be) using a combination of internal and external sources of ideas when innovating (Chesbrough, 2003). The argument is that firms have recently moved from conducting innovation essentially from the ideas and knowledge produced in their own in-house R&D corporate laboratories, into a collaborative mode, where internal and external knowledge outside the firm is exchanged and (re)combined into innovative solutions. That external knowledge can be produced by other firms—here including suppliers—and/or it can be produced by other types of organization such as universities, public research laboratories (Dutrénit, 2010), or organizations like patient associations as well as individual lead users. As a useful literature review reveals,

> the concept [of open innovation] has common currency for at least four reasons. First, it reflects social and economic changes in working patterns, where professionals seek portfolio careers rather than a job-for-life with a single employer. Firms therefore need to find new ways of accessing talent that might not wish to be employed exclusively and directly. Second, globalization has expanded the extent of the labour market that allows for an increased division of labour. Third, improved institutions and organizations such as Intellectual Property Rights (IPR), venture capital (VC), and technology standards allow for trade in ideas. Fourth, new technologies allow for new ways to collaborate and coordinate across geographical distances. (Dahlander and Gann, 2010, p. 699)

It is worth noting that 'open innovation' refers essentially to a context of large firms' in high-tech sectors, where the source of knowledge is essentially the outcome of R&D activities (Chesbrough, 2003). This perspective on large, manufacturing, high-tech firms has been related to SMEs as well (van de Vrande et al., 2009), particularly in relation to territorial forms of innovative interaction (Morgan, 1997) as in industrial districts and clusters (Cooke, 2001a). However, it has been far less integrated in the literature about non-technological innovation.

As mentioned in other chapters of this book, innovation spans widely beyond the high-tech sector into non-technological areas of society and the economy. It is therefore very important to discuss the issues of collaborative innovation in these areas as well, where knowledge is not based on traditional science and technology activities. Instead, innovation in these areas is based on other types of knowledge, like hands-on knowledge and skills in the creative sectors (artistic as well as handcrafts), the procedural knowledge embedded in service products, or the knowledge associated with activities like marketing or managerial procedures, so essential these days for the success of any private or public goods.

Innovation in these non-technological areas is a key driving force for the innovativeness of a society and the economy. This is so in spite of the continuous problems of finding suitable socio-economic indicators to measure those forms of innovation (Bernard et al., 2015; Dutta et al., 2015). In these non-technological innovation areas, collaborative and network-based interactions are equally relevant. Just like in technology innovation, collaboration takes place with different types of organization. Yet, an important difference might be relevant in these interactions: as in these non-technological forms of innovation the interactions with end users and clients might be most relevant and intense, they might as well embody the co-production of complex innovative solutions.

These remarks lead us to consider two central forms of knowledge exchange that take place in these interactions.

The first has to do with the complementary knowledge assets among network partners. Partners' mutual dependency on these different pieces of knowledge is the key for advancing new—collectively created—innovative solutions, and therefore to be ultimately the raison d'être of these innovation networks (Teece, 1986). Complementary knowledge assets are particularly relevant for firms in high-tech sectors, like biotech or software engineering, to engage in innovation networks (Powell et al., 1996; Salavisa et al., 2012). This is the case for new entrants (new entrepreneurial firms) as well as incumbents (typically large firms), which need those complementary assets in order to get access to rapid upscaling frameworks, and to stay ahead in rapidly changing technology-driven markets, respectively (Rothaermel, 2001).

The second form of knowledge exchange in innovation networks is when existing knowledge is shared, ultimately recombined in novel ways to produce innovative solutions to firms or society (Gruber et al., 2013). Studies at the firm level have pointed to the performance of firms pursuing different strategies of knowledge recombination and the ways in which they get access to external knowledge sources (Miller et al., 2007). A recent empirical study focuses instead on the level of individuals, examining the features of patent inventors (e.g. their formal education). The findings show that inventors with a science degree tend to generate patents that are broader in nature (spanning technological boundaries) than inventors with an engineering degree (Gruber et al., 2013).

This indicates that higher education tends to allow for a wider knowledge recombination than other educational backgrounds. These findings resonate with the largely studied dimension of personal ties in sociological approaches to innovation networks. Interpersonal connections in the form of professional, ethnic, or local communities are believed to precede more formal innovation networks. This is particularly relevant in rapidly changing environments and in uncertain technological contexts (Nooteboom, 2004; Molina-Morales and Martínez-Fernández, 2010).

One area where the co-production of novel solutions is generated by the recombination of knowledge in innovation networks is in the public sector. The search for new and more efficient forms of delivering public services to citizens in the expanding welfare state (Sørensen and Torfing, 2011), and to address localized grand challenges associated with growing cities (like transport solutions, air pollution reduction, or waste water management), have motivated local and regional public authorities to engage in intense forms of interaction with the end users and suppliers of these services. These interactions, seeking better delivery of public services and complex urban solutions, usually involve the reorganization of public service production and delivery (often with digital and online approaches—like 'open government'), and the recombination of existing and new technological and non-technological knowledge in diverse knowledge fields in new ways.

Over the past few years, the literature has started examining the importance of the societal dimension of innovative initiatives. In particular, the literature has begun examining cases of civil society-driven innovations beyond (but in interaction with) public authorities' and private for-profit firms' innovation. From the perspective of this book, this reflects the widest possible understanding of innovation interactions, mainly when society is mobilized into finding collective solutions to problems and challenges that have so far not been addressed by firms or public actors. In a sense, such innovation can be perceived as bottom-up societal innovation dynamics, driven essentially for and by social needs, where a wide diversity of forms of interaction is an essential part of that form of innovation. This is why co-creation (as a particular form of interaction) and societal-level innovative activities tend to go hand in hand (Voorberg et al., 2015).

The growing visibility and relevance of the not-for-profit sector, or third sector, is also associated with innovation that seeks to solve or mitigate specific barriers (Anheier et al., 2007). Here the role of philanthropies is of particular relevance, both for technological and non-technological approaches to solving grand social and complex challenges (Maclean et al., 2013). A highly relevant example of this are the so-called 'product development partnerships' in the field of global public health. These are partnerships aiming to produce novel medicines for neglected diseases (malaria, tuberculosis, etc.) and to secure their accessibility in less-developed markets (Muñoz et al., 2015).

Many of these innovative interactions, as well as other forms of innovation and knowledge interaction, involve, in one way or another, the use of information and communication technologies (ICT), as platforms for interaction and for new business-model development. This is related to what Castells has termed the 'network society' in what he sees as the transition from industrialism into 'informationalism' and the subsequent transformation of capitalism as a social and economic form of organization (Castells, 1996).

A similar appraisal of the fundamental changes that ICT brought in the 1990s was captured by Freeman and Soete around the same time. These authors were the pioneers in understanding that ICT is the driving force of a new industrial revolution, which is not only guided by the introduction of technological novelties as such, but to the subsequent deep transformations in societal and economic organization, such as advanced manufacturing and the digital economy opening up for totally new business models (Freeman and Soete, 1997). This is a neo-Schumpeterian perspective on the ways in which this ICT revolution, which started in the early 1970s, is giving birth to a fifth techno-economic paradigm with deep transformative consequences (Perez, 2009).

8.3 Diversity of Innovation Networks and Interactions

Above we addressed the various actors that interact in the innovation system (large/small, high-/low-tech firms, as well as public actors, civil society organizations, philanthropies, etc.) and the way in which they are rapidly expanding forms of networks and interactions. We have also seen that the context in which these interactions take place tends to change rapidly (the advancement of ICT platforms, etc.). It is also worth noting that according to Vonortas the nature of these interactions are both technological and non-technological in character (1997), and that the characteristics of networks differ across industrial sectors (2009a). Given this variation, complexity, and rapid transformation, it is useful to examine the types of innovation networks and interactions from an innovation systems perspective.

The literature offers alternative views. Some of the most acknowledged approaches to networks refer to the strength of the ties that form the innovation networks (weak or strong) (Granovetter, 1983). This perspective is based in the sociological perspective that interpersonal relations are the bedrock of interfirm or interorganizational networks. Other typologies of innovation networks focus on the temporality of the interactions (short project-based interactions, or long and more extensive interactions; Grabher, 2002). The approach on temporality aims at determining the extent to which the innovation networks are recursive and stable, or on the contrary are more ad hoc and changing. The questions of continuity and stability are very relevant. However, most of the empirical studies of innovation networks tend to be cross-sectional (one point in time) rather than temporal (Powell and Grodal, 2005).

The heterogeneity of organizations engaged in interactions is another way to characterize types of innovation networks. This has received considerable attention from 2005 onwards (Corsaro et al., 2012). This is particularly the case when comparing different patterns across industrial sectors and the dynamics of accessing complementary assets (Vonortas, 2009b; Salavisa et al., 2012), and when analysing types of university–industry interactions in relation to academic engagement in external relations and the commercialization of university research outputs (Dahlstrand, 1999; D'Este and Patel, 2007; Perkmann et al., 2013; Bozeman et al., 2013). Most recently, the heterogeneity of the existing knowledge base and of the actors in collaborative partnerships has been positively associated with the problem-solving potential of that consortium (Olsen, 2015).

From the above it follows that knowledge resources and assets are key elements in the study of innovation networks. Therefore, a highly relevant typology of innovation networks, largely anchored in knowledge approaches to economic geography, is based on the types of knowledge that form local innovation networks (Asheim and Coenen, 2005; Tödtling et al., 2006). Some of these knowledge approaches look into the static versus dynamic aspects of knowledge exchange and innovation interactions in those networks: static knowledge exchange here refers to the transfer of 'ready' pieces of information or knowledge from one actor to the other. Cases would be the licensing of a specific technology, the reading of a patent description of another firm or the observation and imitation of other firms. Dynamic knowledge exchange refers to a situation where there is interactive learning among actors through for example cooperation or other joint activities (Lundvall, 1992; Camagni, 1991; Capello, 1999; Lawson, 2000). New research focuses on the different types of knowledge (technological, market, and managerial knowledge) being exchanged and shared in these innovation networks. The findings show that these different types of knowledge are unevenly distributed in those networks, and that interactions are (re)configured in different manners according to that type of knowledge (Sammarra and Biggiero, 2008).

Powell and Grodal have provided an encompassing typology of innovation networks that captures most of the broad notions of collaboration and interaction in an innovation system. Their typology is based on two key dimensions, namely, the formality (contractual basis) or the informality of the interactions on the one hand, and on the closed or fluid membership of the networks on the other hand (Powell and Grodal, 2005). The distinction between formal and informal ties has been a recurrent topic in the study of innovation networks since the mid-1980s, both from the perspective of network dynamics in

Table 8.1. Types of innovation network according to Powell and Grodal

	Informal	Contractual (formal)
Closed membership	*'Primordial'*	*'Supply chain'*
Fluid (open) membership	*'Invisible college'*	*'Strategic'*

Source: edited and simplified from Powell and Grodal, 2005

an innovation system (Freeman, 1991), as well as from the perspective of individual firms' management of these relationships (Dhanaraj and Parkhe, 2006). The second dimension, the closed or fluid membership of networks, is also a feature that has received considerable attention, particularly in relation to the context of localized and cluster-level networks (see more below).

A four-fold typology emerges from the Powell and Grodal distinctions (see Table 8.1): *'primordial'* innovation networks are those of informal nature and closed membership. They are based on common social identity, and the nodes and organizations tend to be rather homogeneous. Of similarly informal nature, but much more fluid and open, are what they call the *'invisible college'*. These are typically based on similar or dissimilar nodes focusing on specific expansion of knowledge, where asset complementarity (Rothaermel, 2001) or knowledge recombination in specific networks (professional, interest-oriented like patients' organizations, etc) plays an important role. Networks focusing on research collaboration, where there are no explicit contractual interactions, is an example of this. These types of networks, however, can become *'strategic networks'* if they become formalized in contracts and other legally-binding agreements among partners. They are still fluid networks insofar as these contractual agreements are limited in time and project-based. Last but not least, the *'supply chain'* types of networks are typically with closed membership, and formalized through contract relations.

Figure 8.1 shows that for the top 30 innovative economies, according to the Global Innovation Index, the intensity of university–industry collaboration might be correlated to the percentage of high-tech and medium-tech output. Figure 8.1 shows on the x-axis university–industry research collaboration. This is measured by the average answer to the survey question: 'In your country, to what extent do business and universities collaborate on research and development (R&D)?' (1 = do not collaborate at all; 7 = collaborate extensively.) On the y-axis of Figure 8.1, high-tech and medium–high-tech output corresponds to the percentage of total manufacturing output according to the OECD classification of technology intensity definition.

Following the Powell and Grodal typology, contractual and closed membership networks are those typically associated with vertically organized *supply chains*. These types of networks exhibit considerable variation whether they are seeking to explore or exploit knowledge. Horizontal forms of collaboration

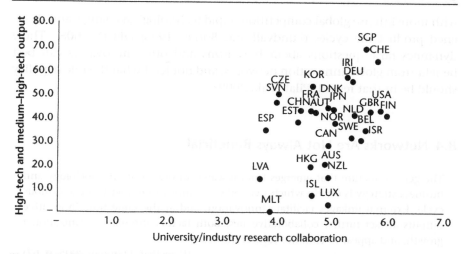

Figure 8.1. University–industry research collaboration and high-tech and medium-tech top 30 economies
Source: Global Innovation Index 2015

tend to be of an explorative nature, whereas vertical forms of collaboration in supply chains tend to seek the exploitation of knowledge into production/commercial activities (Hult et al., 2004). These types of contractual and closed membership networks vary across different industrial sectors, according to the inherent characteristics of the relevant technologies, and the traditions and norms that guide competition or collaboration in that particular industrial sector and its market (Kogut, 2000).

With the rapid advancement of globalization over the past few decades, firms and other innovative organizations have increased the global scope of their R&D and innovation interactions substantially. Innovation networks have been gradually developing global reach (Barnard and Chaminade, 2011; Liu et al., 2013) well beyond traditional geographic proximity. This is particularly the case for multinational companies, who have relocated part of their R&D activities outside their traditional headquarters and into different global locations closer to knowledge sources and to their most relevant global markets (Criscuolo et al., 2005). Some small firms have also followed suit, some of them 'born global' with global innovation and market strategies with a global scope from their very creation (Knight and Cavusgil, 2004). Whereas most of this globalization of innovation and R&D activities takes place among developed countries, a small (Narula, 2010) but increasing number are also taking place in emerging economies (UNCTAD, 2005).

There are several forms and many dimensions in the globalization of innovation activities (Archibugi and Michie, 1995; Archibugi and Filippetti, 2015). Yet, the main logic behind this globalization of innovation networks has to do with more intense global competition, rapid technological change, and short-ened product life cycles (Lundvall and Borrás, 1998; OECD, 2008). These dynamics raise questions about how firms and other innovators can best benefit from global innovation networks, and not least what the role of policy should be in that regard (Pilat et al., 2009).

8.4 Networks Are Not Always Beneficial

The general picture that emerges from research in organizational sociology and business strategy is one in which networks and innovation constitute a virtuous cycle. External linkages facilitate innovation, and at the same time innovative outputs attract further collaborative ties. Both factors stimulate organizational growth, and appear to enhance further innovation.

(Powell and Grodal, 2005, p. 67)

This overly optimistic view about collaborative innovation has been criticized for underestimating the potential downsides of interaction for individual firms (Laursen, 2011). It has also been criticized for not studying when precisely innovation networks contribute (and when not) to the overall innovativeness of the economy (Potter, 2009). This section examines these issues in two steps: first, examining the benefits of innovation networks; and second, examining the situations when networks are not beneficial.

Traditionally, the literature offers a long list of arguments about the positive effects of networks and other forms of organizational interaction for the innovation performance of individual firms (or other organizations), as well as the overall positive effects for the society and economy (Meeus and Faber, 2006). The pillar of these benefits is networks' ability to facilitate interactive learning among participants, and their ability to adapt to rapidly changing contexts. This is because networks allow the expansion and exploitation of complementary knowledge assets and the recombination of existing knowledge into novel solutions.

Partners in networks use each other's knowledge to reposition themselves in the markets and to find new solutions to convoluted challenges. These positive dynamics can be, for example, partners' sharing and spreading costs and risks, or the creation of local critical mass and synergies. This is reflected in local labour markets of skilled workers (Eriksson and Lindgren, 2009), the attraction of more specialized venture capital and financing opportunities (Powell et al., 2002), and the attraction of external talent and skills (Saxenian, 2006), among other examples. It is also reflected in the broadening of the scope of knowledge search in firms and other organizations (here including both R&D and non-R&D activities), resulting in a higher diversification of economic and social activity. It can also result in more rapid and flexible dissemination and scaling up of new solutions and new technologies.

Even if networks and innovation interactions are everywhere and constitute the essence of the social nature of the innovation system, they are not always beneficial. One key reason is that collaboration hinders competition, which is another key driving source of innovation and transformative change. Whereas collaboration in the form of networks might generate synergies by pooling knowledge and other resources of partners together, competition in the market-place and in society (to find new solutions for grand social challenges) is a key dynamic of capitalist economies and of our current globally interdependent societies. 'Innovation is the stimulus to and consequence of competition' (Metcalfe, 2006, p. 106). Since collaboration may diminish levels of competition in one way or another, networks are not always beneficial.

> All economies are knowledge based, a human attribute; they are information based, a social attribute; consequently they are all developing economies, an evolutionary attribute. But what is unique about modern market capitalism is the extent to which knowledge and information are harnessed to change the economic order from within. This is the core of Schumpeter's great legacy to the study of innovation—its cause and significance. (Metcalfe, 2006, p. 110)

As Metcalfe elegantly puts it, competition is essential for the dynamics of change and innovation in our capitalist societies and economies. The neo-Schumpeterian tradition has long acknowledged that. It has done so particularly by paying attention to the role of innovative entrepreneurship and SMEs, in technological sectors (Malerba and Orsenigo, 1996) as well as in territorial dynamics of entrepreneurial discovery in post-Fordist models of industrial organization through flexible specialization (Sabel, 1994)—more recently in the EU model for structural funds allocation called 'smart specialization' (Foray, 2015). It is worth noting that there is extensive evidence of collusive behaviour, with negative consequences for innovation in general (Snyder and Vonortas, 2005).

However, the role of competition, which is behind the innovative dynamics of capitalist economies and societies as envisaged by Schumpeter, has some-how tended to receive less attention in the scholarly literature compared to the positive consequences of networks and collaboration. Evolutionary economists have underlined the importance of selection mechanisms in economic dynamics (Pelikan, 2001).

> To understand innovation-based competition, it is useful to divide the forces at work into two broad categories: variation and differentiation of behaviour, and selection across those behaviours. In turn this leads to the central theorem of competitive capitalism—that more productive activities expand and absorb resources at the expense of less productive alternatives and, in the process, give rise to economic growth and development. (Metcalfe, 2006, p. 115)

8.5 Common Problems with Networking in Innovation Systems

From the above it follows that too much or too little collaboration among actors might generate problems in the innovation system. In situations where there is too much interaction around specific knowledge bases, different forms of lock-in situations might emerge, giving rise to gradual or rapid loss of competitive positions vis-à-vis other more novel solutions along the knowledge frontier. Likewise, in situations where there is too little collaboration and networking among actors, other problems might arrive. Unexploited opportunities, lack of interactive learning, and/or high costs of producing new knowledge might have negative consequences for the individual and collective levels of innovation performance. Consequently, innovation systems need to find a balance between different forms of collaboration and competition.

Different factors might influence such a balance. The pre-existing levels of socio-economic development and overall level of knowledge competences in the economy are crucial factors. Less developed economies suffer from organizational weaknesses, uneven domestic capabilities, and a high technological dependency; therefore, for them the adoption of technology, its adaptation, and its diffusion 'plays a much greater role than original R&D-based development of cutting edge innovations' (Altenburg, 2009, p. 39). In this sense, innovation networks have a fundamental role in issues of technology transfer, adaptation, and diffusion (Feldmann and Breznitz, 2009).

The literature has also identified another set of crucial factors, namely, the areas of industrial specialization and technological regimes dominant in a particular economy. Industrial specialization is a crucial dimension in order to grasp the diversity of dynamics of innovation, and the distinct patterns of learning and complementarities in innovation networks (Malerba, 2009). Furthermore, specific geographical factors play a major role in the evolutionary processes of retention and variation in network structures (Haakonsson and Kirkegaard, 2016). Proximity (a key geographical factor) affects network formation due to actors' communication preferences and mobility opportunities (De Fuentes and Dutrénit, 2016; Haakonsson, 2013). Localized resource profiles (another key geographical factor)—including 'the structural aspects of relationships (e.g. social capital, structural holes) as well as the material, social and institutional resources that these relationships access and transfer' (Glückler, 2007, p. 622)—are other key geographical factors in the formation and evolution of innovation networks.

Overall, the benefits of innovation networks in an innovation system are determined by these general factors. For that reason, it is crucial to examine the particular features of the innovation system before considering the way in which innovation networks and other forms of interaction affect the

---

Box 8.1 INNOVATION NETWORKS AND INTERACTIONS:
MAIN OBSTACLES AND BARRIERS

Unexploited potential due to insufficient interaction and networks.

Network partners do not have complementary knowledge assets.

Lack of critical mass of interactions and networks.

Interactions and networks are creating innovation lock-ins.

No positive network externalities (such as knowledge spill-overs).

---

innovation performance. From a general perspective, and taking the factors above into consideration, innovation networks might suffer from a series of problems or bottlenecks associated with networks and collaborative interactions that are relevant to single out here. Box 8.1 summarizes them.

Firstly, the level of interactions may be insufficient. Innovation systems might suffer from an *unexploited innovation potential* due to an insufficient level of interactions between the different actors in the system. Lack of sufficient interaction can also be a problem due to poor organizations. The reasons might be very different. This is a list of possible institutional and motivational barriers between the organizations, which constitute barriers for university–industry collaboration (Bruneel et al., 2010): poor or too rigid intellectual property rights regulations; lack of trust and social capital; or lack of venture capital to materialize those interactions.

Secondly, the characteristics and competences of networking partners may be irrelevant to each other. It can be a problem if *potential network partners do not have complementary knowledge assets*. It is a problem if potential network partners are not complementing each other, or have highly asymmetric capacities. This refers to situations in which there is limited availability and access to a diverse pool of knowledge. Building additional and differentiated knowledge competences, either collectively (laboratories, knowledge-production centres) or individually (educational levels, labour market resources, etc.) might be crucial to overcome such situations. The lack of complementarity most likely reduces the possibility of positive network externalities in the economy, such as knowledge spill-overs. This might be a situation where there are innovation networking activities taking part in the innovation system, but their positive effects are limited due to the lack of knowledge complementarities.

Thirdly, *the lack of critical mass of innovation interactions with external sources of knowledge and competences from another innovation system* might be an important barrier. Interactions might exist and might be the expression of knowledge complementarities. However, their size may not be proportionate

157

to the size of the economy in question, and there may be very limited inter-action with other actors outside the territory. This lack of critical mass has to do with internal dimensions of the interactions in the innovation system in question, as well as with the external dimension of interactions of actors in an innovation system with actors in another one. Both aspects of lack of critical mass are fundamental.

A fourth type of innovation system obstacle and barrier has to do with the nature of the interactions. Some *interactions create innovation lock-ins*. As we have seen in previous chapters of this book, innovators are always facing the dilemma of whether to develop their products or processes further along the current technology frontier (exploiting existing knowledge), or whether to engage in exploring new sources of knowledge that might give them a com-petitive position in the medium term (exploring new knowledge). This imbal-ance is intrinsic to any form of innovation process.

From the perspective of the innovation system, it is key to have a balance between innovation networks seeking to exploit existing knowledge and those seeking to explore new knowledge trajectories. If the innovation net-works in a system are overwhelmingly exploiting existing knowledge, and too few of the networks are exploring new knowledge, the innovation system might face a problem of innovation lock-in at certain points in time. If innovation networks are becoming too 'conservative' in their business models, they might run the risk of disruptive innovation popping up 'sud-denly' outside the networks, destroying their business model altogether before they are able to react. This risk is as relevant for technology-based innovation as it is for non-technological innovation, as horizontal and enabling tech-nologies (like ICT and the subsequent digital transformation of business models) are having a tremendous effect on both products and processes in virtually all segments of economic and social activity.

A fifth type of obstacle and barrier in an innovation system is when inter-actions and networks do not foster innovation at all. In other words, there are *no positive network externalities* (such as knowledge spill-overs). Seen from the perspective of the whole innovation system, this means that the interactions in the system are not effectively fostering the development of innovations. One possible reason for the limited effect of networks on the innovative performance of individual actors might be associated with the limited absorp-tive capacity of the actors.

As we saw in Chapter 5, the theory of 'absorptive capacity' and the empirical evidence about firms engaging in forms of open innovation shows that there tends to be a strong link between the internal knowledge capacities of a firm and its ability to tap into sources of knowledge from other actors (Cohen and Levinthal, 1990). Firms and other innovators are able to make the most of the knowledge from other actors when they themselves are able to 'understand'

and 'interpret' the value of that external source of knowledge, using it actively in combination with their internal knowledge. 'Absorptive capacity' tells little about the complementarity of that knowledge (another possible problem identified above). Instead, it tells about the importance of internal sources of knowledge of the individual actors when engaging in collaborative endeavours with external partners. There is a positive outcome on innovation performance when the individual firm has a sufficient level of internal knowledge so that it can effectively tap into and use the external knowledge sources. When the level of internal knowledge is too low, firms will be unable to effectively tap into those external sources, making innovation collaborations useless mechanisms to improve their innovation performance. This has important policy implications, which will be addressed below.

It is worth noting that most of the interactions and other forms of collaboration among innovators in innovation systems occur spontaneously according to their changing needs and visions when facing their own individual challenges and when sizing new opportunities. Other times, however, interactions are difficult or problematic from an individual as well as from a collective innovation system perspective, as in the situations examined above. In these situations, there might be a strong case for policy intervention.

8.6 Policy Instruments Fostering Innovation Interactions

This chapter looks at policy instruments that enhance innovation interaction in innovation systems. Given the intrinsic nature of interactions in an innovation system, there might be direct and indirect governmental interventions that affect them (Borrás and Tsagdis, 2008). This chapter examines policy instruments that are directly focusing on enhancing interactions, whereas other chapters look into indirect governmental interventions.

There are many different types of policy instrument that have been deployed by governments. Box 8.2 offers a summary. In fact, cluster and innovation network policy instruments have been rather popular in high-income economies (Andersson et al., 2004) as well as in low-income economies (Ketels et al., 2006), from the end of the 1990s well into the mid-2010s. Whereas an encompassing review of innovation policy instruments in this field is still missing, several relevant analyses of policies in this area are useful for mapping differences in policy instruments across world regions, for example in Europe (Nauwelaers and Wintjes, 2008), Latin America (Altenburg and Meyer-Stamer, 1999), Asia (Kuchiki and Tsuji, 2005), and across the globe (Roelandt et al., 2000). However, a clear-cut identification of policy instruments is difficult as those instruments are highly related to the instruments identified in other activities of the innovation system (e.g. support of R&D

Box 8.2 INNOVATION NETWORKS AND INTERACTIONS: GENERAL TYPES OF MOST COMMON POLICY INSTRUMENTS

---

1. Promoting collaboration between firms, and between university and industry.

2. Promotion of local and regional interactions and networks, either internally in the region, or externally (through foreign direct investment, etc.).

3. Encouragement of collective view or strategy for the region or sector, seeking interactions.

4. Match-making, acquaintance, networking events.

5. Instruments targeting specific actors (e.g. SMEs) in order to foster their embeddedness in networks and interactions.

---

activities, venture capital, education, and knowledge capacity-building, etc.), which have been addressed in other chapters of this book. Yet, innovation network and cluster instruments are typically those targeting diverse aspects of interaction in a sectoral and/or territorial dimension (Nauwelaers and Wintjes, 2008).

Instruments promoting collaboration between firms, and between university and industry. When looking at the most commonly used policy instruments fostering interactions between organizations to enhance innovation, one fundamental dimension is what is being supported and fostered. Here, policy instruments have different foci—see the first set of instruments in Box 8.2. Most typically, innovation policy instruments towards innovation collaboration tend to encourage and support industry's interactions, as well as industry–university (or other research organizations) collaborations (Matt et al., 2012).

This might entail direct economic support (co-funding or full funding) of the coordination costs and/or of the costs of the new collaborative activities/research, or indirect/'soft' incentives fostering collaboration. These are typically done in specific industrial/knowledge areas. Recently, these types of innovation collaboration interactions have been moving beyond the traditional support of R&D activities, and closer into the development and commercialization side of innovation. Gradually, instruments towards innovation networks have introduced requirements to include broader types of actors in the networks (for example, key stakeholders who might eventually be the users/consumers of the outcomes of those collaborations). In other words, policy instruments are stimulating networks to include a wider diversity of actors, in the belief that a wider type of membership will secure a more rapid diffusion of results and a wider impact in society.

A second set of innovation policy instruments fostering interactions are those seeking to *promote local and regional interactions and networks*, either internally in the region or externally (through foreign direct investment, etc.). Naturally, those instruments are more geographically oriented, typically as part of cluster-fostering policies. They may prompt regional actors into collaboration with each other, and/or with external partners. Even if innovation might not be directly the goal of these instruments, they nonetheless might affect it through the improvement of the knowledge base in the territory, by means of access to external sources of knowledge in the form of investment.

A third set of innovation policy instruments are those seeking to *encourage collective views or strategies for the region or sector, seeking interactions*. They do that by coordinating (sectoral and/or regional) actors in developing a collective view or strategy for the sector and/or the region. This form of coordination does not entail direct support of knowledge–production collaboration. Rather, it seeks to raise awareness and to enhance meta-level forms of collaboration by means of aligning overarching strategies for the sector or the territory. It is more an alignment of intentions and aspirations than an alignment of actual research, technological, or non-technological innovative activities.

A fourth set of innovation policy instruments in this field are instruments seeking to improve the mutual acquaintance of the different actors in the system, by means of *match-making and networking events*, expanding the interpersonal informal interactions that, according to some authors mentioned above, constitute the first step for formal interactions and collaborations.

A fifth set of innovation policy *instruments are those directly targeting some specific actors* in the innovation interactions, which typically have some structural difficulties with regard to interaction (e.g. lack of human resources). This is typically the case of policy instruments supporting SMEs, in particular those policies seeking to improve their overall knowledge capacities by giving them preferential access to R&D funding and/or access to different forms of business and technological services; and those aiming to integrate them better into other innovation interactions in the sector or in the region (Garofoli and Musyck, 2003).

Having addressed the different areas in which these policy instruments are focused, we now proceed to examine the mechanisms through which this is done. Namely, we will examine how governments are actually putting this into practice. This is relevant because it generates very different dynamics and directions of the interactions, with potentially negative consequences (as we will see in Section 8.7).

Most innovation network instruments have a bottom-up and self-organizing characteristic, where interested actors might integrate themselves into a network and make an application for support to the public authorities. This self-organization is, however, not always the rule. Some instruments have a much more top-down approach, where specific industrial sectors and actors have been previously identified and targeted by the government and incentives allocated to specific forms of organization. These are typically industrial, scientific, or technological sectors considered strategic by the relevant government.

A second important dimension, which is partly related to the first, has to do with the types of economic sector that policy instruments support. Policy instruments might support interactions in economic sectors that are already strongly represented in the country/region. By contrast, policy instruments might support the creation of competences in new knowledge areas, expecting to create the basis for the emergence of new economic sectors in the country/region. Furthermore, policy instruments might be rather different in terms of exploiting or expanding knowledge bases: either their intention is to expand the knowledge base in existing areas, or to foster exploration of new knowledge into new areas. A third dimension of fostering interactions has to do with the maturity and the pre-existence of those interactions or not. Some instruments aim at building interactions and clusters *ex-novo*, whereas other instruments are directed towards improving, enhancing, or changing the nature of the existing interactions.

The evidence available on the impact of these policy instruments tends to indicate that the overall competence of cluster managers (or the persons leading the implementation and execution of these networking activities), and the early participation of the private sector in regional/national policy strategies, are determinants for the success of these instruments. However, the findings are scarce, diverse (different methodologies), and inconclusive (Uyarra and Ramlogan, 2016).

8.7 Unintended Consequences of Policy: Inducing Three Forms of Lock-In

As shown recently in an extensive collection of the available evaluations of policy instruments related to interactive learning (Cunningham and Ramlogan, 2016), the evidence on the effect and impact of those instruments, however, tends to be inconclusive. The large diversity of policy instruments supporting interactions and innovation networks does not render the study of effects and impacts an easy task. Furthermore, not all scholars agree that there is a good case for pursuing policy intervention for supporting networks (Duranton, 2011; Chatterji et al., 2014) or for clusters (Martin and Sunley, 2003). All of this relates to the issues of the 'when' and 'how' policy

> **Box 8.3** INNOVATION NETWORKS AND INTERACTIONS: UNINTENDED
> CONSEQUENCES OF POLICY
>
> 1. Policy reinforces innovation lock-in.
> 2. Policy reinforces the homogeneity of actors in networks rather than helping
>   interactions among diverse actors.
> 3. Mainly local not international networking.

intervention is called for. This is essentially because in the process of considering policy intervention and the choice of suitable policy instruments, it is key to assess the possible negative effects of policy itself—something that generally has been disregarded in the literature.

There are indeed a number of situations in which lack of clarity of the policy goals and/or poorly designed policy instruments supporting networks might have negative effects on the overall performance of the innovation system. There are at least three such situations, as summarized in Box 8.3.

The first situation is *when policy instruments fostering networks result in an innovation lock-in.* Many innovation network-oriented policies seek generally to improve the competitive position of particular industrial sectors or geographical areas by means of strengthening its technological and knowledge basis. However, if the policy is not designed explicitly to bring in and explore new knowledge, but instead reinforces the existing technological basis fostering the exploitation of that existing knowledge, then a situation of 'innovation lock-in' (the non-advancement in new alternative and potentially disruptive knowledge bases) might occur in the medium term. This could be risky given that technological advances may take place very rapidly, and the industry in question might unexpectedly see its technological position undermined by disruptive technologies for which they were not prepared. For that reason, innovation policy instruments for networking have to seek more 'knowledge-exploring' approaches in order to expand the existing knowledge bases, instead of 'knowledge-exploiting' approaches for which the competitive dynamics of market forces are well suited.

The second potential unintended consequence of policy is when policy instruments reinforce existing patterns of collaboration in innovation networks, which we may call the *homogeneity lock-in.* Existing patterns are often formed by homogeneous or similar types of actors, with similar interests and similar viewpoints. Instead, policy instruments that seek to generate new forms of innovation output by tapping into alternative and complementary competences have to induce diversity and heterogeneity. If instruments are not designed to increase this diversity, but instead reinforce previous homogeneous consortia, the innovation outputs will certainly become less novel and transformative than otherwise. Such a situation does not foster the expansion of knowledge basis by seeking alternative and complementary sources of knowledge exploitation. It would enhance 'homogeneity lock-in' in innovation networks.

A third negative situation generated by poorly designed policy instruments has to do with *the 'geographical lock-in' effect of the instrument*. Policy-makers manage public resources (taxpayers' money, quite simply). For that reason, they might have a natural inclination to ensure that these resources are spent directly in the home country. If such an approach is taken too narrowly, however, it might result in a 'geographical lock-in' of the innovation networks. Such lock-in refers to the situation when interactions are limited to actors within the 'home' geographic area. This would limit the flows and knowledge bases generated by actors in other locations. It is well known that strong geographical knowledge and innovation hubs, like Silicon Valley, are in fact highly dependent on the flows of interactions taking place through personal networks crossing national boundaries (Saxenian, 2006). A too 'local' approach in the design of innovation network policy instruments will limit the inflow of wider knowledge bases, generating the contrary effect as successful innovation hubs show.

8.8 Conclusions for Innovation Policy Design

We have seen in this chapter that interactions are crucial for the innovation process. For that reason, innovation systems are formed by a multitude of different types of interaction which are formal and informal, public and/or private in nature. The outcome is innovation, both for-profit and market-based innovation, as well as not-for-profit and societal-based innovation. The innovation system is complex, consisting of multiple forms of interactions and multiple outcomes of these interactions in terms of innovation.

From the perspective of policy-making, which is the main focus of this book, the balance between stimulating collaboration and competition is an important one. Policy must not blindly pursue collaboration for the sake of it, as it might endanger some fundamental competitive dynamics that characterize innovation in the market and in society at large. Instead, policy intervention must be directed towards situations where there are obvious problems, obstacles, and barriers in the forms and levels of interaction negatively affecting the performance of the innovation system.

With this purpose in mind, this chapter has identified the following deficiencies that serve as the rationale for the development of individual policy instruments specifically targeting those problems. There are at list five (partly overlapping, but clearly identifiable) deficiencies, obstacles, or barriers in the innovation system:

- when there are insufficient levels of interactions so that there is unexploited innovation potential in a given system;
- when the partners in existing innovation networks do not have complementary knowledge assets;
- when there is a lack of critical mass of innovation interactions connecting the actors in an innovation system with external sources of knowledge and competences;
- when some existing innovation interactions are clearly generating and reproducing technological solutions leading to an 'innovation lock-in', an homogeneity lock-in, or a geographical lock-in; and
- when the knowledge base of individual actors (firms and others) are not sufficiently developed in order to profit from their existing interactions with external partners (lack of 'absorptive capacity').

The rapid development of innovation network-oriented policy instruments in many local, regional, and national contexts all over the world is an indication of the popularity among policy-makers of these types of instruments. Yet, beyond this popularity and general preference, policy-makers need to devise instruments in a way that targets real problems in the innovation system, instead of promoting interactions for the sake of it. In some less-developed countries and areas, the problems of absorptive capacity and critical mass in innovation interactions might call for policy instruments improving the knowledge competences of firms and other organizations more broadly, not just the networking per se. Likewise, in middle-income economies, where the challenges are perhaps more related to industrial decline or rapid loss of competitive position of the existing productive sector, the problems that policy-makers must address are more related to the lack of complementary knowledge assets and some clear technological lock-in in the existing innovation networks.

Policy-makers must consider what exactly the problems are that afflict their innovation systems, and whether those problems are amenable to be solved by policy intervention—rather than perceiving networking as a universal solution to a problem that was never truly diagnosed. This is key not just for the sake of developing effective policies solving real-life problems, but also for avoiding poorly designed policy instruments becoming a problem on their own.

9

Changing Institutions

9.1 Introduction

Over the past three decades, economists have become increasingly interested in the role that institutions and regulations play in the economy. This growing interest has drawn them closer to other disciplines in the social sciences such as sociology, law, and political science, which have long acknowledged the role of institutions and regulations in the organizing of social, economic, and political life. For this reason, there is a large body of literature dealing with these matters, both across disciplines and within disciplines. Yet, in spite of some few interdisciplinary efforts, there are still important differences across disciplinary approaches. Likewise, intradisciplinary differences are significant, given the diverse assumptions of social action upon which different theories are based.

This chapter examines the role of institutions (including regulations) from the particular perspective of innovation. In so doing, it takes the point of departure from innovation systems in the understanding that institutions are constitutive elements of the innovation system, while regulations are specific mechanisms of state intervention. More concretely, the general aim of this chapter is to discuss the role of institutions and regulations in the context of the design of innovation policy. The reason for such a focus is that the policy perspective in studies about the role of institutions and regulation has tended to be rather limited. The growing literature on regulatory impact on innovation is providing interesting insights and is perhaps an exception to this rule. But there is more to it.

The chapter starts by acknowledging what we define as 'the double nature of regulations', by which regulations, like any other institution, are constitutive elements of the innovation system. Given the 'visible hand of the state' in regulation, they are at the same time innovation policy instruments. This double nature (constitutive element of the system and innovation policy instrument) is a crucial aspect in understanding the way in which innovation policy is highly engaged in the organizing of the innovation system. This means that the design of innovation policy should not only be based on impact-assessment exercises of regulatory policy instruments' effects. It should also be based on the role of institutions and regulations in reducing uncertainty, managing conflict and cooperation, and providing incentives in the innovation system more generally.

Following from that, the chapter identifies the most salient regulatory areas from the perspective of the innovation system, arguing that the effect of regulation on innovation is not a value statement but an open empirical question. Therefore, three key research questions are formulated: firstly, the extent to which regulation has a positive or negative effect on innovation performance in the system; secondly, whether it has individual costs/benefits for few or wider benefits for the innovativeness of the economy and society; and thirdly, the extent to which regulation is adapting to new (social, economic, and technological) contexts and hence is socially legitimate to induce innovation in a wider social context. More concretely, this chapter examines these three matters in two core regulatory areas in an innovation system, namely, patent regulations and environmental regulations. We will also refer to other chapters in this book where institutions are addressed as part of innovation policy.

Taking a step further, the chapter argues that a systemic approach to innovation policy needs focusing on a second level of matters, namely the problems associated with regulation. These are three: the intrinsic ambiguity of regulation, its degree of enforcement and compliance, and its sociological (rather than normative) legitimacy among socio-economic agents. This has two implications that are fleshed out in Section 9.7. Firstly, it shows that social habits are key to understanding the effects of regulation in the innovation system; and secondly, it provides guidance for the design of innovation policy in a learning context.

9.2 Institutions and Regulation in the Innovation System

Innovations are partly an outcome of interactions that take place within firms, between firms and other organizations, between firms and consumers, etc. Interaction means here that innovations are invariably produced and used in relation to others, and that innovation processes are processes that are socially embedded; that is, processes that occur in a social and economic context. Institutions and regulations are the rules of the game for those interactions and for the social-embeddedness of the innovation process. For that reason, institutions and regulations shape the way in which those interactions and social contextualization take place. In other words, innovation is a social phenomenon, subject to the rules of the game by which any society organizes itself.

Over the past few decades, different strands in the field of economics have looked more carefully at how institutions are actually organizing the economy, and how they can organize it in more efficient and effective ways. Highly inspired by other fields related to human and social sciences, like sociology and anthropology, new institutional economics have developed interesting insights into economic history and economic organization (Menard and Shirley, 2008).

Social theories inspired in rationalist approaches to institutions tend to take the point of departure from the understanding of social action as being intrinsically a rationalist and utility-maximizing behaviour. From the rationalist approach, actors are motivated by individual and materially defined interests, and take a specific position defining their preferences in social interactions. Actors (inter)act following a logic of consequentiality on the basis of their material interests (March and Olsen, 1989), and utility optimize their behaviour. Institutions are perceived by the rationalist approach as specific rules that actors aim to utilize (and if necessary, to bend) in order to achieve their individual goals (Edquist and Johnson, 1997).

Actors might act differently vis-à-vis institutions. They might somehow tend to be opportunistic, making the most of institutions that are not clearly defined, or searching for some specific interpretations of those rules that might benefit their own interests (Mahoney and Thelen, 2010). Hence, from the rationalist perspective of these institutionalist approaches, actors might behave differently, but always following their specific material interests and with a logic that seeks to be consequent with that. From the perspective of the economy, theories inspired by rational approaches tend to look at institutions from the perspective of efficiency. The main issue here is the extent to which institutions constitute efficient rules for market-based interactions. Focus on transaction costs is one such approach (North, 1990).

Alternatively, other strands in the social sciences consider that social action is not always based on rational calculations. Rationality is bounded by social ties and the history of previous decisions. Moreover, social actors might have aspirations other than maximizing individual material interests (like altruism). The axiom of social action is not only the rational pursuit of one's individual interest, but also the need to be accepted. Hence, social behaviour is not really an issue of just 'following the rules' in order to achieve a goal, but mainly an issue of endogenizing those rules as 'the right thing to do' and incorporating them into everyday routines and habits (Hodgson, 1997).

From the perspective of innovation systems these brief theoretical considerations are important for two reasons. Firstly, innovation is the fruit of social action by the innovators. Naturally, innovators engage in innovation activities in the expectation of obtaining some gains. These are normally monetary gains, but can also be of other kinds, like social recognition. The theoretical considerations above remind us that innovators' motivation and incentives to engage in innovative activities are crucial aspects of institutions. Likewise, the theories remind us that the relation between actor (organization) and institution (rule) might be different. In any case, however, institutions shape the way in which actors' interactions take place, and provide some certainty about what to expect from those interactions (Weber and Rohracher, 2012).

Secondly, these theoretical considerations tend to indicate the constitutive nature of institutions. Either perceived exogenously (rational institutionalism) or endogenously (sociological institutionalism), institutions are the 'glue' that organizes a society. This links with our current innovation system perspective, where the whole is greater than the sum of the parts. That is, an innovation system is not just a mere juxtaposition of individual innovators or organizations at a specific territorial level. The system is formed by sets of complex interactions and ways of organizing innovation activities that are unique to that system. Institutions are those constitutive elements that are crucial to understand the idiosyncrasies of each innovation system.

However, the richness of this literature in theoretical as well as in conceptual terms still leaves us with difficulties operating in a coherent analytical perspective. For this reason, some conceptual clarification is needed at this point. We see institutions as 'sets of common habits, routines, established practices, rules, or laws that regulate the relations and interactions between individuals and groups' (Edquist and Johnson, 1997, p. 46). This definition shows that institutions are rather broad, as they include not only politically determined law and formal rules enforced by the state or other authorities, but also socially defined rules of behaviour that tend to be more open-ended and implicitly defined, such as routines and established practices. This definition of institution tells us that an institution is any type of rule of the game that organizes social interactions among individuals and organizations.

Yet, not all institutions in a social order do in fact directly affect innovation processes. For that reason, from the perspective of innovation and innovation systems, some institutions might be more relevant than others. This is particularly the case if we look at some technological or industrial sectors, like for example the agri-food sector. Some institutions might be more relevant than others for the innovativeness of this sector in a given country, for example, the laws around food safety controls, or the eating habits and traditions in that society (i.e. fast or slow food, preference for ecological/non-genetically modified produce). Acknowledging this, we define 'institutional frameworks' as those sets of specific institutions that are most relevant for a given sector or area.

Looking now carefully at the way in which we have formulated these definitions, the verb 'to regulate' comes to the fore. This is so because regulation has for many years been associated with institutions and institutional frameworks. Political scientists in particular have studied the changing role of regulation in contemporary political systems, which has transformed alongside the changing nature of the state and of governance dynamics (Jordana and Levi-Faur, 2004b). Notions like the regulatory state (Majone, 1994) or 'governance' (Pierre and Peters, 2000) have captured these transformations. All this shows that the notion of 'regulation' might be quite complex, and that 'regulating' can mean different things.

For the reasons above, we use a definition of *hard regulation* that refers to the narrow understanding of the concept, namely, 'an authoritative set of rules, accompanied by some mechanism, typically a public agency, for monitoring and promoting compliance with these rules' (Baldwin et al., 1998, p. 3; Jordana and Levi-Faur, 2004a). 'Authoritative' here means legally binding, in the understanding that hard regulation refers to obligatory rules that must be followed by citizens, firms, and organizations. Some of these obligatory regulations come directly from the state, hopefully as the outcome of democratic legislative processes. Other obligatory hard regulations might come from regulatory agencies, which are public organizations to which the state has delegated regulatory powers. These regulatory powers are typically in specific sector and technical areas, as in environmental protection, or drug and medicine regulations, where technical expertise is required. For this reason, hard regulations are a sub-category of institutions.

Taking into consideration the second transformation mentioned above, we need to include a third definition in order to capture the complexity of regulation and institutions in our contemporary economies and societies. This is the case of *soft regulation*, which refers to the formal and explicit set of rules that are not legally binding, e.g. a code of conduct or a voluntary agreement. Soft regulation is formal because we are talking about rules that are explicitly formulated in written text. These are typically put forward in semi-official documents and/or other forms of formalized official communications that serve either to offer moral support and/or apply pressure on actors, while defining collective expectations and what behaviour is (not) acceptable.

Soft regulation differs from hard regulation because the former is not legally binding, hence does not enjoy the enforcement mechanisms of the state. No one can go to jail because they did not follow the wording of a voluntary agreement, but they might in the case of hard regulation because it is compulsory. Likewise, soft regulation constitutes only a part of the notion of institutions because the latter includes all of the former (hard regulation, soft regulation) as well many other types of social rules of the game, namely, the set of implicit, unspoken, and undeclared common habits, routines, or

---

Box 9.1 DEFINITIONS OF INSTITUTION, SOFT REGULATION, AND HARD REGULATION

Institution 'Institutions are sets of common habits, routines, established practices, rules, or laws that regulate the relations and interactions between individuals and groups' (Edquist and Johnson, 1997, p. 46).

Soft regulation Formal and explicit sets of rules that are not legally binding, e.g. a code of conduct.

Hard regulation 'An authoritative set of rules, accompanied by some mechanism, typically a public agency, for monitoring and promoting compliance with these rules' (Baldwin et al., 1998, p. 3; Jordana and Levi-Faur, 2004a).

---

established practices. The strongly informal nature of the latter differs from the (semi-)official and explicit formulation of soft regulations. Box 9.1 summarizes these definitions.

From the above it follows that institutions are the broadest form of rules of the game organizing social interactions, in our case interactions related to innovation activities. Regulations, in their hard and soft forms, are also rules of the game, but they are far more explicit and formalized than many other institutions. Therefore, we can illustrate the relationship between them as Russian dolls encapsulating each other: institutions are the broadest and most generic definition of rules of the game, whereas soft and hard regulations are more specific.

9.3 Important Regulation Areas for Innovation

What particular core areas of regulation are most relevant for innovation activities? In principle, many types of institution or regulation are related to innovation activities because innovation is a complex, diverse, and widespread human activity. However, seen from an innovation policy perspective, some regulations have more relevance than others because they have a more direct effect on the process of innovation and on the way an innovation system is organized (Radosevic, 2012). We consider regulatory areas to be 'core regulatory areas for the innovation system' when they have a horizontal effect on the entire system. 'Horizontal' refers here to regulatory effects that cut across specific industrial or knowledge sectors; and which have a wide effect on the innovative activities of many different socio-economic sectors. This might differ from other, more generic taxonomies of regulation, which are not particularly focused on innovation processes but on regulatory reform more generally (OECD, 1997).

In this chapter we consider that there are at least five important regulatory areas in an innovation system:

1 Intellectual property rights;
2 Fair market competition regulations;
3 Financial and corporate governance regulations;
4 Consumer protection and product liability regulations; and
5 Environmental protection regulations.

The appropriation of immaterial assets and new knowledge by means of IPR is an important area of regulation with a direct impact on innovation activities. As we will see in Section 9.4, there are different ways of appropriating immaterial assets and new knowledge created/developed by firms. These regulations determine the conditions under which innovators (firms and individuals) are able to appropriate immaterial assets (brands, trademarks, designs) and/or new knowledge/expression of ideas produced by them (patents, copyrights, etc.). The expected effects of these regulations are to generate incentives to invest in new knowledge and in the development of immaterial assets, fostering innovation.

Fair market competition regulations in the form of anti-trust law and merger and acquisition control laws are important regulatory areas in the innovation system. These regulations aim at creating a level playing field for all economic actors, securing a context where innovators are able to compete with new ideas and new products in the market on fair conditions. Therefore these regulations reduce uncertainty, as well as manage conflict and cooperation.

Financial and corporate governance regulations are those regulations that define legal requirements for the creation of new firms, filing for bankruptcy, establishing corporate governance structures, etc. These regulations are also core for any innovation system for several reasons. Access to capital at a competitive market-based price, with transparent and law-enforced conditions, is key to any innovator (start-up or established firm). Likewise, corporate governance regulations determining, among others, the conditions and responsibilities in the crucial steps of a firm's life (i.e. legal requirements to create a new firm, file for bankruptcy, receive inheritance, etc.) are also fundamental, reducing uncertainty and defining the framework for conflict resolution and cooperation.

Consumer protection and product liability regulations (typically hard and soft laws defining mandatory or quasi-mandatory standard technical requirements for products, laws for consumer protection, liability, etc.) are also horizontal and key regulatory areas in the innovation system. Innovators are always confronted with the potential risks that their new products might pose to consumers. These regulations are set up in order to determine the standardized specific technical requirements of products, as well as the procedures to make mandatory decisions that limit possible harm to consumers (food safety, product certification, etc.). They also determine the levels and forms of firms' liabilities when harm has been done. As such, these regulatory areas aim essentially at reducing uncertainty and limiting risk.

Last but not least, a fifth important regulatory area with wide effects on the innovation system is the area of environmental protection regulation (understood widely to include energy, transport, natural resources, packaging sectors, etc.). Some innovative products and processes might have negative effects on the natural environment, whereas others might help solve endemic problems of environmental pollution or energy inefficiency. Innovation can in principle go both ways when considering its impact on the environment. For this reason, environmental protection regulations aim at addressing both dimensions of innovation's impact on the environment, dealing with negative environmental externalities. In some cases these regulations aim at creating incentives in specific eco-friendly directions; whereas in others, these regulations aim at setting the legal limits of pollution and assigning liabilities to pollutants.

9.4 The Effects of Regulation and Innovation-Related Issues

Our current societies and economies are heavily regulated, and those regulations have been related to the innovation performance outcomes since the Industrial Revolution. In particular, the advancement of the modern state after World War II has been largely based on increasingly sophisticated regulatory activity on the part of the state, which has shaped the evolution of developed and developing economies and societies, here including innovation performance. This historical co-evolution does not automatically mean that regulation is good or bad, socially fair/unfair, or flexible or rigid through time. It means only that there has been a clear co-evolution process between state-promoted regulatory institutions and innovation (Nelson, 1994). The effect of regulation on innovation is an empirical question, not a value statement.

From a theoretical perspective, institutional economics has identified three generic (expected) effects of regulation (as particular forms of institutions) in the economy, namely, to reduce uncertainty, to manage conflict and cooperation, and to provide incentives (Edquist and Johnson, 1997). Table 9.1 summarizes the expected effects of these particular core regulations on the innovation system, according to these three overall issues.

More recently, however, these theoretical issues have been the object of empirical attention, addressing questions about the actual effect of regulation in the economy, here including the effects on innovation (see Blind, 2012a for

Table 9.1. Five important regulatory areas in the innovation system and their expected effects

Regulatory areas	Expected effects in the innovation system
Immaterial assets and knowledge appropriation regulations (Intellectual Property Rights)	Provides incentives to invest in new knowledge and in the development of immaterial assets, fostering innovation.
Fair market competition regulations (anti-trust law, merger and acquisition control law, etc.)	Creating a level playing field for market interactions reduces uncertainty and manages conflict/cooperation in cross-firm innovation interactions.
Financial and corporate governance regulations (requirements for the creation of new firms, bankruptcy laws, corporate governance regulations, etc.)	Provides incentives to invest by defining rules and fair price of capital as well as reducing uncertainty about conditions and responsibilities in key steps of a firm's life (creation of new firms, bankruptcy, inheritance, etc.).
Consumer protection and product liability regulations (hard and soft law defining technical requirements for products, standards, consumer protection principles, and rights)	Reducing the uncertainty of existing and particularly of new/innovative products, and eventually limiting innovative products' risks to consumers.
Environmental protection regulations	These regulations deal with the negative environmental externalities of products in different ways, sometimes by creating incentives in specific innovative eco-friendly directions, other times by defining the limits and responsibilities of pollutants and forcing them to find innovative alternatives.

an excellent review). It is worth noting that these empirical studies go beyond the three theoretically deduced items above, and include myriad other issues and questions, sometimes rather specific to the regulation in question. From these, we can identify three empirical research questions about the effect of regulation on innovation.

The first closely follows the items mentioned above: what is the effectiveness of the regulation in terms of the costs of compliance and the incentives it generates? This is what Knut Blind has examined in his seminal chapter, where he measures the effects of 'compliance costs on the availability of resources for innovation on the one hand, and the incentives set for performing innovation activities on the other hand' (Blind, 2012b, p. 392). His comparative study of six regulatory frameworks in twenty-one OECD countries over a six-year span shows mixed results. Goods and service regulations and environmental regulations seem to have an overall negative influence on innovation performance at a country level (the benefits of innovation incentives do not outweigh the costs of compliance). Non-restrictive price regulations, IPR regulations, and the regulatory framework encouraging the competitiveness of enterprises seem to have positive effects on innovation performance.

This general approach to the impact of regulation on innovation, which is also based on a cost-benefit focus on costs of compliance, is very useful and relevant, as it serves to provide an overall and comparative view. However, this macro-level perspective loses detail for several reasons. Firstly, it is not able to acknowledge sufficiently the complexity of each regulatory framework (IPR, for example, encompasses a quite broad and diverse type of regulations). Secondly, it does not acknowledge the diversity of the regulatory effects on innovation across different firm sizes, across industrial sectors (patent regulations have different effects on innovation in the biotech sector than in the ICT sector), or across economic regions in the same country.

This leads to a second crucial question about the effect of regulation on innovation, namely, the balance between private benefits and social benefits. This is an issue that lies at the core of state action when regulating. Some regulations, such as IPRs, grant individual proprietary rights to firms or innovators as a mechanism to create incentives to innovate. Other regulations impose obligations and restrictions as a way of shaping specific behaviour (like competition regulations prohibiting cartels, or environmental regulations obliging firms to introduce or avoid specific technologies in their products).

The extent to which these individual rights and/or obligations or restrictions generate private costs/benefits and/or social costs/benefits is an important question. We assume that the state regulates with the expectation that individual costs and benefits in a society will be distributed in a way that will ultimately generate a positive effect over the entire society and economy. Even if some socio-economic agents bear more costs than others, the overall bottom line for the economy and society would need to be positive, e.g. by stimulating innovation. This is, however, an empirical question, as some regulations and their applications might generate unbalanced social outcomes.

One example is USA's medical device regulations, which have encouraged incremental rather than radical innovations on the assumption that the former are safer for patients than the latter. However, the recent case of a hip prosthesis that was unsafe for patients proves that the assumption was wrong. The hip prosthesis was an incremental innovation but became very unsafe, and many patients had to undergo re-operation (Barberá-Tomás and Molas-Gallart, 2014). The case of the hip prosthesis shows that the regulatory authorities' assumption that incremental innovations are safer for patients has proved to be wrong. Regulations of innovation have some important effects.

The third big empirical question about the effect of regulation on innovation has to do with the adaptability and legitimacy of regulation. Here the debates have recently revolved around whether hard or soft forms of regulation are best in innovation-related areas that change rapidly. For example, it has been argued that hard regulation of new and advanced materials might not be the best approach. This is so because hard regulation tends to treat these materials as if they were chemicals, but these materials do not behave as chemicals and there is considerable uncertainty about their properties.

The argument proceeds that the relatively rigid nature of hard regulation does not allow a sufficiently rapid adaptation to the new needs posed by technological advancements. Therefore, the argument continues, soft law in the form of self-regulation by the industry and experts is more rapid and flexible. These arguments, however, tend to disregard the crucial issue of the (social and political) legitimacy problems that soft forms of self-regulation typically entail, particularly when consumer protection or environmental protection are at stake. Therefore, for others, self-regulation as a soft form of regulation may be only a first and preliminary step towards an eventual hard regulation that might secure both adaptability and legitimacy.

These three items (the effectiveness-efficiency of regulation to promote innovation; its social and private benefits in the society and economy; and its adaptability and social acceptance in complex and uncertain technological contexts) constitute potential issues in an innovation system that innovation policy-makers might like to address. As mentioned above, from an empirical perspective, *they are the three important research questions when examining the effects of regulation on the innovation system.*

This chapter examines them in more detail in two core regulatory areas for the innovation system: *patent regulation* (a specific legal figure among other IPR), and *environmental protection regulation*. Both sets of regulation are quite different. The first focuses on granting individual rights in the form of appropriation of new and industrially applicable knowledge, thus generating individual incentives to invest in the production of new knowledge and its utilization. The second, environmental, regulation deals with the negative environmental externalities of innovative and existing products in different ways, sometimes by creating incentives in specific eco-friendly directions, other times by defining the limits and responsibilities of pollutants.

In this book we also deal with the use of institutional rules as an innovation policy instrument in several other chapters. Chapter 6 addresses functional public procurement as a demand-side innovation policy instrument. Public procurement is governed by laws in all countries. In some countries these laws are very detailed. In the EU, directives are issued by the European Commission and they must be translated into national laws by the Member States, as detailed in Chapter 6. Another example is Chapter 10 on public financing of early-stage innovations. Such financing is a matter of complicated relations between private and public financing of innovation processes and how it can be ensured that public financing is operating as a supplement to private financing (by means of fulfilling the additionality condition). The avoidance of duplication and crowding out of private capital requires an appropriate set of institutional rules that are addressed in Chapter 10.

9.5 Patent Regulations and Innovation

IPR are institutions (legal forms) that allow economic actors (individuals, firms, or any organization) to appropriate knowledge or other immaterial assets. Patents are one such legal form that states grant to an individual or organization. Patents are particularly important for innovators because they allow them to obtain a time-limited monopoly over the use of a specific new knowledge. Besides the old discussions on whether or not patents are natural rights, there is a widely accepted view that patents are important for innovation in the economy (Guellec and van Pottelsberghe de la Potterie, 2007).

To obtain a patent, an individual or organization has to file an application to a national patent office—or to the EU's European Patent Office—and make the case. The 'claims' is the specific section of the application where the applicant describes the knowledge for which s/he requests to obtain a patent. Patent offices are specialized regulatory agencies in charge of examining those applications and making the decision to grant (or not) a patent. Those agencies employ scientific and technical experts (patent examiners) who examine the technical nature of those applications. It can take several years between submitting an application and the actual filing (granting) of a patent.

It is worth noting that not all knowledge can be patented. Knowledge that is patentable must generally comply with three criteria: novelty (the knowledge should not have been patented before/not publicly available), 'inventive step' or non-obviousness (the knowledge should not be common sense in the particular field it relates to), and the knowledge must have an industrial applicability. Naturally, these conditions are partly different for each patent regulation, but most national patent regulations follow these three criteria, which are anchored in economic theory (Encaoua et al., 2006).

Over the past two decades there has been a series of public debates about the limits of patentability, or the limits of the subject matter amenable to be patented. This refers specifically to the debates about whether biotech discoveries/inventions and whether software can be patentable. The source of the debates have to do with the three criteria mentioned above, as some authors argue that the clear-cut lines between discovery (not patentable) and invention (patentable) is in reality blurred, and many discoveries are actually being patented (Nelson, 2004). Likewise, other debates revolve around the ethical limits of patenting, particularly in the biotech sector. And yet other debates are around the negative effects of patenting vis-à-vis other more open types of IPR, such as software that is already protected by copyright. The limits of patentability is a topic that remains open to discussion along the rapid changes of patent systems worldwide over the past few years (Borrás and Kahin, 2009).

Due to national jurisdictions, patents are nationally based rights.[1] The rapid globalization of economic and innovative activities has, since the 1990s, put considerable pressure on national patent systems, which has brought forward a rapid internationalization of IPR regimes. This has taken place in different dimensions, and in formal and informal forms. One of the most significant formalized ones is the TRIPS Agreement in the 1990s, signed under the auspices of the World Trade Organization, which linked the issues of IPR to trade policy arrangements (Borrás and Ougaard, 2001).

Likewise, there has been rapidly growing collaboration across the largest patent offices worldwide, particularly the US Patent and Trademark Office, the European Patent Office, and the Japan Patent Office. The role of the World Intellectual Property Organisation, a United Nations organization focusing on IPR in the developing world, has also gained considerable saliency in recent years. Yet the tension between national rights and efforts to create a coherent framework for the exercise of these in the international context is still there, particularly among developed and developing countries, due to their different economic interests in intellectual property.

The economic rationale behind the regulation of patents is that patents stimulate innovation by granting time-limited monopoly powers to patent owners in order to let them exploit new knowledge. This gives patent owners advantages in the market, as no one else is allowed to use that knowledge without the explicit permission (usually with licence payments) of the patent owner. The background of this economic rationale is the non-rival and non-excludable nature of knowledge (which can be easily copied), naturally resulting in new knowledge being rapidly copied by competitors. The nature of knowledge is a powerful disincentive for private investments in knowledge creation, because no economic actor would like to see his or her investment in creating new knowledge to be rapidly copied by competitors. Patents allow patent owners to exploit the new knowledge in exclusivity, thereby stimulating further private investment in knowledge creation. Besides, patents are disclosing knowledge because the claims are publicly available. This is also positive for the economy, because it contributes to transparency about the knowledge frontier.

Over the past decade there has been rapid growth in patenting activity. However, this rapid growth has not been even across countries. Figure 9.1 shows the number of Patent Cooperation Treaty patent applications per million inhabitants during the period 2000–9 in the top 20 most

---

[1] The formal agreement in December 2012 among twenty-five of the twenty-eight EU Member States for the creation of the Unitary Patent will grant the same patent rights across these countries. At the time of writing this book, the Unitary Patent system is not yet operative. All other patent rights in the world are based on national-only jurisdiction.

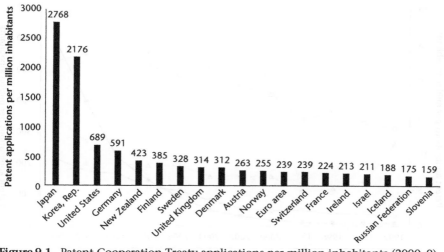

Figure 9.1. Patent Cooperation Treaty applications per million inhabitants (2000–9), top 20 innovative economies
Source: World Bank Data, 2016

innovative economies in the world (according to the Global Innovation Index). As can be seen, Japan and South Korea are the countries with the highest number of patents per inhabitant, with more than 2,000 patents, followed by the USA and Germany with around 600 each. Looking now at Figure 9.2 on the evolution of Patent Cooperation Treaty patent applications, cross-national differences can also be seen in the BRICS countries (Brazil, Russia, India, China, and South Africa). These countries' economies grew rapidly in the period 2000–10 (Fagerberg and Godinho, 2005). Yet the number of patents tends to oscillate through time and across countries (Godinho and Ferreira, 2012). As Figure 9.2 shows, China and Russia have respectively 580 and 170 patents per inhabitant in 2014 (figures following the secondary axis). For their part, Brazil, India, and South Africa (figures following the primary axis) have oscillated more during the period and in 2014 had around 22, 10, and 15 patents per inhabitant, respectively. Hence, differences across countries are very substantial, but in general the number of patents per inhabitant grew during the periods in the figures.

Returning to the theoretical issues mentioned above, the extent to which patent regulations are *actually* stimulating innovation performance in an economy is an empirical question (Rockett, 2010). Several scholars have approached the topic, with mixed results. Similar to the positive findings of Blind above, other authors have found a positive relationship between IPR and economic growth (Eicher and García-Peñalosa, 2008). However, many caveats apply. Firstly, the positive relationship is only present in countries

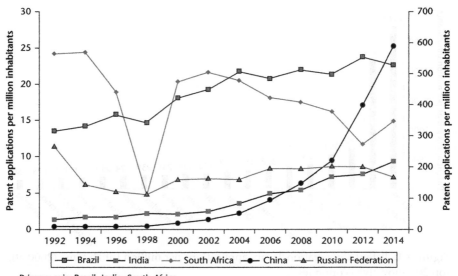

Primary axis: Brazil, India, South Africa
Secondaary axis: China, Russian Federation

Figure 9.2. Evolution of Patent Cooperation Treaty applications per million inhabitants (1992–2014), BRICS countries
Source: World Bank Data

where there are high-quality legal and judicial institutions (rule of law, transparent judicial system, low levels of corruption, etc.; Eicher and García-Peñalosa, 2008). Secondly, and very importantly, IPR and particularly patents have very different impacts in different economies and different industrial sectors (Guellec and van Pottelsberghe de la Potterie, 2007). For this reason, there is no strong evidence showing that stronger protection of IPR would invariably increase innovation performance in an economy (Encaoua et al., 2006).

Economic evidence has shown that the specific features of patent regulation affect the appropriation and exploitation of knowledge in the economy (for a review see Encaoua et al., 2006; Rigby and Ramlogan, 2012). Yet, hard regulations are embedded in a larger set of institutions that include informal interactions. Particularly relevant in this regard is the finding of Lerner in his study of changes in patent applications in sixty nations as a result of changes in national IPR regulations over 150 years (Lerner, 2009). His findings are negative, meaning that strengthened patent regulation has not generated the expected results in the number of patent applications. Partly complementing these findings, Furukawa shows that there is an inverted U-relationship between strong IPR and innovation (Furukawa, 2010). There might be many reasons for these findings, among them, the time-lag issues between regulatory change, patent applications, and innovation outcomes; as well as differences between developed and developing countries; or differences across firm size. Particularly important is the differences across industrial sectors, as some pro-patenting sectors like pharma or biotech are more dependent on patents to secure their business model than, for example, the software engineering sector.

The question about the effectiveness of (strong) patent regulations in terms of stimulating innovation must also be linked to questions related to the costs of obtaining and enforcing patents (efficiency questions). Patent applicants must pay for the application of the patent, and once obtained, they must also pay an annual renewal fee to the patent office (the state). For this reason, patent owners might decide to drop the renewal of a patent some years after they obtained it if it turns out that the patent has not lived up to their initial expectations. It is in fact quite expensive for patent owners to keep a portfolio of patents. In the EU, the debate about costs has been particularly intense, as the costs of translation and of conducting patent litigation cases in different EU country legal systems have traditionally been very high. Reducing those costs has been one of the reasons for the recent efforts to create an EU single 'unitary patent' (Borrás and Kahin, 2009). Furthermore, there is also a cost of defending patents in any legal patent system. This is particularly problematic for SMEs, particularly when there is a litigation case from large companies. This has led to some policy-related discussions about creating accessible and cost-effective forms of 'insurance' for SMEs that could help them defend their patents in these costly litigations.

The second empirical question about patent regulation and the innovation system has to do with the balance between the individual benefits of patent ownership and the overall social benefits that this might generate. There are several interlinked issues related to this question, but perhaps the most exciting has to do with the hypothesis of the 'anti-commons' problem. This is a problem where knowledge, which advances largely in a cumulative way based on previous knowledge, becomes gradually (time-limited) private property reducing the free flow of scientific knowledge and ultimately of scientific advance and innovation.

The debate about the anti-commons is related to several general matters. One is the surge in the number of patents over the last two decades, which might pose difficulties to navigate, particularly for SMEs (Guellec and van Pottelsberghe de la Potterie, 2007). The second has to do with the strength of patent regulations and the judicial aspects of enforcing them (Bessen and Meurer, 2008), which might reduce the 'knowledge pool' available to everyone in an economy (Stiglitz, 2014). Thirdly, the anti-commons has been related to the growth of academic patenting, particularly in Anglo-Saxon universities, a phenomenon that started in the early 1980s with the

Bayh-Dole Act in the USA allowing universities to own the knowledge produced by their employees (Grimaldi et al., 2011). And last but not least, the anti-commons problem has been related to behavioural issues in the predatory practices of patent owners like trolls, blocking or sleeping patents (Torrisi et al., 2016).

The Bayh-Dole Act represented a major shift in the way in which USA research universities had traditionally transferred their knowledge and technology (Feldmann and Breznitz, 2009). In a similar vein, in the early 2000s, most European countries abolished the traditional 'professor privilege'[2] by which professors were entitled to own directly the result of their knowledge. Denmark and Finland did so, but Sweden is the exception that remains (Lissoni et al., 2009). Abolishing that meant it was no longer the professor who personally owned this knowledge, but his/her employer—the university. Little is known yet if the trends towards university patent ownership (Geuna and Rossi, 2011) might represent a reduction in the free accessibility of knowledge (Sampat, 2006), however, some evidence tends to indicate that the overall effect of the anti-commons might be more modest than hitherto assumed (Murray and Stern, 2007).

Patent regulations have been changing in quite substantial ways over recent decades. This has to do not only with the international trends mentioned above with formal treaties and informal collaborations between patent agencies, but also with new views and expectations about the role of patents in the economy and in society. Patents are no longer the turf of technical experts or legal attorneys in ivory towers, but the subject of heated social and political debates about what is just, fair, and ethical, as well as what is economically best. Time and again, there has been a tendency to see the effectiveness of a patent system to be diametrically opposed to its social legitimacy, as if policymakers were confronted with an unsolvable dilemma. This is far from the case in the day-to-day implementation of regulatory decisions and in the political considerations on major changes in the regulatory framework, because the effectiveness of a patent regulatory framework largely depends on the way in which its stakeholders perceive it to be legitimate, valid, and worthwhile (Borrás, 2006).

Two of the most salient examples of the adaptability of patent regulatory frameworks are the US changes introduced by the America Invents Act and the EU creation of the Unitary Patent, both in the 2010s. It is naturally too early to see how these major substantive, administrative, and procedural changes will affect these innovation systems. In any case, they were the outcome of extensive political debates not only among the traditional stakeholders of this

---

[2] Called 'university teachers' exception' in Swedish.

regulatory area (large and small firms, patent attorneys, inventors, etc.), but new stakeholders from civil society organizations interested in the ultimate societal impact of this key regulatory area. The effectiveness of the changes will not only have to do with the way in which the new rules and procedures work as expected, but also how far they are able to engage particular forms of socio-economic behaviour that materialize the expected outcomes of the new framework. In other words, how socially legitimate they are.

9.6 Environmental Regulations and Innovation

Environmental regulations are normally designed to reduce the negative externalities for the environment, hence they are aimed at protecting the natural environment. Innovation might be an outcome of this because environmental regulation, among other things, encourages (by different means) firms and individuals to develop and use innovative eco-friendly solutions. This might in turn generate innovation dynamics in the economy.

However, the extent to which environmental regulations foster innovation is a difficult question to answer in detail for several reasons. Firstly, this might be so because the causal relationship between regulation and innovation might not be direct, but most likely indirect. Many complex factors, not least wider socio-economic and technical factors (based on important technical and sectoral differences) may intervene in different ways. Secondly, there might be a considerable time lag between changes or creation of a new regulation and its possible effects on innovation, as it takes time to develop and diffuse innovations. And thirdly, environmental regulations rarely operate in isolation. Many environmental regulations operate in complex interactions with other regulations (at different levels: regional, national, international, supranational; or regulations of complementary/close sectors) and with other policy instruments of a non-regulatory nature (i.e. economic instruments or voluntary instruments). This interaction with other regulations and other types of policy instrument makes the link between regulation and innovation complex, and therefore it is more accurate to talk about regulatory frameworks' (rather than individual regulations') effect on innovation.

There is currently extensive literature that deals with different aspects of the innovation effects of environmental regulations. This literature has focused on various dimensions of the three questions mentioned in Section 9.5 (on patent regulation).

Regarding the first two questions, since the mid-1990s there has been a lively debate among economists about the extent to which (harder) environmental regulations hinder or enable economic competitiveness and the innovativeness of an economy (Porter and Van der Linde, 1995; Jaffe et al., 1995; Jaffe and Palmer, 1997). These studies have provided theoretical as well as empirical evidence that assumptions regarding the costs of environmental regulations for the competitiveness and innovativeness of firms and of the economy at large are not sustained. More recently, this has been analysed in a more encompassing manner showing that the relations between regulation and economic performance vary across sectors (Stefan and Paul, 2008).

More recently, analytical efforts have expanded into several directions. One such direction looks at the real effects of regulations in contrast to the expected effects that policy-makers had in mind when they designed the regulation (Mazzanti and Zoboli, 2006; Walz et al., 2011). These studies point towards the effects of different policy instruments (and their mixes) in attaining public goals, underlining the importance of looking at the effects of environmental regulations together with other policy instruments (Borrás and Edquist, 2013b; see also Chapter 11 in this book).

Other studies look exclusively at regulatory frameworks' effect on innovation, but instead of looking only at environmental regulations they take all possible forms of regulation that might have had an effect. This puts forward a series of methodological challenges mentioned above. Therefore, many recent efforts have been made in developing assessment methodologies, particularly in an *ex-ante* manner to 'screen' the impact of regulation on innovation performance in specific sectors like water management or raw materials (Peter et al., 2013).

Environmental regulation aims at inducing changes that have a positive impact on the environment. Therefore, when asking about the impact of this regulation on innovation it is important to acknowledge that it is not only a matter of the economic-competitiveness type of innovation but also social change. That is, changes to the way in which society organizes itself and is able to modify behaviour and actions in a way that brings forward solutions to grand challenges like environmental sustainability by means of using existing resources (not always economic resources).

The credibility of environmental regulation and the trust that its enforcement generates in society is paramount here. This normally cannot be achieved solely by a command-and-control involvement of the state through sanctioning and punishment, but a more cooperative mode based on inter-organizational relations and networks that bring forward complementary or alternative forms of collaboration of a non-coercive nature. For this reason, there is a growing literature on collaborative governance in environmental protection (Bäckstrand et al., 2010). The introduction of technological innovations and their wider diffusion in society and economy are largely related to the societal acceptance of these by citizens and consumers at large.

9.7 Conclusions: General Criteria for Designing Innovation Policy

Following the extensive economic literature on institutions, this chapter sees regulation as a particular form of institution that sets the rules for innovators by means of the enforcement of legally binding laws or by means of voluntary non-coercive agreements and standards. Whether hard or soft, regulations must fulfil the generic role of institutions, namely, reducing uncertainty, managing conflict and cooperation, and providing incentives. Institutions are the 'rules of the game' that partly define an innovation system. But regulations are also innovation policy instruments, through which a state or government sets up goals and defines courses of public action fostering innovation. For this reason, regulations have a double nature: they are constitutive elements of the innovation system as rules of the game, and some of them are at the same time specific innovation policy instruments. Questions related to the extent to which regulation enhances innovation or not have been debated in the literature, with mixed results.

Section 9.6 identified three possible problems associated with regulations' relation to innovation. This constitutes a good starting point to identify some general guidelines and criteria from the perspective of innovation policy. Innovation policy aims invariably at promoting and fostering the levels of innovative activity in the economy and society. This requires 'rules of the game' to define the interactions between socio-economic actors in the social process that is innovation. For this reason, when designing innovation policy it is important to take into account the three general problems mentioned.

Following from this, the first guiding criterion for innovation policy in terms of regulation is to be effective and efficient when promoting some specific rights and imposing obligations and restrictions so that it generates incentives and promotes innovation. This might sound obvious, but it requires that policy-makers do not assume *ex-ante* that their expectations when passing or amending a law will be automatically fulfilled. The effects on innovation might be somehow unpredictable if social agents do not behave the way in which it was expected. There might be some intentions of policy-makers and regulators that 'get lost in translation' from the plenary rooms of national parliaments to the everyday life of innovators.

The second guiding criterion when designing innovation policy is the need for regulations to reach overall positive social benefits. Likewise, it requires that policy-makers ensure there is a balance between the costs and benefits of regulation, particularly from the perspective of the general interest and the wider social benefit of regulation for the entire economy and society. Determining this requires a careful regulatory impact assessment on an *ex-ante* (before the law is passed or reformed) and *ex-post* manner (sometime after the law has been enforced, to determine its overall social outcomes).

Last, but not least, regulations need to be adaptive and change through time, as circumstances and new advances in knowledge might require. This is particularly important in innovation-related areas like the ones mentioned above, as innovations advance very rapidly.

10

Public Financing of Early-Stage Innovations

10.1 Introduction

Financing innovation is one of the most crucial preconditions for developing commercially successful products and processes (innovations), and to facilitate their diffusion in the innovation system. It is one of the most important activities in innovation systems (see Box 2.2). Resources for financing innovations come primarily from private actors and in different ways: from internal sources within innovating firms themselves (own capital investments) or from external sources in the private capital markets (stock exchanges, private venture capital (VC) firms, banks or individual 'business angels', among others).

In many countries, public agencies provide finance, for instance, for early-stage innovations, or public actors influence private actors to provide capital for financing innovations in early stages of their development. We will only address those kinds of policy instruments that are directly related to the adoption and transformation of knowledge into new products (and processes) through commercialization and diffusion.

Hence, we will not deal with private funding of innovations in any detail here, as this is a book about innovation policy (which is public action through public policy instruments). However, we will make considerable effort to discuss in which situations private funding is not available and why not. The reason is that such unavailability of private capital means that public involvement is justified. It is a matter of identifying the border between when public intervention is motivated and when it is not. Should there be more or less public intervention, i.e. should the border be moved? This is a crucial policy issue. Another important policy issue is to discuss the characteristics of public financing of innovations. Do they have unintended consequences? Should their characteristics be changed? This is also an important policy issue.

Section 10.2 addresses the rationales for public intervention in innovation funding, i.e. the situations in which policy should be pursued. It builds on the criteria developed in Section 3.5, and provides the basis of the rest of this chapter by specifying what *policy problems* are and how *additionality* can be secured in the financing area. Section 10.3 identifies the diversity of *policy instruments* for financing innovations that governments have developed over the past decades, and it proposes a typology of instruments. These are the instruments with which the policy problems can be mitigated.

To put some flesh on the conceptual bones, we present a description of a case of provision of risk capital by the Swedish state in Section 10.4. It describes a situation where unintended consequences of the policy pursued led to the non-fulfilment of the additionality condition. It also describes how this mistake has begun to be resolved after discussions in the Swedish National Innovation Council (NIC), followed by a government investigation, a bill from the government to the parliament, a decision there and the subsequent creation of a new public risk capital company, wholly owned by the Swedish state, with a capital of 5 billion Swedish crowns (€0.55 billion). This sub-section addresses innovation policy (re)design in action. The chapter concludes with a number of important issues about public financing of innovations.

10.2 Rationales for Public Intervention in Innovation Funding

In this section, we will address rationales or reasons for public intervention in financing to enhance innovation. The key questions are why and when (in what situations) there should be public intervention in the field of innovation financing. It is a matter of identifying *policy problems* in innovation systems that cannot be solved by private actors. See Section 3.5 for the two conditions that must be fulfilled for there to be a reason for public policy intervention in a market economy: a *policy problem* must exist and public organizations must also have the *ability* to solve or mitigate the policy problem. The identification of policy problems in a detailed manner should precede the definition of policy objectives, which should in turn be clear and explicit (see Section 3.6). In this chapter we will apply these conditions to the area of risk capital funding. The question of *additionality* (or market supplementation) is closely related to the identification of policy problems.

In the following sub-sections we characterize some important obstacles and barriers that might require public intervention with regard to financing.

10.2.1 *Lack (or Low Levels) of Private Funding in Early Stages*

Most analysts tend to agree that financing of the transformation of knowledge into innovation in early stages is not taken care of completely or sufficiently by private actors in the system of innovation (Edquist, 2002; del-Palacio et al.,

2012; Hall and Lerner, 2010). Public seed funding is motivated when there are no, or not enough, private initiatives financing early stages of innovative firms. In such cases business angels or other private capital are simply not available or prepared to take the role of financing.

If private capital is available, there is, of course, no need for public funding. This means that a public funding agency should not compete with private organizations in an 'unfair' manner on the basis of public taxpayers' money. On the contrary, the public agency should add something to the innovation system that no other actor is able to contribute, i.e. 'additionality' should be at hand. This means that private initiatives should not be duplicated or crowded out by public actors (see Section 10.5.1 on lack of additionality; Leleux and Surlemont, 2003).

As indicated above, public funds (financial subsidies) should only come forward in situations where private firms and private capital markets do not offer financing. But the question is not only in which situations the public sector should finance innovation activities, but also how. When we know in which situations public funding should be made available, we can analyse which public policy instruments there should be—and we will do so in Section 10.3. In this chapter we, again, concentrate on policy, i.e. on what public organizations should or should not do. In this case the issue is public financing of commercialization of innovations.

The expression 'the valley of death' is extensively used in the context of financing of early-stage innovative firms. The expression is meant to capture the idea that there might be a lack of (or insufficient level of private) financial resources in the early phases of the transformation of knowledge into innovations, particularly in the early growing stages of firm development. Small innovative firms may successfully have passed the very first phase of investment (the very early phase financed by friends, family, business angels, and small public grants), but find themselves without sufficient capital willing to invest in their early growing stage: in the development of their product and in their scaling up of early market-access phases.

For large incumbent firms that introduce new products to achieve renewal or diversification, financing can be based on accumulated profits or based on an easier access to capital markets. Similarly, incremental improvements in products and processes made by established firms are more easily financed from private sources than radical innovations pursued by new start-up firms.

The availability of private funding for innovation is often not a problem in later stages in the innovation process, when the product is developed and when it is quite clear that there is a market demand for it—or when there are even sales and profits. Hence there is normally no need for public funding in these later stages. However, in the very early stages of the innovation process, when the innovation is just a vague idea or possibility, and when the product has not yet successfully entered the market, i.e. when the process still has to pass the valley of death, then private funding might not be available because of uncertainty or large risks—often related to uncertainties about the potential market. This calls for public seed funding.

There are large differences between the various sectors of production. The development of pharmaceuticals and biotech products may take fifteen years and may be very capital consuming for long periods—before any income from sales can materialize. The investments in developing the product may be very large and it may take a long time to get it accepted by the authorizing agencies. On the other hand, products in the ICT sector and in service sectors (e.g. Facebook) need much less capital in the early stages and the time to market is much shorter. These differences between sectors are important.

10.2.2 *High Uncertainty and Risk*

The main reason for providing public seed funding for innovation is the uncertainty and large risks for firms making such investments. This means that the expected probability of failure of innovative firms is much larger than in economic activities in general. It is therefore crucial that public seed investments are sometimes made by public agencies in early-stage innovations (if there are no private alternatives). In countries where there is a large portfolio of public seed capital investments, failures may be balanced by successes. But it is also important that it is accepted by the general public, policy-makers, and politicians that a considerable proportion of seed capital investments will fail. It is simply a part of the game.

In addition to leading to a large number of failures, early-stage seed funding may also lead to a few cases where the pay-off is extremely large. However, these cases cannot be predicted as the processes are evolutionary ones. Neither can it be established *ex ante* if the average pay-off on the public seed capital investments will be large, small—or negative. That the resulting average pay-off may be negative has to be accepted. This is actually why private organizations are not, in the first place, willing to provide the financing—and why public intervention is therefore called for. Accordingly, a *subsidy* must be included as part of public seed capital investments—otherwise it would not be policy.

Accepting the possibility that the average pay-off may be negative means that policy-motivated seed-funding organizations *cannot be organized as firms listed on stock exchanges*. This has been tried. The dismantling of the so-called wage-earner funds in Sweden in the 1990s led to the creation of two holding companies, Atle and Bure. They were equipped with 6.5 billion Swedish crowns. They were later listed on the Swedish stock exchange. Thereafter the remaining state ownership in the two companies was transferred to Industrifonden (another public VC company). The consequence was that the two firms stopped investing in high-risk early-stage seed funding, the purpose for which they were initially created. They transformed themselves into ordinary investment firms, trying to maximize profits—which meant investing mainly in much more mature projects (Isaksson, 1999; Riksrevisionen, 2014).

When Atle and Bure were listed on the stock exchange, they started to duplicate, compete with—and probably crowd out—what private funders could potentially do, i.e. the additionality condition was then no longer fulfilled. There is simply no need for such public funding. If Atle and Bure had remained true seed-funding agencies (while still listed on the stock exchange), and if the average pay-off thereby would have been negative, they would have been risking bankruptcy and their stock market value would have fallen drastically. This is another way of saying that public seed funding should include an element of subsidies, which cannot be handled as a pure market activity, as it is policy.

Here, we should recall that our definition of an holistic public innovation policy is that it includes all actions by public organizations that influence or may influence innovation processes (see Section 3.2). Hence, we must be aware of the appropriate border between private and public action, i.e. where there should be public intervention to solve 'problems' that private organizations cannot solve. Where should the line of demarcation be? This is discussed in the case of financing in this chapter.

10.2.3 If Policy Is the Problem

However, public policy includes those actions that are already carried out by public organizations. What are the characteristics or features of these actions? And should they be changed? If the characteristics are not appropriate, why and how should they be changed? In other words, the solutions attempted by public policy might not be working well or be the best ones. They might be unable to address the obstacles and barriers, or they may even be aggravating the situation. Policies might have unintended negative consequences. If so, policies must, of course, be changed.

Accordingly, a crucial issue to address is when there is actually a need for public financing of innovation and when there is not. This requires detailed analysis and is not easy to find out in an exact manner. It is a matter of establishing that private innovation financing is not available in certain situations where there is a need for such financing in the innovation system, i.e. that we do have cases of additionality.[1] This is all the more complicated

---

[1] See Section 3.5 for a general discussion of additionality in the context of criteria for when public intervention is motivated and in which situations it is not.

since the potential availability of private financing is changing along the process of the development of the innovation. Risks often decrease over time when the process of developing the innovation proceeds and the availability of private risk capital thereby increases.

If the development of the product or the company goes well, then private investors will show up and want to take over. After all, the idea is that the public intervention should gradually make itself not needed over time—when the valley of death has been passed. A tricky question to answer is then exactly when, i.e. in which situations, the public funding should be withdrawn. Hence, issues to discuss in this context are when and how this should happen and who should benefit from successes—a question that we will return to later in this chapter.

The opposite possibility is that the need for public funding 'never' disappears. This begs the question of for how long, and in what quantities, the public funding should continue before it is accepted that the attempt to finance the innovation has failed. In other words, when should public funding be terminated if private investors do not take over (Munari and Toschi, 2015; Nightingale et al., 2009)? This is a difficult issue to analyse because it can be argued that some kinds of innovation need more public support for longer time periods than others. There are important differences across production sectors in this respect.

The risk and the stakes are high when dealing with public funding and public regulatory frameworks. One feature of policy instruments for financing in this context is patient public capital supporting the financing of new innovative firms. The state has a particular capacity for patient capital (long-term investments; Mazzucato, 2013), which should not be focusing only on large firms with radical innovation potential; but most particularly for nurturing new innovation-led entrepreneurial activities. Likewise policies must be ready to take new directions and redirect their modus operandi, should the need for their intervention cease or reduce significantly. In other words, policy-makers should devise policy instruments (and policy mixes) that can be easily transformed if the innovation system context so requires (Wilson, 2015).

Last but not least, the organizational capacity of civil servants is paramount in this complex policy area (Borrás, 2011). Policy-makers' organizational capacity refers to their knowledge and expertise competences in this field, as well as their analytical abilities and organizational resources. 'Governments should invest in appropriate methodologies which can accurately measure investment trends in the early stage venture capital market, and specifically angel investment activity' (Mason, 2009).

10.3 Innovation Policy Instruments for Financing Innovations

In general terms, the policy instruments promoting the availability of capital in the innovation system can be classified in the following way: *Equity programmes, tax incentives, investment regulations, business angels' networks, second-tier stock markets, and other related policy instruments*—see Box 10.1. This section presents them one by one, explaining their approaches and organization, providing real-life examples of countries that have used them with more or less success. Section 10.4 will present a case study of a radical change in the provision of public risk capital in a situation when additionality was not at hand. Thereafter follows a section with conclusions.

Box 10.1 POLICY INSTRUMENTS RELATED TO PUBLIC FUNDING OF INNOVATIONS

Equity programmes

- Direct public support: public agency investing public funds into firms.
- Hybrid funds: public and private co-investment requirements, where investment decisions are typically made by a private agency.
- Funding private venture capital industry: public support to the private venture capital industry through buy-out options, loans, or loan guarantees.

Tax incentives

- Tax deductions on investments in new or small firms.
- Tax deductions on the gains from venture capital investments.
- Tax exemptions or deductions to newly created firms.

Investment regulations

- Legal conditions for institutional investors' (pension funds, insurance companies, and banks) investments in venture capital activities.
- Bankruptcy regulations.
- Legal conditions and procedures for foreign capital investments.

Business angel networks

- Economic support to creation and activities of business angel networks (or clubs).

Second-tier stock markets

- Regulatory and funding support for the creation of second-tier stock markets.

Other related instruments

- Public loans and loan guarantees to entrepreneurial and small innovative firms.

Source: own elaboration

10.3.1 *Equity Programmes*

Starting with the first group of instruments, *equity programmes* are programmes created by governments using public funds to stimulate, in different ways, the availability of equity in the economy (particularly for new innovative firms), addressing some of these firms' financial needs by using public funds in a proactive way. Yet, these programmes can take many different forms. Firstly, they can grant direct support to entrepreneurial firms through a public agency which makes investment decisions and takes an ownership role in the new company. This is the case of Vækstfonden in Denmark, or several regional funds in Sweden, investing directly in different early phases of new firms with different levels of success (Edquist, 1999; Isaksson, 1999).

Hybrid funds are the second type of equity support instrument, also called fund-in-fund. These are similar to the previous ones, but with an important difference, namely, that the investment decision is taken by a private organization which manages the public funds, usually with the requirement that the public investment in new companies is done with the co-investment of private funds.

A third, and the most common approach, is *public support to the private VC industry*.[2] This is often done through public buy-out options, low interest rate loans, and/or public loan guarantees to private VC firms. This is the case of Finland's Industriinvestering AB (FII) created in the mid-1990s; the SBIC programme in the USA since the mid-1950s, or the newly created EU Jeremie programme and its implementation in Lithuania (Snieska and Venckuviene, 2011). In a literature review of evaluations of these types of equity programme, Ramlogan and Rigby found that most impact assessments focused on employment or turnover, but not on the innovation outcomes (Ramlogan and Rigby, 2012a).

In a few developed countries, these three types of 'equity programme' instruments co-exist with each other in a rather proactive role of public funding into VC activities. As we will see in Section 10.5, the performance of these policy instruments might not be as smooth or unproblematic as it might seem at first glance.

10.3.2 *Tax Incentives*

Tax incentives are a second important group of policy instrument. Here, governments use different forms of tax incentives in order to stimulate private

---

[2] VC is a sub-set of risk capital and private equity. It refers to investments of a proprietary nature (like risk capital) and in unlisted companies (like private equity), but it is a sub-set of those, because VC usually entails *an active ownership role from the investor* controlling or advising the development of the company (usually in the board of directors), and it is usually done on a time-limited basis (with a clear exit strategy from the investor).

investment in VC activities, and the VC industry in general. These policy instruments are essentially of three kinds, namely, *tax deductions on investments in new or small firms*; *tax deductions on the gains from VC investments*; and *tax exemptions or deductions directly to newly created firms*. One interesting example of the first type of policy instrument is the Canadian Labour Sponsored Venture Capital Funds. This is a tax relief provision for individual investors (usually involving small amounts) in investment funds that are partly owned and/or managed by trade unions. The tax incentives come with some important requirements, like an obligation to invest for a minimum of eight years, and a maximum amount of investment.

Regarding the second type of tax incentive (targeting the gains from investments in VC activities), relevant research results tend to indicate generally that 'reductions in the corporate capital gains tax rate increase the share of both high-tech and early stage investment' (Da Rin et al., 2006, p. 1699). Regarding the third type, deductions on the taxation levels of newly created firms, a recent USA–Sweden comparison shows that the heavier tax burden on entrepreneur firms in Sweden partly explains the less developed VC market in Sweden (Lerner and Tåg, 2013). Besides, lower personal income taxation in the USA more generally has an important effect on levels of entrepreneurship more generally (Cullen and Gordon, 2007). Having seen these three types of tax-related policy instrument, it is worth noting the general perception among experts that 'Tax incentives can be a "blunt" instrument (i.e. difficult to target effectively); so careful design, monitoring, evaluation and adjustment is necessary to ensure that the intended results are achieved' (Wilson, 2015, p. 16).

10.3.3 *Investment Regulations*

The third large group of policy instruments for private VC is what we can call *investment regulations*. This refers to regulatory frameworks with direct impact on the incentives and dynamics of the financial system, particularly on the availability of private VC. These include, for example, the regulatory *legal* conditions for the *institutional investors' (pension funds, insurance companies and banks) investments in venture capital activities* (traditionally the three largest private organizational investors). Another type of relevant regulatory framework is *bankrupcy regulations*, particularly the way in which it deals with assets.

Finally, another type of investment regulation that is directly relevant for private VC is the *legal conditions and procedures for foreign capital investments* in the country. A cross-country analysis has shown that the regulatory framework has paramount importance for the supply and demand of private VC. In particular, the analysis found that 'favourable fiscal and legal environments facilitate the establishment of venture capital and private equity funds and increase the supply of capital. Similarly, liberal bankruptcy laws stimulate entrepreneurialism and increase the demand for venture capital' (Armour and Cumming, 2006, p. 630).

10.3.4 *Support to Business Angel Networks*

Public support to business angel networks (BANs) is the fourth group of policy instruments addressing the private VC sector. As mentioned before, business angels are individual investors, and therefore on the informal side of the VC industry. BANs, also called 'clubs', are networks that match individual investors (angels) with entrepreneurs. They bring together a wide variety of entrepreneurship projects with many different possible investors. Hence, the larger the network the larger the investment opportunities for entrepreneurs. For that reason, the networks/clubs tend to reduce transaction costs for both investors and entrepreneurs. BANs might emerge spontaneously, like Le Club XXI Siècle targeting immigrant entrepreneurs; or the Harvard Business School Alumni Angels Association, targeting the alumni community; or they might emerge with the active support of public policies, like the programme launched by CORFO in 2006 by the Chilean government (Romaní et al., 2013); or the Danish DBAN national programme created in 2000 (Lindgaard Christensen, 2011). Indeed, policies supporting BANs have developed since the late 1990s, particularly in Europe.

These policy instruments usually have multiple goals. Beyond the goal of matching investors with entrepreneurs, they also promote the professionalization of the informal investors, their training, and sharing experiences; they increase their visibility in view of attracting more informal investments of this kind; and last but not least, they aim at reducing asymmetric information problems, increasing the transparency in this market.

However, the success of these publicly supported BANs is mixed. Several factors might be at play, some of which are internal to the policy instrument, like the strategic management decisions about which BANs and areas to support; the 'correct patience' of the public funding committed to the BANs—avoiding both premature and delayed exit strategies; or most importantly, the extent to which public actors supporting BANs act in combination with other actors.

This latter point is quite relevant. In emerging economies or low-income economies, the 'investment readiness' of entrepreneurs might be a problem. This refers to the demand side of the private VC market, where the entrepreneurial culture and competences are not strong. Hence, BANs are most effective if combined with other types of instruments seeking to strengthen the entrepreneurial systems and upgrade the competences of entrepreneurs vis-à-vis potential investors (Romaní et al., 2013). There is a natural complementarity between policy instruments towards BANs and 'accelerators' that provide short-term training and networking for entrepreneurs (Cohen and Hochberg, 2014).

10.3.5 *Second-Tier Stock Markets*

A fifth group of policy instruments are focusing on *second-tier stock markets* (or new stock markets). Two of the most successful and iconic second-tier stock markets were NASDAQ (USA) and AIM (UK). Since the mid-1990s, several European countries developed a series of initiatives towards the creation of similar types of market at the national level, most of them with limited success (Posner, 2005). The pan-European second-tier market NASDAQ was created during that time, conceived as an electronic securities exchange headquartered in Brussels. Largely equivalent to the original NASDAQ in the USA, the creation of the pan-European NASDAQ was closely linked to initiatives by the European Commission, aiming at creating a pan-European market rather than national markets (Weber and Posner, 2000). However, it was short-lived due to the dot.com bubble. Euro-NM, a parallel initiative by a network of the Amsterdam, Brussels, Frankfurt, Paris, and Milan stock exchanges around the same time, was also short-lived (Revest and Sapio, 2010).

Figure 10.1 shows the number of listed companies at AIM and the aggregated levels of their market value during the period 1995–2015. When examining the figure, it is worth noting the exponential growth of this particular second-tier market in the first period from 1995 to 2007, and the strength of the financial crisis when it hit this particular market. The last three years in the figure (2013 to 2015) show relatively stable levels of the number of firms as well as their market value. Perhaps this might indicate slightly less volatility than before.

10.3.6 *Other Instruments*

'*Other instruments*' refers to programmes and public initiatives directed towards financing small firms. Examples of this are public loans, loan guarantees, and grants that governments give to small innovative firms as seed capital. Strictly speaking, these are not VC because they do not entail ownership, and because there is a direct requirement for firms to repay their loans. Most OECD countries have at least one such scheme (Wilson, 2015, p. 15).

Taken together, these instruments have different effects. Some of them aim at conveying direct support to innovation dynamics in small firms, in a way that public funds or incentives generate innovation dynamics themselves. Other instruments seek more indirect effects, focusing on fostering the supply side of private VC availability, with the goal of stimulating private investors in

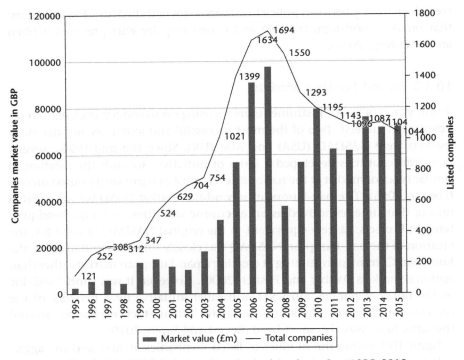

Figure 10.1. AIM's listed companies and market value, 1995–2015
Source: AIM Statistics Archive, 2016

the field. Hence, this is directed more towards fostering a crowding-in effect, of attracting available private resources into the innovation system.

The different structures of a financial sector shape different forms of private funding for innovative activities. The Anglo-Saxon countries, with 'outsider-dominated financial systems', have higher stock market capitalization than other countries such as Germany (with an 'insider-dominated' financial system; Hirsch-Kreinsen, 2011). This can be exemplified by the success of second-tier stock markets in the USA and UK in contrast with the less successful story of these new markets in Europe. Likewise, the policy mix and the institutional features of the economy have been key factors for understanding the differences of private VC markets in Sweden and the USA (Lerner and Tåg, 2013).

10.4 Provision of Risk Capital by the Swedish State: An Example

Since financing is absolutely crucial for developing commercially successful innovations and facilitating their diffusion, it is an important activity in all innovation systems (see Box 2.2). Resources for the financing of innovations come primarily from *private* actors, for example, from innovating firms themselves (internal capital markets), stock exchanges, private VC funds and firms, banks, or individuals (business angels). However, in many countries—including the USA—*public* agencies also provide such financing, in the form of seed capital, for instance, in support of innovation activities. Such public activity may certainly be—and is—an important element of an (holistic) innovation policy.

In Section 3.5 we discussed the *identification of policy problems* and *additionality*. We returned to some of this in the beginning of Section 10.2 in this chapter. We will now illustrate this discussion with the case of public financing of early-stage innovation in Sweden.

10.4.1 *Lack of Additionality in Swedish Public Risk Capital Provision*

A crucial issue to address in the innovation policy design phase is whether or not there is an actual need for public financing of innovation. This requires detailed analysis, but such analysis is indeed possible and necessary to undertake (see further below in this section). It is a matter of establishing whether or not private innovation financing is available in certain situations where funding is needed for the efficient operation of the innovation system, i.e. that we do have cases of policy problems and additionality. This is all the more complicated as the potential availability of private financing changes as the innovation processes develop. Risks often decrease over time and the availability of private risk capital may increase or decrease.

Risk capital provision was discussed at the first meeting of the Swedish NIC in February 2015.[3] Previous analyses were undertaken by Svensson (2011) and Riksrevisionen (2014). According to Svensson, only 16 per cent of all public support for equity investment in Sweden targeted the seed stage. He also points out that the seed stage presents the lowest risk of the government crowding out private funding. At the same time, the bylaws of many public funding agencies (agencies in which the state is represented on the boards) require the funding actors not to make losses or to make a profit (rather than providing a subsidy). As a consequence, the funding agencies seek projects

---

[3] The NIC was created by Swedish prime minister Stefan Löfven in February 2015. It is personally chaired by the prime minister, which is unusual for similar councils in other countries. Another atypical characteristic of the Swedish NIC is that it has a dominant and wide focus on innovation policy, i.e. when public organizations influence innovation processes. In other countries, such councils focus predominantly on science and/or research policy and treat innovation policy, if at all, as an 'appendix' to research. The development and operation of NIC is described in detail in Edquist 2018a and 2018b.

with low risk, i.e. projects in mature or late stages of innovation development (OECD, 2012b; Svensson, 2011).

Accordingly, 84 per cent of the public funding was allocated to firms that had already made sales and were in a period of expansion. This means that public capital was crowding out private capital, and that public funds were used for purposes that were not motivated. This is extremely problematic from an additionality point of view. In principle it was, according to Svensson, only the Innovation Bridge that invested in companies that did not yet have any sales. According to Svensson, this funding organization is closest to the theoretical ideal and should therefore get larger resources, and ALMI should drop the requirement that the companies in which they invest must have documented demand. If so, it could fill a gap in the financing available in early, start-up phases (Svensson, 2011, p. 33).[4]

The analysis by Svensson summarized above was followed by a report on public provision of risk capital by the highest-level Swedish auditor, Riksrevisionen, an agency created and governed by parliament (Riksrevisionen, 2014). This report presented similar conclusions, as summarized below.

According to Riksrevisionen, the rate of return (profit) requirement on public funding of private companies should be at a 'low level'. The public financing should also be 'market-supplementing', i.e. it should increase the supply of risk capital in early phases where private actors do not invest to a sufficient degree. Further, the public funding should contribute to facilitating private actors to offer financing from their side. At the same time, public risk capital funding organizations should operate 'under the same conditions' as private organizations. 'Through risk sharing on equal terms with private actors', the combined supply of financing can be oriented towards early investment phases (Riksrevisionen, 2014, p. 43). The state also decided that some of the public organizations should allocate their capital only to certain geographical areas or sectors of production. This applied to 60 per cent of the resources. As we will see, these state objectives, here expressed by Riksrevisionen, are highly contradictory (p. 29).

Riksrevisionen (2014, p. 48) divided investments into the following stages: 'seed', 'start-up', 'early growth', 'expansion', and 'mature'. The 'seed' and 'start-up' phases can be considered to be early phases. The agency found that private financers were mainly active in the three later phases, with the mature phase dominating. According to Riksrevisionen, the 'seed' phase received only 0.2 per cent of public capital in 2011–12, which must be considered to be extremely low. About 28 per cent of the public capital went to the 'start-up' phase. Hence, more than 70 per cent of the funds went to the

---

[4] The Innovation Bridge and ALMI were merged in 2013—see below.

more mature phases (Riksrevisionen 2014, p. 49). Clearly, the additionality condition was, according to the numbers presented by Riksrevisionen, fulfilled only for a small part of the public investments.

Two of the six public risk capital providers had direct profit demands that were the same as that on the private market (Riksrevisionen, 2014, p. 43). For ALMI regional investments, the requirement is that investments are made on a commercial basis. This is considered to be fulfilled if specific investments are made 'simultaneous to and with at least as large an investment as private commercial organizations and on the same conditions' (Riksrevisionen, 2014, p. 32). This is obviously incompatible with having a 'low-level' profit requirement.

In addition, all of the public risk capital providers except one were required to collaborate in financing projects with private organizations and on the same conditions (Riksrevisionen, 2014, p. 44). To operate 'on the same conditions' means, in practice, that public organizations should have a market-based rate of return for specific investments.

It should be mentioned here that it seems to be clear that the actual returns are much lower in early stages than in later ones. For example, the Sixth Pension Fund (*Sjätte AP-fonden*) shows a return of plus 16.3 per cent for their investments in 'mature companies' and a return of minus 14.2 per cent for their investments in 'expansion companies' (Riksrevisionen, 2014, p. 46).[5]

The idea or rationale behind the demand on public risk capital organizations to collaborate in financing projects together with private organizations is that this should contribute to moving the frontier for the risk level of projects that private organizations invest in (Riksrevisionen, 2014, pp. 46–7). Since investments in early phases are riskier and less profitable (on average), private investors can be expected to demand higher returns on these investments than on investments in later stages. If public risk capital providers should collaborate with and act under the same conditions as private ones, this implies that the expected return demand of public risk capital providers must also be higher in early stages.

Occasionally—or perhaps exceptionally—it happens, however, that such risky investments become extremely profitable. In such cases, there are examples of public seed capital organizations that have not demanded 'their' share of the resulting super-profits. One example is the Linköping Technology Bridging Foundation in Sweden, evaluated in Edquist (1999).

---

[5] It should also be mentioned that this fund is not included in the category of 'public risk capital providers' here. The main reason is that the vast majority of its investment goes to 'mature companies'. It is rather a part of the pension system than of public efforts to provide risk capital. (Riksrevisionen, 2014, p. 48).

We saw, however, that practically no public funds were invested as seed capital and only limited amounts have been invested in later, but still early, stages. Therefore, it seems natural to conclude that the demand for collaboration on equal terms between public and private risk capital providers has instead made public organizations invest in mature stages, where private organizations are spontaneously active. Hence, the demands with regard to the rate of return of the public risk capital providers are also incompatible with the objective that public risk capital providers be market-supplementing. Joint investments with private organizations on equal terms do not function as a mechanism to make private risk capital providers invest in earlier phases. It seems to have the opposite result. This goes completely against the explicit objective of the policy—which is to make private investors invest in earlier stages through co-investments on equal terms.

The Swedish example illustrates a 'spontaneous' tendency not uncommon in public innovation funding organizations to drift into funding of later stages in the innovation process—instead of concentrating on the early stages, where innovating companies do not yet have any sales. The provision of such funding actually competes with private providers of capital, which may partly be explained by the fact that public risk capital providers often make co-investments with private investors—spontaneously or demanded by the statutes.

The co-investment strategy drew public capital to late stages rather than attracting private capital to early stages. In fact, the additionality condition was, according to research by both Svensson (2011) and Riksrevisionen (2014), not fulfilled in most of the cases where public risk capital was invested. This was a policy mistake and it recreated a policy problem.

Such mistakes may be caused by incorrect analyses of policy problems, a lack of additionality, public capital crowding out private capital, that profit demands on public capital providers drives public capital to later stages in the development of innovations, lobbyism, etc. These issues will be addressed in Section 10.5.

In this context, it is important that 'policy problems' may include consequences of previous policies, i.e. actions already carried out by public organizations (see Section 3.5). If the characteristics of these actions are not appropriate, it is a policy (re)design issue to determine why and how they should be changed.

In other words, public organizations need to figure out whether the solutions attempted by public policy might not be working well or are the best ones. It could be that the public organization is unable to solve the policy problems, or may even be aggravating them. If so, policies must, of course, be changed. Innovation policy design thus includes the identification of what should be achieved by new policies, but also how existing policies should be changed. An important part of innovation policy is to evaluate previous policies and, sometimes, correct policy mistakes.

10.4.2 How to Achieve Public/Private Co-investments in Early Stages

Public risk capital providers may invest by themselves in early stages of the development of firms and innovations. Because of uncertainty and high risk, such investment will probably yield a low—or even negative—average rate of return. This could mitigate a 'policy problem' in the system of innovation, since private investors are reluctant to invest in these early stages. This solution can be used, in principle.

However, a common argument against it is that public administrators might not have the skill to handle such investments in a satisfactory manner. Again, in principle, the public organization might recruit administrators that are as skilled as the ones working in private risk capital firms. A complicating factor is also that the probable low or negative rates of return on seed stage investment would make the public funds decrease in size and even disappear over time. The motivation for accepting that would be to see it in a perspective of social costs and benefits, not private ones. A social cost-benefit analysis should be carried out.

If the available public risk capital funds are themselves invested in mature companies, there would be no additionality and no market-supplementing effect, but competition with private risk capitalists and even crowding out. Such public investments are not motivated from a policy point of view and should not be pursued.

As we have seen, individual private investors will avoid early-stage investment. This is actually why we, in the first place, have a policy problem with regard to early-stage investment in the innovation system. The trick is to draw these resources to seed stages.

Public investors should, in principle, accept less favourable conditions (lower returns or higher risks) than private investors, if they invest individually and simultaneously in early stages of the same company. However, in such a case, the company where the investments are made would prefer only the public investor. The private one would be crowded out, as the public competition based on taxpayers' money would be unfair. The public organizations would appropriate the best projects, leaving sub-optimal ones to be financed by private risk capital providers (Leleux and Surlemon, 2003, p. 99). Hence, co-investments between public and private risk capital providers on the same conditions in early stages do not work, if additionality should characterize public risk capital provision. The trick is to create an incentive also for private investors to invest in early stages in some way.

There are two ways to increase the supply of risk capital to early stages:

1 The public risk capital organization invests by itself in early-stage phases and with a subsidy in the form of a low or negative return. This option would mean that public and private risk capital providers are not active in the same arenas.

2 A private and a public risk capital provider creates a consortium before any investments in companies are made. One characteristic of the consortium should be that a subsidy is involved in the form of an agreement that the public unit gets a lower rate of return or accepts a higher risk than the private unit. A second characteristic would be that the consortium uses this subsidy to invest all the resources of the consortium in early stages. This would draw private money to seed stages. The subsidy to private investors would be motivated by the social benefit that the state is expecting from it. The necessary size of that subsidy remains to be estimated.

10.4.3 *The Transformation of Swedish Public Risk Capital Provision*

On the basis of the two studies referred to above, Charles Edquist stressed at the first meeting of the Swedish NIC in February 2015 that the additionality condition was not being fulfilled by Swedish state risk capital provision practices. The minister of enterprise and innovation Mikael Damberg and his state secretary raised the same issue in a later presentation at the same meeting. Throughout the subsequent discussion in the NIC, there was general agreement that additionality (market supplementation) should be assured, and that one way of achieving that would be to attach a subsidy to the provision of public risk capital.

The minister appointed an investigation immediately after that meeting and the investigator (Hans Rystad) presented his results on 15 June 2015 (Statens Offentliga Utredningar, 2015, p. 64). The issue was again discussed at the NIC meeting in September 2015. The investigation findings were then sent out for comments and review and the ministry, on this basis, presented a bill to parliament in March 2016 (Regeringens Proposition, 2015, p. 110). This bill was debated in parliament in June 2016 and a decision was taken on 1 July 2016. It accepted the proposals in the bill (thus indicating unity among the political parties).

Very soon after the decision in parliament (on 1 July 2016), the minister created a new public risk capital company called Saminvest AB, wholly owned by the Swedish state, with a capital of 5 billion Swedish crowns (€0.55 billion). At that point Saminvest AB was staffed and consolidated. The management of

Saminvest AB was called to the NIC meeting on 28 August 2017 to report. The company had, at that time, not yet started investment operations.

To complete this process (from discussion in the NIC to a decision in parliament and the creation of the public risk capital company) in eighteen months is enormously fast for a state system. We believe that the fact that it was discussed in NIC, created and chaired by the prime minister, was a partial explanation for this speed of action. The mere existence of the NIC gave innovation policy issues a much higher status and degree of importance within the government itself and within the public agencies, i.e. in the entire state apparatus. The swiftness of the action by the ministry of enterprise and innovation is the second explanation for the rapidity. However, the process of starting actual investment operations at the administrative level has been slower.

At the NIC meeting in August 2017, the management of Saminvest AB reported that it would invest in privately managed risk capital funds, so-called fund-in-fund investments with co-investments on equal terms with private risk capital providers. They also informed the NIC that no subsidy was planned.[6] At the same time, it was reported that the Saminvest funds should primarily be invested where private capital is not available to a sufficient degree, i.e. where there is greatest need for market-supplementing investments.

In the light of the previous discussion in this chapter, this is contradictory. That such co-investments may be problematic and may draw public capital to late stages was indicated by the history of public risk capital provision recounted above. It is a problem that should be solved by the directives to Saminvest from the government and then be dealt with by the board and management of Saminvest AB. In addition, it should regularly be followed up by the government. All these problems are related to the fulfilment of the additionality condition.

On 18 January 2018, it was reported in the Swedish press that Saminvest had made its first investment of 160 million Swedish crowns in a Norwegian life science fund called Hadean Ventures Capital I AB. The chief executive officer of Saminvest AB (Peder Hasslev) was also reported to have said that Saminvest AB wants a yield on their investment 'adjusted to conditions on the market', i.e. the same as for private investors. (Karlsson, 2018). In December 2017, Saminvest AB also invested 180 million Swedish crowns in Spintop Investment Partners III AB and 100 million Swedish crowns in Luminar Ventures AB. Hence 440 million crowns have been offered. However, only

---

[6] The return on invested capital shall be 'positive', according to the instructions from the owner, i.e. the state. According to the Annual Report of Saminvest AB for the second half of 2016, the 'long term value development shall be the best possible'.

21 million crowns had been paid out by March 31, 2018 (Saminvest, 2017, 2018).

The written objectives of Saminvest AB are fairly clear: to pursue financing activities geared towards innovative firms with a high potential for growth by means of indirect investments that are market-supplementing.[7] This would mean a major reallocation from late to early stages. However, the practice of Saminvest AB may not deliver on this and the policy mistakes in earlier periods mentioned above may be repeated if adjustments are not made. The question to the board and daily leadership of Saminvest AB is: how will they ensure that the investments go to early stages? Obviously, it has not happened in earlier attempts with similar policies. The trick is to get private investors to invest where they do not want to. Will Saminvest AB make its investments conditional in some sense to achieve the additionality objective by the allocation of resources to early stages?

With regard to the design of policy in this field, substantial progress has been made. When it comes to actual practical implementation of the policy, it is less clear. Hence, problems may still remain in the operation of Swedish public risk capital provision. One is that additionality has to be more clearly identified by means of analysis of the need for public risk capital in various sectors and, as discussed above, in different stages of development. Another problem is the need to determine the appropriate size of the subsidy attached to the public risk capital provision.[8] A third problem is whether explicit requirements on investments in early stages should be associated with the subsidy. Several billion crowns remain to be invested.

10.5 Public Financing of Innovations: Some Conclusions

As indicated, funding of innovation processes is a very important activity in all innovation systems. The largest part of this financing is provided by private organizations, but sometimes there are reasons for public organizations to supply risk funding to facilitate and enhance innovation processes. Such public funding is most often called for in the early stages of the commercialization process. When such funding is provided it is done by means of different innovation policy instruments. In this chapter, we have discussed when and how this is pursued—and how it should be done.

---

[7] http://www.saminvest.se/

[8] As stressed above, a substantial subsidy may be required to make early stage investment viable—as the risk of failure in these stages is the basis for the need for public risk capital in the first place.

In Chapter 3, an holistic innovation policy was defined as a policy that seeks to include all public actions that influence or may influence innovation processes. This contrasts with partial innovation policy, which focuses on only one or a few of the many determinants of innovation processes. A special case of partial policy is a linear view which focuses mainly or strongly on research as a determinant of innovation. The linear view dominates policy in most countries. To the extent that, for example, public risk capital provision (or functional innovation procurement) is given a larger role in innovation policy, the policy gradually moves in the direction of a more holistic innovation policy (see Box 2.2).

We will briefly comment on six issues directly related to public seed funding. These are:

1 lack of additionality;
2 profit demands and relations between public and private funding;
3 how to supply risk capital to early-stage investment;
4 acceptance of public losses and need for cashing in profits;
5 the relation between public R&D funding and public seed funding; and
6 public seed capital becoming 'intelligent'.

10.5.1 *Lack of Additionality*

The public risk capital providers should be 'market-supplementing' and should not compete with or crowd out private suppliers. In other words, there must be additionality for public seed funding to be motivated. We discussed this issue at a general level in Section 10.2. In Section 10.4, we used the case of Sweden to achieve specificity in the discussion. However, the issues that we address below are of a general nature and are highly relevant for the innovation systems in most countries.

As indicated by the Swedish example, there seems to be a 'spontaneous' tendency for public innovation funding organizations to drift into funding in later stages in the innovation process—instead of concentrating on the early stages. The additionality condition was shown not to be fulfilled for most of the public risk capital invested in Sweden. The provision of such funding competes with private providers of capital. It is not a matter of innovation policy, but of private firms exposed to public competition by using taxpayers' money.

In order to secure that the additionality condition is fulfilled, a detailed analysis is necessary. It has to be found out whether private funding is available in certain situations where there is a need for such financing in the innovation system. This is complicated as the potential availability of private financing changes along the process of innovation. Risks often decrease over time, when the process of developing the innovation proceeds and the availability of private risk capital increases. This means that the analysis has to be renewed constantly. It is complicated to pursue such analyses. The description of the Swedish case in Section 10.4 shows, however, that it is possible.

10.5.2 Profit Demands and Relations between Public and Private Funding

On the basis of the Swedish case described and analysed in Section 10.4, we discussed the issues of profit demands by public (and private) risk capital providers and whether they should collaborate or not.

The conclusion is that the requirement of collaboration on equal terms is not working if additionality shall characterize public risk capital provision, i.e. public funds shall be allocated to early stages. Instead, the return requirement for public risk capital organizations should be lower than for private investors, or they should accept a higher risk for the same rate of return. However, if the public organizations demand lower rates of return than private organizations, then they will crowd out private investors and it may lead to unfair competition—if they are active in the same arenas. One way to solve this is to ensure that private and public risk capital providers are not active in the same arenas, to the largest extent possible. Thereby, we return to the additionality requirement. Public risk capital providers should be active where private actors are not. This is mainly the seed capital stage. Thus, public risk capital providers should concentrate on the seed capital stage. But often they do not.

There should be no demands that public risk capital-providing organizations should co-finance with private actors on the same terms. This implies that the demands with regard to rates of return must be allowed to be lower than for private financing organizations.

The criteria for public risk capital investment should be (a) that the firms cannot raise such capital from private organizations, and (b) that the public funding agency judges that the idea or innovation developed by a firm is likely to have a large potential, i.e. it is important for the innovation system (see Section 3.5). When the public 'policy' organizations become subject to a 'commercial' profit requirement or objective, this actually operates as a mechanism behind the 'spontaneous' tendency that pushes the public funding agencies to drift into late-stage funding and into competition with private organizations. Thereby they 'lose' their policy function. The mechanism behind this is, at least partly, not 'spontaneous' but the result of a flawed policy design. More specifically, it is a matter of an 'institution' (or rule) created by the state not being appropriate.

The issues discussed in this sub-section are highly relevant for the final design and operation of the new public risk company Saminvest AB in Sweden. As indicated above, problems may remain in the operation of Swedish public risk capital provision. One problem is that the need for public risk capital (additionality) has to be more clearly identified by means of analysis—in terms of sectors and stages of development. Another is that the size of the subsidy that is involved in the public risk capital provision has to be defined. A substantial subsidy may be required to make early-stage investment viable—as the risk of failure in these stages is the basis for the need for public risk capital in the first place.

Judging from the reporting by the leadership of Saminvest AB at the Swedish NIC meeting in August 2017, there is no subsidy at all planned—which we consider quite problematic. The fund-in-fund solution chosen means co-investment between Saminvest AB and private capital providers. That such co-investment may be problematic and may draw public capital to late stages was indicated by the history of public risk capital provision told above. (The additionality condition was not fulfilled.) It is a problem that should be solved by the directives to Saminvest from the government and then dealt with by the board and management of Saminvest AB. In addition, it should be regularly followed up by the government. All these problems are related to the additionality condition.

10.5.3 *How to Supply Risk Capital to Early-Stage Investment*

Two ways to increase the supply of risk capital for early seed stage innovations follow:

1 Public risk capital organizations invest by themselves in early stages, and a subsidy in the form of low expected average returns is involved.

2 Private and public risk capital providers create consortia before any investments in companies are made. One characteristic of the consortia should be that subsidies are involved in the form of an agreement that the public unit gets a lower rate of return or accepts a higher risk than the private unit. A second characteristic of the consortia is that this subsidy is used to invest all the resources of the consortium in early stages. In this way public money would draw private money to seed stages. The subsidy to private investors should be motivated by the social benefit that the state is expecting from it.

Neither of these mechanisms has been extensively used to secure access to risk capital for early-stage investment in Sweden.

10.5.4 *Acceptance of Public Losses and Need for Cashing in Profits*

The reasons why private organizations are unwilling or unable to provide risk capital in seed phases are uncertainty and large risks. If public funders step in, then the risk of failure is very high. This has to be accepted by the administrators of the public VC organizations, other public financing bodies and their boards, the ministries above them, politicians, and the general public.

A high risk of failure is simply in the cards. It is the role of public funders to absorb these risks—and failures. Losses must be acceptable and accepted for public risk capital provision to constitute an innovation policy instrument. This means that the performance of public risk capital organizations should not be measured in terms of private costs and benefits, but in terms of social ones.

Occasionally—or perhaps exceptionally—it happens, however, that such risky investments become extremely profitable. In such cases, there are examples of public seed capital organizations that have not demanded 'their' share of the resulting super-profits. If super-profits are the result of public risk capital provision in some exceptional cases, it is important that the public investing agencies capture these profits to the largest extent possible—and that they use these resources for investment in other (risky) projects.

10.5.5 *The Relation between Public R&D Funding and Public Seed Funding*

When an innovation is based on publicly funded research, the metaphor of the 'valley of death' may imply that there are public resources available for R&D to a larger extent than there are resources available for the commercialization of the research results. The borderline between publicly funded R&D and the commercialization of results is, however, not a precise and distinct one. In addition, publicly provided R&D funding is normally not made available for profit, and no paying back of the funds is required. This is true even if there are no results at all, i.e. the R&D funding is a complete failure, but also if there are very good R&D results. Hence, public R&D funding is not at all dependent on or subject to 'commercial conditions'.

In some countries, it is even so that the researchers pursuing publicly funded research individually own the results of that research.[9] The different characteristics of R&D funding and seed funding for innovation may be a reason not to let the activity spin off too early from the 'safe' realm of R&D (perhaps in a university) to the 'tough' world of commercialization of research

---

[9] This is the so-called teacher's exception in patent law in some countries. It was addressed in Chapter 9 on institutions.

results. To delay the spin-off is actually an alternative to providing public funds for absorbing uncertainty and large risks in the early phases of commercialization of knowledge into innovation. This alternative should be used to a larger extent.

10.5.6 *Public Seed Capital Should Become 'Intelligent'*

Knowledge and funding can also be related in a different way. The success or failure of a process of commercialization is, of course, partly a result of how 'intelligently' the funds are used. Innovators or innovating organizations do not only need financial resources, they also need knowledge of different kinds. It may be technical knowledge directly related to the field of the attempted innovation, be it electronics, biosensors, or computer games. Sometimes the innovators themselves hold such knowledge, sometimes it has to be supplemented with technical knowledge from related fields.

It may also be a question of knowledge about how innovation processes are most efficiently pursued, i.e. it may be knowledge about patents, leadership, organization, or marketing. The latter kind of knowledge may be held by business angels or private or public innovation financing organizations with previous experience of commercialization of innovations. The financial capital needs to be supplemented by knowledge to turn the combination into 'intelligent' seed capital. Devising 'intelligent' financing instruments should be a target for policy-makers. The capacity of civil servants is paramount in this complex and specific policy area. Expert competence and capacity of policy-makers and politicians is crucial for the quality of the policy (Lerner, 2002).

11

The Choice of Innovation Policy Instruments

11.1 Introduction

The purpose of this chapter is to discuss the different types of instruments of innovation policy, to examine how governments and public agencies in different countries and different times have used these instruments differently, to explore the political nature of instrument choice and design (and associated issues), and to elaborate a set of criteria for the selection and design of the instruments in relation to the formulation of holistic innovation policy. In the everyday process of policy-making, many instruments are developed as a mere continuation of existing schemes, or with poor consideration of the expected effects. This chapter argues that innovation policy instruments must be designed carefully and on the basis of an innovation system perspective, so that they are combined into mixes that address the complex problems of the innovation processes. These mixes are often called 'policy mixes', though we prefer the term 'instrument mix'. The wide combination of instruments in such mixes is what makes innovation policy 'holistic'.

As discussed extensively in Chapter 3 of this book, problems to be mitigated by innovation policy must be identified and specified according to the activities in innovation systems. A policy problem is a low performance of (a part of) the innovation system, i.e. a 'problem' exists if the objectives in terms of innovation intensity are not achieved by private organizations. Once there is a general picture of the causes of the policy problems or deficiencies in the innovation system, then it is possible to identify, on this basis, the policy instruments that might mitigate the problems and, most importantly, how to combine them into a specific mix. If the main cause of a problem is a lack of adequate levels of research, then the different policy instruments for enhancing levels of R&D should be in focus. If there is a lack of demand for certain product innovations, then a specific set of demand-side instruments such as public procurement-enhancing innovation and specific regulations can be used in an instrument mix that targets that specific problem. Chapter 3 discusses these matters in detail.

The current chapter examines the role of policy instruments in the context of holistic innovation policy, the types of policy instrument in innovation policy, the problem-oriented nature that defines the criteria for that design and choice, and the politics involved in that. With this purpose in mind, Section 11.2 begins by discussing the importance of the choice of policy instruments in relation to the innovation system, and the three dimensions that are crucial in this regard. Section 11.3 identifies the different types of policy instruments and defines their combination in instrument mixes, in a general sense. Section 11.4 takes this up into the concrete area of interest, namely innovation policy, providing examples and discussing the specificities of policy instrumentation in an innovation system context. Section 11.5 examines in detail how these policy instruments are related to the problems that might relate to the different activities of the innovation system, with the understanding that policy instruments should mitigate the problems that might occur in the system. Section 11.6 acknowledges that the choice and design of policy instruments in innovation policy is a political process, and the importance of legitimacy of instruments in the context of advanced democratic societies. Lastly, Section 11.7 summarizes the arguments, emphasizing the problem-mitigation approach to the choice and design of instruments, conducted from an holistic innovation policy perspective.

11.2 The Choice of Instruments

The choice of instruments is a crucial decision regarding the formulation of an innovation policy. This entails three important dimensions: *firstly*, a primary selection of the specific instruments most suitable among the wide range of different possible instruments; *secondly*, the concrete design and/or 'customization' of the instruments for the context in which they are supposed to operate; and *thirdly*, the design of an instrument mix, or set of different and complementary policy instruments, to address the problems identified.

Sometimes innovation policy instruments are chosen on an individual basis, meaning on the basis of their individual features alone. Typically, however, innovation policy instruments are combined in mixes, implying that the selection of instruments takes into consideration their complementary or balancing effects on solving or mitigating the problems in the innovation system.[1] When selecting instruments it is important to look at both the

---

[1] The general relations between innovation policy objectives (ultimate and direct), policy problems, additionality, and policy instruments are addressed in Chapter 3.

individual features and the complementary/synergetic/contrasting effects of an instrument in relation to the specific mix in which it is embedded. A crucial dimension when discussing the choice of innovation policy instruments is the issue of adapting the instrument to the specific problems in the innovation system and, most importantly, to the specific features of the administrative structures. In other words, policy instruments need a certain degree of adaptation and 'customization' to the changing needs of the system and the capacities of public administrators.

One example that demonstrates the importance of policy instrument choice is the comparison of the innovation policies in the ICT sectors of Israel, Taiwan, and Ireland during the 1990s, as shown in Box 11.1.

As shown in Section 3.5, direct innovation policy objectives must be formulated in terms of identifying problems in the innovation system, and there is no way to identify 'problems' specifically enough on the basis of theory alone. Problems can be identified by means of different sources of policy learning, namely measurements, comparative studies, and different analyses. The most widely used, and perhaps the most influential, sources of information for the identification of problems in the innovation system are innovation indicators. Innovation indicators typically come from a variety of regular statistical series at national and international levels (the most famous set of international indicators is based on the 'Oslo manual' and the OECD's

---

Box 11.1 INNOVATION POLICIES IN THE ICT SECTORS OF ISRAEL, TAIWAN, AND IRELAND

In developing their ICT industries, Israel, Taiwan, and Ireland focused on similar goals for economic growth and socio-economic development in their innovation policies. They targeted specific goals for developing physical infrastructures, invested in education, deregulated markets (notably telecommunications), and paid special attention to SMEs, as the engines of ICT sector economic growth. But, as Breznitz indicates:

> their micro-level policies—those at the level of industry and firm—were distinctively different. Since the late 1960s Ireland has focused mainly on foreign direct investment-based industrial development policies. Israel has focused on inducing industrial R&D activities through public grants, with project ideas originating solely in private industry. In Taiwan the ruling party relied on such public research agencies as the Industrial Technology Research Institute (ITRI) to lead R&D efforts and diffuse the results throughout private industry.   (Breznitz, 2007, p. 7)

That is, even when the three states had very similar goals, the trajectories that they followed and the instruments they chose for the implementation of those goals were different. This is what Breznitz calls 'micro-level policies' and what we call 'policy instrument choice'. The three countries made different instrument choices for virtually the same overall goals, and all three have been rather successful in achieving them.

---

own statistical series), or from innovation surveys, which provide more detailed and firm-based data about innovation trends. An additional database is the Community Innovation Survey.[2]

A second source of learning for innovation policy-making is foresight exercises, which produce expert-based analyses of future trends in specific technological fields (Weber et al., 2009). Likewise, benchmarks and best cases have also become popular in the advanced economies over the past few years (Makkonen and van der Have, 2013). Benchmarks are typically quantitative targets set up by public agencies and governments on the basis of best case performance.

Another example of an extensively used source of learning in innovation policy-making these days is independent expert assessments of innovation policy performance (e.g. ex-post and ex-ante evaluation of policies), which is typically done in national contexts. More recently, however, international organizations have increasingly engaged in external assessment of national policies, particularly the OECD (with very influential assessment exercises of innovation policies for higher education systems) and the EU (where EU27 Member States exchange best practice and peer review each other).

11.3 Types of Policy Instrument and Instrument Mixes

A conventional and general *definition of public policy instruments* is 'a set of techniques by which governmental authorities wield their power in attempting to ensure support and effect (or prevent) social change' (Vedung, 1998, p. 21). This definition puts an emphasis on the purposive nature of policy instruments. Policy instruments have a purpose: namely, to induce change (or to avoid change) in a particular way, which is believed to stimulate innovation, i.e. influence the direct innovation policy objectives. The instruments may be intended to influence both the direction and speed of innovation.

The purposive nature of the instruments is to remind us that the instruments are put in place to achieve some specific goals. Obviously, the instruments of innovation policy are focused on fostering innovation. However, as mentioned in Section 11.1, innovation is rarely a goal in itself but a means to achieve broader goals, such as economic growth, increased employment, environmental protection, military capacity, or public health, to name some of the most important ultimate objectives. In other words, innovation policy instruments are intended to influence innovation processes and thereby

---

[2] That the interpretation of the many innovation-related indicators is a tricky thing is shown in Edquist and Zabala-Iturriagagoitia 2018. There it is, for example, shown that the well-known composite indicator of the Innovation Union Scoreboard is flawed.

contribute to fulfilling these ultimate political goals by means of achieving the direct objectives formulated in innovation terms.

The Vedung definition above is interesting for a second reason: it also emphasizes the effectiveness and popular support dimensions of innovation policy instruments: 'to ensure support and effect social change'. As we will see in this chapter, political support and the effectiveness of the instruments are very important aspects of innovation policy, as is the understanding that there are important differences and changing traditions in the combinations of policy instruments in innovation policy, the so-called instrument mixes. Strictly speaking, each policy instrument used by a government or public agency is unique. Instruments are typically chosen, designed, and implemented with a specific problem in mind, in a specific policy context (innovation policy in this case), at a specific point in time, and in a specific political-ideological situation.

Generally speaking, there are three main categories of instruments used in public policy: (1) regulatory instruments, (2) economic and financial instruments, and (3) soft instruments. This three-fold typology is what has popularly been identified as the 'sticks', the 'carrots', and the 'sermons' of public policy instruments (Bemelmans-Videc et al., 2003). Admittedly, the scholarly literature offers alternative classifications of policy instruments (Linder and Peters, 1998; Hood and Margetts, 2007). However, the three-fold division used here remains the most accepted in the literature on instruments and continues to be the most widely used in practical contexts (de Bruijn and Hufen, 1998; Salamon, 2002). The added value of focusing on it is two-fold. Firstly, it allows us to make sense of complexity and to navigate in an ocean of different instruments in innovation policy. Secondly, it allows us to define some useful criteria for the choice and design of instruments in the formulation phase of innovation policy (in the next sections of this chapter).

The first type, regulatory instruments, uses legal tools for the regulation of social and market interactions. The logic behind this type of instrument is the willingness of the government to define the frameworks of the interactions taking place in society and in the economy. Naturally, there are many different types, but common to them all is that these regulatory instruments (laws, rules, directives, etc.) are obligatory in nature, meaning that actors are obliged to act within some clearly defined boundaries of what is allowed and what is not. Obligatory measures are typically backed by threats of sanctions in cases of non-compliance. These sanctions can be very different in nature (fines and other economic sanctions, or temporary withdrawal of rights), depending on the content of the regulation and the definition of legal responsibility. Some authors believe that sanctioning is the most crucial property of regulatory instruments (focusing on the imposition and hierarchical side of regulation). Others see the normative authority of governments as the most important feature of these instruments (hence focusing on the normative-positive side of obligatory regulation) (Lemaire, 1998). From the point of view of innovation policy, regulatory instruments are, for example, used for the definition of market conditions for innovative products and processes, or for governing financing of innovation processes or public procurement.

Economic and financial instruments are the second type of policy instruments and provide specific pecuniary incentives (or disincentives) and support specific social and economic activities. Generally speaking, they can involve economic means in cash or kind, and they can be based on positive incentives (encouraging or promoting certain activities) or on disincentives (discouraging or restraining certain activities). Box 11.2 presents some examples of economic instruments according to these different sub-types.

As Box 11.2 shows, economic instruments are very broad in nature. In some countries there is traditionally extensive use of economic instruments providing economic means in kind, whereas in others there is wider use of economic means in cash. As we will see in Section 11.4, economic and financial instruments have been extensively used in the field of innovation policy.

Soft instruments are the third main type of policy instrument and are characterized by being voluntary and non-coercive. With soft instruments, those who are 'governed' are not subjected to obligatory measures, sanctions,

---

Box 11.2 EXAMPLES OF ECONOMIC POLICY INSTRUMENTS

Economic means in cash

POSITIVE INCENTIVES (ENCOURAGING AND PROMOTING)
Cash transfers
Cash grants
Subsidies
Reduced-interest loans
Loan guarantees

DISINCENTIVES (DISCOURAGING AND RESTRAINING)
Taxes
Charges
Fees
Customs duties
Tariffs

Economic means in kind

POSITIVE INCENTIVES
Government provision of goods and services
Private provision of goods and services under government contracts
Vouchers

Source: Vedung, 1998

---

or direct incentives or disincentives by the government or its public agencies. Instead, soft instruments provide recommendations, make normative appeals, or offer voluntary or contractual agreements. Examples of these instruments are campaigns, codes of conduct, recommendations, voluntary agreements and contractual relations, and public and private partnerships. These instruments are very diverse, but are generally based on persuasion, the mutual exchange of information among actors, and less hierarchical forms of cooperation between public and private actors.

The growing use of soft instruments is at the heart of fundamental transformations in the public administration of most countries (particularly visible in Europe and the USA). This has been termed 'governance', meaning that the extensive use of these instruments has transformed the role of the government from being a provider and regulator to being a coordinator and facilitator (Jordana and Levi-Faur, 2004b). What is important at this stage is to underline the fact that there has also been a rapid growth in the number of these types of instruments in the field of innovation policy, as we will see in Section 11.4.

11.4 Innovation Policy Instruments

The three-fold typology of policy instruments above is applicable to innovation policy (see Figure 11.1). Instruments such as intellectual property rights, environmental regulations, tax exemptions, competitive public research funding, support for technology transfer offices, soft loans for innovations in specific industries, or industrial and public-private partnerships for knowledge infrastructure are widely used in innovation policy in many countries.

Figure 11.1. Examples of policy instruments in innovation policy
Source: own elaboration

Regulatory instruments using law and binding regulations are important in the field of innovation policy, for example the regulation of intellectual property rights (in particular, but not only, patent regulations), the regulation of research and higher education organizations like universities and public research organizations (most importantly the statutory nature of the organizations, and researchers' employment regulations), competition (anti-trust) policy regulations concerning R&D and innovative activities by firms in the market, public procurement directives, bioethics and other regulations related to innovative activities, and last but not least some specific industrial sector regulations with effects on innovative activities. Regulatory instruments are 'rules of the game' for knowledge and innovation processes in innovation policy. Because regulations are obligatory, these rules of the game are formal and compulsory and constitute an important part of the institutional set-up of a system of innovation.

It is important to keep in mind that the relationship between regulatory instruments and innovation can be *direct* or *indirect*. A direct relationship refers to the situation where regulations have been designed with the explicit purpose of affecting knowledge and innovative activities. An example of this is when patent and university laws are changed in order to allow universities to own patents and to create the necessary organizational arrangements to stimulate the commercialization of knowledge (Mowery and Ziedonis, 2000).

However, regulatory instruments might sometimes be important for innovation processes in an indirect way. This is the case when the final purpose of a specific regulatory instrument is not to foster innovation but when this happens in an indirect way, as pointed out in our definition of innovation policy in Chapter 3. An example of this is when an environmental regulation forbids a specific polluting chemical substance or forces a reduction in industrial waste. This induces product innovations or process innovations because the regulation forces firms to find alternative solutions (Edquist et al., 2001a). As with the other types of instruments, regulatory instruments can have an important impact on the innovation process, due not only to the way in which these instruments are selected and designed, but also how they are implemented and enforced.

Regarding the second type of instruments (economic and financial instruments), innovation policy has traditionally made extensive use of these. This is particularly the case for instruments stimulating positive incentives in cash and in kind. One of the most widely used instruments is 'in-block' public support to research organizations, primarily public universities and public research organizations (Dutrénit, 2010). However, there are other fundamental instruments using economic incentives, for example tax incentives and support to venture and seed capital. There has been a significant trend towards selecting and designing 'market-based' or 'market-like' economic incentives in the past two decades. A case in point is the increase of schemes using competitive research funding (Lepori et al., 2007) and public seed funding.

Another significant observation at this stage is that most of the existing economic instruments largely influence the development and diffusion of innovations (products and processes) from the supply side rather than the demand side. However, scholars and policy-makers alike are starting to recognize the importance of developing instruments that influence innovation processes from the demand side. This is due to the demand side being crucial in terms of some of the most important dynamics in the innovation process (the role of users and customers in all sorts of innovation process) and to a series of fundamental pure public goods (for example clean air) with a rather weak demand side (green technologies). Instruments focusing on the demand side can help redress these specific types of weakness. One example is public procurement for innovation, addressed in Chapter 6.

'Soft instruments' are our third main category of instruments. These instruments have been increasingly used in innovation policy over the past two decades. However, it is important to keep in mind that even if their relative importance is increasing, these instruments are largely a complement to regulatory and economic instruments. Nonetheless, they might constitute important new forms and new approaches to public action in terms of innovation.

There are many different forms of soft instruments. Examples of these are:

- voluntary technical standards at the national or international level (Blind, 2004);
- codes of conduct for firms, universities, or public research organizations (for example, the code of conduct for the recruitment of researchers in Europe, advocating transparency in recruitment procedures);
- management contracts with public research organizations (an instrument defining an agreement between policy-makers and managers of these organizations, setting up the strategic goals for that public organization);
- public-private partnerships sharing costs, benefits, and risks in the provision of specific public goods (for example, in the field of knowledge infrastructure); and
- campaigns and public communication instruments (for example, diffusion of scientific knowledge by using events like 'research days' or TV documentaries).

Because innovation is a very complex phenomenon, the new soft instruments might be able to address different aspects of the innovation process and innovation system that the previous regulatory and economic instruments could not do properly. Sometimes soft instruments address 'old' issues of innovation policy, but they do so in a different way.

11.5 Innovation Policy Problems, Instrument Mixes, and National Styles

When designing innovation policy, the selection of innovation policy instruments must be done in relation to the actual policy problems identified in the innovation system. In Section 11.1, we stressed that a *policy problem* has to be identified as low performance of the innovation system, i.e. low innovation intensity for a certain category of innovations compared to the input resources. There, we also discussed various ways to identify such problems. In addition, we pointed out that it is necessary to know the main *causes* of the problems in order to be able to choose appropriate innovation policy instruments. Policy instruments must be selected, customized to the nature of the problem to be solved as well as its causes, and combined in mixes with complementary policy instruments. As we will show below, innovation policy instruments are closely related to the different activities of the innovation system. These activities were identified in detail in Chapter 2 of this book and can be seen as the determinants of the development and diffusion of innovations. Hence the 'problems' to be mitigated by innovation policy are closely related to the identification of deficiencies or bottlenecks related to these activities.

As explained in detail in Chapter 2 (Box 2.2) of this book, the ten activities of innovation systems are divided into four groups. Although the list of activities is a preliminary and hypothetical one, the important thing to stress here is that it includes many determinants in *addition* to those commonly mentioned in the literature (typically, the creation of knowledge and financing of innovation activities). The reason for stressing this is that these additional activities also influence innovation processes. Concentrating only on R&D and financing may lead—or rather, actually leads to—a linear supply-push view of the innovation process and innovation policy.[3] Efforts must be made to avoid this, if an innovation policy that looks at the whole innovation system—i.e. an holistic policy—is to be achieved. As mentioned earlier in Chapters 2 and 3 of the book, our list also includes the activities in the system that influence innovation processes from the demand side.

Another relevant issue to consider when looking at these ten different activities of the innovation system in relation to the design of innovation policy is that the innovation policy instruments might be situated at different

---

[3] R&D does *not* automatically lead to innovations, i.e. to new product and processes, and thereby to economic growth. Knowledge is not enough—it has to be transformed into innovations in order to create growth and employment. R&D is only one of the many inputs/determinants of innovation—it is not always necessary, and it is never sufficient to achieve innovation-based growth. The other nine activities are also important.

levels of government. The vertical division of powers across different levels of government affects the extent to which federal/central, regional/community, or local/municipal are in charge of designing specific policy instruments. Sometimes the division of powers is clear in the sense that these levels of government have exclusive powers, whereas other times those powers are shared. For example, support to incubators is typically shared across different levels of government but others, such as support and regulation of public research organizations, are concentrated in one level of government. Hence, it is always very important to understand the idiosyncrasies of state structures and the multilevel division of powers when studying the way in which policy instruments have been designed and developed.

When looking at the ten different activities in an innovation system, a relevant issue to analyse is the appropriate balance between *demand*-side innovation policy instruments and *supply*-side instruments, mentioned in Section 11.4. The dominance of 'science and technology' policies pursued so far has meant a too strong emphasis on supply-side instruments. We argue that there is a need for a new generation of innovation policy instruments, especially demand-side instruments, such as public procurement for innovation.

Hence, the ten activities mentioned in the paragraphs above can be related to different (several or many) kinds of innovation policy instruments. This will be done here by designing a matrix of the relations between the ten activities and various policy instruments (Table 11.1). It must be emphasized that the matrix just serves to exemplify relations between activities and instruments and certainly does not present a complete picture. As we saw in Section 11.3, there are many innovation policy instruments that can be used. The matrix shows the activities and some traditional types of instruments related to them.

As indicated in Table 11.1, it may be helpful to use the ten activities as a checklist when selecting innovation policy instruments to achieve direct policy objectives—and thereby also ultimate policy objectives. An holistic innovation policy involves all ten activities. It is performed by public organizations that use policy instruments of the kind listed in Table 11.1.

Smits and Kuhlmann (2004) argue that the formulation of innovation policy has entered into a phase in which policy instruments are becoming systemic. In their view, this is mostly visible in the area of 'cluster approach' policy instruments (Borrás and Tsagdis, 2008), because these instruments are managing interfaces, deconstructing and organizing systems, providing a platform for learning, providing strategic intelligence, and stimulating demand (Smits and Kuhlmann, 2004). Their point is that 'systemic instruments' might co-exist with traditional policy instruments of a traditional linear mode.

Table 11.1. Activities in innovation systems and types of innovation policy instrument

Types of policy instrument		Activities in the innovation system									
		Provision of R&D	Competence-building	New product markets	Articulation of quality requirements	Creating and changing organizations	Creating and changing institutions	Interactive learning	Incubation activities	Financing innovation	Consultancy services
Regulation	Intellectual property rights	X		X					X		
	Competition law	X			X		X				
	Ethical regulations	X					X				X
Economic transfer	'In-block' support of R&D	X	X	X							
	Competitive funding of R&D									X	
	Tax exemptions		X	X							
	Public procurement to enhance innovation				X	X					
Soft instruments	'In-block' support for innovation-promotion					X			X		X
	Voluntary standards		X		X	X					
	Public-private partnerships					X					
	Codes of conduct					X					

Note: the number of policy instruments is much larger—only a sample is included here for reasons of space. A full development of this matrix might include 50–100 policy instruments for the ten activities.

In our view, policy instruments should be seen in a slightly different way, in that instruments as such are not seen as systemic or not. What makes them systemic is the way in which policy instruments are combined and customized into mixes that aim at addressing the concrete problems identified in an innovation system. In other words, it is not the instruments alone that make an innovation policy systemic. It is the instrument mixes that make it systemic—if they are designed, combined, customized, and implemented in a way that addresses the complex and multidimensional nature of the causes of the problems (Mohnen and Röller, 2005).

The focus on instrument mixes (or 'policy mixes', as some prefer to call them) has received considerable attention from policy-makers over the past few years. In their review of the way in which this notion has been used, Flanagan et al. underline the complexity of policy instruments and argue that the actor and the institutional context in which instruments operate are crucial in determining their effects (Flanagan et al., 2011). Most of the recent efforts by policy-makers to deal with instrument mixes have sought to enhance levels of public and/or private R&D expenditures (Serris, 2004).[4] This is relevant, but it only reflects one specific activity in an innovation system, and it may be conducive to partial and linear innovation policies (see Sections 3.2 and 3.3 of this book).

A definition of innovation policy instrument mix is the specific combination of innovation-related policy instruments which interact explicitly or implicitly in influencing innovation intensity. It is worth pointing out here that there are no perfect models or 'optimal' policy instruments that fit all purposes. On the contrary, instrument mixes are very different and varied depending on the context for which they are designed. The very specific and unique nature of each innovation system, with its individual strengths and weaknesses, as well as concrete problems and bottlenecks, on the one hand, and the very specific national/regional traditions regarding state–market–society relations on the other, mean that any 'one-size-fits-all' attempt is irrelevant. This is to say that policy mixes are specifically designed and implemented with specific problems and causes in specific systems in mind, and they tend to follow distinct patterns of national policy styles. Innovation policy mixes are different because the innovation systems are different, the policy problems are different, and the socio-political and historical contexts of policy-making are different across countries and regions—and over time.

Having said that, however, the diversity of designs, experiences, and results of these instrument mixes might provide good sources for mutual

---

[4] In the late 2000s, the EU launched a project for monitoring and analysing the instrument mixes of EU Member States that are conducive to higher levels of R&D investments. See http://ec. europa.eu/invest-in-research/monitoring/document_en.htm.

policy-learning. While acknowledging differences and idiosyncrasies across countries, it is still possible to dissect and analyse why some instrument mixes are better than others at addressing complex problems in the innovation system.

One last issue that is important to underline here is that differences in the outcomes from instrument mixes might not necessarily be related to the nature of the selection, customization, and combination of different policy instruments, but to their actual implementation. This is to say that the way in which the instrument mixes are put into practice is as important as their design. Policy making and policy learning are, after all, largely influenced by the organizational capacity of the public administration managing and enforcing them (Borrás, 2011).

11.6 The Politics of Innovation Policy Instruments

The formulation of innovation policy invariably entails a selection—of which objectives (ultimate and direct) to emphasize, which problems to address in the policy, which policy instruments to choose, etc. By definition this selection can never be politically neutral. In other words, policy objectives and policy instruments are not neutral devices. This is as true for any type of policy as it is for innovation policy. Having said that, it is important to consider the legitimacy of the instruments, namely the degree of popular and political endorsement of different innovation policy instruments.

In advanced representative democratic systems, political parties tend to disagree on the type of policy instruments to be chosen and how they should be designed. The same applies to the citizens and the public in general, as their implicit or explicit endorsement of policy instruments is crucial for the sustainability and effectiveness of the policy instrument. An instrument that is no longer legitimate runs the risk of being popularly contested or falling into disuse, hence making its correct implementation difficult. This might compromise its effectiveness and expected results. If contestation is fierce and widespread, governments and their public agencies might reconsider the specific contents of an instrument, or even the entire instrument as such.

Popular contestation and party politics can be particularly strong in the formulation phase of innovation policy, which is our main focus of interest here. One of the most recent examples of strong popular contestation and adversarial party politics during the phase of formulation of innovation policy instruments is the proposal for a directive on software patents in the EU. Box 11.3 summarizes the example.

In the case in Box 11.3, the contending parties disagreed about the regulation as such (software being subject to patentability), but agreed on the overall

---

Box 11.3 LEGITIMACY OF AN INSTRUMENT: THE CASE OF SOFTWARE
PATENTS IN THE EU

The question of what can be patented and what cannot is a fundamental issue in innovation systems because patent laws are highly relevant regulatory policy instruments providing incentives to inventors. The limits of patentability have always been a topic for consideration among patent experts (patent attorneys, patent examiners, and highly specialized legal practitioners), but very rarely is it an issue that interests the general public. However, in the late 1990s and early 2000s, this became one of the most hotly disputed issues in EU politics. The proposal of the European Commission for harmonizing national regulations allowing software to be patentable across the EU was strongly opposed by the open source community, and strongly supported by big industry. The proposal for a directive 'on the patentability of computer-implemented inventions' more popularly known as software patents, put forward by the Commission in 2002, was rejected by broad opposition in the European Parliament. Leifeld and Haunss suggest that this was basically due to the fact that the coalition against software patents managed to set the tone of the debate in spite of their very limited economic resources (Leifeld and Haunss, 2012). From the perspective that interests us here, namely the politics of innovation policy instruments, this case indicates that the legitimacy of an instrument is strongly related to the legitimacy and popular acceptance of the instrument and, in the case of patents, strongly related to their effectiveness (Borrás, 2006).

goal of fostering innovation and thereby economic growth. There are, however, cases where contention regarding an instrument reflects fundamental differences of opinion on alternative goals. This is particularly the case of regulations related to life sciences. The rapid advance of life sciences has occasionally put the goals of economic growth and industrial exploitation in direct conflict with some pre-established fundamental values and ethical norms in society (bioethics). Examples of politically sensitive instruments are the regulations regarding the use of embryonic stem cells in research, the authorization of genetically modified organisms in the environment and the market, and the limits of research testing on animals and humans. All these examples show that, although innovation policy instruments seem to be 'low politics', occasional strong contestations show the essential political nature of innovation policy formulation.

Another important dimension of political contention is the nature of public action itself. In particular, whether or not state intervention is motivated, and whether one or the other innovation policy instrument should be used, have been debated intensively on the basis of political ideology and values. From our point of view, the nature of public action must be carefully analysed, and constructive discussions can be pursued on the basis of these analyses. It is not particularly interesting to argue that private organizations or public ones are the most suitable when it comes to influencing innovation processes. We want to see this empirically: specific analysis, constructive pragmatism, and common sense rather than ideological dogmatism are needed to find out who should do what and with what instruments.

11.7 Conclusions: Innovation Policy Instruments and Mixes

Selecting policy instruments is a crucial part of policy-making. Instruments of innovation policy need to be understood as the operational forms of intervention by governments and public agencies. Even if instruments have a purposive nature (instruments for something), it does not mean that all innovation policy instruments have been consciously chosen and designed. As a matter of fact, the selection and use of innovation policy instruments is not always based on clearly defined overall governmental objectives of innovation policy; nor are they always based on a clear identification of problems. Unfortunately, many instruments are selected by means of an ad hoc set of decisions (or non-decisions), largely based on a continuation of previous schemes, or on lobby activity of specific interest groups, rather than on the visionary considerations of an holistic innovation policy and a critical assessment of the actual problems that need action.

In this chapter, we have argued that the design of innovation policy must include specifying ultimate objectives, translating them into direct objectives and, on this basis, identifying problems that are not solved by private organizations. These problems are related to low performance of the innovation system, i.e. low innovation intensity of a certain category of innovations, for which the direct objective is high intensity. In order to be able to design innovation policy instruments to mitigate the problems identified, it is also necessary to know the most important causes of the problems identified. These causes are related to the activities or determinants of the development and diffusion of innovations. The instruments are also related to these activities as outlined in Table 11.1.

Hence, the identification of the problems and their activity-related causes should be the basis for the selection of policy instruments. The combination of instruments is a crucial part of the innovation policy. Some might be instruments created *ex novo*, but in most cases, instruments are changed and adapted to new problems and combined with other instruments to address the problems.

Rarely are innovation policy instruments ready or 'prêt-à-porter' for the task at hand. Most of the time, if not always, policy instruments must be designed, redesigned, and adapted to the specific problems in the innovation systems and their uses. Instrument design can change over time according to changing preferences, changing objectives, and changing problems in the innovation system.

Each policy instrument is unique. Even if some policy instruments are similar in their ways of defining and approaching a problem, there will always be substantial differences not only in terms of the concrete details of how the instruments are chosen and designed, but also in terms of the overall social, political, economic, and organizational context in which the instruments are applied.

12

Building the Theoretical Foundations for an Holistic Innovation Policy

12.1 Introduction

An holistic innovation policy is defined in this book as a policy that integrates all public actions that influence or may influence innovation processes. This chapter has two parts: (1) a summary of the book and (2) a proposed research agenda.

First, this chapter summarizes the book. It does so by addressing *holistic innovation policy* and by dealing with the three themes pointed out in the subtitle of the book, in three sub-sections:

- the theoretical foundations of an holistic innovation policy (Section 12.2);
- the identification of policy problems and additionality (Section 12.3); and
- the choice of innovation policy instruments (Section 12.4).

These sub-sections present some of the content of earlier chapters, including policy implications of our analysis.

Secondly, we present what we see as *an agenda for future innovation policy and research* (Section 12.5).

Except for the policy and research agenda, there is nothing new in this chapter, and it *can be read independently of the rest of the book*. There are no references to the literature. However, there are references to earlier chapters of the book. The reader should consult those chapters for the detailed analysis and arguments behind the content of this chapter—as well as for references to the literature.

12.2 Theoretical Foundations for an Holistic Innovation Policy

12.2.1 *Innovation Systems: The Systems Activities Approach*

The so-called *linear model* of how innovations develop tended to dominate in the early days of research on innovation and also in innovation policy.

It was based on the assumption that innovations are mainly applied scientific knowledge. The model was called 'linear' because innovations were assumed to be generated by a process consisting of well-defined, consecutive stages, e.g. basic research, applied research, and development work, resulting in new products and processes that ultimately influence growth and employment as well as solutions to societal and environmental problems. It was a supply-push view and stresses mainly research as a determinant of innovations. However, research does not automatically lead to innovations, and research is never sufficient to achieve innovations.

The *systems of innovation (SI) approach*, which has diffused rapidly since the 1990s, has completely replaced the linear view in the field of innovation research (but not in innovation policy-making). This approach, in its different versions, usually defines innovation in terms of determinants of innovation processes, although different determinants are emphasized in different versions. In Chapter 2, we tried to clarify these and other conceptual and theoretical matters in some detail as a way of setting up the foundations of the rest of the book.

Research within the innovation systems approach has long paid most attention to the *components* (e.g. organizations and institutions) of systems. Less has been said about the dynamic *processes* that occur in the systems and how they change.

To address what occurs in SIs, one can consider what we refer to as *activities*. Activities are factors that influence the direction and speed of the development and diffusion of innovations, for example, research and development (R&D), public procurement, and the financing of innovations.

We believe that an emphasis on activities or determinants within innovation systems will become even more crucial for the development of both innovation theory and innovation policies in the future. It is also by influencing these determinants that enterprises and public agencies can affect the innovation processes through their strategies and policies.

Our definition of an innovation system includes not only the innovations themselves but also all important economic, social, political, organizational, institutional, and other factors (activities) that influence the development, diffusion, and use of innovations. Accordingly, our definition of innovation systems is based on a particular specification of the SI approach where ten activities (or determinants of innovation processes) define an innovation system. This definition of an innovation system is much broader and more general than most other variants, as it includes all determinants of innovation processes in addition to the innovations themselves. We call this the *systems activities approach*. A list of the activities in innovation systems or determinants of innovation processes is presented in Box 2.2. The activities are also presented in more detail in Chapter 2 and analysed in Chapters 4–10.

The systems activities approach is our theorizing about innovation systems and their dynamics, which is done in the context of a continuous development from previous (theoretical) work on innovations and innovation systems. Innovation systems may be national, regional, or sectoral. These three perspectives may be clustered as variants of a single generic SI approach. Much of the discussion here is based on the premise that these different variants of SIs coexist and complement each other. Whether the most appropriate conception of the SI, in a certain context, should be national, sectoral, or regional depends, to a large extent, on the questions one wants to ask.

In Section 2.2, we also specified our concept of innovation as new creations of economic and societal importance, usually performed by firms—in collaboration and interdependence with other organizations that are parts of innovation systems. We made a distinction between process innovations and product innovations and stressed that the new creations do not become innovations until they are spread to a considerable degree. Prototypes or test series do not qualify as innovations.

The list of activities (also called functions in other lists) in Box 2.2 is preliminary, hypothetical, and one among several possible lists. These activities are the hypothetical determinants of the development and the diffusion of innovations. The list will certainly be revised when our knowledge of the determinants of innovation processes has improved. Nonetheless, this list can be used as a checklist or signpost to discuss the factors that—probably—affect innovation processes. This is important, as innovation processes are very complex and influenced by a variety of factors. Among other things, the list can serve as a tool to avoid mono-causality, i.e. an overly strong emphasis on one single activity (be it research or seed funding) and a neglect of others (be it institutions or innovation-enhancing functional public procurement) when causally explaining innovation processes and when selecting innovation policy instruments to mitigate policy problems.

After unfolding and specifying each of these ten activities in Chapter 2, we devoted seven chapters (4–10) in this book to discussing most of them. Each of these chapters carefully considers why the specific activity addressed is crucial for the innovation process and innovation system. We also addressed those policy problems that are generated by policy itself.

However, before addressing each activity per chapter, we specified our view on innovation policy as an holistic and problem-based one in Chapter 3. One reason for doing this is that we do not consider innovation policy to be a separate 'activity' in innovation systems. We consider innovation policy to be a part of all activities in such systems (more about this in Section 12.2.2).

12.2.2 *Holistic Innovation Policy*

Chapter 3 of this book develops the core of the argument regarding the specific assumptions, conceptual specifications, and theoretical propositions about the role and limits of innovation policy. As indicated there, the SI approach has contributed considerably to discussions of innovation policy. The theoretical basis for the holistic approach to innovation policy proposed in this book is built on a certain version of the SI approach and on the identification of concrete policy problems that afflict the innovation systems, including unintended consequences of implemented policies. It also includes a procedure for the selection of policy instruments. Following from that, Chapter 3 argues that most innovation policies are still partial, not holistic; that innovation policy must be separated from research policy; and that innovation policy learning can only take place using an analytical model that helps in understanding the dynamics of the innovation system, what worked, how, and why.

Innovation policy aims at influencing the speed and direction of innovation processes. For that reason, policy is inextricably related to the dynamics of the innovation system, which it aims at redressing, shaping, and transforming. The large diversity of innovation systems means that there are no ready-made solutions that policy can provide: there is no one-size-fits-all policy. Policy must be designed and implemented based on an identification of the concrete policy problems that afflict the innovation system. The identification of such policy problems will be addressed in Section 12.3.

In recent years, innovation policy has increasingly been discussed using terms such as 'broad-based innovation policies', 'systemic innovation policies', 'a demand-pull view', and 'demand-oriented policy instruments'. These terms refer to a broad perspective on innovation policy. In Chapter 3, we called this perspective an holistic approach to innovation policy (see also below). While adding terms such as demand-oriented innovation policy instruments to a linear view certainly increases the degree of holism of innovation policy, this is not sufficiently comprehensive to warrant it being truly holistic.

In this book, *an holistic innovation policy is defined as one that integrates all public actions that influence or may influence innovation processes*. It takes all determinants of innovation into account. It is not driven by the supply side only, but has a much wider scope. It requires a broad view of the determinants of innovation processes, which means that it also requires a version of the innovation systems approach that is very broad (as mentioned in Section 12.2.1 and developed in detail in Chapter 2). The list of ten activities (Box 2.2) is our preliminary attempt to provide a conceptual basis for such a comprehensive approach, in an instrumental way. It can also serve as a basis for further developing the notion of an holistic approach to innovation policy.

It must be recognized, however, that innovation policies are still normally practised in a *partial* way, focusing on only one or a few of the determinants of innovation processes or activities in innovation systems. *Partial* and *holistic* innovation policies represent the extremes on a continuum from very partial to fully holistic ones, and we therefore speak of the *degree* to which an innovation policy is partial or holistic. Partial innovation policies are of different kinds but often focus strongly on the role of research for innovation—in the *linear* tradition. Hence, linear innovation policy is a special case of partial innovation policies, actually the most common one.

This means that innovation policy practice is currently massively lagging behind innovation studies and innovation research when it comes to being broad-based, demand-oriented, or holistic. Innovation policies are partial rather than holistic, and most of these partial policies are of a linear kind. A truly *holistic innovation policy* would explicitly integrate all public actions that influence or may influence innovation processes—for example, by addressing all the activities influencing innovation processes in a coordinated manner.

The holistic policy approach proposed here is an attempt to provide a framework that counteracts and transcends partial and linear policies. As mentioned above, we do not include public innovation policy as one of the ten activities in Box 2.2 for the simple reason that public innovation policy is a part of *all* the ten activities. All the activities are carried out by organizations in innovation systems, and these systems include both private and public organizations for most activities. As an example, in all innovation systems, R&D is funded and performed by public organizations (universities, public research institutes) and by private organizations (enterprises). What is important is the *division of labour between private and public organizations* with regard to the design and implementation of each of the activities. The portion of the various activities carried out by public organizations actually *constitutes* innovation policy. This division of labour was addressed in Section 2.5. In this summary chapter it will now be addressed in Section 12.3.

12.3 Identification of Policy Problems and Additionality

An holistic innovation policy includes not only identifying determinants of innovations but also selecting innovation policy instruments based on these determinants. However, as such, the determinants and instruments say nothing about the objectives of innovation policy. They have to be specified politically. An holistic innovation policy can be instrumental and useful across very different types of politically defined objectives—see below.

In Section 3.6, we made a distinction between ultimate and direct innovation policy objectives. Ultimate innovation policy objectives may be economic (economic progress, economic growth, employment, competitiveness, etc.), environmental (e.g. long-term sustainable development), social (e.g. justice), or they may be related to (other) challenges, such as ensuring health, security, etc. These ultimate objectives of innovation policy have to be specified separately and exogenously in political processes. These specifications are carried out within the formal political system, by means of, for example, elections, parliaments, and governments. However, the objectives are also affected by diverse activities outside political organizations and institutions, such as in debates, research activities, civil society initiatives, demonstrations, and lobbyism. Politicians are rather more interested in the consequences of innovations than in the innovations per se.

Innovation policy instruments, to be discussed in Section 12.4, can only influence these ultimate objectives in an indirect way. Direct innovation policy objectives, on the other hand, must be identified and specified in innovation terms and can be achieved by means of innovation policy instruments. This means that the ultimate socio-political objectives must be 'translated' into direct objectives. For example, we need to know how the ultimate objectives of economic growth and environmental protection are related to (certain kinds of) innovations and how these innovations can be enhanced to fulfil the ultimate objectives.

This means that direct objectives have their basis in policy problems. Hence, it is crucial to be able to identify such policy problems. No policy at all is better than a policy that is not based on a clearly identified policy problem.

Why and in which situations then should an innovation policy be pursued and when should it not, i.e. what is the rationale for pursuing innovation policy? As indicated in Sections 3.5 and 12.2, innovation policy within an holistic approach is seen as a division of labour between private and public organizations. Within such an approach, two conditions must be fulfilled for there to be reasons for public innovation policy initiatives in a market economy:

- Private organizations must prove to be unwilling or unsuccessful in achieving the objectives formulated; i.e. a policy problem must exist.
- The state (national, regional, local) and its public organizations must also have the ability to solve or mitigate the policy problem.

These two conditions show the central importance of the issue of additionality in solving policy problems. That is, innovation policy must not replace, duplicate, or crowd out what private actors (can) accomplish, but rather support or supplement the actions of the private sector. Additionality is, in fact, sometimes referred to as 'market-supplementing'. Additionality is closely related to the identification of policy problems and to determining how and to what extent the public sector can best support and 'add to' what private actors can accomplish and are willing to undertake.

This means that only activities that are important for the innovation system, but are, at the same time, not carried out by private organizations, should be stimulated or performed by public organizations—and, of course, only if they have the ability to do so. A policy problem is always related to low innovation performance of the innovation system. The performance (or productivity) of an innovation system is the relationship between what goes into (a certain part of) the system and what comes out; it is a relation between innovation inputs and innovation output. The output is—simply—innovations. There is a policy problem when there is low innovation performance (output as compared to input) of the SI.

When we are examining the policy problems that might plague the innovation system, we should not disregard the problems that are generated by the negative effects (or lack of any effect) of public policy initiatives. They may be unintended consequences of policy action itself, as indicated in Section 3.7.

We use the term 'policy problem' instead of 'failure' in order to avoid the connotations that the traditional economics notion of 'market failure' has. This is conscious and intentional. A 'market failure' implies a comparison between an existing SI and an ideal or optimal system. Since it is not possible to specify an optimal innovation system, the notion of 'market failure' loses its meaning and applicability. In order to avoid leading thoughts in the wrong direction, we therefore prefer to talk about 'policy problems' instead of 'market failures'.

As defined in Box 3.1, a policy problem is always related to low innovation performance of the innovation system. There is a policy problem when there is low innovation performance (output as compared to input) of the SI; in other words, the low *innovation performance* of a certain category of innovations (product, process, etc.) as compared to the resources invested for that purpose. The existence of a policy problem in a concrete context (region, country, etc.) has to be identified through empirical analysis. This book provides the theoretical and conceptual foundations upon which that analysis can be framed. Put differently, a 'policy problem' exists if the objectives in terms of innovation performance are not achieved by private organizations (see Section 3.6 and Box 3.1 about objectives of innovation policy). Following from that, there might be some obstacles and barriers in the innovation systems. They are the possible deficiencies, imbalances, bottlenecks, etc. in the activities of the innovation system that might be the causes behind the low innovation performance of that system.

There are certainly limits to what innovation policy can do. Some societal problems cannot be solved by means of innovations at all. Examples are social problems that have to be addressed by political and legal processes and policies. Neither can all problems that are caused by innovation-related conditions be solved by pursuing innovation policy. There are cases where public organizations do not have the ability to solve identified innovation policy problems not solved by private organizations. In other words, these problems are not solvable by innovation policy (see Sections 3.5 and 12.3).

In addition, new problems can be created by innovation policy itself. This refers to the unintended consequences of policy intervention. In other words, one important argument of this book is that we should not disregard the problems that are generated by the negative effects (or lack of any effect) of innovation policy initiatives themselves. One such source of policy-created problems are cases where the additionality condition was not fulfilled by a previous policy.

12.4 Some Obstacles and Barriers in Innovation Systems Characterized in This Book

In this book we have characterized several important items in an attempt to provide a theoretically inspired and clear logic about what can go wrong in the innovation system (policy problems in terms of low innovation performance), what can be done from an innovation policy perspective (policy instruments), and what the obstacles and barriers are that are generated by policy itself as negative unintended consequences of policies.

Table 12.1 summarizes the obstacles and barriers in innovation systems, policy instruments, and unintended negative consequences of policy along the different innovation system activities analysed in Chapters 4 to 10 of this book.

Knowledge creation and R&D is a crucial activity in innovation systems. Four obstacles and barriers might afflict innovation systems: inadequate levels of private investment in R&D, poor complementarity between investment sources in R&D, high uncertainty and long time lags between investment and private returns, and poor social rates of return of research investments. Most of these obstacles and barriers are described in the literature, as R&D and knowledge creation is one of the activities in innovation systems that have received significant attention among policy-makers and experts. Among the most common policy instruments devoted to tackling these issues, we can find a series of important economic and financial instruments like direct public funding to R&D-performing organizations, competition-based public funding, and tax incentives to firms' R&D activities. Intellectual property rights are another important instrument (particularly patent regulations), as well as public-private partnerships. However, these policy instruments might

Table 12.1. The obstacles and barriers characterized in this book

Areas of the innovation system	Obstacles and barriers in the innovation system	Commonly used policy instruments	Unintended negative consequences of policy
Knowledge production and Research and development (R&D)	Inadequate levels of investment in R&D. Poor complementarity between investment sources in R&D. High uncertainty and long time lag between investment and private returns. Poor social rates of return of research investments.	Direct public funding. Competition-based public funding. Tax incentives. Intellectual property rights. Public-private partnerships.	Lack of additionality and crowding out. If public funding does not promote disruptive knowledge creation. If unbalanced public support between curiosity-driven R&D and strategic R&D If focus on the quantity not on the quality of R&D. Undefined goals of public R&D investment.
Education, training, and skills formation	Insufficient skills and competences Time lag between firms' short-term needs and long-term development of skills and knowledge. Imbalances between internal and external sources of competence in firms.	Regulation, organization, and funding of the education systems including vocational training. Migration policies (including reverse brain-drain instruments).	Old-fashioned pedagogics and not developing knowledge competences for twenty-first century. Insufficient and inflexible vocational training.
Functional procurement as demand side	Lack of innovation dynamics in the economy and in the public sector. Innovation lock-in. Opportunity costs if not developing technology and innovative solutions to complex societal and economic problems.	Public procurement instruments that enhance innovations, e.g. functional specifications and functional procurement. Public procurement—innovation.	If description of products is a basis for public procurement. If repetitive description of existing products. If demand for obsolete products. If lack of enhancement of innovation in public procurement.
Change of organizations: entrepreneurship and intrapreneurship	Weak levels of entrepreneurship and new entrants in the economy. Low-quality entrepreneurship. Low organizational capacity and innovation by established firms. Poor selection environment does not reward entrepreneurial activity.	Instruments creating variation and selection environment. Instruments promoting entrepreneurial culture. Disseminating best practices of innovation management practices.	Ineffective policies unable to create variation and selection. Policies strengthen the incumbents discouraging new entrants.
Interaction and networking	Unexploited potential due to insufficient interaction and networks. Network partners do not have	Instruments promoting collaboration between academia and industry. Promoting of local and regional interactions and networks.	If policy reinforces innovation lock-in. If policy reinforces the homogeneity of actors in networks rather than diversity.

(*continued*)

Table 12.1. *Continued*

Areas of the innovation system	Obstacles and barriers in the innovation system	Commonly used policy instruments	Unintended negative consequences of policy
	complementary knowledge assets. Lack of critical mass of interactions with external sources. If interactions and networks are creating innovation lock-ins. No positive network externalities (such as knowledge spill-overs).	Encouraging collective view or strategy for the region or sector seeking interactions. Match-making, acquaintance, networking events. Instruments targeting specific sectors (e.g. SMEs) in order to foster their embeddedness in networks.	If policy emphasizes local not international networking.
Changing institutions	Lack of incentives to invest in immaterial assets. Lack of a level playing field for market interactions. High level of contextual uncertainty. Negative economic and knowledge externalities.	Intellectual property rights. Competition regulations. Financial and corporate governance regulations. Consumer protection and product liability regulations. Environmental protection regulations.	Limited effectiveness of the regulation if generating insufficient incentives and/or high costs of compliance. If there is an imbalance between private benefits and social benefits of the instruments. If standards promote technical lock-in. If lack of adaptability of regulation and red tape.
Public financing of early-stage innovations	Lack or low levels of private funding in early stages (capital market supply is underdeveloped, for example with few, unspecialized venture capital firms, few business angels, etc.). High uncertainty and risk.	Equity programmes. Tax incentives. Investment regulations that generate incentives. Support to business angel networks. Second-tier stock markets.	Lack of additionality and crowding-out effects. If there are profit demands on public funding. If public risk capital goes to mature sectors.

Source: own elaboration

generate some negative consequences themselves, like the lack of additionality and crowding-out effect of public R&D support over private R&D support; if public funding does not promote disruptive knowledge creation; if there is an unbalanced public support between curiosity-driven R&D and strategic R&D; if there is a focus on the quantity rather than the quality of R&D in the innovation system; and if there are undefined goals of public R&D investment.

Education, training, and skills is another crucial activity in innovation systems associated with the development of competences at the individual level. This is an area that has received little scholarly attention in relation to innovation systems and their overall innovation performance. Three important issues here might afflict innovation systems. The first is the insufficient level of skills and competences in the innovation system due to low levels of education and/or brain drain. This afflicts many countries, particularly low-income countries. A second issue is the time lag between firms' short-term needs on the one hand, and the long-term development of skills and knowledge at the individual level, on the other hand. This time lag is rather problematic and is a considerable bottleneck in situations of very rapid technological change. And thirdly, some innovation systems might have an imbalance between the internal and external sources of competence in firms.

The most common policy instruments used in this context are related to the organization, funding, and regulation of the education systems, here including vocational training. Migration policies, either focusing on attracting a highly specialized workforce or aiming at reversing brain drain, are also quite relevant. The unintended consequences of these policy instruments might be that old-fashioned pedagogics and learning modes are not suitable for current needs, hence promoting irrelevant knowledge competences. Another obstacle or barrier, which is quite important in low- and high-income countries, is insufficient levels and inflexible forms of vocational training.

Demand-side activities, especially functional public procurement, is another key activity of innovation systems. Functional procurement describes the problem that shall be solved instead of the product that shall be bought. In this way, functional public procurement enhances creativity, innovation, and competition in a very large part of the economy. There are at least three issues that typically affect the innovation system: firstly, the lack of innovation dynamics in the economy and in the public sector. Secondly, there might be innovation lock-in in some industries. And thirdly, the obstacles related to the opportunity costs when not developing technology and innovative solutions to complex societal and economic challenges. Policy instruments in this area are still in their infancy, as they require substantial organizational capacities from civil servants to define the functions of innovative products. In particular, public procurement instruments that enhance innovations, e.g. functional specifications and functional procurement, have a very large potential as demand-side innovation policy instruments. There might be some unintended consequences of policy, most importantly, if the description of products is the basis for public procurement, if there is a repetitive description of existing products, if there is a demand for obsolete products, and if there is a lack of enhancement of innovation in procurement.

Organizational change associated with entrepreneurship and intrapreneurship is a fourth relevant activity in innovation systems. Here, issues in the system might be related to weak levels of entrepreneurship and new entrants into the economy, low quality of entrepreneurship, low organizational capacity and innovation within established firms, and a poor selection environment that does not reward entrepreneurial activity. Policy-makers have developed a series of entrepreneurship-related policy instruments that aim at creating variation and selection, instruments promoting entrepreneurial culture, and instruments disseminating best practices of innovation management within firms. However, a series of policy-generated unintended negative consequences might arise when ineffective policies are unable to create variation and selection in the economy, and when policies strengthen the incumbents discouraging new entrants.

Innovation-related interactions and networks are essential aspects of innovation systems. Innovators interact in many different ways, bringing innovative solutions to the society and to the market. However, networks might suffer from some barriers and obstacles. The most important are: the unexploited potential due to insufficient interaction and networks, network partners do not have the complementary knowledge assets, the lack of critical mass of interactions with external sources, if interactions and networks are creating innovation lock-ins, and if there are no positive network externalities (such as knowledge spill-overs). During the past decades many countries and regions have developed network-oriented policy instruments. There is a wide diversity of policy instruments, but these can be organized around five main focus areas. These are: policy instruments promoting collaboration between academia and industry, policy instruments promoting local and regional interactions and networks, policy instruments encouraging a collective view or strategy for the region or sector seeking interactions, policy instruments for match-making, acquaintance, and networking events, and policy instruments targeting specific sectors (e.g. SMEs) in order to foster their embeddedness in networks. The eagerness of many governments to support and encourage those interactions and networks might, however, result in negative unintended consequences: for example, if policy reinforces innovation lock-in dynamics among network partners, if policy reinforces the homogeneity of actors in networks rather than their diversity, or if policy emphasizes local interactions and networks rather than international networking. These unintended consequences might ultimately diminish the innovativeness of the economy in significant ways.

Institutions and institutional change is another key determinant of innovation systems. Here, the obstacles and barriers may be related to a lack of incentives to invest in immaterial assets, lack of a level playing field for market interactions, high level of contextual uncertainty, and negative economic and knowledge externalities. There is a wide range of policy instruments that aim at tackling these issues. The most relevant of those are intellectual property rights, competition regulations, financial and corporate governance regulations, consumer protection and product liability regulations, and environmental protection regulations. This wide range of policy instruments might have unintended consequences in the innovation system. Regulations may be ineffective, either because they generate insufficient incentives and/or because of the very high costs of compliance. Other difficulties might arise if there is an imbalance between the private benefits and the social benefits of the instruments; if standards are promoting technical lock-in rather than new innovative solutions, or if there is a lack of adaptability of regulation and red tape.

The last activity that has been studied in this book is the financing of innovation. Chapter 10 put particular focus on public financing of early-stage innovations. The deficiencies in the innovation system might be several, mainly associated with a lack or low levels of private funding in early stages (capital market supply is underdeveloped, for example if there are few unspecialized venture capital firms, few business angels, etc.), and/or there are high levels of uncertainty and risk. Policy-makers have devised a series of policy instruments to target those problems, including equity programmes supporting seed-funding activities through soft loans, public grants, or even public equity investments in new firms. Tax incentives to investors are another important type of policy instrument, as well as investment regulations that generate incentives. Other policy instruments support business angel networks, or the creation of second-tier stock markets.

However, these policy instruments might generate other problems themselves, among others, when there is a lack of additionality and crowding-out effects, if there are profit demands on public financing, or if public risk capital goes to mature sectors.

12.5 The Choice of Policy Instruments

This section is based upon Chapter 11. There we argued that the design of innovation policy must include specifying ultimate objectives, translating them into direct objectives, and, on this basis, identifying problems that are not solved by private organizations. These problems are related to low performance of the innovation system, i.e. low innovation intensities of certain categories of innovations, for which the direct objective is high intensity, or they may be directly related to the activities in innovation systems, i.e. the determinants or causes of innovation processes.

We have argued that currently there are tendencies for innovation policies to become less partial and more holistic in some contexts. Truly holistic innovation policies require that all the determinants of innovation processes, exemplified with the ten activities, are taken into account when selecting policy instruments. We have proposed that this is done by means of a broad version of the SI approach. However, the use of the innovation systems approach for actual policy purposes is still often a matter of lip service and the content of innovation policies is still dominated by the linear model. Too much emphasis is put on R&D at the expense of looking into the other crucial activities in the innovation system.

The affinity between determinants, activities, and policy instruments is close; instruments being the publicly performed part of determinants. On the basis of policy objectives, politicians and policy-makers must try to identify policy problems. This will give them the basis to find out which instruments might be used to mitigate or solve the policy problems, i.e. they must find out which policy instruments are best and are most suitable for them to use.

When policy-makers know the policy problems in an SI, they might consider which policy instruments to use in order to do something about them. Policy-makers must identify the (main) causes of the policy problems beforehand in order to be able to select policy instruments intended to mitigate or solve the problems. This means that we have to grapple with the fact that dealing with causal explanations in the social sciences is a very demanding task.

Actually, this relates back to our specific version of the SI approach and the ten activities in innovation systems which we consider to be hypothetical determinants of innovation processes. On the basis of our broad definition of 'innovation system', it is reasonable to include policy instruments that correspond to many, or all, of these determinants of innovation processes (activities in innovation systems) when discussing which innovation policy instruments should be used when pursuing innovation policy.

Related to this issue is the question of how innovation systems change. At the end of Sections 2.3 and 3.5, we argued that innovation systems are not automatic 'machines' that produce innovations in a mechanical way. They are partly self-organized (e.g. by markets), but they are also coordinated by policy and politics.

Self-organized systems can change because of crises or other shocks. Hence, systems might be partly self-transforming. However, policy and politics play crucial roles in the change of innovation systems, as they are part and parcel of the systems. Policies are designed because of problems existing in the systems and their implementations are conscious efforts to change the systems. Additionality and market supplementation means that policy operates in a different way than markets and can therefore be an important mechanism of system change. In addition, changes in the objectives of innovation policy might radically alter the operation of the systems.

When narrowing down the perspective to achieving direct innovation policy objectives, the relation between policy problems and policy instruments is instrumental—it is a matter of cause and effect. In an ideal world, policy problems are identified by means of systematic and comparative empirical analysis, and policy instruments are thereafter rationally selected and implemented to mitigate or solve the problems. The instruments are intended to causally influence the problem in a direct way. However, the real world of policy-making and policy decision might not be rational. Moreover, it is important to understand that this relationship (between problem identification and instrument choice) is very different from talking about the linear model and linear innovation policy—see Chapter 2 and Section 12.1. Several instruments are normally used simultaneously in a supplementary and multidimensional way. Therefore, a 'mix' of policy instruments is used to mitigate policy problems. We therefore think that it is more accurate to speak about 'instrument mixes' than about 'policy mixes'.

Our focus on 'activities' within SIs also emphasizes strongly what happens in the systems—rather than focusing on their components. We have stressed (in Chapter 2) that our version of the SI approach focuses more on *changes* of institutions and organizations than on the components of institutions and organizations as such. In this sense, the systems activities approach provides a more dynamic perspective than other perspectives. Our approach can therefore capture how various activities that influence specific innovation processes may change the performance with regard to these innovations—and thereby how the whole system changes. Of course, the resulting innovations as such are also novelties introduced into the innovation system and the society.

Fulfilling direct objectives is a means of achieving ultimate objectives, i.e. in a mediated way. Hence, innovation policy instruments have to be selected in order to achieve direct objectives, and thereby indirectly to achieve the ultimate objectives. In order to solve or mitigate a policy problem of a low innovation performance by means of innovation policy, we need to know (be able to measure) the innovation performance for specific categories of innovation. Ideally, we also need to know which determinants/activities influence the innovation intensities and how, at least the most important ones.

Once we have specified the (ultimate and direct) objectives of innovation policy and have a general picture of the policy problems and their causes, it is possible to design policies to attempt to solve or mitigate those policy problems. Policy objectives are essential in order to influence both the direction and speed of innovations, by means of innovation policy.

12.6 Agenda for Innovation Policy and Innovation Research

Most things included in the previous sections of this chapter are a summary of the contents in this book. This final section is different. We will present our view on what could be a future agenda for innovation policy and research underpinning it.

We have, in this book, tried to develop theoretical foundations of an holistic innovation policy approach by providing a conceptual and analytical framework for gathering evidence and making sense of it. Holistic innovation policy is a policy that takes into consideration the whole innovation system, meaning a policy that is designed to look into all determinants of innovation processes, for example, the ten different activities that characterize innovation systems.

A continuation along the holistic policy trajectory would profit greatly from further theoretical research on the basis of the partial/linear versus holistic categories. The utopian end result could be a general theory of (the determinants of) innovations. It would attempt to identify all important determinants of the development and diffusion of innovations and their relative weights for different classes of innovation—knowledge that we do not currently possess. Thereby the most important instruments of innovation policy would also be identified.

Some people argue that it is not possible to talk about causality and explanation in an innovation context. We agree that causality is a complex matter in the social sciences. However, we cannot do without knowing about the main causes, determinants, and policy instruments if we want to understand innovation processes in innovation systems or if we want to be able to pursue effective innovation policies.

A research effort as the one described above would also include substantial efforts to measure product and process innovations as outputs of innovation systems. This would be crucial as an evidence base for identifying policy problems, and thereby for the design of innovation policies. All the determinants (activities) of innovations would, in such an attempt, be considered to be input measures.

This would make it possible to calculate something corresponding to *total* factor productivity (or multifactor productivity) of innovation systems instead of a partial productivity or efficiency measure. This would 'in principle' be a way to escape the partial/linear/mono-causal view.

Such an effort would absorb many calendar years and maybe a couple of hundred man years. But given the enormous significance of innovation as a force of change in our socio-economic, environmental, and political systems, this is highly motivated. As a matter of fact, innovation is at least as important for society as education and training. Hence, resources larger than those allocated to the OECD Pisa measurements are strongly motivated. It would be a relevant objective for the OECD Blue Sky innovation indicator work. Alternatively, the effort could be made in a large academic collaboration project.

Such a (theoretical) effort would, of course, be gradual and start by identifying the most important and obvious determinants of innovation. As a matter of fact, such a process has already started through the development and consolidation of the SI approach, through different lists of determinants (functions, activities) that have been developed by different contributors, and through current efforts in a similar direction by some international organizations. A further step could be to evaluate and compare the existing lists of functions and activities in innovation systems. As we have seen earlier, the activities approach can be used to define an innovation system, and it also has the potential to be instrumental in the development of a theory about the determinants of innovation processes.

Much more effort and evidence-based analysis should also be invested in ensuring the additionality condition is fulfilled when innovation policies are designed and redesigned. This requires further conceptual and theoretical research, as well as empirical analyses of relevant indicators and data on innovations and their determinants, to provide underpinnings for such design. It is essential that innovation policy becomes evidence-based to a greater degree.

Lack of additionality has several roots. It is often related to a lack of previous analysis and careful discussion of reasons for public intervention. This calls for more effort into identifying and analysing policy problems in the innovation system and the potential solutions that might come from public action. We believe that it should *always* be established that the additionality condition is fulfilled before policy action is taken. A solid conceptual and theoretical framework is required to provide a basis for such analyses, ultimately guiding decisions to devise and reshape relevant policy instruments.

Our impression from interacting with politicians and policy-makers in the field of innovation policy is that some of them are not particularly used to thinking in additionality terms. At the same time, it is important that the state and its organizations are doing only things that private organizations cannot or are not doing. This means that public organizations, through policy initiatives, are acting in a way that supplements what market actors do. They can also try to stimulate private actors to solve the policy problems identified by providing incentives for them to do so.

In practice, the linear view still dominates over holistic innovation policies in all countries, and innovation policy is normally subsumed under and treated as a part of research policy (see Section 3.4). Developing an holistic innovation policy would mean establishing it as a separate policy area. This would, in one respect, make it similar to research policy—which has been an independent policy area in many countries for decades. But it would also make innovation policy partly separate and independent from research policy. We would argue that such a separation between innovation policy and research policy is very important to make the linear view lose its hegemonic dominance.

Of course, if we use broad definitions of innovation policy and research policy (as we propose), there must be overlap between the two policy areas, with them 'intruding' into each other's 'territories'. This can be generalized: they also intrude into the territories of additional policy areas, such as labour market policies, public procurement policies, defence equipment policies, energy policies, transport policies, health-care policies, environmental policies, and regional policies. The effect of the resulting 'intrusion' or 'trespassing' makes it clear to everyone that policy areas do partly overlap and that they therefore must be coordinated. Innovation policy and research policy should be separate from each other in the design phase—but it must be ensured that they support each other when implemented.

Identifying innovation policy problems is not easy. It requires detailed measuring of innovation output by means of statistical analyses and identifying the main causes of the problems. Such detailed analyses provide very important guidance for policy-makers and politicians. It means that the decisions to pursue innovation policy initiatives (or not) do not need to be a matter only of political ideology. Instead, the issue of whether or not there should be innovation policy initiatives in specific situations can be analysed and discussed on the basis of evidence instead of ideology. In that way, political consensus can be reached on whether to pursue policies or not—and how.

Bibliography

Acemoglu, D. (1997) 'Training and Innovation in an Imperfect Labour Market'. *Review of Economic Studies*, Vol. 64, No. 3, pp. 445–64.

Ács, Z.J., Autio, E., and Szerb, L. (2014) 'National Systems of Entrepreneurship: Measurement Issues and Policy Implications'. *Research Policy*, Vol. 43, No. 3, pp. 476–94.

Aghion, P., David, P.A., and Foray, D. (2009a) 'Can We Link Policy Practice with Research on STIG Systems? Toward Connecting the Analysis of Science, Technology and Innovation Policy with Realistic Programs for Economic Development and Growth'. In Foray, D. (ed.), *The New Economics of Technology Policy*. Cheltenham: Edward Elgar.

Aghion, P., David, P.A., and Foray, D. (2009b) 'Science, Technology and Innovation for Economic Growth: Linking Policy Research and Practice in "STIG Systems"'. *Research Policy*, Vol. 38, No. 4, pp. 681–93.

Altbach, P. and Balán, J. (eds) (2007) *Transforming Research Universities in Asia and Latin America: World Class Worldwide*. Baltimore, MD: Johns Hopkins University Press.

Altenburg, T. (2009) 'Building Inclusive Innovation Systems in Developing Countries: Challenges for Innovation Systems Research'. In Lundvall, B.-Å., Joseph, K.J., Chaminade, C., and Vang, J. (eds), *Handbook of Innovation Systems and Developing Countries: Building Domestic Capabilities in a Global Setting*. Cheltenham: Edward Elgar, pp. 33–56.

Altenburg, T. and Meyer-Stamer, J. (1999) 'How to Promote Clusters: Policy Experiences from Latin America'. *World Development*, Vol. 27, No. 9, pp. 1693–713.

Álvarez, I. and Molero, J. (2005) 'Technology and the Generation of International Knowledge Spillovers: An Application to Spanish Manufacturing Firms'. *Research Policy*, Vol. 34, No. 9, pp. 1440–52.

Amable, B., Barré, R., and Boyer, R. (1997) 'Diversity, Coherence and Transformations of Innovation Systems'. In Barré, R., Gibbons, M., Maddox, J., Martin, B., and Papon, P. (eds), *Science in Tomorrow's Europe*. Paris: Economica International.

Andersen, E.S., Lundvall, B.-Å., and Sorrn-Friese, H. (2002) 'Editorial: Special Issue on Innovation Systems'. *Research Policy*, Vol. 31, pp. 185–90.

Andersson, T., Serger Scwaag, S., Sörvik, J., and Hansson Wise, E. (2004) *The Cluster Policies Whitebook*. Malmö: International Organisation for Knowledge Economy and Enterprise Development.

Anheier, H.K., Simmons, A., and Winder, D. (eds) (2007) *Innovation in Strategic Philanthropy: Local and Global Perspectives*. New York: Springer.

Bibliography

Aragón-Correa, J.A., García-Morales, V.J., and Cordón-Pozo, E. (2007) 'Leadership and Organizational Learning's Role on Innovation and Performance: Lessons from Spain'. *Industrial Marketing Management*, Vol. 36, No. 3, pp. 349–59.

Archibugi, D. and Filippetti, A. (2015) 'Editors' Introduction'. *The Handbook of Global Science, Technology, and Innovation*. Chichester: John Wiley & Sons, pp. 1–11.

Archibugi, D. and Michie, J. (1995) 'The Globalisation of Technology: A New Taxonomy'. *Cambridge Journal of Economics*, Vol. 19, pp. 121–40.

Armour, J. and Cumming, D. (2006) 'The Legislative Road to Silicon Valley'. *Oxford Economic Papers*, Vol. 58, No. 4, pp. 596–635.

Arrow, K.J. (1962) 'The Economic Implications of Learning by Doing'. *Review of Economic Studies*, Vol. 29, No. 3, pp. 155–73.

Asheim, B.T. and Coenen, L. (2005) 'Knowledge Bases and Regional Innovation Systems: Comparing Nordic Clusters'. *Research Policy*, Vol. 34, No. 8, pp. 1173–90.

Asheim, B. and Coenen, L. (2006) 'Contextualising Regional Innovation Systems in a Globalising Learning Economy: On Knowledge Bases and Institutional Frameworks'. *Journal of Technology Transfer*, Vol. 31, No. 1, pp. 163–73.

Audretsch, D.B. and Feldmann, M.P. (2004) 'Knowledge Spillovers and the Geography of Innovation'. In Henderson, V.J. and Thisse, J.-F. (eds), *Handbook of Urban and Regional Economics*. Amsterdam: Elsevier.

Audretsch, D.B., Keilbach, M.C., and Lehmann, E.E. (2006) *Entrepreneurship and Economic Growth*. Oxford: Oxford University Press.

Audretsch, D.B., Falck, O., Heblich, S., and Lederer, A. (eds) (2011) *Handbook of Research on Innovation and Entrepreneurship*. Cheltenham: Edward Elgar.

Autio, E., Kanninen, S. and Gustafsson, R. (2008) 'First- and Second-Order Additionality and Learning Outcomes in Collaborative R&D Programs'. *Research Policy*, Vol. 37, No. 1, pp. 59–76.

Baldwin, R., Scott, C., and Hood, C. (1998) 'Introduction'. In Baldwin, R., Scott, C., and Hood, C. (eds), *A Reader on Regulation*. Oxford: Oxford University Press, pp. 1–55.

Barberá-Tomás, D. and Molas-Gallart, J. (2014) 'Governance and Technological Change: The Effects of Regulation in Medical Devices'. In Borrás, S. and Edler, J. (eds), *The Governance of Socio-Technical Systems: Explaining Change*. Cheltenham: Edward Elgar, pp. 96–110.

Barnard, H. and Chaminade, C. (2011) *Global Innovation Networks: Towards a Taxonomy*. Lund: CIRCLE.

Bartels, F.L., Koria, R., and Andriano, L. (2016) 'Effectiveness and Efficiency of National Systems of Innovation: A Comparative Analysis of Ghana and Kenya'. *African Journal of Science, Technology, Innovation and Development*, Vol. 8, No. 4, pp. 343–56.

Bartlett, D. and Dibben, P. (2002) 'Public Sector Innovation and Entrepreneurship: Case Studies from Local Government'. *Local Government Studies*, Vol. 28, No. 4, pp. 107–21.

Baumol, W.J. (2002) 'Entrepreneurship, Innovation and Growth: The David-Goliath Symbiosis'. *Journal of Entrepreneurial Finance*, Vol. 7, No. 2, pp. 1–10.

Baumol, W.J., Litan, R.E., and Schramm, C.J. (2007) *Good Capitalism, Bad Capitalism, and the Economics of Growth and Prosperity*. New Haven, CT: Yale University.

Bemelmans-Videc, M.-L., Rist, R.C., and Vedung, E. (eds) (2003) *Carrots, Sticks and Sermons: Policy Instruments and Their Evaluation*. London: Transaction.

Bergek, A., Jacobsson, S., Carlsson, B., Lindmark, S., and Rickne, A. (2008) 'Analyzing the Functional Dynamics of Technological Innovation Systems: A Scheme of Analysis'. *Research Policy*, Vol. 37, No. 3, pp. 407–29.

Bergek, A., Jacobsson, S., Hekkert, M., and Smith, K. (2010) 'Functionality of Innovation Systems as a Rationale for and Guide to Innovation Policy'. In Smits, R.E., Kuhlmann, S., and Shapira, P. (eds), *The Theory and Practice of Innovation Policy: An International Research Handbook*. Cheltenham: Edward Elgar, pp. 115–44.

Bergman, K., Ejermo, O., Fischer, J., Hallonsten, O., Høgni Kalsø, H., and Moodysson, J. (2010) *Effects of VINNOVA Programmes on Small and Medium-Sized Enterprises: The Cases of Forska&Väx and VINN NU*. Stockholm: Vinnova.

Bernard, A.L., Escalona Reynoso, R., Saisana, M., Guadagno, F., and Wunsch-Vincent, S. (2015) 'Benchmarking Innovation Performance at the Global and Country Levels'. In Dutta, S., Lanvin, B., and Wunsch-Vincent, S. (eds), *The Global Innovation Index 2015: Effective Innovation Policies for Development*. Geneva: WIPO, pp. 65–80.

Bessen, J.E. (2015) *Learning by Doing: The Real Connection between Innovation, Wages, and Wealth*. New Haven, CT: Yale University Press.

Bessen, J.E. and Meurer, M.J. (2008) *Patent Failure: How Judges, Bureaucrats, and Lawyers Put Innovators at Risk*. Princeton, NJ: Princeton University Press.

Biegelbauer, P. and Borrás, S. (eds) (2003) *Innovation Policies in Europe and the US: The New Agenda*. Aldershot: Ashgate.

Black, G.C. (2006) 'Geography and Spillover: Shaping Innovation Policy through Small Business Research'. In Guston, D.H. and Sarewitz, D. (eds), *Shaping Science and Technology Policy: The Next Generation of Research*. Madison, WI: University of Wisconsin Press, pp. 77–101.

Blind, K. (2004) *The Economics Of Standards: Theory, Evidence, Policy*. Cheltenham: Edward Elgar.

Blind, K. (2012a) *The Impact of Regulation on Innovation*. Manchester: Manchester University Press.

Blind, K. (2012b) 'The Influence of Regulations on Innovation: A Quantitative Assessment for OECD Countries'. *Research Policy*, Vol. 41, No. 2, pp. 391–400.

Boekholt, P. (2010) 'The Evolution of Innovation Paradigms and Their Influence on Research, Technological Development and Innovation Policy Instruments'. In Smits, R.E., Kuhlmann, S., and Shapira, P. (eds), *The Theory and Practice of Innovation Policy: An International Research Handbook*. Cheltenham: Edward Elgar, pp. 333–59.

Borrás, S. (2003) *The Innovation Policy of the European Union: From Government to Governance*. Cheltenham: Edward Elgar.

Borrás, S. (2006) 'The Governance of the European Patent System: Effective and Legitimate?' *Economy and Society*, Vol. 35, No. 4, pp. 594–610.

Borrás, S. (2009) *The Widening and Deepening of Innovation Policy: What Conditions Provide for Effective Governance?* Lund: Lund University, Sweden.

Borrás, S. (2011) 'Policy Learning and Organizational Capacities in Innovation Policies'. *Science and Public Policy*, Vol. 38, No. 9, pp. 725–34.

Borrás, S. (2015) 'Reforms of National Innovation Policies in Europe: Coordinating Sensemaking across Countries'. In Borrás, S. and Seabrooke, L. (eds), *Sources of*

National Institutional Competitiveness: Sensemaking and Institutional Change. Oxford: Oxford University Press, pp. 60–77.

Borrás, S. (2016) 'Organisations in Innovation Systems: Entrepreneurship, Intrapreneurship and Public Policy'. *DBP Working Papers*. Copenhagen: Department of Business and Politics, Copenhagen Business School.

Borrás, S. and Edquist, C. (2013a) *The Choice of Innovation Policy Instruments*. Lund: CIRCLE.

Borrás, S. and Edquist, C. (2013b) 'The Choice of Innovation Policy Instruments'. *Technological Forecasting and Social Change*, Vol. 80, No. 8, pp. 1513–22.

Borrás, S. and Edquist, C. (2013c) *Competence Building: A Systemic Approach to Innovation Policy*. Lund: CIRCLE.

Borrás, S. and Edquist, C. (2014) *Institutions and Regulations in Innovation Systems: Effects, Problems and Innovation Policy Design*. Lund: CIRCLE.

Borrás, S. and Edquist, C. (2015a) 'Education, Training and Skills in Innovation Policy'. *Science and Public Policy*, Vol. 42, No. 2, pp. 215–27.

Borrás, S. and Edquist, C. (2015b) 'Innovation Policy for Knowledge Production and R&D: The Investment Portfolio Approach'. In Crespi, F. and Quatraro, F. (eds), *The Economics of Knowledge, Innovation and Systemic Technology Policy*. New York: Routledge, pp. 361–82.

Borrás, S. and Kahin, B. (2009) 'Patent Reform in Europe and the US'. *Science and Public Policy*, Vol. 36, No. 8.

Borrás, S. and Ougaard, M. (2001) 'Patentløsninger: Intellektuel ejendomsret, EU og WTO'. *GRUS*, Vol. 22, No. 64, pp. 25–42.

Borrás, S. and Tsagdis, D. (2008) *Cluster Policies in Europe: Firms, Institutions and Governance*. Cheltenham: Edward Elgar.

Borrás, S., Chaminade, C., and Edquist, C. (2009) 'The Challenges of Globalization: Strategic Choices for Innovation Policy'. In Marklund, G., Vonortas, N., and Wessner, C. (eds), *The Innovation Imperative: National Innovation Strategies in the Global Economy*. Cheltenham: Edward Elgar, pp. 7–23.

Bosch, G. and Charest, J. (2008) 'Vocational Training and the Labour Market in Liberal and Coordinated Economies'. *Industrial Relations Journal*, Vol. 39, No. 5, pp. 428–47.

Bozeman, B. and Sarewitz, D. (2011) 'Public Value Mapping and Science Policy Evaluation'. *Minerva*, Vol. 49, No. 1, pp. 1–23.

Bozeman, B., Fay, D., and Slade, C. (2013) 'Research Collaboration in Universities and Academic Entrepreneurship: The-State-of-the-Art'. *Journal of Technology Transfer*, Vol. 38, No. 1, pp. 1–67.

Braczyk, H.-J., Cooke, P., and Heidenreich, M. (eds) (1998) *Regional Innovation Systems*. London: University College London.

Breschi, S. and Malerba, F. (1997) 'Sectoral Innovation Systems: Technological Regimes, Schumpeterian Dynamic, and Spatial Boundaries'. In Edquist, C. (ed.), *Systems of Innovation: Technologies, Institutions and Organisations*. London: Pinter.

Breznitz, D. (2007) *Innovation and the State: Political Choice and Strategies for Growth in Israel, Taiwan and Ireland*. New Haven, CT: Yale University Press.

Brockmann, M., Clarke, L., and Winch, C. (eds) (2011) *Knowledge, Skills and Competence in the European Labour Market: What's in a Vocational Qualification?* London: Routledge.

Bruneel, J., D'Este, P., and Salter, A. (2010) 'Investigating the Factors that Diminish the Barriers to University–Industry Collaboration'. *Research Policy*, Vol. 39, No. 7, pp. 858–68.

Bush, V. (1945) 'Science: The Endless Frontier'. *Transactions of the Kansas Academy of Science (1903–)*. Vol. 48, No. 3, pp. 231–64.

Bäckstrand, K., Khan, J., Kronsell, A., and Lövbrand, E. (eds) (2010) *Environmental Politics and Deliberative Democracy: Examining the Promise of New Modes of Governance.* Cheltenham: Edward Elgar.

Camagni, R. (1991) 'Local "Milieu", Uncertainty and Innovation Networks: Towards a New Dynamic Theory of Economic Space'. In Camagni, R. (ed.), *Innovation Networks*. London: Belhaven Press, pp. 121–44.

Capello, R. (1999) 'SME Clustering and Factor Productivity: A Milieu Production Function Model'. *European Planning Studies*, Vol. 7, pp. 719–35.

Carlsen, H., Johansson, L., Wikman-Svahn, P., and Dreborg, K.H. (2014) 'Co-evolutionary Scenarios for Creative Prototyping of Future Robot Systems for Civil Protection'. *Technological Forecasting and Social Change*, Vol. 84, pp. 93–100.

Carlsson, B. (ed.) (1995) *Technological Systems and Economic Performance: The Case of Factory Automation*. Dordrecht: Kluwer.

Carlsson, B. (ed.) (1997) *Technological Systems and Industrial Dynamics*. Frankfurt: Springer.

Carlsson, B. and Jacobsson, S. (1997) 'Diversity Creation and Technological Systems: A Technology Policy Perspective'. In Edquist, C. (ed.), *Systems of Innovation: Technologies, Institutions and Organizations*. London: Pinter.

Carneiro, R. (2003) 'On Knowledge and Learning for the New Millennium'. In Coinceicao, P., Heitor, M.V., and Lundvall, B.-Å. (eds), *Innovation, Competence Building and Social Cohesion in Europe: Towards a Learning Society*. Cheltenham: Edward Elgar, pp. 186–205.

Castellacci, F. and Natera, J.M. (2013) 'The Dynamics of National Innovation Systems: A Panel Cointegration Analysis of the Coevolution between Innovative Capability and Absorptive Capacity'. *Research Policy*, Vol. 42, No. 3, pp. 579–94.

Castells, M. (1996) *The Rise of the Network Society*. Cambridge, MA: Blackwell.

Chaminade, C. (2011) 'Are Knowledge Bases Enough? A Comparative Study of the Geography of Knowledge Sources in China (Great Beijing) and India (Pune)'. *European Planning Studies*, Vol. 19, No. 7, pp. 1357–73.

Chaminade, C. and Edquist, C. (2006) 'From Theory to Practice: The Use of the Systems of Innovation Approach in Innovation Policy'. In Hage, J.T. and Meeus, M. (eds), *Innovation, Science and Institutional Change: A Research Handbook*. Oxford: Oxford University Press.

Chaminade, C. and Edquist, C. (2010) 'Rationales for Public Policy Intervention in the Innovation Process: A Systems of Innovation Approach'. In Kuhlman, S., Shapira, P., and Smits, R. (eds), *The Theory and Practice of Innovation Policy: An International Research Handbook*. Cheltenham: Edward Elgar.

Chatterji, A., Glaeser, E., and Kerr, W. (2014) 'Clusters of Entrepreneurship and Innovation'. *Innovation Policy and the Economy*, Vol. 14, pp. 129–66.

Chesbrough, H. (2003) *Open Innovation: The New Imperative for Creating and Profiting from Technology*. Boston, MA: Harvard Business School.

Citi, M. (2014) 'Revisiting Creeping Competences in the EU: The Case of Security R&D Policy'. *Journal of European Integration*, Vol. 36, No. 2, pp. 135–51.

Cohen, S. and Hochberg, Y.V. (2014) *Accelerating Startups: The Seed Accelerator Phenomenon*. http://dx.doi.org/10.2139/ssrn.2418000.

Cohen, W.M. and Levinthal, D.A. (1990) 'Absorptive Capacity: A New Perspective on Learning and Innovation'. *Administrative Science Quarterly*, Vol. 35, No. 1, pp. 128–52.

Cooke, P. (2001a) *Knowledge Economies: Clusters, Learning and Co-operative Advantage*. New York: Routledge.

Cooke, P. (2001b) 'Regional Innovation Systems, Clusters, and the Knowledge Economy'. *Industrial and Corporate Change*, Vol. 10, No. 4, pp. 945–74.

Cooke, P., Gomez Uranga, M., and Etxebarria, G. (1997) 'Regional Innovation Systems: Institutional and Organisational Dimensions'. *Research Policy*, Vol. 26, No. 4, pp. 475–91.

Corsaro, D., Cantù, C., and Tunisini, A. (2012) 'Actors' Heterogeneity in Innovation Networks'. *Industrial Marketing Management*, Vol. 41, No. 5, pp. 780–9.

Cowan, R., David, P.A., and Foray, D. (2000) 'The Explicit Economics of Knowledge Codification and Tacitness'. *Industrial and Corporate Change*, Vol. 9, No. 2, pp. 211–53.

Criscuolo, P., Narula, R., and Verspagen, B. (2005) 'Role of Home and Host Country Innovation Systems in R&D Internationalisation: A Patent Citation Analysis'. *Economics of Innovation and New Technology*, Vol. 14, No. 5, pp. 417–33.

Crossan, M.M. and Apaydin, M. (2010) 'A Multi-Dimensional Framework of Organizational Innovation: A Systematic Review of the Literature'. *Journal of Management Studies*, Vol. 47, No. 6, pp. 1154–91.

Crow, M. and Bozeman, B. (1998) *Limited by Design: R&D Laboratories in the US National Innovation System*. New York: Columbia University Press.

Cullen, J.B. and Gordon, R.H. (2007) 'Taxes and Entrepreneurial Risk-Taking: Theory and Evidence for the US'. *Journal of Public Economics*, Vol. 91, No. 7–8, pp. 1479–505.

Culpepper, P.D. and Thelen, K. (2008) 'Institutions and Collective Actors in the Provision of Training: Historical and Cross-National Comparisons'. In Mayer, K.U. and Solga, H. (eds), *Skill Formation: Interdisciplinary and Cross-National Perspectives*. Cambridge: Cambridge University Press, pp. 21–49.

Cunningham, P. and Ramlogan, R. (2016) 'The Impact of Innovation Networks'. In Edler, J., Cunningham, P., Gök, A., and Shapira, P. (eds), *Handbook of Innovation Policy Impact*. Cheltenham: Edward Elgar, pp. 279–317.

Curtin, P., Stanwick, J., and Beddie, F. (2011) *Fostering Enterprise: The Innovation and Skills Nexus—Research Readings*. Adelaide: National Centre for Vocational Education Research.

D'Este, P. and Patel, P. (2007) 'University–Industry Linkages in the UK: What Are the Factors Underlying the Variety of Interactions with Industry?' *Research Policy*, Vol. 36, No. 9, pp. 1295–313.

Da Rin, M., Nicodano, G., and Sembenelli, A. (2006) 'Public Policy and the Creation of Active Venture Capital Markets'. *Journal of Public Economics*, Vol. 90, No. 8–9, pp. 1699–723.

Dahlander, L. and Gann, D.M. (2010) 'How Open Is Innovation?' *Research Policy*, Vol. 39, No. 6, pp. 699–709.

Dahlstrand, Å.L. (1997) 'Growth and Inventiveness in Technology-Based Spin-Off Firms'. *Research Policy*, Vol. 26, No. 3, pp. 331–44.

Dahlstrand, Å.L. (1999) 'Technology-Based SMEs in the Göteborg Region: Their Origin and Interaction with Universities and Large Firms'. *Regional Studies*, Vol. 33, No. 4, pp. 379–89.

Dalhammar, C. and Leire, C. (2012) *Miljöanpassade upphandling och innovationsupphandling som styrmedel. En rapport till Upphandlingsutredningen*. Lund: Lund University.

Davidsson, P. (2016) *Researching Entrepreneurship: Conceptualization and Design*. Heidelberg: Springer.

Davies, A., Fidler, D., and Gorbis, M. (2011) *Future Work Skills 2020*. Palo Alto, CA: Institute for the Future and Apollo Research Institute.

de Bruijn, H.A. and Hufen, H.A.M. (1998) 'The Traditional Approach to Policy Instruments'. In Peters, G.B. and Nispen, F.K.M. (eds), *Public Policy Instruments: Evaluating the Tools of Public Administration*. Cheltenham: Edward Elgar, pp. 11–32.

De Ferranti, D., Perry, G.E., Gill, I., Guasch, J.L., Maloney, W.F., Sánchez-Páramo, C., and Schady, N. (eds) (2003) *Closing the Gap in Education and Technology*. Washington: World Bank.

De Fuentes, C. and Dutrénit, G. (2016) 'Geographic Proximity and University–Industry Interaction: The Case of Mexico'. *Journal of Technology Transfer*, Vol. 41, No. 2, pp. 329–48.

del-Palacio, I., Zhang, X.T., and Sole, F. (2012) 'The Capital Gap for Small Technology Companies: Public Venture Capital to the Rescue?' *Small Business Economics*, Vol. 38, No. 3, pp. 283–301.

Dhanaraj, C. and Parkhe, A. (2006) 'Orchestrating Innovation Networks'. *Academy of Management Review*, Vol. 31, No. 3, pp. 659–69.

Dietmer, L. (2011) 'Building Up of Innovative Capacities of Workers'. In Curtin, P., Stanwick, J., and Beddie, F. (eds), *Fostering Enterprise: The Innovation and Skills Nexus-Research Findings*. Adelaide: National Centre for Vocational Education Research, pp. 38–51.

Diez, M.A. (2001) 'The Evaluation of Regional Innovation and Cluster Policies: Towards a Participatory Approach'. *European Planning Studies*, Vol. 9, No. 7, pp. 907–23.

Domanski, D., Howaldt, J., and Kaletka, C. (2014) *Theoretical Approaches to Social Innovation: A Critical Literature Review*. Brussels: European Commission.

Drejer, A., Christensen, K.S., and Ulhøi, J.P. (2004) 'Understanding Intrapreneurship by Means of State-of-the-Art Knowledge Management and Organisational Learning Theory'. *International Journal of Management and Enterprise Development*, Vol. 1, No. 2, pp. 102–19.

Duranton, G. (2011) 'California Dreamin': The Feeble Case for Cluster Policies'. *Review of Economic Analysis*, Vol. 3, pp. 3–45.

Dutrénit, G. (2004) 'Building Technological Capabilities in Latecomer Firms: A Review Essay'. *Science, Technology and Society*, Vol. 9, No. 2, pp. 209–41.

Dutrénit, G. (2010) 'Introduction to Special Issue: Interactions between Public Research Organisations and Industry in Latin America: A Study on Channels and Benefits from the Perspective of Firms and Researchers'. *Science and Public Policy*, Vol. 37, No. 7, pp. 471–2.

Bibliography

Dutrénit, G., Puchet Anyul, M., and Teubal, M. (2011) 'Building Bridges between Co-evolutionary Approaches to Science, Technology and Innovation and Development Economics: An Interpretive Model'. *Innovation and Development*, Vol. 1, No. 1, pp. 51–74.

Dutta, S., Lanvin, B., and Wunsch-Vincent, S. (eds) (2015) *The Global Innovation Index 2015: Effective Innovation Policies for Development*. Geneva: WIPO.

Edler, J. (2006) *Demand-Oriented Innovation Policy Office of Technology Assessment at the German Bundestag*. Working Report no. 99.

Edler, J. (2009) 'Demand Policies for Innovation in EU CEE Countries'. *Manchester Business School Research Paper*. Manchester: Manchester University Press.

Edler, J. and Georghiou, L. (2007) 'Public Procurement and Innovation: Resurrecting the Demand Side'. *Research Policy*, Vol. 36, No. 7, pp. 949–63.

Edler, J., Fier, H., and Grimpe, C. (2011) 'International Scientist Mobility and the Locus of Knowledge and Technology Transfer'. *Research Policy*, Vol. 40, No. 6, pp. 791–805.

Edquist, C. (1993) 'Innovationspolitik för förnyelse av svensk industri' ('Innovation Policy for Renewal of Swedish Industry, in Swedish'). *Tema T Rapport*. Linköping: University of Linköping, Department of Technology and Social Change.

Edquist, C. (ed.) (1997) *Systems of Innovation: Technologies, Institutions and Organizations*. London: Pinter.

Edquist, C. (1999b) *Teknikbrostiftelsen i Linköping: En utvärdering av dess roll som offentlig såddfinansiär i det regionala innovationssystemet* (*The Technology Bridge Foundation in Linköping: An Evaluation of Its Role as a Public Provider of Seed Capital in the Regional System of Innovation*). Linköping.

Edquist, C. (2002) *Innovationspolitik för Sverige: Mål, skäl, problem och åtgärder* (*Innovation Policy for Sweden: Objectives, Rationales, Problems and Measures*). Stockholm.

Edquist, C. (2003) 'The Role of Policy in Stimulating Product and Process Innovation'. Division of Innovation, Lund Institute of Technology, Lund University.

Edquist, C. (2005) 'Systems of Innovation: Perspectives and Challenges'. In Fagerberg, J., Mowery, D.C., and Nelson, R.R. (eds), *The Oxford Handbook of Innovation*. Oxford: Oxford University Press.

Edquist, C. (2011) 'Design of Innovation Policy through Diagnostic Analysis: Identification of Systemic Problems (or Failures)'. *Industrial and Corporate Change*, Vol. 20, No. 6, pp. 1725–53.

Edquist, C. (2014a) 'Efficiency of Research and Innovation Systems for Economic Growth and Employment: Report for the European Research and Innovation Area Committee'. *Innovation Papers*. Lund: CIRCLE.

Edquist, C. (2014b) 'Holistic Innovation Policy—Why, What and How? With Examples from Sweden'. Lundvall Symposium 'Innovation Policy–Can It Make a Difference?' Aalborg.

Edquist, C. (2014c) *Offentlig upphandling och innovation* (*Public Procurement and Innovation*). Stockholm: Konkurrensverket (Swedish Competition Authority).

Edquist, C. (2014d) 'Striving towards a Holistic Innovation Policy in European Countries—But Linearity Still Prevails!' *STI Policy Review*, Vol. 5, No. 2, pp. 1–19.

Edquist, C. (2015) *Innovation-Related Public Procurement as a Demand-Oriented Innovation Policy Instrument*. Lund: CIRCLE, Lund University.

Edquist, C. (2016a) *Funktionsupphandling för ökad innovation* (Functional *Procurement for Increased Innovation*). Debate article in Upphandling 24. https://upphandling24. se/funktion supphandling-for-okad-innovation/.

Edquist, C. (2016b) *Så kan upphandling förbättras* (*Public Procurement Can Be Improved in This Way*). Stockholm: Dagens Industri.

Edquist, C. (2017) *Developing Strategic Frameworks for Innovation Related Public Procurement: Thematic Report Topic A of the Mutual Learning Exercise (MLE) Innovation Related Public Procurement*. Brussels: European Commission. https://rio.jrc.ec.europa.eu/en/ file/11394/download?token=vqnTgOSi.

Edquist, C. (2018a) *Towards a Holistic Innovation Policy: Can the Swedish National Innovation Council Serve as a Role Model?* Lund: CIRCLE, Lund University.

Edquist, C. (2018b) 'Towards a Holistic Innovation Policy: Can the Swedish National Innovation Council (NIC) Be a Role Model?' *Research Policy*, October. https://doi.org/ 10.1016/j.respol.2018.10.008.

Edquist, C. and Chaminade, C. (2006) Industrial Policy from a System-of-Innovation Perspective. *European Investment Bank Papers*, Vol. 11, No. 1–2, pp. 108–39.

Edquist, C. and Hommen, L. (1999) 'Systems of Innovation: Theory and Policy from the Demand Side'. *Technology in Society*, Vol. 21, pp. 63–79.

Edquist, C. and Johnson, B. (1997) 'Institutions and Organisations in Systems of Innovation'. In Edquist, C. (ed.), *Systems of Innovation: Technologies, Institutions and Organisations*. London: Pinter, pp. 41–63.

Edquist, C. and Zabala-Iturriagagoitia, J.M. (2012) 'Public Procurement for Innovation as Mission-Oriented Innovation Policy'. *Research Policy*, Vol. 41, No. 10, pp. 1757–69.

Edquist, C. and Zabala-Iturriagagoitia, J.M. (2015) 'Pre-Commercial Procurement: A Demand or Supply Policy Instrument in Relation to Innovation?' *R&D Management*, Vol. 45, No. 2, pp. 147–60.

Edquist, C., Hammarqvist, P., and Hommen, L. (2000a) 'Public Technology Procurement in Sweden: The X2000 High Speed Train'. In Edquist, C., Hommen, L., and Tsipouri, L. (eds), *Public Technology Procurement and Innovation*. Boston, MA: Springer, pp. 79–98.

Edquist, C., Hommen, L., and Tsipouri, L. (eds) (2000b) *Public Technology Procurement and Innovation*. Dordrecht: Kluwer Academic.

Edquist, C., Hommen, L., and McKelvey, M. (2001a) *Innovation and Employment: Process Versus Product Innovation*. Cheltenham: Edward Elgar.

Edquist, C., Rees, G., Lorenzen, M., and Vincent-Lancrin, S. (2001b) *Cities and Regions in the New Learning Economy*. Paris: OECD.

Edquist, C., Malerba, F., Metcalfe, S., Montobbio, F., and Steinmueller, E.W. (2004) 'Sectoral Systems: Implications for European Innovation Policy'. In Malerba, F. (ed.), *Sectoral Systems of Innovation in Europe: Concepts, Issues and Analyses of Six Major Sectors in Europe*. Cambridge: Cambridge University Press, pp. 427–61.

Edquist, C., Luukkonen, T., and Sotarauta, M. (2009) 'Broad-Based Innovation Policy'. In Ylä-Anttila, P. and Rouvinen, P. (eds), *Evaluation of the Finnish National Innovation System*. Helsinki: ETLA, pp. 11–69.

Edquist, C., Vonortas, N.S., and Zabala Iturriagagoitia, J.M. (2014) 'Introduction'. In Edquist, C., Vonortas, N.S., Zabala Iturriagagoitia, J.M., and Edler, J. (eds), *Public Procurement for Innovation*. Cheltenham: Edward Elgar.

Edquist, C. Zabala-Iturriagagoitia, J.M., Buchinger, E., and Whyles, G. (2018a) *Mutual Learning Exercise on Innovation-Related Procurement: Final Report*. Brussels: European Commission. https://rio.jrc.ec.europa.eu/en/file/11394/download?token=vqnTgOSi.

Edquist, C., Zabala-Iturriagagoitia, J.M., Barbero, J., and Zofío, J.L. (2018b) 'On the Meaning of Innovation Performance: Is the Synthetic Indicator of the Innovation Union Scoreboard Flawed?' *Research Evaluation*, pp. rvy011–rvy.

Edurne, M., Mikel, N., and Mikel, Z.I.J. (2014) 'Coordination-Mix: The Hidden Face of STI Policy'. *Review of Policy Research*, Vol. 31, No. 5, pp. 367–89.

Edvinsson, L. and Malone, M. (1997) *Intellectual Capital: Realizing your Company's True Value by Finding Its Hidden Brainpower*. New York: Harper Collins.

Eicher, T. and García-Peñalosa, C. (2008) 'Endogenous Strength of Intellectual Property Rights: Implications for Economic Development and Growth'. *European Economic Review*, Vol. 52, No. 2, pp. 237–58.

Encaoua, D., Guellec, D., and Martínez, C. (2006) 'Patent Systems for Encouraging Innovation: Lessons from Economic Analysis'. *Research Policy*, Vol. 35, No. 9, pp. 1423–40.

Ergas, H. (1987) 'The Importance of Technology Policy'. In Dasgupta, P. and Stoneman, P. (eds), *Economic Policy and Technological Performance*. Cambridge: Cambridge University Press, pp. 192–245.

Eriksson, R. and Lindgren, U. (2009) 'Localized Mobility Clusters: Impacts of Labour Market Externalities on Firm Performance'. *Journal of Economic Geography*, Vol. 9, No. 1, pp. 33–53.

Estellés-Arolas, E. and González-Ladrón-de-Guevara, F. (2012) 'Towards an Integrated Crowdsourcing Definition'. *Journal of Information Science*, Vol. 38, No. 2, pp. 189–200.

European University Association (2011) *Global University Rankings and Their Impact*. Brussels: European University Association.

Fagerberg, J. (2017) 'Innovation Policy: Rationales, Lessons and Challenges'. *Journal of Economic Surveys*, Vol. 31, No. 2, pp. 497–512.

Fagerberg, J. and Godinho, M.M. (2005) 'Innovation and Catching-Up'. In Fagerberg, J., Mowery, D.C., and Nelson, R.R. (eds), *The Oxford Handbook of Innovation*. Oxford: Oxford University Press, pp. 514–42.

Fagerberg, J. and Srholec, M. (2009) 'Innovation Systems, Technology and Development: Unpacking the Relationships'. In Lundvall, B.-Å., Joseph, K.J., Chaminade, C., and Vang, J. (eds), *Handbook of Innovation Systems and Developing Countries: Building Domestic Capabilities in a Global Setting*. Cheltenham: Edward Elgar, pp. 83–115.

Feldman, M. (2000) 'Location and Innovation: The New Economic Geography of Innovation, Spillovers, and Agglomeration'. In Clark, G.L., Meric, S., Gertler, M.S., and Feldman, M.P. (eds), *The Oxford Handbook of Economic Geography*. Oxford: Oxford University Press, pp. 373–94.

Feldmann, M.P. and Breznitz, S.M. (2009) 'The American Experience in University Technology Transfer'. In McKelvey, M. and Holmén, M. (eds), *Learning to Compete in European Universities*. Cheltenham: Edward Elgar.

Flanagan, K., Uyarra, E., and Laranja, M. (2011) 'Reconceptualising the "Policy Mix" for Innovation'. *Research Policy*, Vol. 40, No. 5, pp. 702–13.

Flatten, T.C., Engelen, A., Zahra, S.A., and Brettel, M. (2011) 'A Measure of Absorptive Capacity: Scale Development and Validation'. *European Management Journal*, Vol. 29, No. 2, pp. 98–116.

Foray, D. (2001) 'Intellectual Property and Innovation in the Knowledge-Based Economy'. *Beleisstudies Technologie Economie*, Vol. 37, pp. 13–43.

Foray, D. (2015) *Smart Specialisation: Opportunities and Challenges for Regional Innovation*. London: Routledge.

Foray, D., Mowery, D.C., and Nelson, R.R. (2012) 'Public R&D and Social Challenges: What Lessons from Mission R&D Programs?' *Research Policy*, Vol. 41, No. 10, pp. 1697–702.

Forester, J. (1984) 'Bounded Rationality and the Politics of Muddling Through'. *Public Administration Review*, Vol. 44, No. 1, pp. 23–31.

Fortin, J.-M. and Currie, D.J. (2013) 'Big Science vs. Little Science: How Scientific Impact Scales with Funding'. *PLoS ONE*, Vol. 8, No. 6, p. e65263.

Freeman, C. (1987) *Technology Policy and Economic Performance: Lessons from Japan*. Cambridge: Cambridge University Press.

Freeman, C. (1991) 'Networks of Innovators: A Synthesis of Research Issues'. *Research Policy*, Vol. 20, No. 5, pp. 499–514.

Freeman, C. and Soete, L. (1997) *The Economics of Industrial Innovation*. London: Routledge.

Freitas, I.M.B. (2007) 'New Instruments in Innovation Policy: The Case of the Department of Trade and Industry in the UK'. *Science and Public Policy*, Vol. 34, No. 9, pp. 644–56.

Furukawa, Y. (2010) 'Intellectual Property Protection and Innovation: An Inverted-U Relationship'. *Economics Letters*, Vol. 109, No. 2, pp. 99–101.

Gabrielsson, J., Politis, D., and Tell, J. (2012) 'University Professors and Early Stage Research Commercialisation: An Empirical Test of the Knowledge Corridor Theory'. *International Journal of Technology Transfer and Commercialisation*, Vol. 11, No. 3–4, pp. 213–33.

Gabrielsson, J., Politis, D., and Dahlstrand, Å.L. (2013) 'Patents and Entrepreneurship: The Impact of Opportunity, Motivation and Ability'. *International Journal of Entrepreneurship and Small Business*, Vol. 19, No. 2, pp. 142–66.

Gabrielsson, J., Dahlstrand, Å.L., and Politis, D. (2014) 'Sustainable High-Growth Entrepreneurship'. *International Journal of Entrepreneurship and Innovation*, Vol. 15, No. 1, pp. 29–40.

Galli, R. and Teubal, M. (1997) 'Paradigmatic Shifts in National Innovation Systems'. In Edquist, C. (ed.), *Systems of Innovation: Technologies, Institutions and Organizations*. London: Pinter.

Garcia, R. and Calantone, R. (2002) 'A Critical Look at Technological Innovation Typology and Innovativeness Terminology: A Literature Review'. *Journal of Product Innovation Management*, Vol. 19, No. 2, pp. 110–32.

Garofoli, G. and Musyck, B. (2003) 'Innovation Policies for SMEs: An Overview of Policy Instruments'. In Asheim, B.T., Isaksen, A., Nauwelaers, C., and Tödtling, F. (eds), *Regional Innovation Policy for Small-Medium Enterprises*. Cheltenham: Edward Elgar.

Garrouste, P. and Ioannides, S. (eds) (2001) *Evolution and Path Dependence in Economic Ideas: Past and Present*. Cheltenham: Edward Elgar.

Gartner, W.B. (1988) ' "Who Is an Entrepreneur?" Is the Wrong Question'. *American Journal of Small Business*, Spring, pp. 11–32.

Geiger, R.L. (2004) *To Advance Knowledge: The Growth of American Research Universities 1900–1940*. New Brunswick, NJ: Transaction.

Georghiou, L. (2002) 'Impact and Additionality of Innovation Policy'. In Boekholt, P. (ed.), *Innovation Policy and Sustainable Development: Can Public Innovation Incentives Make a Difference?* Flanders: IWT Studies, pp. 58–65.

Georghiou, L. and Clarysse, B. (2006) 'Introduction and Synthesis'. In OECD (ed.), *Government R&D Funding and Company Behaviour: Measuring Behavioural Additionality*. Paris: OECD.

Geuna, A. and Rossi, F. (2011) 'Changes to University IPR Regulations in Europe and the Impact on Academic Patenting'. *Research Policy*, Vol. 40, No. 8, pp. 1068–76.

Glückler, J. (2007) 'Economic Geography and the Evolution of Networks'. *Journal of Economic Geography*, Vol. 7, No. 5, pp. 619–34.

Godin, B. (2006) 'The Linear Model of Innovation: The Historical Construction of an Analytical Framework'. *Science, Technology and Human Values*, Vol. 31, No. 6, pp. 639–67.

Godin, B. and Lane, J.P. (2013) 'Pushes and Pulls: Hi(S)tory of the Demand Pull Model of Innovation'. *Science, Technology and Human Values*, Vol. 38, No. 5, pp. 621–54.

Godinho, M.M. and Ferreira, V. (2012) 'Analyzing the Evidence of an IPR Take-Off in China and India'. *Research Policy*, Vol. 41, No. 3, pp. 499–511.

Grabher, G. (2002) 'Cool Projects, Boring Institutions: Temporary Collaboration in Social Context'. *Regional Studies*, Vol. 36, No. 3, pp. 205–14.

Granovetter, M.S. (1983) 'The Strength of Weak Ties: A Network Theory Revisited'. *Sociological Theory*, Vol. 1, pp. 201–33.

Grimaldi, R., Kenney, M., Siegel, D.S., and Wright, M. (2011) '30 Years after Bayh–Dole: Reassessing Academic Entrepreneurship'. *Research Policy*, Vol. 40, No. 8, pp. 1045–57.

Gruber, M., Harhoff, D., and Hoisl, K. (2013) 'Knowledge Recombination across Technological Boundaries: Scientists vs. Engineers'. *Management Science*, Vol. 59, No. 4, pp. 837–51.

Guellec, D. and van Pottelsberghe de la Potterie, B. (2007) *The Economics of the European Patent System: IP Policy for Innovation and Competition*. Oxford: Oxford University Press.

Guinet, J. (2009) *Boosting Innovation: Some Lessons from the Experience of OECD Countries*. Paris: OECD.

Guston, D. (2000) *Between Politics and Science: Assuring the Integrity and Productivity of Research*. Cambridge: Cambridge University Press.

Guthrie, J. and Petty, R. (2000) 'Intellectual Capital Literature Review'. *Journal of Intellectual Capital*, Vol. 1, No. 2, pp. 155–76.

Guzman, J. and Stern, S. (2016) 'The State of American Entrepreneurship: New Estimates of the Quantity and Quality of Entrepreneurship for 15 US States, 1988–2014'. *NBER Working Paper No. 22095*, p. 108.

Guzman, J. and Stern, S. (2017) 'Nowcasting and Placecasting Entrepreneurial Quality and Performance'. In Haltiwanger, J., Hurst, E., Miranda, J., and Schoar, A. (eds), *Measuring Entrepreneurial Businesses: Current Knowledge and Challenges*. Washington, DC: NBER, pp. 63–109.

Gök, A. and Edler, J. (2012) 'The Use of Behavioural Additionality Evaluation in Innovation Policy'. *Research Evaluation*, Vol. 21, No. 4, pp. 306–18.

Haakonsson, S. (2013) 'Offshoring of Innovation: Global Innovation Networks in the Danish Biotech Industry'. In Pedersen, T., Bals, L., Ørberg Jensen, P.D., and Larsen, M.M. (eds), *The Offshoring Challenge: Strategic Design and Innovation for Tomorrow's Organization*. London: Springer, pp. 303–23.

Haakonsson, S.J. and Kirkegaard, J.K. (2016) 'Configuration of Technology Networks in the Wind Turbine Industry: A Comparative Study of Technology Management Models in European and Chinese Lead Firms'. *International Journal of Technology Management*, Vol. 70, No. 4, pp. 281–99.

Haakonsson, S.J. and Slepniov, D. (2018) 'Technology Transmission across National Innovation Systems: The Role of Danish Suppliers in Upgrading the Wind Energy Industry in China'. *European Journal of Development Research*, Vol. 30, No. 3, pp. 462–80.

Hage, J.T. (1999) 'Organizational Innovation and Organizational Change'. *Annual Review of Sociology*, Vol. 25, pp. 597–622.

Hall, B. and Lerner, J. (2010) 'The Financing of R&D and Innovation'. In Hall, B. and Rosenberg, N. (eds), *Handbook of the Economics of Innovation*. Amsterdam: Elsevier, pp. 610–38.

Hall, B., Mairesse, J., and Mohnen, P. (2010) 'Measuring the Returns to R&D'. In Hall, B. and Rosenberg, N. (eds), *Handbook of the Economics of Innovation*. Amsterdam: Elsevier, pp. 1033–82.

Harhoff, D. and Kane, T.J. (1997) 'Is the German Apprenticeship System a Panacea for the US Labor Market?' *Journal of Population Economics*, Vol. 10, No. 2, pp. 171–96.

Hart, D.M. (ed.) (2003) *The Emergence of Entrepreneurship Policy: Governance, Start-Ups and Growth*. Cambridge: Cambridge University Press.

Hartley, J. (2005) 'Innovation in Governance and Public Services: Past and Present'. *Public Money and Management*, Vol. 25, No. 1, pp. 27–34.

Hazelkorn, E. (2013) 'Reflections on a Decade of Global Rankings: What We've Learned and Outstanding Issues'. *Beiträge zur Hochschulforschung*, Vol. 35, No. 2, pp. 8–33.

Hekkert, M.P., Suurs, R.A.A., Negro, S.O., Kuhlmann, S., and Smits, R.E.H.M. (2007) 'Functions of Innovation Systems: A New Approach for Analysing Technological Change'. *Technological Forecasting and Social Change*, Vol. 74, No. 4, pp. 413–32.

Henrekson, M. and Stenkula, M. (2010) 'Entrepreneurship and Public Policy'. In Acs, Z. J. and Audretsch, D.B. (eds), *Handbook of Entrepreneurship Research*. New York: Springer, pp. 595–637.

Hicks, D. (2012) 'Performance-Based University Research Funding Systems'. *Research Policy*, Vol. 41, No. 2, pp. 251–61.

Hirsch-Kreinsen, H. (2011) 'Financial Market and Technological Innovation'. *Industry and Innovation*, Vol. 18, No. 4, pp. 351–68.

Hodgson, G.M. (1997) 'The Ubiquity of Habits and Rules'. *Cambridge Journal of Economics*, Vol. 21, No. 6, pp. 663–84.

Hood, C.C. and Margetts, H.Z. (2007) *The Tools of Government in the Digital Age*. London: Palgrave.

Hsu, Y.-H. and Fang, W. (2009) 'Intellectual Capital and New Product Development Performance: The Mediating Role of Organizational Learning Capability'. *Technological Forecasting and Social Change*, Vol. 76, No. 5, pp. 664–77.

Hult, G.T.M., Ketchen, D.J. and Slater, S.F. (2004) 'Information Processing, Knowledge Development, and Strategic Supply Chain Performance'. *Academy of Management Journal*, Vol. 47, No. 2, pp. 241–53.

Høyrup, S. (2010) 'Employee-Driven Innovation and Workplace Learning: Basic Concepts, Approaches and Themes'. *Transfer: European Review of Labour and Research*, Vol. 16, No. 2, pp. 143–54.

Isaksson, A. (1999) *Effekter av venture capital i Sverige (Impact of Venture Capital in Sweden)*. Stockholm: NUTEK.

Jaffe, A.B. (1998) 'The Importance of "Spillovers" in the Policy Mission of the Advanced Technology Program'. *Journal of Technology Transfer*, Vol. 23, No. 2, pp. 11–19.

Jaffe, A.B. and Palmer, J. (1997) 'Environmental Regulation and Innovation: A Panel Data Study'. *Review of Economics and Statistics*, Vol. 79, No. 4, pp. 610–19.

Jaffe, A.B., Peterson, S.R., Portney, P.R., and Stavins, R.N. (1995) 'Environmental Regulation and the Competitiveness of US Manufacturing: What Does the Evidence Tell Us?'. *Journal of Economic Literature*, Vol. 33, No. 1, pp. 132–63.

Jasanoff, S. (ed.) (1995) *Handbook of Science and Technology Studies*. London: SAGE.

Jensen, M.B., Johnson, B., Lorenz, E., and Lundvall, B.Å. (2007) 'Forms of Knowledge and Modes of Innovation'. *Research Policy*, Vol. 36, No. 5, pp. 680–93.

Johnson, B., Lorenz, E., and Lundvall, B.-Å. (2002) 'Why All This Fuss about Codified and Tacit Knowledge?' *Industrial and Corporate Change*, Vol. 11, pp. 245–62.

Jones, B. (2012) *Innovation and Human Resources: Migration Policies and Employment Protection Policies*. Manchester: Manchester Institute of Innovation Research, University of Manchester.

Jones, B. and Grimshaw, D. (2012) *The Effects of Policies for Training and Skills on Improving Innovation Capabilities in Firms*. Manchester: Manchester Institute of Innovation Research, University of Manchester.

Jones, Barbara and Grimshaw, Damian (2016) 'The Impact of Skill Formation Policies on Innovation'. In Edler, J., Cunningham, P., Abdullah, G., and Shapira, P. (eds), *Handbook of Innovation Policy Impact* (Cheltenham: Edward Elgar), pp. 108–28.

Jones, B. and Miller, B. (2007) *Innovation Diffusion in the New Economy: The Tacit Component*. London: Routledge.

Jordan, G.B., Hage, J., and Mote, J. (2008) 'A Theories-Based Systemic Framework for Evaluating Diverse Portfolios of Scientific Work, Part 1: Micro and Meso Indicators'. *New Directions for Evaluation*, Vol. 2008, No. 118, pp. 7–24.

Jordana, J. and Levi-Faur, D. (eds) (2004a) *The Politics of Regulation: Institutions and Regulatory Reforms for the Age of* Governance. Cheltenham: Edward Elgar.

Jordana, J. and Levi-Faur, D. (2004b) 'The Politics of Regulation in the Age of Governance'. In Jordana, J. and Levi-Faur, D. (eds), *The Politics of Regulation: Institutions and Regulatory Reforms for the Age of Governance*. London: Routledge, pp. 1–28.

Joss, S. (1999) 'Public Participation in Science and Technology Policy—and Decision-Making—Ephemeral Phenomenon or Lasting Change?' *Science and Public Policy*, Vol. 26, No. 5, pp. 290–3.

Kahlenborn, W., Moser, C., Frijdal, J., and Essig, M. (2011) *Strategic Use of Public Procurement in Europe: Final Report to the European Commission*. Berlin: Adelphi.

Karlsson, C. (2018) 'Statliga miljoner till bolag i utecklingsfasen' ('State Millions to Companies in the Development Phase'). *Dagens Industri*.

Kesting, P. and Ulhøi, J.P. (2010) 'Employee-Driven Innovation: Extending the License to Foster Innovation'. *Management Decision*, Vol. 48, No. 1, pp. 65–84.

Ketels, C., Lindqvist, G., and Sölvell, Ö. (2006) *Cluster Initiatives in Developing and Transition Economies*. Stockholm: Center for Strategy and Competitiveness.

Kim, L. (1997) *Imitation to Innovation: The Dynamics of Korea's Technological Learning*. Boston, MA: Harvard Business School Press.

Kitagawa, F. (2004) 'Universities and Regional Advantage: Higher Education and Innovation Policies in English Regions'. *European Planning Studies*, Vol. 12, No. 6, pp. 835–52.

Klein, P.G., Mahoney, J.T., McGahan, A.M., and Pitelis, C.N. (2010) 'Toward a Theory of Public Entrepreneurship'. *European Management Review*, Vol. 7, No. 1, pp. 1–15.

Klein, P.G., Mahoney, J.T., McGahan, A.M., and Pitelis, C.N. (2013) 'Capabilities and Strategic Entrepreneurship in Public Organizations'. *Strategic Entrepreneurship Journal*, Vol. 7, No. 1, pp. 70–91.

Klein Woolthuis, R., Lankhuizen, M., and Gilsing, V. (2005) 'A System Failure Framework for Innovation Policy Design'. *Technovation*, Vol. 25, No. 6, pp. 609–19.

Kline, S.J. (1985) 'Innovation Is Not a Linear Process'. *Research Management*, Vol. 28, No. 4, pp. 36–45.

Kline, S.J. and Rosenberg, N. (1986) 'An Overview of Innovation'. In Landau, R. and Rosenberg, N. (eds), *The Positive Sum Game*. Washington, DC: National Academy Press.

Knight, G.A. and Cavusgil, S.T. (2004) 'Innovation, Organizational Capabilities, and the Born-Global Firm'. *Journal of International Business Studies*, Vol. 35, No. 2, pp. 124–41.

Kogut, B. (2000) 'The Network as Knowledge: Generative Rules and the Emergence of Structure'. *Strategic Management Journal*, Vol. 21, No. 2, pp. 405–25.

Kuchiki, A. and Tsuji, M. (eds) (2005) *Industrial Clusters in Asia: Analyses of Their Competition and Cooperation*. London: Palgrave Macmillan.

Kuhlmann, S. (2003) 'Evaluation of Research and Innovation Policies: A Discussion of Trends with Examples from Germany'. *International Journal of Technology Management*, Vol. 26, No. 2–4, pp. 131–49.

Kuhlmann, S. and Ordonez-Matamoros, G. (2016) 'Governance of Innovation in Emerging Countries: Understanding Failures and Exploring Options'. In Kuhlmann, S. and Ordonez-Matamoros, G. (eds), *Research Handbook on Innovation Governance for Emerging Economies: Towards Better Models*. Cheltenham: Edward Elgar.

Kuhlmann, S. and Rip, A. (2014) *The Challenge of Addressing Grand Challenges: A Think Piece on How Innovation Can Be Driven towards the 'Grand Challenges' as Defined under the Prospective European Union Framework Programme Horizon 2020*. Twente: Twente University.

Kuhlmann, S. and Rip, A. (2018) 'Next-Generation Innovation Policy and Grand Challenges'. *Science and Public Policy*, pp. scy011–scy.

Kuhlmann, S., Shapira, P., and Smits, R.E. (2010) 'Introduction: A Systemic Perspective: The Innovation Policy Dance'. In Smits, R.E., Kuhlmann, S., and Shapira, P. (eds), *The Theory and Practice of Innovation Policy: An International Research Handbook*. Cheltenham: Edward Elgar, pp. 1–22.

Kutnetsor, Y. (ed.) (2006) *Diaspora Networks and the International Migration of Skills*. Washington, DC: World Bank.

Köhler, C., Laredo, P., and Rammer, C. (2012) The Impact and Effectiveness of Fiscal Incentives for R&D. *Nesta*, January.

Lach, S. (2002) 'Do R&D Subsidies Stimulate or Displace Private R&D? Evidence from Israel'. *Journal of Industrial Economics*, Vol. 50, No. 4, pp. 369–90.

Lam, A. (2005) 'Organizational Innovation'. In Fagerberg, J., Mowery, D.C., and Nelson, R.R. (eds), *The Oxford Handbook on Innovation*. Oxford: Oxford University Press, pp. 115–47.

Landström, H. (2005) *Pioneers in Entrepreneurship and Small Business Research*. Boston, MA: Springer.

Laursen, K. (2011) 'User–Producer Interaction as a Driver of Innovation: Costs and Advantages in an Open Innovation Model'. *Science and Public Policy*, Vol. 38, No. 9, pp. 713–23.

Laursen, K. and Salter, A. (2006) 'Open for Innovation: The Role of Openness in Explaining Innovation Performance among UK Manufacturing Firms'. *Strategic Management Journal*, Vol. 27, No. 2, pp. 131–50.

Lawson, C. (2000) 'Collective Learning, System Competences and Epistemically Significant Moments'. In Keeble, D. and Wilkinson, F. (eds), *High-technology Clusters, Networking and Collective Learning*. Aldershot: Ashgate, pp. 182–98.

Lazonick, W. (2005) 'The Innovative Firm'. In Fagerberg, J., Mowery, D.C., and Nelson, R.R. (eds), *The Oxford Handbook of Innovation*. Oxford: Oxford University Press, pp. 29–55.

Leifeld, P. and Haunss, S. (2012) 'Political Discourse Networks and the Conflict over Software Patents in Europe'. *European Journal of Political Research*, Vol. 51, pp. 382–409.

Leleux, B. and Surlemont, B. (2003) 'Public versus Private Venture Capital: Seeding or Crowding Out? A Pan-European Analysis'. *Journal of Business Venturing*, Vol. 18, No. 1, pp. 81–104.

Lemaire, D. (1998) 'The Stick: Regulation as a Tool of Government'. In Bemelmans-Videc, M.L., Rist, R.C., and Verdung, E. (eds), *Carrots, Sticks and Sermons: Policy Instruments and Their Evaluation*. London: Transaction, pp. 59–76.

Lepori, B., van den Besselaar, P., Dinges, M., Potí, B., Reale, E., Slipersaeter, S., Thèves, J., and van der Meulen, B. (2007) 'Comparing the Evolution of National Research Policies: What Patterns of Change?' *Science and Public Policy*, Vol. 34, No. 6, pp. 372–88.

Lepori, B., Masso, J., Jabłecka, J., Sima, K., and Ukrainski, K. (2009) 'Comparing the Organization of Public Research Funding in Central and Eastern European Countries'. *Science and Public Policy*, Vol. 36, No. 9, pp. 667–81.

Lerner, J. (2002) 'When Bureaucrats Meet Entrepreneurs: The Design of Effective "Public Venture Capital" Programmes'. *Economic Journal*, Vol. 112, No. 477, pp. F73–F84.

Lerner, J. (2009) 'The Empirical Impact of Intellectual Property Rights on Innovation: Puzzles and Clues'. *American Economic Review*, Vol. 99, No. 2, pp. 343–8.

Lerner, J. and Tåg, J. (2013) 'Institutions and Venture Capital'. *Industrial and Corporate Change*, Vol. 22, No. 1, pp. 153–82.

Lindblom, C.E. (1959) 'The Science of "Muddling Through"'. *Public Administration Review*, Vol. 19, No. 2, pp. 79–88.

Linder, S.H. and Peters, B.G. (1998) 'The Study of Policy Instruments: Four Schools of Thought'. In Peters, B.G. and Nispen, F.K.M. (eds), *Public Policy Instruments: Evaluating the Tools of Public Administration*. Cheltenham: Edward Elgar, pp. 33–45.

Lindgaard Christensen, J. (2011) 'Should Government Support Business Angel Networks? The Tale of Danish Business Angels Network'. *Venture Capital*, Vol. 13, No. 4, pp. 337–56.

Lindholm Dahlstrand, Å. and Johannisson, B. (2013) 'Introduction: The Challenges, the Journey and the Lessons'. In Lindholm Dahlstrand, Å. and Johannisson, B. (eds), *Enacting Regional Dynamics and Entrepreneurship: Bridging the Territorial and the Functional*. Abingdon: Routledge.

Lipsey, R.G., Carlaw, K.I., and Bekar, C.T. (2005) *Economic Transformations: General Purpose Technologies and Long Term Economic Growth*. New York: Oxford University Press.

Lissoni, F., Lotz, P., Schovsbo, J., and Treccani, A. (2009) 'Academic Patenting and the Professor's Privilege: Evidence on Denmark from the KEINS Database'. *Science and Public Policy*, Vol. 36, No. 8, pp. 595–607.

Liu, J., Chaminade, C., and Asheim, B. (2013) 'The Geography and Structure of Global Innovation Networks: A Knowledge Base Perspective'. *European Planning Studies*, Vol. 21, No. 9, pp. 1456–73.

Liu, X. and White, S. (2001) 'Comparing Innovation Systems: A Framework and Application to China's Transitional Context'. *Research Policy*, Vol. 30, No. 7, pp. 1091–114.

Lorenz, E. (2011) 'Do Labour Markets and Educational and Training Systems Matter for Innovation Outcomes? A Multi-Level Analysis for the EU-27'. *Science and Public Policy*, Vol. 38, No. 9, pp. 691–702.

Lorenz, E. and Lundvall, B.-Å. (2011) 'Accounting for Creativity in the European Union: A Multi-Level Analysis of Individual Competence, Labour Market Structure, and Systems of Education and Training'. *Cambridge Journal of Economics*, Vol. 35, No. 2, pp. 269–94.

Lorenz, E., Lundvall, B.-Å., Kraemer-Mbula, E., and Rasmussen, P. (2016) 'Work Organisation, Forms of Employee Learning and National Systems of Education and Training'. *European Journal of Education*, Vol. 51, No. 2, pp. 154–75.

Ludger, D., Hauschildt, U., Rauner, F., and Zelloth, H. (eds) (2013) *The Architecture of Innovative Apprenticeship*. Dordrecht: Springer.

Lundvall, B.-Å. (1985) *Product Innovation and User–Producer Interaction*. Aalborg: Aalborg University Press.

Lundvall, B.-Å. (1988) 'Innovation as an Interactive Process: From User–Producer Interaction to the National System of Innovation'. In Dosi, G., Teece, D., and Chytrys, J. (eds), *Technical Change and Economic Theory*. London: Pinter.

Lundvall, B.-Å. (ed.) (1992) *National Systems of Innovation: Towards a Theory of Innovation and Interactive Learning*. London: Pinter.

Lundvall, B.-Å. (2007) 'National Innovation Systems: Analytical Concept and Development Tool'. *Industry and Innovation*, Vol. 14, No. 1, pp. 95–119.

Lundvall, B.-Å. and Borrás, S. (1998) *The Globalising Learning Economy: Implications for Innovation Policy*. Brussels: European Commission.

Lundvall, B.-Å. and Johnson, B. (1994) 'The Learning Economy'. *Journal of Industrial Studies*, Vol. 1, No. 2, pp. 23–42.

Lundvall, B.-Å., Johnson, B., Andersen, E.S., and Dalum, B. (2002) 'National Systems of Production, Innovation and Competence Building'. *Research Policy*, Vol. 31, No. 2, pp. 213–31.

Lundvall, B.- Å., Joseph, K., Chaminade, C., and Vang, J. (2009) 'Innovation Systems and Developing Countries: An introduction'. In Lundvall, B.A., Joseph, K., Chaminade, C., and Vang, J. (eds), *Innovation Systems and Developing Countries: Building Domestic Capabilities in a Global Setting*. Cheltenham: Edward Elgar.

Macaulay, L., Moxham, C., Jones, B., and Miles, I. (2010) 'Innovation and Skills'. In Maglio, P.P., Kieliszewski, C.A., and Spohrer, J.C. (eds), *Handbook of Service Science*. New York: Springer, pp. 717–36.

Maclean, M., Harvey, C., and Gordon, J. (2013) 'Social Innovation, Social Entrepreneurship and the Practice of Contemporary Entrepreneurial Philanthropy'. *International Small Business Journal*, Vol. 31, No. 7, pp. 747–63.

Mahoney, J. and Thelen, K. (eds) (2010) *Explaining Institutional Change: Ambiguity, Agency and Power*. Cambridge: Cambridge University Press.

Majone, G. (1994) 'The Rise of the Regulatory State in Europe'. *West European Politics*, Vol. 17, pp. 77–101.

Makkonen, T. and Lin, B. (2012) 'Continuing Vocational Training and Innovation in Europe'. *International Journal of Innovation and Learning*, Vol. 11, No. 4, pp. 325–38.

Makkonen, T. and van der Have, R. (2013) 'Benchmarking Regional Innovative Performance: Composite Measures and Direct Innovation Counts'. *Scientometrics*, Vol. 94, No. 1, pp. 247–62.

Malerba, F. (2009) 'Increase Learning, Break Knowledge Lock-Ins and Foster Dynamic Complementarities: Evolutionary and System Perspectives on Technology Policy in Industrial Dynamics'. In Foray, D. (ed.), *The New Economics of Technology Policy*. Cheltenham: Edward Elgar.

Malerba, F. and Orsenigo, L. (1996) 'Schumpeterian Patterns of Innovation Are Technology-Specific'. *Research Policy*, Vol. 25, No. 3, pp. 451–78.

March, J.G. (1991) 'Exploration and Exploitation in Organizational Learning'. *Organization Science*, Vol. 2, No. 1, pp. 71–87.

March, J.G. (2010) *The Ambiguities of* Experience. Ithaca, NY: Cornell University Press.

March, J.G. and Olsen, J.P. (1989) *Rediscovering Institutions: The Organizational Basis of Politics*. New York: Free Press.

Martin, J.F. (1996) *The EU Public Procurement Rules: A Critical Analysis*. Oxford: Clarendon Press.

Martin, R. and Sunley, P. (2003) 'Deconstructing Clusters: Chaotic Concept or Policy Panacea?' *Journal of Economic Geography*, Vol. 3, No. 1, pp. 5–35.

Mason, C.M. (2009) 'Public Policy Support for the Informal Venture Capital Market in Europe: A Critical Review'. *International Small Business Journal*, Vol. 27, No. 5, pp. 536–56.

Matt, M., Robin, S., and Wolff, S. (2012) 'The Influence of Public Programs on Inter-Firm R&D Collaboration Strategies: Project-Level Evidence from EU FP5 and FP6'. *Journal of Technology Transfer*, Vol. 37, No. 6, pp. 885–916.

Maukola, J. (2015) 'Sweden Set to Switch Tracks'. *Research Europe*, 19 March.

Mazzanti, M. and Zoboli, R. (2006) 'Economic Instruments and Induced Innovation: The European Policies on End-of-Life Vehicles'. *Ecological Economics*, Vol. 58, No. 2, pp. 318–37.

Mazzucato, M. (2013) 'Financing Innovation: Creative Destruction vs. Destructive Creation'. *Industrial and Corporate Change*, Vol. 22, No. 4, pp. 851–67.

Mazzucato, M. (2016) 'From Market Fixing to Market-Creating: A New Framework for Innovation Policy'. *Industry and Innovation*, Vol. 23, No. 2, pp. 140–56.

McKelvey, M. and Holmén, M. (2009) 'Introduction'. In McKelvey, M. and Holmén, M. (eds), *Learning to Compete in European Universities: From Social Institution to Knowledge Business*. Cheltenham: Edward Elgar, pp. 1–18.

McKelvey, M. and Ljungberg, D. (2017) 'How Public Policy Can Stimulate the Capabilities of Firms to Innovate in a Traditional Industry through Academic Engagement: The Case of the Swedish Food Industry'. *R&D Management*, Vol. 47, No. 4, pp. 534–44.

McKelvey, M., Zaring, O., and Ljungberg, D. (2015) 'Creating Innovative Opportunities through Research Collaboration: An Evolutionary Framework and Empirical Illustration in Engineering'. *Technovation*, Vol. 39–40, pp. 26–36.

Meeus, M. and Faber, J. (2006) 'Interorganizational Relations and Innovation: A Review and Theoretical Extension'. In Meeus, M. and Hage, J. (eds), *Innovation, Science and Institutional Change*. Oxford: Oxford University Press, pp. 67–87.

Menard, C. and Shirley, M.M. (eds) (2008) *Handbook of New Institutional Economics*. Berlin: Springer.

Metcalfe, S. (1995) 'The Economic Foundations of Technology Policy: Equilibrium and Evolutionary Perspectives'. In Stoneman, P. (ed.), *Handbook of the Economics of Innovation and Technological Change*. Oxford: Blackwell, pp. 409–512.

Metcalfe, S. (2006) 'Innovation, Competition and Enterprise: Foundations for Economic Evolution in Learning Economies'. In Hage, J. and Meeus, M. (eds), *Innovation, Science, and Institutional Change*. Oxford: Oxford University Press, pp. 105–21.

Metcalfe, S. (2007) 'Innovation Systems, Innovation Policy and Restless Capitalism'. In Malerba, F. and Brusoni, S. (eds), *Perspectives on Innovation*. Cambridge: Cambridge University Press.

Miles, I. (2005) 'Innovation in Services'. In Fagerberg, J., Mowery, D.C., and Nelson, R.R. (eds), *The Oxford Handbook on Innovation*. Oxford: Oxford University Press, pp. 433–58.

Miller, D.J., Fern, M.J., and Cardinal, L.B. (2007) 'The Use of Knowledge for Technological Innovation within Diversified Firms'. *Academy of Management Journal*, Vol. 50, No. 2, pp. 307–25.

Moed, H.F., Glänzel, W., and Schmoch, U. (eds) (2010) *Handbook of Quantitative Science and Technology Research: The Use of Publication and Patent Statistics in Studies of S&T Systems*. Dordrecht: Kluwer Academic.

Mohnen, P. and Röller, L.-H. (2005) 'Complementarities in Innovation Policy'. *European Economic Review*, Vol. 49, No. 6, pp. 1431–50.

Molas-Gallart, J. (2012) 'Research Governance and the Role of Evaluation: A Comparative Study'. *American Journal of Evaluation*, Vol. 33, No. 4, pp. 583–98.

Molina-Morales, F.X. and Martínez-Fernández, M.T. (2010) 'Social Networks: Effects of Social Capital on Firm Innovation'. *Journal of Small Business Management*, Vol. 48, No. 2, pp. 258–79.

Morgan, K. (1997) 'The Learning Region: Institutions, Innovation and Regional Renewal'. *Regional Studies*, Vol. 31, No. 5, pp. 491–503.

Mowery, D.C. and Rosenberg, N. (1998) *Paths of Innovation: Technological Change in 20th-Century America*. Cambridge: Cambridge University Press.

Mowery, D.C. and Sampat, B.N. (2005) 'Universities in National Innovation Systems'. In Fagerberg, J., Mowery, D.C., and Nelson, R.R. (eds), *The Oxford Handbook of Innovation*. Oxford: Oxford University Press.

Mowery, D.C. and Ziedonis, A.A. (2000) 'Numbers, Quality, and Entry: How Has the Bayh-Dole Act Affected US University Patenting and Licensing'. In Jaffe, A.B., Josh, L., and Scott, S. (eds), *Innovation Policy and the Economy*. Cambridge, MA: MIT Press.

Munari, F. and Toschi, L. (2015) 'Assessing the Impact of Public Venture Capital Programmes in the United Kingdom: Do Regional Characteristics Matter?' *Journal of Business Venturing*, Vol. 30, No. 2, pp. 205–26.

Muñoz, V., Visentin, F., Foray, D., and Gaulé, P. (2015) 'Can Medical Products Be Developed on a Non-Profit Basis? Exploring Product Development Partnerships for Neglected Diseases'. *Science and Public Policy*, Vol. 42, No. 3, pp. 315–38.

Murovec, N. and Prodan, I. (2009) 'Absorptive Capacity, Its Determinants, and Influence on Innovation Output: Cross-Cultural Validation of the Structural Model'. *Technovation*, Vol. 29, No. 12, pp. 859–72.

Murray, F. and Stern, S. (2007) 'Do Formal Intellectual Property Rights Hinder the Free Flow of Scientific Knowledge? An Empirical Test of the Anti-Commons Hypothesis'. *Journal of Economic Behavior and Organization*, Vol. 63, No. 4, pp. 648–87.

Mytelka, L.K. and Smith, K. (2002) 'Policy Learning and Innovation Theory: An Interactive and Co-evolving Process'. *Research Policy*, Vol. 31, No. 8–9, pp. 1467–79.

Narula, R. (2010) *Much Ado about Nothing or Sirens of a Brave New World? MNE Activity from Developing Countries and Its Significance for Development*. Paris: OECD Development Centre.

Nauwelaers, C. and Wintjes, R. (2008) 'Innovation Policy, Innovation in Policy: Policy Learning within and across Systems and Clusters'. In Nauwelaers, C. and Wintjes, R.

(eds), *Innovation Policy in Europe: Measurement and Strategy.* Cheltenham: Edward Elgar.

Nelson, R.R. (1959) 'The Simple Economics of Basic Scientific Research'. *Journal of Political Economy*, Vol. 67, No. 3, pp. 297–306.

Nelson, R.R. (ed.) (1993) *National Innovation Systems: A Comparative Analysis.* Oxford: Oxford University Press.

Nelson, R.R. (1994) 'The Co-evolution of Technology, Industrial Structure, and Supporting Institutions'. *Industrial and Corporate Change*, Vol. 3, No. 1, pp. 47–63.

Nelson, R.R. (2004) 'The Market Economy, and the Scientific Commons'. *Research Policy*, Vol. 33, No. 3, pp. 455–71.

Nelson, R.R. (2009) 'Building Effective "Innovation Systems" versus Dealing with "Market Failures" as Ways of Thinking about Technology Policy'. In Foray, D. (ed.), *The New Economics of Technology Policy.* Cheltenham: Edward Elgar.

Nelson, R.R. and Rosenberg, N. (1993) 'Technical Innovation and National Systems'. In Nelson, R.R. (ed.), *National Innovation Systems: A Comparative Analysis.* Oxford: Oxford University Press, pp. 3–22.

Nelson, R.R. and Winter, S. (1982) *An Evolutionary Theory of Economic Change.* Cambridge, MA: Harvard University Press.

Nicholls, A., Simon, J., and Gabriel, M. (eds) (2015) *New Frontiers in Social Innovation Research.* London: Palgrave.

Nightingale, P. (2003) 'If Nelson and Winter Are Only Half Right about Tacit Knowledge, Which Half? A Searlean Critique of "Codification"'. *Industrial and Corporate Change*, Vol. 12, No. 2, pp. 149–83.

Nightingale, P. and Coad, A. (2014) 'Muppets and Gazelles: Political and Methodological Biases in Entrepreneurship Research'. *Industrial and Corporate Change*, Vol. 23, No. 1, pp. 113–43.

Nightingale, P., Murray, G., Cowling, M., Baden-Fuller, C., Mason, C., Siepel, J., Hopins, M., and Dannreuther, C. (2009) *From Funding Gaps to Thin Markets: UK Government Support for Early-Stage Venture Capital.* London: NESTA and BVCA.

Nonaka, I. (1994) 'A Dynamic Theory of Organizational Knowledge Creation'. *Organization Science*, Vol. 5, No. 1, pp. 14–37.

Nooteboom, B. (2004) *Inter-Firm Collaboration, Learning and Networks: An Integrated Approach.* London: Routledge.

North, D.C. (1990) *Institutions, Institutional Change and Economic Performance.* Cambridge: Cambridge University Press.

OECD (1997) *The OECD Report on Regulatory Reform: Volume I: Sectoral Studies.* Paris: OECD.

OECD (2001) *Cities and Regions in the New Learning Economy: Education and Skills.* Report prepared by Charles Edquist, Gareth Rees, Mark Lorentzen and Stéphan Vincent Lancrin. Paris: OECD.

OECD (2002) *Frascati Manual: Proposed Standard Practice for Surveys on Research and Experimental Development.* Paris: OECD.

OECD (2005) *The Measurement of Scientific and Technological Activities. Oslo Manual: The Guidelines for Collecting and Interpreting Innovation Data*, 3rd edn. Paris: OECD.

OECD (2007) *The Internationalisation of Business R&D: Evidence, Impacts and Implications*. Paris: OECD.

OECD (2008) *Open Innovation in Global Networks*. Paris: OECD.

OECD (2011) *Skills for Innovation and Research*. Paris: OECD.

OECD (2012a) *New Sources of Growth Knowledge-Based Capital Driving Investment and Productivity in the 21st Century: Interim Project Findings*. Paris: OECD.

OECD (2012b) *OECD Reviews of Innovation Policy: Sweden*. Paris: OECD.

OECD (2016) *Public Procurement for Innovation: Good Practices and Strategies*. Paris: OECD.

Oerlemans, L. and Meeus, M. (2005) 'Do Organizational and Spatial Proximity Impact on Firm Performance?' *Regional Studies*, Vol. 39, No. 1, pp. 89–104.

Oh, D.-S., Philips, F., Park, S., and Lee, E. (2016) 'Innovation Eco-Systems: A Critical Examination'. *Technovation*, Vol. 54, August.

Olsen, A.Ø. (2015) 'In Search of Solutions: Inertia, Knowledge Sources and Diversity in Collaborative Problem-Solving'. Copenhagen: Copenhagen Business School.

Pelikan, P. (2001) 'Self-Organizing and Darwinian Selection in Economic and Biological Evolutions: An Enquiry into the Sources of Organizing Information'. In Foster, J. and Metcalfe, J.S. (eds), *Frontiers of Evolutionary Economics: Competition, Self-Organization and Innovation Policy*. Cheltenham: Edward Elgar, pp. 121–50.

Perez, C. (2009) 'Technological Revolutions and Techno-Economic Paradigms'. *Cambridge Journal of Economics*, Vol. 34, No. 1, pp. 185–202.

Perkmann, M., Tartari, V., McKelvey, M., Autio, E., Broström, A., D'Este, P., Fini, R., Geuna, A., Grimaldi, R., Hughes, A., Krabel, S., Kitson, M., Llerena, P., Lissoni, F., Salter, A., and Sobrero, M. (2013) 'Academic Engagement and Commercialisation: A Review of the Literature on University–Industry Relations'. *Research Policy*, Vol. 42, No. 2, pp. 423–42.

Peter, V., van der Veen, G., Doranova, A., and Miedzinski, M. (2013) *Screening of Regulatory Framework*. Brussels: Technopolis.

Phelps, C., Heidl, R., and Wadhwa, A. (2012) 'Knowledge, Networks, and Knowledge Networks'. *Journal of Management*, Vol. 38, No. 4, pp. 1115–66.

Pierre, J. and Peters, B.G. (2000) *Governance, Politics and the State*. Basingstoke: Macmillan.

Pierre, J. and Peters, G.B. (2005) *Governing Complex Societies: Trajectories and Scenarios*. London: Palgrave.

Pilat, D., De Backer, K., Basri, E., Box, S., and Cervantes, M. (2009) 'The Development of Global Innovation Networks and the Transfer of Knowledge'. In Chandra, V., Eröcal, D., Padoan, P.C., and Primo Braga, C.A. (eds), *Innovation and Growth Chasing a Moving Frontier*. Paris: OECD and World Bank, pp. 85–106.

Pitelis, C.N. (2010) 'Economics: Economic Theories of the Firm, Business and Government'. In Coen, D., Grant, W., and Wilson, G. (eds), *The Oxford Handbook of Business and Government*. Oxford: Oxford University Press.

Pitelis, C.N. (2012) 'Clusters, Entrepreneurial Ecosystem Co-creation, and Appropriability: A Conceptual Framework'. *Industrial and Corporate Change*, Vol. 21, No. 6, pp. 1359–88.

Piva, M., Santorelli, E., and Vivarelli, M. (2006) 'Technological and Organizational Changes as Determinants of the Skill Bias: Evidence from the Italian Machinery Industry'. *Managerial and Decision Economics*, Vol. 27, No. 1, pp. 63–73.

Politis, D., Gabrielsson, J., and Shveykina, O. (2012) 'Early-Stage Finance and the Role of External Entrepreneurs in the Commercialization of University-Generated Knowledge'. *Venture Capital*, Vol. 14, No. 2–3, pp. 175–98.

Porter, M. and Van der Linde, C. (1995) 'Toward a New Conception of the Environment-Competitiveness Relationship'. *Journal of Economic Perspectives*, Vol. 9, No. 4, pp. 97–118.

Porto Gómez, I., Zabala-Iturriagagoitia, J.M., and Aguirre Larrakoetxea, U. (2018) 'Old Wine in Old Bottles: The Neglected Role of Vocational Training Centres in Innovation'. *Vocations and Learning*, Vol. 11, No. 2, pp. 205–21.

Posner, E. (2005) 'Sources of Institutional Change: The Supranational Origins of Europe's New Stock Markets'. *World Politics*, Vol. 58, No. 1, pp. 1–40.

Potter, J. (2009) 'Policy Issues in Clusters, Innovation and Entrepreneurship'. In Potter, J. and Miranda, G. (eds), *Clusters, Innovation and Entrepreneurship*. Paris: OECD.

Powell, W.W. and Grodal, S. (2005) 'Networks of Innovators'. In Fagerberg, J., Mowery, D., and Nelson, R.R. (eds), *The Oxford Handbook of Innovation*. Oxford: Oxford University Press, pp. 56–85.

Powell, W.W., Koput, K.W., and Smith-Doerr, L. (1996) 'Interorganizational Collaboration and the Locus of Innovation: Networks of Learning in Biotechnology'. *Administrative Science Quarterly*, Vol. 41, No. 1, pp. 116–45.

Powell, W.W., Koput, K.W., Bowie, J.I., and Smith-Doerr, L. (2002) 'The Spatial Clustering of Science and Capital: Accounting for Biotech Firm–Venture Capital Relationships'. *Regional Studies*, Vol. 36, No. 3, pp. 291–305.

Prahalad, C.K. (2012) 'Bottom of the Pyramid as a Source of Breakthrough Innovations'. *Journal of Product Innovation Management*, Vol. 29, No. 1, pp. 6–12.

Prahalad, C.K. and Hamel, G. (1990) 'The Core Competence of the Corporation'. *Harvard Business Review*, May–June, pp. 79–91.

Prantl, S. (2011) 'Entry Regulation and Firm Entry: Evidence from Germany Reunification'. In Audretsch, D., Falck, O., Heblich, S., and Lederer, A. (eds), *Handbook of Research on Innovation and Entrepreneurship*. Cheltenham: Edward Elgar, pp. 74–87.

Radosevic, S. (2007) *National Systems of Innovation and Entrepreneurship: In Search of a Missing Link*. London: University College London.

Radosevic, S. (2012) 'Innovation Policy Studies between Theory and Practice: A Literature Review Based Analysis.'. *STI Policy Review*, Vol. 3, No. 1, pp. 1–45.

Radosevic, S. and Yoruk, E. (2013) 'Entrepreneurial Propensity of Innovation Systems: Theory, Methodology and Evidence'. *Research Policy*, Vol. 42, No. 5, pp. 1015–38.

Ramlogan, R. and Rigby, J. (2012a) *Access to Finance: Impacts of Publicly Supported Venture Capital and Loan Guarantees*. London and Manchester: NESTA and Manchester University Press.

Ramlogan, R. and Rigby, J. (2012b) *The Impact and Effectiveness of Entrepreneurship Policy*. Manchester: Manchester University Press.

Regeringens Proposition (2015) 'Staten och kapitalet: Struktur för finansiering av innovation och hållbar tillväxt' ('State and Capital: Structure for Financing of Innovation and Sustainable Growth'). Stockholm.

Regeringskansliet Finansdepartementet (2017) Nationella upphandlingsstrategin (The National Procurement Strategy). Stockholm.

Revest, V. and Sapio, A. (2010) 'Financing Technology-Based Small Firms in Europe: What Do We Know?' Small Business Economics, Vol. 39, No. 1, pp. 179–205.

Rigby, J. and Ramlogan, R. (2012) The Impact and Effectiveness of Support Measures for Exploiting Intellectual Property. Manchester: Manchester University Press.

Riksrevisionen (2014) Statens insatser för riskkapitalförsörjning: i senaste laget (State Efforts for Risk Capital Supply: In Late Stages). Stockholm.

Rockett, K. (2010) 'Property Rights and Invention'. In Bronwyn, H.H. and Nathan, R. (eds), Handbook of the Economics of Innovation. North-Holland: Elsevier, pp. 315–80.

Roelandt, T.J.A., Gilsing, V., and Sinderen, J.v. (2000) 'New Policies for the New Economy: Cluster-Based Innovation Policy: International Experiences'. Unpublished paper.

Rolfstam, M. (2009) 'Public Procurement as an Innovation Policy Tool: The Role of Institutions'. Science and Public Policy, Vol. 36, No. 5, pp. 349–60.

Romaní, G., Atienza, M., and Amorós, J.E. (2013) 'The Development of Business Angel Networks in Latin American Countries: The Case of Chile'. Venture Capital, Vol. 15, No. 2, pp. 95–113.

Romero-Jordán, D., Delgado-Rodríguez, M.J., Álvarez-Ayuso, I., and de Lucas-Santos, S. (2014) 'Assessment of the Public Tools Used to Promote R&D Investment in Spanish SMEs'. Small Business Economics, Vol. 43, No. 4, pp. 959–76.

Rothaermel, F.T. (2001) 'Incumbent's Advantage through Exploiting Complementary Assets via Interfirm Cooperation'. Strategic Management Journal, Vol. 22, No. 6–7, pp. 687–99.

Rotolo, D., Rafols, I., Hopkins, M., and Leydesdorff, L. (2013) 'Mapping the De Facto Governance of Emerging Science and Technologies'. SSRN Electronic Journal, January.

Rubalcaba, L. (2006) 'Which Policy for Innovation in Services?' Science and Public Policy, Vol. 33, No. 10, pp. 745–56.

Sabel, C.F. (1994) 'Flexible Specialisation and Regional Economics'. In Amin, A. (ed.), Post-Fordism: A Reader. Oxford: Blackwell, pp. 101–56.

Salamon, L.M. (2002) The Tools of Government: A Guide to the New Governance. Oxford: Oxford University Press.

Salavisa, I., Sousa, C., and Fontes, M. (2012) 'Topologies of Innovation Networks in Knowledge-Intensive Sectors: Sectoral Differences in the Access to Knowledge and Complementary Assets through Formal and Informal Ties'. Technovation, Vol. 32, No. 6, pp. 380–99.

Salomon, J.-J. (1977) 'Science Policy Studies and the Development of Science Policy'. In Spiegel-Rösing, I. and Price, D. (eds), Science, Technology and Society: A Cross-Disciplinary Perspective. London: SAGE, pp. 67–83.

Saminvest (2017) Årsredovisning 2017 (Annual Report 2017). Stockholm.

Saminvest (2018) Delårsrapport kvartal 1, 2018 (Quarterly Report 1, 2018). Stockholm.

Sammarra, A. and Biggiero, L. (2008) 'Heterogeneity and Specificity of Inter-Firm Knowledge Flows in Innovation Networks'. *Journal of Management Studies*, Vol. 45, No. 4, pp. 800–29.

Sampat, B.N. (2006) 'Universities and Intellectual Property: Shaping a New Patent Policy for Government Funded Academic Research'. In Guston, D.H. and Sarewitz, D. (eds), *Shaping Science and Technology Policy: The Next Generation of Research*. Madison, Wi: University of Wisconsin Press, pp. 55–76.

Sanchez, M.P., Chaminade, C., and Olea, M. (2000) 'Management of Intangibles: An Attempt to Build a Theory'. *Journal of Intellectual Capital*, Vol. 1, No. 4, pp. 312–27.

Saxenian, A. (2006) *The New Argonauts. Regional Advantage in a Global Economy*. Cambridge, Ma: Harvard University Press.

Schenk, E. and Guittard, C. (2011) 'Towards a Characterization of Crowdsourcing Practices'. *Journal of Innovation Economics*, Vol. 1, No. 7, pp. 93–107.

Scherer, F.M. and Harhoff, D. (2000) 'Technology Policy for a World of Skew-Distributed Outcomes'. *Research Policy*, Vol. 29, No. 4–5, pp. 559–66.

Schmoch, U., Rammer, C., and Legler, C. (eds) (2006) *National Systems of Innovation in Comparison: Structure and Performance Indicators for the Knowledge Society*. Dordrecht: Springer.

Schot, J. (2001) 'Towards New Forms of Participatory Technology Development'. *Technology Analysis and Strategic Management*, Vol. 13, No. 1, pp. 39–52.

Schot, J. and O'Donovan, C. (2016) 'Rethinking Society for the 21st Century: Developing a Science and Technology Studies Perspective'. Blog: https://www.ipsp.org/blog/rethinking-society-21th-century-developing-science-technology-studies-perspective.

Schumpeter, J.A. (1942/2005) *Capitalism, Socialism and Democracy*. London: Routledge.

Schwaag-Serger, S., Wise, E., and Arnold, E. (2015) *National Research and Innovation Councils as an Instrument of Innovation Governance: Characteristics and Challenges*. Stockholm: Vinnova.

Serris, J. (2004) *Report of the CREST Expert Group on Public Research Spending and Policy Mixes*. Brussels: European Commission.

Shane, S.A. (2003) *A General Theory of Entrepreneurship: The Individual–Opportunity Nexus*. Cheltenham: Edward Elgar.

Shane, S.A. and Venkataraman, S. (2000) 'The Promise of Entrepreneurship as a Field of Research'. *Academy of Management Review*, Vol. 25, No. 1, pp. 217–26.

Skogli, E. and Nellemann, R.G. (2016) *Utredning om insentiver/ordninger for risikoavlastning for innovative offentlige anskaffelser (Incentives/Schemes for Risk Relief for Innovative Public Procurement)*. Oslo: MENON Business Economics.

Smith, A., Courvisanos, J., Tuck, J., and McEachern, S. (2012) *Building the Capacity to Innovate: The Role of Human Capital*. Adelaide: National Centre for Vocational Education Research.

Smith, K. (2000) 'Innovation as a Systemic Phenomenon: Rethinking the Role of Policy'. *Enterprises and Innovation Management Studies*, Vol. 1, No. 1, pp. 73–102.

Smith, R. (2008) 'Aligning Competencies, Capabilities and Resources'. *Research Technology Management: Journal of the Industrial Research Institute*, September–October, pp. 1–11.

Smits, R. and Kuhlmann, S. (2004) 'The Rise of Systemic Instruments in Innovation Policy'. *International Journal of Foresight and Innovation Policy*, Vol. 1, No. 1–2, pp. 4–32.

Snieska, V. and Venckuviene, V. (2011) 'Hybrid Venture Capital Funds in Lithuania: Motives, Factors and Present State of Development'. *Engineering Economics*, Vol. 22, No. 2.

Snyder, C.M. and Vonortas, N.S. (2005) 'Multiproject Contact in Research Joint Ventures: Evidence and Theory'. *Journal of Economic Behavior and Organization*, Vol. 58, No. 4, pp. 459–86.

Statens Offentliga Utredningar (2015) 'En fondstruktur för innovation och tillväxt', *SOU*, Vol. 205, No. 64.

Steedman, H. (2003) 'Low Skills: A Social Problem for Europe'. In Conceicao, P., Heitor, M.V., and Lundvall, B.-Å. (eds), *Innovation, Competence Building and Social Cohesion in Europe*. Cheltenham: Edward Elgar, pp. 206–18.

Stefan, A. and Paul, L. (2008) 'Does It Pay to Be Green? A Systematic Overview'. *Academy of Management Perspectives*, Vol. 22, No. 4, pp. 45–62.

Steinmueller, E.W. (2006) 'Learning in the Knowledge-Based Economy: The Future as Viewed from the Past'. In Antonelli, C., Foray, D., Hall, B., and Steinmueller, E.W. (eds), *New Frontiers in the Economics of Innovation and New Technology: Essays in Honour of Paul David*. Cheltenham: Edward Elgar, pp. 207–38.

Steyaert, C. and Hjorth, D. (2006) 'Introduction: What Is Social in Social Entrepreneurship?' In Steyaert, C. and Hjorth, D. (eds), *Entrepreneurship as Social Change: A Third Movements in Entrepreneurship Book*. Cheltenham: Edward Elgar.

Stiglitz, J.E. (2014) *Intellectual Property Rights, The Pool of Knowledge and Innovation*. Cambridge, MA: NBER.

Stokes, D.E. (1997) *Pasteur's Quadrant: Basic Science and Technological Innovation*. Washington, DC: Brookings Institution.

Strandburg, K.J. (2005) 'Curiosity-Driven Research and University Technology Transfer'. *American Law and Economics Association Annual Meetings*.

Sutton, R.I. and Staw, B.M. (1995) 'What Theory Is Not'. *Administrative Science Quarterly*, Vol. 40, pp. 371–84.

Svensson, R. (2011) 'När är statsligt stöd till innovativa företag och entreprenörer effektivt?' ('When Is State Support to Innovative Companies and Entrepreneurs Efficient?'). *Svenskt Näringsliv*.

Swedberg, R. (2006) 'Social Entrepreneurship: The View of the Young Schumpeter'. In Steyaert, C. and Hjorth, D. (eds), *Entrepreneurship as Social Change: A Third Movements in Entrepreneurship Book*. Cheltenham: Edward Elgar.

Swedberg, R. (2012) 'Theorizing in Sociology and Social Sciences: Turning to the Context of Discovery'. *Theory and Society*, Vol. 41, No. 1, pp. 1–40.

Sørensen, E. and Torfing, J. (2011) 'Enhancing Collaborative Innovation in the Public Sector'. *Administration and Society*, 7 September.

Technopolis Group (2011) *Evaluation of ICREA 2001–2011*. Brighton: Technopolis.

Teece, D.J. (1986) 'Profiting from Technological Innovation: Implications for Integration, Collaboration, Licensing and Public Policy'. *Research Policy*, Vol. 15, No. 6, pp. 285–305.

Teece, D.J. (2010) 'Technological Innovation and the Theory of the Firm: The Role of Enterprise-Level Knowledge, Complementarities, and (Dynamic) Capabilities'. In Bronwyn, H.H. and Nathan, R. (eds), *Handbook of the Economics of Innovation*. North-Holland: Elsevier, pp. 679–730.

Teece, D.J., Pisano, G., and Shuen, A. (1997) 'Dynamic Capabilities and Strategic Management'. *Strategic Management Journal*, Vol. 18, No. 7, pp. 509–33.

Teixeira, A.A.C. (2014) 'Evolution, Roots and Influence of the Literature on National Systems of Innovation: A Bibliometric Account'. *Cambridge Journal of Economics*, Vol. 38, No. 1, pp. 181–214.

Tidd, J. and Bessant, J. (2013) *Managing Innovation: Integrating Technological, Market and Organizational Change*. Hoboken, NJ: Wiley.

Toner, P. (2011) *Workforce Skills and Innovation: An Overview of Major Themes in the Literature*. Paris: OECD.

Toner, P. and Woolley, R. (2016) 'Perspectives and Debates on Vocational Education and Training, Skills and the Prospects for Innovation'. *Revista Española de Sociología*, Vol. 25, No. 3, pp. 319–42.

Toner, P., Marceau, J., Hall, R., and Considine, G. (2004) *Innovation Agents: Vocational Education and Training Skills and Innovation in Australian Industries and Firms*. Adelaide: National Centre for Vocational Education Research.

Torrisi, S., Gambardella, A., Giuri, P., Harhoff, D., Hoisl, K., and Mariani, M. (2016) 'Used, Blocking and Sleeping Patents: Empirical Evidence from a Large-Scale Inventor Survey'. *Research Policy*, Vol. 45, No. 7, pp. 1374–85.

Tsipouri, L. (2012) 'Comparing Innovation Performance and Science in Society in the European Member States'. *Science and Public Policy*, Vol. 39, No. 6, pp. 732–40.

Tödtling, F. and Trippl, M. (2005) 'One Size Fits All? Towards a Differentiated Regional Innovation Policy Approach'. *Research Policy*, Vol. 34, No. 8, pp. 1203–19.

Tödtling, F., Lehner, P., and Trippl, M. (2006) 'Innovation in Knowledge Intensive Industries: The Nature and Geography of Knowledge Links'. *European Planning Studies*, Vol. 14, No. 8, pp. 1035–58.

UNCTAD (2005) *World Investment Report: Transnational Corporations and the Internationalization of R&D*. New York and Geneva: UNCTAD.

US Government Accountability Office (2005) *Federal Science, Technology, Engineering, and Mathematics Programs and Related Trends*. Washington, DC: US Government Accountability Office.

Uyarra, E. (2010) 'Conceptualizing the Regional Roles of Universities, Implications and Contradictions'. *European Planning Studies*, Vol. 18, No. 8, pp. 1227–46.

Uyarra, E. and Flanagan, K. (2010) 'Understanding the Innovation Impacts of Public Procurement'. *European Planning Studies*, Vol. 18, No. 1, pp. 123–43.

Uyarra, E. and Ramlogan, R. (2016) 'The Impact of Cluster Policy on Innovation'. In Edler, J., Cunningham, P., Gök, A., and Shapira, P. (eds), *Handbook of Innovation Policy Impact*. Cheltenham: Edward Elgar, pp. 196–238.

van de Vrande, V., de Jong, J.P.J., Vanhaverbeke, W., and de Rochemont, M. (2009) 'Open Innovation in SMEs: Trends, Motives and Management Challenges'. *Technovation*, Vol. 29, No. 6–7, pp. 423–37.

van den Ende, J. and Dolfsma, W. (2002) 'Technology Push, Demand Pull and the Shaping of Technological Paradigms'. *Journal of Evolutionary Economics*, Vol. 15, No. 1, pp. 83–99.

van den Hove, S. (2007) 'A Rationale for Science–Policy Interfaces'. *Futures*, Vol. 39, No. 7, pp. 807–26.

van Praag, M. (2011) 'Who Values the Status of the Entrepreneur?' In Audretsch, D.B., Falck, O., Heblich, S., and Lederer, A. (eds), *The Handbook of Research on Innovation and Entrepreneurship*. Cheltenham: Edward Elgar.

Varsakelis, N.C. (2006) 'Education, Political Institutions and Innovative Activity: A Cross-Country Empirical Investigation'. *Research Policy*, Vol. 35, No. 7, pp. 1083–90.

Vedung, E. (1998) 'Policy Instruments: Typologies and Theories'. In Bemelmans-Videc, M.L., Rist, R.C., and Vedung, E. (eds), *Carrots, Sticks and Sermons: Policy Instruments and Their Evaluation*. London: Transaction.

Vincent, L. (2008) 'Differentiating Competence, Capability and Capacity'. *Innovating Perspectives*, Vol. 16, No. 3, pp. 1–2.

von Hippel, E. (2005) 'Democratizing Innovation: The Evolving Phenomenon of User Innovation'. *Journal für Betriebswirtschaft*, Vol. 55, No. 1, pp. 63–78.

Vonortas, N.S. (1997) *Cooperation in Research and Development*. New York: Springer.

Vonortas, N.S. (2009a) 'Innovation Networks in Industry'. In Malerba, F. and Vonortas, N.S. (eds), *Innovation Networks in Industries*. Cheltenham: Edward Elgar, pp. 27–41.

Vonortas, N.S. (2009b) 'Innovation Networks in Industry'. In Malerba, F. and Vonortas, N.S. (eds), *Innovation Networks in Industries*. Cheltenham: Edward Elgar.

Voorberg, W.H., Bekkers, V.J.J.M., and Tummers, L.G. (2015) 'A Systematic Review of Co-Creation and Co-Production: Embarking on the Social Innovation Journey'. *Public Management Review*, Vol. 17, No. 9, pp. 1333–57.

Wallace, M.L. and Rafols, I. (2015) 'Research Portfolio Analysis in Science Policy: Moving from Financial Returns to Societal Benefits'. *Minerva*, Vol. 53, No. 2, pp. 89–115.

Wallsten, S.J. (2000) 'The Effects of Government-Industry R&D Programs on Private R&D: The Case of the Small Business Innovation Research Program'. *RAND Journal of Economics*, Vol. 31, No. 1, pp. 82–100.

Walz, R., Schleich, J., and Ragwitz, M. (2011) 'Regulation, Innovation and Wind Power Technologies: An Empirical Analysis for OECD Countries'. DIME Final Conference, 6–8 April, Maastricht.

Weber, S. and Posner, E. (2000) 'Creating a Pan-European Equity Market: The Origins of EASDAQ'. *Review of International Political Economy*, Vol. 7, No. 4, pp. 529–73.

Weber, K.M. and Rohracher, H. (2012) 'Legitimizing Research, Technology and Innovation Policies for Transformative Change: Combining Insights from Innovation Systems and Multi-Level Perspective in a Comprehensive "Failures" Framework'. *Research Policy*, Vol. 41, No. 6, pp. 1037–47.

Weber, K.M. and Truffer, B. (2017) 'Moving Innovation Systems Research to the Next Level: Towards an Integrative Agenda'. *Oxford Review of Economic Policy*, Vol. 33, No. 1, pp. 101–21.

Weber, K.M., Kubeczko, K., Kaufmann, A., and Grunewald, B. (2009) 'Trade-Offs between Policy Impacts of Future-Oriented Analysis: Experiences from the

Innovation Policy Foresight and Strategy Process of the City of Vienna'. *Technology Analysis and Strategic Management*, Vol. 21, No. 8, pp. 953–69.

Weber, K.M., Harper, J.C., Könnölä, T., and Carabias Barceló, V. (2012) 'Coping with a Fast-Changing World: Towards New Systems of Future-Oriented Technology Analysis'. *Science and Public Policy*, Vol. 39, No. 2, pp. 153–65.

Weick, K.E. (1995) 'What Theory Is Not, Theorizing Is'. *Administrative Science Quarterly*, Vol. 40, No. 3, pp. 385–90.

Wesseling, J.H. and Edquist, C. (2018) 'Public Procurement for Innovation to Help Meet Societal Challenges: A Review and Case Study'. *Science and Public Policy.*, Vol. 45, No. 4, pp. 493–502.

Whitley, R. (2008) 'Universities as Strategic Actors: Limitations and Variations'. In Engwall, L. and Weaire, D. (eds), *The University in the Market*. London: Portland Press, pp. 23–37.

Wilson, K.E. (2015) *Policy Lessons from Financing Innovative Firms*. Paris: OECD.

Zabala-Iturriagagoitia, J.M. (2012) 'New Product Development in Traditional Industries: Decision-Making Revised'. *Journal of Technology Management and Innovation*, Vol. 7, pp. 31–51.

Zabala-Iturriagagoitia, J.M. (2014) 'Innovation Management Tools: Implementing Technology Watch as a Routine for Adaptation'. *Technology Analysis and Strategic Management*, Vol. 26, No. 9, pp. 1073–89.

Zeschky, M., Widenmayer, B., and Gassmann, O. (2011) 'Frugal Innovation in Emerging Markets'. *Research-Technology Management*, Vol. 54, No. 4, pp. 38–45.

Zweig, D., Fung, C.S., and Han, D. (2008) 'Redefining the Brain Drain: China's "Diaspora Option"'. *Science Technology and Society*, Vol. 13, No. 1, pp. 1–33.

275

Index

Index

Index

Index

Index

Sammara, A. 151
Sampat, B.N. 72, 182
Sanchez, M.P. 89
sanctions, and regulatory instruments 216
Sapio, A. 197
Sarewitz, D. 67
Saxenian, A. 99, 154, 164
scale modelling 70
Scandinavian countries, entrepreneurship and
  intrapreneurship 141
Schenk, E. 96
Scherer, F.M. 65
Schmoch, U. 78
Schot, J. 2, 9
Schumpeter, J.A. 5, 132, 135–6, 155
  neo-Schumpeterian tradition 155
  Schumpeter Mark I and Mark II 136
Schwaag-Serger, S. 44
science
  basic science and applied science 57, 58
  science-based innovations 17
scientific knowledge, and innovation
  systems 20–1
scientific production 2
scientific progress 18
second-tier stock markets 193b, 197, 198
sectoral innovation systems 24
seed funding 35, 189, 190–1, 199, 200,
  203, 204
  issues related to 207–11
  public 219, 220
selection policies, and
  entrepreneurship 138–9, 140t
self-organized innovation systems 48,
  161–2, 242
self-regulation 176
Semta 98
Serris, J. 224
service sector 17, 18, 190
Shane, S.A. 137, 138
Shekarabi, Ardalan 122, 123, 126
Shirley, M.M. 168
SIs (systems of innovation) approach 2–4, 15,
  20, 21–4, 230–1, 245
  changes in 48
  and choice of policy instruments 241–2
  components of 19b, 230
  constituents of 20b
  defining 19b
  and holistic innovation policy 39, 232
  institutions and regulation 167–71
  main role of 19b
  networks and interactions in 145, 146–50
    common problems with 156–9
  organizations in 20, 21, 132, 133
    typology of 133–5, 134t
  policy implications syndrome 3–4

and policy-making 37
provision of constituents for 24, 25b,
  32–5
see also systems activities approach
skewed innovation policies 2
Skill Biased Technological Change
  hypothesis 104
skills 2, 11, 84, 85, 86
  and competences 83, 98, 105
    continuous skills development 92, 94,
      97–8, 100
    external competences 94–6
    'hard' skills 92
    internal competences 88t, 90, 92–3
    offshore manufacturing activities 101
    "soft" skills 92, 95
  and human capital 89
  and migration policy 98–9
  obstacles and barriers in innovation
    systems 237t, 238–9
Skogli, E. 118
Slepniov, D. 22
small firms
  access to venture capital 13
  creation of 136
  public financing of 189
SMEs (small and medium-sized firms) 32
  and competence-building 85
  and innovative interactions 147, 155
  and patent regulation 181
  policy instruments promoting 160b, 161
  R&D in innovation systems 59f
  and vocational training 98
Smith, A. 86, 94
Smith, K. 3, 5
Smith, R. 83
Smits, R. 222
Snieska, V. 194
Snyder, C.M. 155
social action, institutions and regulation
  167, 168
social capital 156
social competences 86
social development 15
social entrepreneurship 138
social innovation 12, 18
social media, and crowdsourcing 96
social problems, and the limits of innovation
  policy 50
social rate of return, on R&D investment 65–6,
  66b, 67, 81
social security
  flexicurity 94
  regulations 139, 140t
socio-economic context of innovation
  systems 1
socio-economic development

292

Index